D. M. Armstrong is an eminent Australian philosopher whose work over many years has dealt with such subjects as the nature of possibility, concepts of the particular and the universal, causes and laws of nature, and the nature of human consciousness.

This collection of essays, all specially written for this volume, explores the many facets of Armstrong's work, concentrating on his more recent interests. There are four sections in the book: possibility and identity, universals, laws and causality, and philosophy of mind. The contributors comprise an international group of philosophers from the United States, England, and Australia. An interesting feature of the volume is that Armstong himself has written responses to each of the essays. There is also a complete bibliography of Armstrong's writings.

The volume will be essential reading for metaphysicians and philosophers of mind, as well as for epistemologists and philosophers of science.

Contributors: John Bigelow, Keith Campbell, Evan Fales, Peter Forrest, Frank Jackson, David Lewis, William G. Lycan, C. B. Martin, D. H. Mellor, Peter Menzies, J. J. C. Smart.

ONTOLOGY, CAUSALITY AND MIND

Ontology, Causality and Mind

Essays in Honour of D. M. Armstrong

Edited by

JOHN BACON

KEITH CAMPBELL

LLOYD REINHARDT

University of Sydney

CAMBRIDGE
UNIVERSITY PRESS

Published by the Press Syndicate of the University of Cambridge
The Pitt Building, Trumpington Street, Cambridge CB2 1RP
40 West 20th Street, New York, NY 10011-4211, USA
10 Stamford Road, Oakleigh, Victoria 3166, Australia

First published 1993

Printed in the United States of America

Library of Congress Cataloging-in-Publication Data
Ontology, causality and mind : essays in honour of D.M. Armstrong /
edited by John Bacon, Keith Campbell, Lloyd Reinhardt.
p.   cm.
Includes bibliographical references.
ISBN 0-521-41562-4 (hc)
1. Philosophy. I. Armstrong, D. M. (David Malet), 1926– .
II. Bacon, John, 1940– . III. Campbell, Keith, 1938– .
IV. Reinhardt, Lloyd.
B29.069   1993
110 – dc20   92-469
                                                  CIP

A catalog record for this book is available from the British Library.

ISBN 0-521-41562-4 hardback

Contents

IV CONSCIOUSNESS AND SECONDARY QUALITIES

Preface

David Armstrong was born in 1926 into a naval family in Melbourne, Australia. After schooling in England and at Geelong Grammar School in Victoria, and a period of service in the Royal Australian Navy, he entered the University of Sydney in 1947.

The Sydney Philosophy Department was at that time dominated by John Anderson, the charismatic and isiosyncratic Scottish philosopher. While Armstrong never adopted many of Anderson's views on particular issues in logic, metaphysics, epistemology and ethics, he has always regarded Anderson as the crucial influence in his intellectual formation. In common with his teacher, he has steadily pursued the classic substantive issues of metaphysically motivated philosophizing. Both engaged in the search for a synoptic, rationally compelling world view framed by a naturalism of empiricist inspiration.

From Sydney, Armstrong went on to Exeter College, Oxford, and took the then recently established B.Phil. degree in 1954. Oxford was at that time the heartland of the linguistic analytic movement in philosophy, with Ryle and Austin as pre-eminent figures. Armstrong worked principally with H. H. Price, the specialist in the philosophy of perception, who was always more traditional in his approach to the problems of philosophy. While Armstrong picked up analytic tools in Oxford, he never adopted the view that all, or even many, of philosophy's conundrums are mere symptoms of linguistic pathology rather than genuine questions.

After Oxford, he spent a brief period (1954–55) teaching at Birkbeck College in the University of London, then seven years at the University of Melbourne, earning the Ph.D. there while teaching at the same time. Since 1964 he has held John Anderson's chair as Challis Professor of Philosophy in Sydney. His imminent retirement is the occasion for this tribute.

Armstrong's philosophy, presented now in ten books and nearly fifty major papers, has ranged over many of the main issues in epistemology and metaphysics. Rather unusually, it has tended to move from the more specific and concrete to the more abstract and general. He has been concerned throughout to elaborate and defend a philosophy which is economical, unified and compatibly continuous with the established results of the natural sciences. Several themes run through it all: a naturalism that holds all reality to be spatiotemporal, a materialism that aims to account for all mental phenomena without appeal beyond the categories of physical being, and an empiricism that both vindicates and draws strength from the methods and successes of the natural sciences.

In *Perception and the Physical World* (1961), Armstrong confronted then fashionable phenomenalist tendencies with a direct realism that had no place for mentalistic items. He urged the various objections to sense-data and the identification problem they face. He developed an account of perceiving in terms of inclinations to belief, which took him farther away from the classic empiricist doctrines of perception by way of ideas.

A Materialist Theory of the Mind (1968) was the first full-dress presentation of central-state materialism, an equally naturalist, scientifically more plausible successor to behaviorism in the philosophy of mind. This major and highly influential work presented an analysis of mental phenomena in terms of what they are apt to cause or be caused by. It proceeded to point out that the most likely items to fit those places in the causal networks of human perception, feeling, memory and action had recently come to light: they are structures, states and processes in the central nervous system.

Belief and knowledge were treated only lightly in *A Materialist Theory of the Mind*. In *Belief, Truth and Knowledge* (1973), Armstrong developed an idea of Ramsey's that beliefs are maps by which we steer, sub-maps of one great action-guiding belief map in our head. Against causal theories, he made a significant contribution to the development of the reliabilist account of the distinction between knowledge and mere true belief.

During the seventies, Armstrong turned his attention to the classical problem of universals. In the two volumes of *Universals and Scientific Realism* (1978), he built a case for an immanent realism about universals with three main themes, of profound originality and considerable influence: first, that contemporary confidence in set theory to sustain some version of nominalism is unjustifiable, and nominalism is desperately implausible; second, that an empiricist philosophy need not, and should not, bear the nominalist burden; and third, that the identification of actually existing universals is a task for which the fundamental sciences alone are equipped. There are far fewer universals than one might suppose, and to determine which ones there are calls for a substantive piece of contingent scientific theorizing.

This scientific realism about universals was promptly put to work in developing a philosophy of the laws that apparently govern the cosmos. *What Is a Law of Nature?* (1983a) argues that the regularity theories of law, deriving from Hume, are all fatally flawed, mainly in their incapacity to account for the accidental–nomic distinction. It goes on to urge that laws relating (classes of) particular events or occurrences rest on a relation of necessitation holding between the universals involved, thus setting forth one variant of what is now known as the Dretske–Tooley–Armstrong theory of laws.

The concern with necessity provides a linking thread to Armstrong's next major project, *A Combinatorial Theory of Possibility* (1989a). Here he attempts to build – upon a foundation in the Tractarian thought of Wittgenstein, Cresswell and Skyrms – an account of nonactual possibilities as fictive reorderings of strictly actual cosmic constituents. Thus possible-world realism is repudiated, ersatzism is skirted, and naturalism is upheld. Here again, Armstrong's view of universals, as abstractions from states of affairs on an equal footing with particulars, stands him in good stead.

In the theory of perception, the analysis of knowledge, the philosophy of mind, the problem of universals, the question of laws, and now the philosophy of possibility, Armstrong has not only contributed to the discussion but played a large part in establishing philosophy's agenda and setting the terms of its debates.

Philosophy is a very hard subject with a very long history. It is very hard to say something new and important on any one major question. This makes it all the more remarkable that anyone should have had new and important things to say on a whole range of questions. But Armstrong has done more than make a massive contribution to philosophical doctrine; he has also shown us a way of doing philosophy. He has made an admirable contribution to the style in which we philosophize. It is easy when tackling very hard problems to lapse into obscurity or hide behind it. Armstrong's philosophical writings are examples of how to discuss the hardest questions in philosophy without sacrificing the kind of clarity that makes progress possible. We have him to thank for bringing us so much interesting and important philosophical news, and for doing it with such style and clarity.[1]

For some of us, working with Armstrong has meant acquiring respect and affection for a fellow intellectual with whom we disagree deeply on both philosophical and political matters, which must be among the most rewarding experiences of academic life. We call Armstrong an 'intellectual' in his own sense, embracing an interest in social and political matters that goes well beyond theory to advocacy. Although often referred to as a conservative or a right-winger, Armstrong characterizes himself as a liberal conservative. He has always championed human rights and he has always opposed tyranny. He has always taught, even when it was less fashionable than it now is, that these ends could best be served by a free market and free trade.

In the academy, Armstrong's 'politics' – motivated by scrupulous support for the highest standards – led him to oppose many of the changes that have overtaken universities in recent decades. This stance has cost him friends. It has also done much to sustain a self-respecting and livable departmental environment.

It would be quite anomalous if our differences with Armstrong did not extend also to philosophy. For example, one of us is deeply attracted to the work of the later Wittgenstein. While Armstrong does not go so far as Russell in condemning that work, he is annoyed by its influence and does not think very highly of its main themes. Yet despite these areas of difference, which have occasioned a fair number of sharp exchanges, and despite Armstrong's pre-Kantian proclivities (as some might see them), his place in our philosophical and intellectual life is cherished and unforgettable.

As will be evident from the introductions to Armstrong's replies herein, his impact upon his fellow philosophers has not been limited to published disputation or academic statesmanship. Quite apart from the influence of his substantive views and the example of his clear style, those of us who have been affected by him value almost more than anything else the inspirational force of his personality. In his presence, philosophy *feels* important. This has been his priceless gift to colleagues and students, the secret of the coherence of the Department of Traditional and Modern Philosophy, aptly called 'Armstrong's department' in most of the world. It is our hope that this volume will convey a sense of that presence to the reader, along with our gratitude to the honoree.

We thank our contributors for agreeing to provide the substance of this *Festschrift,* for getting their papers in on time and for brooking occasional editorial queries gracefully. Our thanks go likewise to David Armstrong for the care and despatch with which he wrote his replies to each contributor. Finally, we should like to acknowledge the support of Greg Currie, whose suggestion helped initiate this book.

NOTE

1. This paragraph is a modified version of Frank Jackson's remarks on introducing Armstrong's last appearance as Challis Professor before the Australasian Association of Philosophy in Melbourne, 10 July 1991.

REFERENCES

Armstrong, D. M. 1961. *Perception and the Physical World* (London: Routledge & Kegan Paul).

1968. *A Materialist Theory of the Mind* (London: Routledge & Kegal Paul).

1973. *Belief, Truth and Knowledge* (Cambridge University Press).

1978. *Universals and Scientific Realism,* 2 vols. (Cambridge University Press).

1983a. *What Is a Law of Nature?* (Cambridge University Press).

1989a. *A Combinatorial Theory of Possibility* (Cambridge University Press).

Contributors

John Bigelow, a Canadian educated in New Zealand and Australia, has worked in Melbourne, Australia, for the past fifteen years, first at La Trobe University and now at Monash University, where he holds a chair in the Philosophy Department. He is author of *The Reality of Numbers* (Oxford University Press, 1988) and, with Robert Pargetter, of *Science and Necessity* (Cambridge University Press, 1990). He is a prolific contributor to the journals, either alone or with Robert Pargetter, Brian Ellis, Susan Dodds or John Campbell. In this volume, he continues exploration of the power of an uninhibitedly realistic view of universals of many types.

Keith Campbell, for many years a colleague of David Armstrong, is now, after a period at the University of Maryland, his successor in the Challis Chair of Philosophy at the University of Sydney. He is the author of *Body and Mind* (Macmillan 1972, Notre Dame 1985), *Metaphysics: An Introduction* (Wadsworth, 1976), *A Stoic Philosophy of Life* (University Press of America, 1986) and *Abstract Particulars* (Blackwell, 1990). The essay in this collection is his fourth contribution to the problems involved in developing an adequate philosophy of colour and of colour vision.

Evan Fales is Associate Professor of Philosophy at the University of Iowa, a school celebrated for its attachment to ontology. He is author of *Causation and Universals* (Routledge, 1990), and here he contrasts that work's necessitarian view with Armstrong's sense of natural law as resting on a contingent yet necessitating relation between universals.

Peter Forrest, one of Armstrong's pupils, is now Professor of Philosophy at the University of New England in northern New South Wales. Forrest is author of *The Dynamics of Belief: A Normative Logic* (Blackwell, 1986) and *Quantum Metaphysics* (Blackwell, 1988), as well as contributions to the journals, some in collaboration with Armstrong. His background in mathematics undergirds his discussion of Realist theses in first philosophy and the philosophy of science.

Frank Jackson holds the Chair in Philosophy in the Research School of Social Sciences in the Australian National University, Canberra. He has made contributions to many debates in philosophy, is author of *Perception: A Representative Theory* (Cambridge University Press, 1977) and *Conditionals* (Blackwell, 1987) and is editor of *Conditionals* (Oxford University Press, 1991). His contribution to this volume concerns an ongoing discussion of the connection between being intelligent and behaving in ways characteristic of intelligence.

David Lewis teaches philosophy at Princeton University and is a regular visitor to Australia. He is the author of *Convention* (Harvard University Press, 1969), *Counterfactuals* (Blackwell, 1973), *Philosophical Papers* (2 volumes, Oxford University Press, 1983 and 1986), *On the Plurality of Worlds* (Blackwell, 1986), *Parts of Classes* (Blackwell, 1991), and of articles in several branches of philosophy. Here he discusses a puzzle about things that exist in many not-quite-identical versions, and proposes a solution using Armstrong's idea that extensive overlap may approximate identity.

William G. Lycan, following a period at Ohio State University, is now William Rand Kenan Jr. Professor of Philosophy at the University of North Carolina at Chapel Hill, and currently a Fellow of the Center for Advanced Study in the Behavioral Sciences in Palo Alto, California. He is author of *Knowing Who,* with Steven Boer (MIT Bradford, 1986), *Logical Form in Natural Language* (MIT Bradford, 1984), *Consciousness* (MIT Bradford, 1987), *Judgement and Justification* (Cambridge University Press, 1988), and editor of *Mind and Cognition* (Blackwell, 1990). His essay in this volume raises problems for Armstrong's fictive combinatorialism in the philosophy of possibility.

C. B. Martin, after a period at the University of Adelaide, South Australia, became a colleague of Armstrong when he succeeded Alan Stout in a Chair at the University of Sydney. While in Australia, and subsequently as visiting Professor at Harvard, Columbia and Michigan and in his post as Professor at the University of Calgary in Canada, he has presented causal accounts of reference, perception and memory, and of causality and realism, whose influence is shown in his *Festschrift: Cause, Mind, and Reality* (ed. Heil, Kluwer, 1989). Martin is author of *Religious Belief* (Cornell University Press, 1959) and editor, with Armstrong, of a collection of articles on Locke and Berkeley. In this volume he propounds a realistic conception of intrinsic causal powers as essential to a proper understanding of causality, in both physical and mental contexts.

D. H. Mellor is Professor of Philosophy in the University of Cambridge. His work has ranged across a broad spectrum in metaphysics, philosophy of science and philosophy of mind. He is the author of *The Matter of Chance* (1971), *Real Time* (1981) and *Matters of Metaphysics* (1991), all published by Cambridge University Press, as are his edited works: *Prospects for Pragmatism: Essays in Memory of F. P. Ramsey* (1980), *Science, Belief and Behaviour: Essays in Honour of R. B. Braithwaite* (1980), *F. P. Ramsey: Philosophical Papers* (1990) and *Ways of Communicating* (1990). His essay in this volume uses Ramsey's work on laws, theories and universals to answer a question posed but not settled by Armstrong's theory of universals: namely, how they relate to the meanings of predicates.

Peter Menzies, a former colleague of Armstrong, holds a position as Research Fellow in the Research School of Social Sciences of the Australian National University, Canberra. His work has concentrated on developing a viable comprehensive philosophy of causation, which has been appearing in the journals. In this essay, he criticizes regularity and necessitation theories of laws of nature and offers a new account of physical necessity in terms of certain agent modalities.

J. J. C. Smart has for many years been a leading figure in Australian philosophy, first at the University of Adelaide, then at La Trobe University and finally in a chair of philosophy in the Australian National University's Research School of Social Sciences, from which he retired in 1985. He is author of *An Outline of a System of Utilitarian Ethics* (Melbourne University Press, 1961), *Philosophy and Scientific Realism* (Routledge, 1963), *Between Science and Philosophy* (Random House, 1968), *Utilitarianism: For and Against* (with Bernard Williams, Cambridge University Press, 1973), *Ethics, Persuasion, and Truth* (Routledge, 1984), *Essays, Metaphysical and Moral* (Blackwell, 1987) and *Our Place in the Universe* (Blackwell, 1989). Blackwell also published a *Festschrift* for Smart, *Metaphysics and Morality,* edited by Philip Pettit, Richard Sylvan and Jean Norman, in 1987. In opposition to Armstrong, Smart remains a staunch defender of a Humean account of natural law, and his essay in this volume continues the debate.

I

Possibility and Identity

1

Armstrong's New Combinatorialist Theory of Modality

WILLIAM G. LYCAN

1

For over thirty years now, David Armstrong has been defending the doctrine he calls Naturalism, capital N. Naturalism is roughly the view that everything that exists (a) is located in (our) physical spacetime and (b) makes some causal contribution to the spatiotemporal world.[1] In the face of the many apparent counterexamples to that generalization, Armstrong has written a series of books, beginning with *Perception and the Physical World* (1961), attacking the counterexamples one by one.

He started with what I consider the low hurdles, arguing that neither perceptual experience nor sensation (*Bodily Sensations,* 1962) occasions any departure from Naturalism. In *A Materialist Theory of the Mind* (1968), he went on to treat thinking, feeling, and all the rest of the mental, deploying his well-known Causal Analysis of mental concepts – a bigger job, certainly, but well within Armstrong's powers to accomplish. Knowledge and epistemic justification came tumbling after; *Belief, Truth and Knowledge* (1973) spun nicely off Chapters 9 and 10 of its predecessor.[2]

Easy, all too easy. But suddenly the going got tougher: What of *universals*? Since unlike many Naturalists Armstrong scorns what he calls 'Ostrich Nominalism' and firmly believes in properties and other universals, he found himself committed to providing a Naturalistic account of them. That task is at least an order of magnitude or two more taxing than that of Naturalizing just mind and knowledge. It required two volumes (*Universals and Scientific Realism,* vols. 1 and 2, 1978), as well as real metaphysical ingenuity. His theory of universals suggested an account of laws of nature (*What Is a Law of Nature?*, 1983a), even more recondite a subject matter because of its modal element, but Armstrong was undaunted.

At that point a lesser philosopher might have rested. (I certainly would have.) The Naturalizing of mind, epistemology, universals and natural law might reasonably be thought an exemplary life's work, entitling the author to a permanent holiday with pay and free champagne. But such are Armstrong's vision, integrity and energy that he has advanced without pause to the next frontier. His most recent book, *A Combinatorial Theory of Possibility* (1989a)[3] defends Naturalism against what is probably its worst enemy: modality itself. (Not that he has forgotten mathematics and set theory, see below.)

I believe that the Naturalizing of modality is vastly more difficult than were all Armstrong's previous Naturalist efforts combined.[4] In fact, I believe that to provide *any* plausible theory of modality, never mind a Naturalistic one, would be an astounding feat.[5] (And none of the currently fashionable theories, plausible or not, is Naturalistic.)[6] Thus, despite my sympathy for Armstrong's great attempt, I was a priori very pessimistic. And despite my admiration for Armstrong's actual theory, I think a posteriori that it fails. But let us see.

2

Armstrong starts with the idea inaugurated by Quine (1969)[7] that Lycan (1979) called 'Combinatorialism' – the idea of treating 'possible worlds' as set-theoretic or otherwise combinatorial rearrangements of whatever are in fact the basic elements of our own actual world. But he faces an obstacle right at the outset: Most combinatorialists help themselves to set theory, because some abstract individuating and ordering device seems clearly required to fund the notion of 'a rearrangement of' the basic elements of this world. That means trouble for Armstrong, since a Naturalist is not entitled to nonphysical items like sets, at least so long as those items remain acausal and nonspatiotemporal.[8]

But following Skyrms (1981), Armstrong gives the Combinatorialist idea a bold Tractarian twist, endorsing the claim that the existence of this possibility or that one is determined by 'the mere existence of' the basic elements involved (p. 37; cf. Wittgenstein's 1922 *Tractatus* 3.4). If that claim is really true, then perhaps Armstrong need not actually produce any set-theoretic or other abstract-object mock-up in order to see 'other possible worlds' as rearrangements of the metaphysical atoms of this world. (Further, he announces that his version of Combinatorialism will display a 'fictionalist element', of which more shortly.) Let us see how this goes.

Armstrong begins with his already defended Tractarian ontology of states of affairs (1978), maintaining that both 'properties' and 'individuals' are only aspects of and abstractions from states of affairs. States of affairs are causal and spatiotemporal, so Naturalism is maintained; Naturalism would be violated only if Armstrong were to permit uninstantiated properties, which he notoriously does not. The world's ultimate building blocks are the atomic states of affairs, those consisting of a simple individual's having a simple property. As for Wittgenstein, every atomic state of affairs is logically independent of all the others (1989a, p. 41), and in particular, all simple properties and relations are compossible (p. 49).

Now, to the issue: What is a *merely possible* state of affairs? That, as Armstrong says (p. 45), requires a revision of his previous use of the phrase 'state of affairs', since up till now he has used it to mean an actual element of the actual world. He begins with the notion of a false atomic statement. A merely possible state of affairs is what a false atomic statement purports to describe, and is ostensibly referred to by a gerund phrase, as in '*a*'s being G'. A nonactual *world* is a conjunctive aggregate of possible states of affairs. Armstrong begins with what he calls 'Wittgenstein worlds' (p. 48), roughly those conjunctive states of affairs that involve all and only the actual basic individuals and properties of our world. In subsequent chapters he provides for contracted worlds that contain fewer individuals or properties, and for expanded worlds containing more individuals, though he argues against 'alien universals'. (There are many other refinements and elaborations, but I think none that will affect my assessment of Armstrong's basic position on mere possibilia.)⁹

What is *combinatorial* about all this is (I presume) that the terms occurring in even a false atomic statement must denote – the subject must denote an actual simple, and the predicate must denote a universal that is actually instantiated by something. Thus if a whole merely possible world is a maximal heap of atomic states of affairs, the heap will be composed of actual individuals and actually instantiated universals merely rearranged, as is both the Combinatorial and the Naturalist way.

Again, it is a *heap* or conjunction, rather than set or any other assembled abstract entity. Armstrong emphasizes that he is not what Lewis (1986a) calls an 'Ersatzer'; he is not proffering a stock of actual entities to simulate or go proxy for 'possibilia'. Rather, he 'treat[s] . . . mere possibilities as non-existents' (p. 46).

A merely possible state of affairs does not exist, subsist or have any sort of being. It is no addition to our ontology. It is 'what is not'. It would not even be right to say that we can *refer* to it, at any rate if reference is taken to be a relation.

'Reference to' mere possibilia has the same linguistic, metaphysical and presumably epistemological status as does ostensible reference to ideal entities in science (ideal gases, frictionless planes, perfect vacuums); at least, Armstrong calls such ideal items '[t]he parallel' by which he officially explains the ontological status of his possibilia.

That is the fictionalist part. It is important to see that Armstrong's fictionalism is no afterthought, but is vital to his project: A given possibility, an actual or merely possible state of affairs, is a particular, Armstrong argues (p. 52); it is not repeatable within a single world. And the gerund phrase that designates or ostensibly refers to a state of affairs is a singular term, albeit a nominalized sentence. Thus, although there may be some sense in which a particular possibility is determined by 'the mere existence of' the basic elements that figure in it, the possibility is not exhausted by those elements' existing separately or even by their Leonard–Goodman sum. It is rather, according to Armstrong, a unified particular from which the elements are merely 'abstracted'. If we were formalizing Armstrong's ontology, we would need a gerund operator, a singular-term–forming functor applying to name–predicate pairs; a's being G would have to be expressed as something like $B\{a, G\}$.

Armstrong seems to grant all that (p. 46): 'When we talk about possibilities, we are talking about something represent*ed*, not a representation. (An ideal gas is not a representation.)' A possibility is a *thing* represented, but it is not on its face an actual thing. Thus it might seem that Armstrong must Ersatz if he is to save his Actualism; but unhappily, to Ersatz would forfeit Naturalism. The only way to avoid Ersatzing consistently with Actualism and the fact that possibilities are particulars is to insist that the mere possibilities simply do not exist and hence that descriptions of them are fictional.

3

Once we understand the semantics and the ontology of ideal entities, we can apply it to our nonactual 'worlds'. But now, what of the semantics and the ontology of fiction?

Armstrong himself says that what we need is 'an Actualist, one-world, account' of fictional statements (pp. 49–50). (Evidently he is assuming that statements about ideal entities in science *are* literally fictional and so would yield to a general semantics of fiction. This assumption is plausible, but notice that we need not accept it; some other treatment of ideal entities might be preferable, and then we would have the choice of which treatment to extend to the merely possible worlds.)

Ideal scientific entities have a relevant noteworthy feature: There is some inclination to say that statements about them are literally true, not literally false though true-in-fiction. Armstrong shares that inclination,[10] which could be gratified if we were to understand the relevant statements counterfactually – namely, as prefaced by 'If there were any . . .' ('If there were any perfect vacuum, light would travel through it [in such-and-such a manner]'). But to extend *that* treatment of ideal entities to nonactual worlds would be to revert to the tactic of paraphrasing statements about possibilia in counterfactual terms. 'There might have been a golden mountain' would be explicated in the usual way as 'Some possible world contains a golden mountain', which in turn would be understood as fictionally asserting the existence of maximal conjunctive states of affairs that realize, inter alia, a mountain made of gold. Since (I presume) this fiction would be a true one by Armstrong's lights,[11] the counterfactual treatment of ideal entities would paraphrase it as something like (A) 'If there were any array of possible worlds (i.e., any array of maximal conjunctive states of affairs besides the actual one that fit the Leibnizian picture of logical space), there would be one that realized a golden mountain'.

(A) is hard to process and probably genuinely hard to understand. (Does the antecedent express the anti-Naturalistic and perhaps Meinongian supposition that there are after all many *worlds* besides our own actual one?) But even if we understand what (A) says, we shall have further trouble computing its truth-value; I do not know how to tell what would be the case 'if Meinongianism were correct', though perhaps the Meinongian *picture* is clear enough to warrant the inference that there would be a nonactual world containing a golden mountain.

In any case, there are deeper objections to explicating ordinary modal statements in counterfactual terms.[12] First, although we seem to understand counterfactuals in ordinary conversation, they have proved to be among the most troublesome and elusive expressions there are. There truth conditions have remained genuinely mysterious; in philosophical or linguistic discussion of counterfactuals, people blank out or disagree even over simple data. Counterfactuals are not good ontology for purposes of serious, back-to-the-wall philosophizing.[13]

The past twenty-five years have seen great progress in the general understanding of counterfactuals, beginning with Stalnaker (1968) and Lewis (1973). But that progress has resulted precisely from the considered and well-motivated use of possible-worlds semantics. Therefore we have overwhelmingly strong reason to explicate counterfactuals in terms of possible worlds; and any such reason is *eo ipso* reason not to paraphrase talk of possible worlds in terms of unexplicated counterfactuals. The upshot is that although the counterfactual view of truths about ideal entities may be fine for Armstrong's standard scientific examples, it will not do if carried over to possibilia.

[Notice two further points about ideal entities. First: Whether or not we think of truths about ideal entities as being *paraphrasable by* counterfactuals, we may agree that scientific talk of ideal entities *licences* the same counterfactuals. Thus, any obscurity or weirdness in counterfactuals like (A) embarrasses Armstrong's analogy. Second: Scientific idealization is often justified on the grounds that empirical consequences are unaffected. That too is a counterfactual matter; the idea is that empirical predictions are just (or approximately) as they would be if the idealizations held in fact, and that is why the idealizations are permitted. On Armstrong's analogy, then, it should turn out that empirical predictions are just (or approximately) as they would be if there really were worlds other than our own. But what sense could Armstrong, or we, make of that claim?]

4

Some philosophers have resisted the aforementioned inclination and held that, as things are, physics is just plain *false* so far as it does commit itself to ideal entities. (They may add that reference to ideal entities is in principle eliminable from physics, so that physics can in principle be stated in such a way as to make it, and not just its empirical consequences, true.)[14] Such a treatment would never do for Armstrong's purpose, for he wants everyday modal statements, at least, to come out literally true. He needs at least some sense in which possible-worlds statements are true, even though there is a more robust sense in which they are false.

Perhaps there are better ways than the counterfactual way of understanding truths stated in terms of ideal entities as literal, but none has come to me. Let us then, after all, stay with the idea of fictional truth. The obvious compromise (as between the counterfactual view of truths about ideal items and simply rejecting the notion of truths about ideal items), is to say that a modal statement is literally true if and only if the corresponding possible-worlds statement is fictionally-true, even though the statement itself is not literally true. And my impression is that Armstrong would endorse that compromise.

We must then give the Actualist semantics of fictional-truth itself. But as Armstrong plainly recognizes (p. 49), standard possible-worlds accounts of fictional truth are forbidden him. Nor, of course, can he turn to Meinongian accounts such as Castañeda's (1989). He must leave the mainstream and seek elsewhere.[15]

Before surveying the prospects for the semantics of fiction, I want to mention a remaining troublesome feature of ideal entities in science: typically they are degenerate or otherwise special cases of what would otherwise be real physical entities, where an important magnitude takes an impossible value (often 0). That is, they are limiting cases, which is why we have so little trouble understanding the idealized language. (It also encourages the counterfactual analysis of ideal entities.) But Armstrong's merely possible worlds do not have this feature; they are not ideal limiting cases smoothly continuous with real physical objects. This too suggests that the analogy is not very helpful and that Armstrong would do better to stick by a fictionalist account less strictly tied to the foibles of ideal scientific items.

5

What worldless fictional semantics shall he choose, then? Armstrong is offhand (p. 50): 'I do not know in detail what account to give, but it would be truly surprising if no such satisfying account were available'. And that, it seems, is that.

How can Armstrong thus shrug off what seems clearly to be the biggest problem facing his theory of modality? I offer a psychobiographical conjecture, inviting him to confirm or reject it at his leisure. It is supported by nothing in Armstrong (1989a), but is suggested by some passages in his previous works (e.g. 1973) and encouraged by any number of conversations. Here is the conjecture: For Armstrong, Naturalism is not a regulative ideal, or a distant goal to be achieved (if ever) only by overcoming terrible obstacles, requiring ingenuity, great skill, and the grace of one's muse. For him Naturalism is a presumed fact – if not *accompli,* but for some details. His Causal Argument (cf. note 1) has shown it to be so, if we had not already been persuaded by our good hard-headed respect for science and our disdain for superstition. Now, if one does thus take Naturalism for granted, then – given any phenomenon or item that is uncontroversially a part of everyday human life – it will be obvious that the item admits of some Naturalistic treatment or other, and it will not much matter which. The practice of producing and understanding fictions, in particular, is a quotidian human activity, performed using nothing but physical minds, mouths and pens. So there will be no great difficulty fitting fiction and its products into nature; they already are in nature.

If that is the way Armstrong is thinking, the problem is dialectical. We do have powerful motives for Naturalism, but the obstacles must equally be recognized, for they are dismaying. Attempts have been made to Naturalize modality, by philosophers whose brilliance is a byword, and the attempts have not succeeded; as I said in Section 1, there is not even a satisfactory *non*-Naturalistic theory of modality. Modal facts remain an ostensible counterexample to Naturalism.

So too, one cannot assume that a good theory of fiction (in particular) is just around the corner. For fiction is all too close to modality; fictional entities are nonactual possibilia, save for those which are impossibilia. The analysis of modality in terms of fiction is a step, but not a large step. Let us therefore pursue a few avenues toward a non–possible-worlds semantics of fictional truth.

6

First, there are syntactic/inferential accounts. For example, a statement
S will be true-in a fiction F just in case S is a deductive consequence of
some member of F (F being construed as a set of sentences or formulas
that regiments F), where 'deductive' means proof-theoretic rather than
merely semantic.[16]

But to apply an account of this sort to Armstrong's 'Wittgenstein worlds'
would result in a specifically linguistic form of Ersatzism, whose mock-
ups would be parochial to a particular formal language. First, it would
require an actual fiction in which to ground Armstrong's ideal entities.
Let us inaccurately but alliteratively call such a fiction 'Leibniz's Lie'; it
says that alongside the actual world there exists an inconceivably huge
panoply of other worlds, exhibiting structure S (of the sort needed to
support intensional logic). The structure S must somehow be spelt out,
in detail, because all our subsequent statements about 'worlds' must be
strictly deducible from the Lie; and the Lie must be expressed in a particular language, say a formalized version of English, in order for deducibility to be defined on it. Then a statement like 'Some possible world contains a golden mountain' will be fictionally-true if and only if there is a
formally correct deduction of the statement from the Lie.

This is not Ersatzism *in propria persona,* since it does not deliberately
or directly furnish a set of actual world-simulacra. But it creates such a
set indirectly: For any given world to 'exist' for purposes of logic and
semantics is (according to Armstrong) for that world to exist-in-fiction,
which is in turn for the statement of its existence to be actually deducible
from Leibniz's Lie and thus for that statement actually to exist. Thus, to
every world there corresponds its existentially quantified specification-in-
formalized-English, and if that correspondence holds then we might as
well accept the specifications as Ersatz worlds and be done with it. But
Armstrong does not want that. Moreover, a parochially linguistic Ersatzism faces well-known problems of its own.[17]

This last problem for the syntactic/inferential account actually expands
into a general difficulty for any fictionalism regarding the Wittgenstein
worlds, syntactic/inferential or not: Again, fictional-truth *tout court* requires a fiction. Statements are fictionally true or pretend-true only because there actually exist stories and other fictions for them to be true-in.
But who authored a fiction according to which any one or more of the
Wittgenstein worlds existed? It is not obvious that Leibniz's Lie actually
exists.[18]

There is a further, though related difficulty. In order for 'Some possible world contains a golden mountain' or any other specific possibilistic

quantification to be deducible from Leibniz's Lie, the Lie must contain the appropriate stock of specific predicates, such as 'golden' and 'mountain'. Thus the Lie cannot be a merely schematic description of a set of worlds, but must syntactically imply the existence (at some world) of everything that is in fact possible. But the Lie was supposed to be an actual fiction, historically tokened by someone in the real world. So for Armstrong's purposes (assuming he were to pursue the syntactic/inferential strategy) someone would have to have actually said something about gold and mountains that entails the existence of a golden mountain. Philosophers using Meinong's famous example have done so, no doubt, but the same is not true for every single adjective–noun pair that in fact describes a possible object.

Armstrong's Combinatorialism might eventually rescue this syntactic/ inferential incarnation from this objection, for someone – at least Armstrong himself – might actually say something about 'all combinations' of predicates, along with a handy definition of a 'combination" and some level-crossing principle to handle use–mention problems, and add all that to an original fiction that manages to contain all the primitive predicates. However, something of the sort would have to be worked out at length, and we may be sure the details would be nasty. The syntactic/inferential strategy is not hopeless, but neither is it very promising.

7

Secondly, there are local-ambiguity theories of fiction, according to which the words occurring in a fictionally true statement have other than their literal meanings – at least, the copula in a subject–predicate sentence has a special meaning, which might be expressed as 'fictionally-is':[19] It is not true that Sherlock Holmes lived in Baker Street (for the perfectly real Baker Street is not such that any Sherlock Holmes ever lived in it[20]); what is true is only that Holmes fictionally-did live in Baker Street.

I myself do not believe that there is any sense in which sentences like 'Sherlock Holmes lived in Baker Street' are true save when they are used as abbreviating 'In fiction F, ...' statements. But it is clear that if I am wrong and such a sentence *is* ever true at face value in virtue of its copula's having taken a fictionalized sense, then the sentence's nonexistent subject has turned Meinongian Object. If for 'Sherlock Holmes lived in Baker Street' to be true is for Sherlock Holmes to fictionally-have lived in Baker Street, then Holmes is being treated as having ontological status of some sort. But for Armstrong, Holmes does not exist, subsist or have any sort of being.

Also, were Armstrong to pursue the present line, the fictional copula would itself still need a semantics. What is the truth-condition of

'Sherlock Holmes fictionally-did live in Baker Street'? If we are denied possible worlds as well as any form of Meinongianism, I am at a loss.

8

Thirdly, there are speech–act accounts of fictional truth.[21] On such a view, someone who asserts a fictional sentence meaning it fictionally is not making a literal declarative statement, but is engaging in a pretense. The felicity conditions on such pretend-statements do not include literal truth (*contra* Plato, it is simply not a criticism of a work of fiction to point out that the work is not literally true). Of course fictional statements have many other kinds of felicity conditions, but not ones that are immediately relevant to modal metaphysics.

The trouble for speech–act accounts is that they still must distinguish between fictional truth and fictional falsity. The accounts differ in their means of explicating 'pretend-true' and distinguishing pretend-true from pretend-false statements.[22] But note that for Armstrong's purposes they will have to do that job without recourse to possible worlds, and if their proponents want to differ significantly from syntactic/inferential accounts, then neither can pretend-truth be just a matter of syntactic deducibility from a particular fiction.

Speech–act theorists often sympathize with Gricean analyses of linguistic meaning and illocutionary force in terms of a speaker's (richly nested) propositional attitudes, and that strategy seems especially appropriate to the explication of fictive acts. Perhaps the difference between fictional truth and fictional falsity has to do with speakers' intentions and beliefs; though often the real world must cooperate in some ways if a statement is to be fictionally-true, far less is demanded of the world by fictional-truth than by literal truth. But here again, it is hard to see how the analysis would go without recourse to one or more of the means already denied to Armstrong – possible worlds, Meinongian objects, a syntactic/inferential approach to the "In fiction F" operator, and so on.

I do not know what further alternative approaches there may be to fictional truth. But in any case it seems clear that Armstrong has most of the interesting work still ahead of him, even if we agree that 'it would be truly surprising if no . . . satisfying [actualist, one-world] account were available'.

9

I would raise a final question for Armstrong's modal metaphysic. It is an internal question, not to say an ad hominem: He describes his theory as a

Fictionalist Combinatorialism; and as I have said, he is entirely serious about the Fictionalist part. But if the Fictionalism will eventually triumph over the difficulties I have raised and work out satisfactorily, *why bother with the Combinatorialism?* For Fictionalism itself guarantees Actualism. If 'other worlds' exist no more than ideal entities do, and if statements about them are at best fictionally-true, then that is modal metaphysics enough; there is no need for extraneous restrictions on how the 'worlds' may be constituted according to the fiction. They would not have to be rearrangements of the actual atoms; they would not have to be Naturalistic; they would not even have to be logically possible entities in their own right. For they are fictional, and their parent fictions can say anything we like without ontological cost to reality. In particular, we could take Lewis's (1986a) virulently Concretist theory of worlds as a fiction, and help ourselves to that theory's technical advantages without paying the price of admission. Lewis calls Ersatzism 'paradise on the cheap', but Fictionalism would be even cheaper.

Armstrong seems to address this point (p. 50):

I used to think that . . . Lewis's multiverse taken as a fiction would serve. The trouble with this idea is that the fiction would be a fiction of a monstrously swollen actuality. But the merely possible worlds are *alternatives* to the actual world and to each other. [Italics original]

But I do not entirely follow that. I do see what Armstrong means by 'a monstrously swollen actuality', which alludes to his argument (pp. 16–17) that, if Lewis is right in thinking that there *exist* other physical space-times merely dislocated from ours, then they are actual regions of reality rather than merely possible 'worlds'. But remember fiction's rampant, utterly anarchical freedom: A fiction can say anything. A fiction could say even that Lewis's outrageous theory is true as it stands (and not just as reconstrued by Armstrong or by anyone else) – even if the latter statement is logically incoherent.

So, why not be Fictionalist Lewisians, or Fictionalist Meinongians or Fictionalist anything else, rather than Fictionalist Combinatorialists? Armstrong's answer cannot lie in basic modal metaphysics at all. Fictionalism is too powerful a strategy. If successful, it solves ontological problems almost before they have arisen; no further basic metaphysics is called for. Nor, as I have mentioned, is Combinatorialism needed to preserve Naturalism, for there is nothing wrong with contra-Naturalistic fiction.

Rather, I think Armstrong's Combinatorialism is relegated to an ideological role and perhaps some tasks of fine-tuning. Its main functions seem to be to enforce 'actual-world chauvinis[m]' (p. 56) and to *remind us of* Armstrong's Naturalism. An obvious example of both is Armstrong's vigorous rejection of 'alien' universals in Chapter 4 (a rejection with sub-stantive modal consequences, not least that Armstrong must abandon S5 for S4).[23] Combinatorialism also militates against the empty world (pp. 63–4) and so solves the ancient cosmological conundrum; it sug-gests a modal epistemology that 'makes possibility epistemically accessi-ble' (p. 102); it licenses a Humean 'Distinct-Existences Principle' (p. 115) that does a bit of work; and the like, here and there. It is no wonder Arm-strong favors Combinatorialism, for a dedicated Naturalist's notion of an 'alternative possibility' would be a very concrete notion of the physical recombining of Nature's actual constituents. It is a pity, for Armstrong and for us all, that Combinatorialism requires one to choose between Ersatzing and Fictionalism.[24]

10

My critique of Armstrong's theory of possibility has been harsh, for I do not believe the theory has come anywhere near success. But my skepticism should occlude neither my sympathy nor my admiration for Armstrong's project. As I said in the beginning, I think modality is the toughest nut in Nature (or out of it, as the case may be), and I do not believe *anyone's* theory has come anywhere near success or is likely to do so in our life-times. Armstrong's zeal and fortitude deserve our thanks.[25]

NOTES

1. Armstrong's exact definition of 'Naturalism' has varied slightly from work to work. His defense of Naturalism consists largely in his well-known Causal Argument, whose most recent version is presented in Chapter 1 of Armstrong (1989a); see also Chapter 12 of Armstrong (1978).
2. Nor, he would have added, does anything in the philosophy of language or linguistic semantics require any exception to Naturalism, for meaning is a func-tion of mind (Armstrong 1971; he regards that article as superseded by Bennett 1976). As for ethical value, Armstrong is not a moral realist in the first place, but falls in with the view of Mackie (1977).
3. All my subsequent page and chapter references will be to that work unless marked otherwise.
4. Assuming, at least, that one is a modal realist in the first place. One might simply refuse to countenance modal distinctions, and/or regard statements of possibility and necessity as false or meaningless. But one would thereby de-prive oneself of almost everything one might think of to say on most everyday topics.
5. That is why in my own work (e.g. Lycan 1991b) I have accepted David Lewis's (1986a) agenda of trying to show why an Ersatzist theory of modality is su-perior on balance to Lewis's own mad-rhinoceros version of modal realism,

rather than trying to refute Lewis's outrageous view outright. That his theory has some bizarre consequences cannot in itself be taken to show that an obviously better theory is possible.

6. The Positivist theory of necessity as truth by convention was wonderfully Naturalistic (assuming some Naturalization of truth and convention themselves). But it has few advocates nowadays, because of the perceived infirmity of the very notion of truth 'by' convention; Lycan (1991a) argues that this perception is correct. More sophisticated metalinguistic theories derive from Sellars (1948), but have never caught on.

7. But the best known and best developed version of Combinatorialism has been Cresswell's (1972, 1973).

8. Later, in Chapter 9, he sketches a program for Naturalizing set theory. But he has an additional reason for eschewing sets in pursuing the present project (p. 47): 'It seems that sets are supervenient on their members, that is, ultimately, things which are not sets. Supervenience, however, is a notion to be defined in terms of possible worlds, and hence in terms of possibility. It seems undesirable, therefore, to make use of sets in defining possibility'.

9. He provides for 'relative atoms' in case it should turn out that matter is indefinitely divisible (Chapter 5); he refines Wittgenstein's Humean compossibility assumption at some length (Chapters 6 and 8); and he elaborates the underlying theory of universals (Chapters 7–10), finally attempting to subsume mathematics and logic.

10. 'Some statements about ideal gasses, frictionless planes and economic men are true, while others are false' (p. 50).

11. This is not, of course, to say that there actually does exist a golden mountain, but only that 'Some possible world contains a golden mountain' is one of the statements that would be accepted rather than rejected by modal metaphysicians, in the same sense as some statements about ideal gases are accepted rather than rejected by physicists.

12. Such an explicative program is an instance of what Lycan (1979) called the 'paraphrastic' approach to possibilia. The following critical points are digested from that essay.

13. As I quietly put it in Lycan (1979), 'Resting a philosophical theory on unexplicated counterfactuals is like hoping one may cross a freezing river by hopping across the heaving ice floes'.

14. Cf. Field's (1980) fictionalist theory of numbers.

15. He adds that in any case 'the notion of the fictional . . . has no special link with possibility', for there are impossible fictions (p. 49). Agreed: no *special* link, in that sense. But certainly a very important link, in that fictional entities are nonactual objects of intelligible discourse.

16. Any plausible theory of fictional truth will expand this strict deductive-closure criterion by also including further sentences deduced or induced with the aid of real-world information brought to bear on the reader's interpretation of the text. See Lewis (1978) and Ross (1987), but for present purposes try to ignore and abstract away from the couching of their accounts in terms of possible worlds.

17. Armstrong might reply that those very problems (e.g., there being fewer than continuum-many sentences of any actual formal language) constitute a sufficient reason for *not* simply taking the specifications as world surrogates, and so much the worse for my argument. But each problem translates

straightforwardly into a reason against the original claim that for a world to exist is for a statement of its existence to be deducible from the Lie.

18. It might be replied that although a fiction is needed, an author is not: fictions may be Platonic entities existing in their own right, and only sometimes stumbled upon by creative writers. In that sense, perhaps, there is a fiction corresponding to each of the Wittgenstein worlds. However: (a) as before, this would collapse Armstrong's alleged Combinatorialism into Adams's 'world-story' form of Ersatzism; and (b) no Naturalist can appeal to Platonic entities, 'fictions' or anything else. A fiction may be a universal rather than a particular, but for Armstrong the only universals are immanent Scotist universals, only formally abstracted from actual physical states of affairs (1978; see also Armstrong's 1989b taxonomy of theories of universals).

19. It would not help to maintain just that the quantifiers have special meanings, for that was our original problem about mere possibilia. It is of course possible to locate the fictional/literal ambiguity of a sentence somewhere other than in the sentence's copula. One might hold that the predicates involved are paronymous, or even that the component singular terms shift their reference. (Chapter 11 of Castañeda 1989 contains a useful critical review of these options.) For that matter, one might suppose that the ambiguity consisted in the presence or absence of an underlying 'story' or 'In fiction F' operator, though that would merely bring us back to the problem of providing a semantics for that operator and hence to the options already surveyed.

20. Even in its nineteenth-century 200 block, which was half a mile south of the renumbered present-day 200 section. I am sorry to see that the latter is now falsely marked as the fictional home of Holmes.

21. For example, Currie (1990).

22. Cf. Currie (1990).

23. Armstrong himself does not feel that 'must' as chafing, but only as the expression of what a good Naturalist and actual-world chauvinist should *want* to think about modal logic. Armstrong does go on to permit alien individuals, since it is fairly obvious that there might have been more quarks or leptons than in fact there are, and he grants (p. 60) that this counts as a qualification of the Combinatorialist idea.

24. In its inception, Combinatorialism was offered simply as a way of Ersatzing, a mere implementation of the Ersatzer program. It was made particularly plausible by examples such as 'possible chess game', 'possible sentence' and the like which obviously yield to Combinatorialist treatment (so long as one has an *individuator,* a singular-term–forming operator used to designate alternative arrangements of the relevant basic elements).

25. I am very grateful to David Armstrong for intense discussion of this and many other topics over the years, and even more so to him and his colleagues for making me riotously welcome in the Department of Traditional and Modern Philosophy, University of Sydney, in 1978, 1983 and 1986.

REFERENCES

Armstrong, D. M. 1961. *Perception and the Physical World* (London: Routledge & Kegan Paul).

1962. *Bodily Sensations* (London: Routledge & Kegan Paul).

1968. *A Materialist Theory of the Mind* (London: Routledge & Kegan Paul).

1971. 'Meaning and Communication', *Philosophical Review* 80: 427–47.

1973. *Belief, Truth and Knowledge* (Cambridge University Press).

1978. *Universals and Scientific Realism,* 2 vols. (Cambridge University Press).

1983a. *What Is a Law of Nature?* (Cambridge University Press).

1989a. *A Combinatorial Theory of Possibility* (Cambridge University Press).

1989b. *Universals: an Opinionated Introduction* (Boulder, CO: Westview).

Bennett, Jonathan. 1976. *Linguistic Behaviour* (Cambridge University Press).

Castañeda, Hector-Neri. 1989. *Thinking, Language, and Experience* (Minneapolis, MN: University of Minnesota Press).

Cresswell, M. J. 1972. 'The World is Everything that is the Case', *Australasian Journal of Philosophy* 50: 1–13. Reprinted in Loux (1979), pp. 129–45.

1973. *Logics and Languages* (London: Methuen).

Currie, Gregory. 1990. *The Nature of Fiction* (Cambridge University Press).

Field, Hartry. 1980. *Science without Numbers* (Princeton University Press).

Lewis, David. 1973. *Counterfactuals* (Cambridge, MA: Harvard University Press).

1978. 'Truth in Fiction', *American Philosophical Quarterly* 15: 37–46. Reprinted in *Philosophical Papers,* vol. 1 (Oxford: Blackwell, 1983), pp. 261–75.

1986a. *On the Plurality of Worlds* (Oxford: Blackwell).

Loux, Michael J. (ed.) 1979. *The Possible and the Actual* (Ithaca, NY: Cornell University Press).

Lycan, William G. 1979. 'The Trouble with Possible Worlds'. In Loux (1979), pp. 274–316.

1991a. 'Definition in a Quinean World'. In *Definitions and Definability: Philosophical Perspectives,* ed. J. H. Fetzer, D. Schatz and G. Schlesinger (Dordrecht: Kluwer).

1991b. 'Two – No, Three – Concepts of Possible Worlds', *Proceedings of the Aristotelian Society* 91: 215–27.

Mackie, J. L. 1977. *Ethics: Inventing Right and Wrong* (New York: Penguin).

Quine, W. V. 1969. 'Propositional Objects'. In *Ontological Relativity and Other Essays* (New York: Columbia University Press), pp. 139–60.

Ross, J. 1987. 'The Semantics of Media', Ph.D. thesis, Wellington: Victoria University.

Sellars, Wilfrid. 1948. 'Concepts as Involving Laws and Inconceivable without Them', *Philosophy of Science* 15: 287–315. Reprinted in *Pure Pragmatics and Possible Worlds: the Early Essays of Wilfrid Sellars,* ed. Jeffrey Sicha (Atascadero, CA: Ridgeview).

Skyrms, Brian. 1981. 'Tractarian Nominalism', *Philosophical Studies* 40: 199–206. Reprinted in Armstrong (1989a), pp. 145–52.

Stalnaker, Robert C. 1969. 'A Theory of Conditionals'. In *Studies in Logical Theory,* ed. Nicholas Rescher, *American Philosophical Quarterly* Monograph Series, no. 2 (Oxford: Blackwell).

Wittgenstein, Ludwig. 1922. *Tractatus Logico-Philosophicus,* tr. F. P. Ramsey, ed. C. K. Ogden (London: Routledge & Kegan Paul).

Reply to Lycan

D. M. ARMSTRONG

Bill Lycan has visited our department in Sydney for half a year on two different occasions. After his first visit, I told him that any time he wanted I would write him a reference saying that there could be no better visitor to a department. The intellectual stimulation he gave us, his teaching, the way he threw himself into everything that was going on (including some amateur acting), and his liveliness and humour at all times made it an enormous pleasure to have him with us. A few years later he was back with us. I thought that the second visit had to be an anticlimax. In fact it was just as enjoyable and intellectually valuable as the first time. I know nothing to his discredit during these visits except his fanatical determination to discuss Wilfrid Sellars' 'grain' argument about colour in a paper or papers, which grew ever longer and where the argument was alleged to contain an ever greater number of steps.

Possibility

There is an important, if informal, principle of sociology which says that people are promoted to the level of their incapacity. This ensures plenty of dead-wood at or near the top. Lycan's opening remarks suggest to me that something of the same sort occurs in my defence of Naturalism, understood as the view that the spatiotemporal manifold constitutes all that there is. My problem is self-inflicted. By attempting to resolve successively greater difficulties for this thesis, and, at the last, by trying to give a Naturalist account of modality, I ensure that I fall into every greater implausibility.

It may be so. It must be conceded that modality poses great difficulties. It must be conceded also that my fictionalist account of possible worlds, to which Lycan directs his criticism, suffers because I have not worked out a Naturalist doctrine of fictions. But, as Lycan suggests, I do have a fairly confident belief that such a doctrine can be worked out. An inability to work out an account of fiction compatible with Naturalism would seem to be an extraordinary hurdle at which to fall.

The first point to make is a negative one. *Pace* Lycan, fiction is not very close to modality. Lycan states (Section 5) that 'fictional entities are nonactual possibilia, save for those which are impossibilia'. Precisely; fictional entities are nonexistents, but they have no particular modal status. A Cheshire cat that leaves behind its grin is as fictionally acceptable as a Cinderella that leaves behind her glass slipper. Impossible things cannot, of course, be caught within a framework of possible worlds, only approximations to such things can be so caught (see Lewis on impossible fictions in the postscript to his 'Truth in Fiction', 1983a). The moral I draw from this is that a possible-worlds treatment of fiction is misdirected.

The next step is to bring the fiction of possible worlds under the subcategory of *useful* fictions. Or, because there are different sorts of usefulness, to bring this fiction under the category of fictions that are, explicitly, *intellectually* useful. The kinship with the scientific fictions that even a scientific realist must countenance, such things as ideal gases, is then manifest. Of course, despite this kinship, there may still be a wide gap between the useful fictions of scientists and what I am claiming is the useful fiction of possible worlds.

Lycan mentions what he takes to be differences between scientific fictions and the alleged fiction of possible worlds. He points out that 'true' statements about ideal entities in science licence counterfactuals (Section 3); and that such entities are typically degenerate or limiting cases (Section 4). He states that the same cannot be said of possible worlds. But, first, there are counterfactuals where the consequent is simply permitted rather than ensured or made probable ('If this had been done, then that might have happened'). Presumably, although no example springs to my mind, ideal entities in science could figure in the antecedent of such counterfactuals. Possible worlds may be thought of as scenarios for the world that are permitted, once all sorts of restrictions (though not all restrictions) are thought away. They are also limiting cases, because the restrictions left in place are minimal.

But however this may be, we do find natural scientists employing conceptions that are very close to that of possible worlds. Physicists and others talk about 'ensembles' of states of a system or about 'phase-spaces'. The idea here is that some system subject to physical laws is under consideration; this system can be in various possible states. The totality of all these physically possible states constitutes the ensemble or phase-space of the states. It would seem plausible to say that these totalities involve a fictional element, for no one thinks that the physical system under consideration will actually *be* in all these states. Most of the states are *merely* possible, which means, at least according to me, that they have no existence. They are fictions.

Certain restrictions are placed upon such ensembles. Certain physical laws, if not all physical laws, remain in force. Many states that a philosopher would consider possible states are excluded. But the problem for a philosopher who wants to introduce the notion of possible worlds is no more than this: to introduce much more relaxed constraints, without abandoning all constraints. It would not be relevant here to discuss just what those relaxed constraints should be. Different philosophers may very reasonably adopt different constraints. (Consider, for instance, the position of those who maintain that the laws of nature hold 'in all possible worlds'. The ensembles that they admit will not be all that different from those admitted by the physicists.)

Lycan may fairly object to all this that I have merely been assuming, without showing, that ensembles or phase-spaces are fictions. And he may further fairly object that, even if they are fictions, the problem of giving an account of fiction has still been squibbed. But it seems a plausible hypothesis, one involving a minimum of metaphysics, that such ensembles are fictions. And if they are, then surely it does something to tame the problem of the fictional if the natural scientist is as involved with it, and involved in the same general way, as the philosopher.

Lycan does ask an important question, though, when he asks why, if fictionalism about possible worlds is true, we should bother about Combinatorialism? Why not, for instance, simply adopt Lewis's theory but treat it as a fiction? In a nice thrust, Lycan points out that, since fictions can be incoherent, I need not worry about whether the theory is logically coherent or not.

In the first place, would I not have to worry about whether the fiction was *conservative?* When Hartry Field (1980) argued that mathematics is fictional, he did not deny that it is useful; he therefore argued that it is conservative. If you put in truths about the physical world in at one end of the sausage machine, you must get nothing but truths about the physical world out at the other. He found proof of the conservativeness of mathematics a difficult undertaking, and has not yet completed it. I want the fiction of possible worlds to be of use in philosophy, so do I not need some argument to show that it does not mislead? Proof is hardly appropriate for a question about the metaphysics of modality. But I take Combinatorialism to be a reasonably plausible theory of possibility, satisfying some quite deep intuitions, and one way to develop it is as a Fictionalist Combinatorialism about possible worlds.

But an epistemic point may be even more important here. Consider the question raised by Lewis (1986a) of whether a talking donkey is possible. Assuming that the laws of nature rule out such a beast in our world, a claim of possibility is for Lewis a claim about some other, totally inaccessible, world. In my 1989a (Chapter 7, Section IV) I argue that, given combinatorial principles, scientific and semantic information from our world can be brought to bear on the question. Indeed, such information as we already have suggests what most philosophers would offhand take to be the case – that a talking donkey *is* possible. Lewis can get this result also, because he uses combinatorial principles as one of the principles to be used in deciding what is the case in other possible worlds. But suppose we ask what reason Lewis has for thinking that combinatorial principles apply in those other worlds. He can only argue from the intuitive appeal that such principles have. There can be no question of checking the principles against the worlds. In these circumstances I think that a theory that makes combinatorial principles part of the very essence of possibility has an advantage.

But perhaps a fictionalist approach is quite wrong. In that case I would try, as Cresswell and others have done, to use sets of actually existing elements as substitutes for possibilities. I am not delighted with this way out because it involves taking representations as substitutes for the possibilities that they represent. But perhaps I am too delicate in this matter. Lycan, in any case, does not raise this objection. Rather, he says that 'a Naturalist is not entitled to nonphysical items like sets, at least so long as those items remain acausal and nonspatiotemporal' (Section 2, first paragraph). In a footnote, however, he indicates that I do sketch 'a program for Naturalizing set theory'. I hope I have advanced that program further in my 1991 paper 'Classes Are States of Affairs'. The key is the question of singletons, that is, unit sets, because as pointed out by Lewis (1991) many-membered sets appear to be nothing more than mereological wholes composed of singletons. Singletons I take to be states of affairs having a subject–attribute form. The attribute in question is that of *unithood,* the higher-order property of having some unit-making property. A unit-making property is one that picks out the subject as one thing, so that a many-membered set becomes what it surely should be: a collection of its members, each taken as a unit, each taken as a one.

Many states of affairs are perceivable, and there is no difficulty in the perception that a particular has some unit-making property or other. That the particular has unithood, as opposed to some specific unit-making property, would seem to be an abstraction by the intellect (in the old, legitimate, Lockean sense: selective and partial consideration) from what is perceived.

It remains true, as Lycan points out, that an account of possibilities as sets does involve me in technical difficulties, at any rate if I want to take singletons as supervenient upon their members. For I use a definition of supervenience in terms of possible worlds. Some adjustment in my position would be necessary here to avoid circularity, and I am not sure how that adjustment should go.

But, in conclusion, I do not think that the status of my possible worlds, whether as fictions or sets of elements, constitutes the most serious difficulty for my theory of possibility. I am far more worried that the theory will turn out to be circular in a deep manner. The theory purports to analyze the very idea of possibility in terms of the fictional combination of wholly distinct elements. It may be that this idea involves a covert appeal to modal notions; it is with some trepidation that I await attempts to argue this. If they succeeded, I would retreat to a claim to have uncovered the true structure of modality – this structure would then be an irreducible feature of being. It should, I hope, still be possible to argue that *mere* possibilities do not exist. If so, irreducible modality would still be compatible with Naturalism.

REFERENCES

Armstrong, D. M. 1989a. *A Combinatorial Theory of Possibility* (Cambridge University Press).

1991. 'Classes Are States of Affairs'. *Mind* 100: 189–200.

Field, Hartry. 1980. *Science without Numbers* (Princeton University Press).

Lewis, David. 1983a. Postscripts to 'Truth in Fiction'. In *Philosophical Papers,* vol. 1 (Oxford: Blackwell), pp. 276–80.

1986a. *On the Plurality of Worlds* (Oxford: Blackwell).

1991. *Parts of Classes* (Oxford: Blackwell).

2

Many, but Almost One

DAVID LEWIS

The Problem of the Many

Think of a cloud – just one cloud, and around it clear blue sky. Seen from the ground, the cloud may seem to have a sharp boundary. Not so. The cloud is a swarm of water droplets. At the outskirts of the cloud the density of the droplets falls off. Eventually they are so few and far between that we may hesitate to say that the outlying droplets are still part of the cloud at all; perhaps we might better say only that they are near the cloud. But the transition is gradual. Many surfaces are equally good candidates to be the boundary of the cloud. Therefore many aggregates of droplets, some more inclusive and some less inclusive (and some inclusive in different ways then others), are equally good candidates to be the cloud. Since they have equal claim, how can we say that the cloud is one of these aggregates rather than another? But if all of them count as clouds, then we have many clouds rather than one. And if none of them count, each one being ruled out because of the competition from the others, then we have no cloud. How is it, then, that we have just one cloud? And yet we do.

This is Unger's (1980) 'problem of the many'. Once noticed, we can see that it is everywhere, for all things are swarms of particles. There are always outlying particles, questionably parts of the thing, not definitely included and not definitely not included. So there are always many aggregates, differing by a little bit here and a little bit there, with equal claim to be the thing. We have many things or we have none, but anyway not the one thing we thought we had. That is absurd.

Think of a rusty nail, and the gradual transition from steel, to steel with bits of rust scattered through, to rust adhering to the nail, to rust merely resting on the nail. Or think of a cathode, and its departing electrons. Or think of anything that undergoes evaporation or erosion or abrasion. Or think of yourself, or any organism, with parts that gradually come loose in metabolism or excretion or perspiration or shedding of dead skin. In each case, a thing has questionable parts, and therefore is subject to the problem of the many.

If, as I think, things perdure through time by having temporal parts, then questionable temporal parts add to the problem of the many. If a person comes into existence gradually (whether over weeks or over years or over nanoseconds doesn't matter for our present purpose) then there are questionable temporal parts at the beginning of every human life. Likewise at the end, even in the most sudden death imaginable. Do you think you are one person? – No, there are many aggregates of temporal parts, differing just a little at the ends, with equal claim to count as persons, and equal claim to count as you. Are all those equally good claims good enough? If so, you are many. If not, you are none. Either way we get the wrong answer. For undeniably you are one.

If, as some think but I do not,[1] ordinary things extend through other possible worlds, then the problem of the many takes on still another dimension. Here in this world we have a ship, the *Enigma;* there in another world is a ship built at about the same time, to plans that are nearly the same but not quite, using many of the same planks and some that are not the same. It is questionable whether the ship in that other world is *Enigma* herself, or just a substitute. If *Enigma* is a thing that extends through worlds, then the question is whether *Enigma* includes as a part what's in that other world. We have two versions of *Enigma,* one that includes this questionable other-worldly part and one that excludes it. They have equal claim to count as ships, and equal claim to count as *Enigma.* We have two ships, coinciding in this world but differing in their full extent. Or else we have none; but anyway not the one ship we thought we had.

The Paradox of 1001 Cats

Cat Tibbles is alone on the mat. Tibbles has hairs $h_1, h_2, \ldots, h_{1000}$. Let c be Tibbles including all these hairs; let c_1 be all of Tibbles except for h_1; and similarly for $c_2, \ldots, c_{1000}$. Each of these c's is a cat. So instead of one cat on the mat, Tibbles, we have at least 1001 cats – which is absurd. This is P. T. Geach's (1980, pp. 215–16) paradox of 1001 cats.

Why should we think that each c_n is a cat? Because, says Geach, 'c_n would clearly be a cat were the hair h_n plucked out, and we cannot reasonably suppose that plucking out a hair *generates* a cat, so c_n must already have been a cat' (p. 215). This need not convince us. We can reply that plucking out h_n turns c_n from a mere proper part of cat Tibbles into the whole of a cat. No new cat is generated, since the cat that c_n becomes the whole of is none other than Tibbles. Nor do c_n and Tibbles ever become identical *simpliciter* – of course not, since what's true about c_n's past still differs from what's true about Tibbles's past. Rather, c_n becomes the whole of cat Tibbles in the sense that c_n's post-plucking temporal part is identical with Tibbles's post-plucking temporal part. So far, so good; except for those, like Geach, who reject the idea of temporal parts. The rest of us have no paradox yet.

But suppose it is spring, and Tibbles is shedding. When a cat sheds, the hairs do not come popping off; they become gradually looser, until finally they are held in place only by the hairs around them. By the end of this gradual process, the loose hairs are no longer parts of the cat. Sometime before the end, they are questionable parts: not definitely still parts of the cat, not definitely not. Suppose each of $h_1, h_2, \ldots, h_{1000}$ is at this questionable stage. Now indeed all of $c_1, c_2, \ldots, c_{1000}$, and also c which includes all the questionable hairs, have equal claim to be a cat, and equal claim to be Tibbles. So now we have 1001 cats. (Indeed, we have many more than that. For instance there is the cat that includes all but the four hairs h_6, h_{408}, h_{882}, and h_{907}.) The paradox of 1001 cats, insofar as it is a real paradox, is another instance of Unger's problem of the many.

To deny that there are many cats on the mat, we must either deny that the many are cats, or else deny that the cats are many. We may solve the paradox by finding a way to disqualify candidates for cathood: there are the many, sure enough, but the many are not all cats. At most one of them is. Perhaps the true cat is one of the many; or perhaps it is something else altogether, and none of the many are cats. Or else, if we grant that all the candidates are truly cats, we must find a way to say that these cats are not truly different from one another. I think both alternatives lead to successful solutions, but we shall see some unsuccessful solutions as well.

Two Solutions by Disqualification: None of the Many Are Cats

We could try saying that not one of the c's is a cat; they are many, sure enough, but not many cats. Tibbles, the only genuine cat on the mat, is something else, different from all of them.

One way to disqualify the many is to invoke the alleged distinction between things and the parcels of matter that constitute them. We could try saying that the c's are not cats. Rather, they are cat-constituting parcels of matter. Tibbles is the cat that each of them constitutes.[2]

This dualism of things and their constituters is unparsimonious and unnecessary. It was invented to solve a certain problem, but a better solution to that problem lies elsewhere, as follows. We know that the matter of a thing may exist before and after the thing does; and we know that a thing may gain and lose matter while it still exists, as a cat does, or a wave or a flame. The dualists conclude that the matter is not the thing; constitution is not identity; there are things, there are the parcels of matter that temporarily constitute those things; these are items of two different categories, related by the special relation of constitution. We must agree, at least, that the temporally extended thing is not the temporally extended parcel of matter that temporarily constitutes that thing. But constitution may be identity, all the same, if it is identity between temporal parts. If some matter constitutes a cat for one minute, then a minute-long temporal segment of the cat is identical to a minute-long temporal segment of the matter. The cat consists entirely of the matter that constitutes it, in this sense: The whole of the cat, throughout the time it lives, consists entirely of temporal segments of various parcels of matter. At any moment, if we disregard everything not located at that moment, the cat and the matter that then constitutes it are identical.[3]

So only those who reject the notion of temporal parts have any need for the dualism of things and constituters. But suppose we accept it all the same. At best, this just transforms the paradox of 1001 cats into the paradox of 1001 cat-constituters. Is that an improvement? We all thought there was only one cat on the mat. After distinguishing Tibbles from her constituter, would we not still want to think there was only one cat-constituter on the mat?

Further, even granted that Tibbles has many constituters, I still question whether Tibbles is the only cat present. The constituters are cat-like in size, shape, weight, inner structure, and motion. They vibrate and set the air in motion – in short, they purr (especially when you pat them). Any way a cat can be at a moment, cat-constituters also can be; anything a cat can do at a moment, cat-constituters also can do. They are all too cat-like not to be cats. Indeed, they may have unfeline pasts and futures, but that doesn't show that they are never cats; it only shows that they do not remain cats for very long. Now we have the paradox of 1002 cats: Tibbles the constituted cat, and also the 1001 all-too-feline cat-constituters. Nothing has been gained.

I conclude that invoking the dualism of cats and cat-constituters to solve the paradox of 1001 cats does not succeed.

A different way to disqualify the many appeals to a doctrine of vagueness in nature. We could try saying that cat Tibbles is a vague object, and that the c's are not cats but rather alternative precisifications of a cat.

In one way, at least, this solution works better than the one before. This time, I cannot complain that at best we only transform the paradox of 1001 cats into the paradox of 1001 cat-precisifications, because that is no paradox. If indeed there are vague objects and precisifications, it is only to be expected that one vague object will have many precisifications.

If the proposal is meant to solve our paradox, it must be meant as serious metaphysics. It cannot just be a way of saying 'in the material mode' that the words 'Tibbles' and 'cat' are vague, and that this vagueness makes it indefinite just which hairs are part of the cat Tibbles. Rather, the idea must be that material objects come in two varieties, vague and precise; cats are vague, the *c*'s are precise, and that is why none of the *c*'s is a cat.

This new dualism of vague objects and their precisifications is, again, unparsimonious and unnecessary. The problem it was made to solve might better be solved another way. It is absurd to think that we have decided to apply the name 'Tibbles' to a certain precisely delimited object; or that we have decided to apply the term 'cat' to each of certain precisely delimited objects. But we needn't conclude that these words must rather apply to certain *im*precisely delimited, vague objects. Instead we should conclude that we never quite made up our minds just what these words apply to. We have made up our minds that 'Tibbles' is to name one or another Tibbles-precisification, but we never decided just which one; we decided that 'cat' was to apply to some and only some cat-precisifications, but again we never decided just which ones. (Nor did we ever decide just which things our new-found terms 'Tibbles-precisification' and 'cat-precisification' were to apply to.) It was very sensible of us not to decide. We probably couldn't have done it if we'd tried; and even if we could have, doing it would have been useless folly. Semantic indecision will suffice to explain the phenomenon of vagueness.[4] We need no vague objects.

Further, I doubt that I have any correct conception of a vague object. How, for instance, shall I think of an object that is vague in its spatial extent? The closest I can come is to superimpose three pictures. There is the *multiplicity* picture, in which the vague object gives way to its many precisifications, and the vagueness of the object gives way to differences between precisifications. There is the *ignorance* picture, in which the object has some definite but secret extent. And there is the *fadeaway* picture, in which the presence of the object admits of degree, in much the way that the presence of a spot of illumination admits of degree, and the degree diminishes as a function of the distance from the region where the object is most intensely present. None of the three pictures is right. Each one in its own way replaces the alleged vagueness of the object by precision. But if I cannot think of a vague object except by juggling these mistaken pictures, I have no correct conception.[5]

I can complain as before that we end up with a paradox of 1002 cats: Tibbles the vague cat, and also the 1001 precise cats. Once again, the cat-precisifications are all too cat-like. More so than the cat-constituters, in fact: The precisifications are cat-like not just in what they can do and how they can be at a moment, but also over time. They would make good pets – especially since 1001 of them will not eat you out of house and home!

Don't say that the precisifications cannot be cats because cats cannot be precise objects. Surely there could be cats in a world where nature is so much less gradual that the problem of the many goes away. It could happen that cats have no questionable parts at all, neither spatial nor temporal. (In this world, when cats shed in the spring, the hairs *do* come popping off.) So it is at least possible that cat-like precise objects are genuine cats. If so, how can the presence of one vague cat spoil their cathood?

I conclude that invoking the dualism of vague objects and their precisifications to solve the paradox of 1001 cats does not succeed.

A Better Solution by Disqualification: One of the Many Is a Cat

Since all of the many are so cat-like, there is only one credible way to deny that all of them are cats. When is something very cat-like, yet not a cat? – When it is just a little less than a whole cat, almost all of a cat with just one little bit left out. Or when it is just a little more than a cat, a cat plus a little something extra. Or when it is both a little more and a little less.

Suppose we say that one of our many is exactly a cat, no more and no less; and that each of the rest is disqualified because it is a little less than a cat, or a little more, or both more and less. This invokes no unparsimonious and unnecessary dualisms; it disqualifies all but one of the many without denying that they are very cat-like; it leaves us with just one cat. All very satisfactory.

The trouble, so it seems, is that there is no saying which one is a cat. That is left altogether arbitrary. Settling it takes a semantic decision, and that is the decision we never made (and shouldn't have made, and maybe couldn't have made). No secret fact could answer the question, for we never decided how the answer would depend on secret facts. Which one deserves the name 'cat' is up to us. If we decline to settle the question, nothing else will settle it for us.[6]

We cannot deny the arbitrariness. What we can deny, though, is that it is trouble. What shall we do, if semantic indecision is inescapable, and yet we wish to carry on talking? The answer, surely, is to exploit the fact that very often our unmade semantic decisions don't matter. Often, what you want to say will be true under all different ways of making the unmade decision. Then if you say it, even if by choice or by necessity you leave the decision forever unmade, you still speak truthfully. It makes no difference just what you meant, what you say is true regardless. And if it makes no difference just what you meant, likewise it makes no difference that you never made up your mind just what to mean. You say that a famous architect designed Fred's house; it never crossed your mind to think whether by 'house' you meant something that did or that didn't include the attached garage; neither does some established convention or secret fact decide the issue; no matter, you knew that what you said was true either way.

This plan for coping with semantic indecision is van Fraassen's (1966) method of *supervaluations*. Call a sentence *super-true* if and only if it is true under all ways of making the unmade semantic decisions; *super-false* if and only if it is false under all ways of making those decisions; and if it is true under some ways and false under others, then it suffers a super-truth-value gap. Super-truth, with respect to a language interpreted in an imperfectly decisive way, replaces truth *simpliciter* as the goal of a cooperative speaker attempting to impart information. We can put it another way: Whatever it is that we do to determine the 'intended' interpretation of our language determines not one interpretation but a range of interpretations. (The range depends on context, and is itself somewhat indeterminate.) What we try for, in imparting information, is truth of what we say under all the intended interpretations.

Each intended interpretation of our language puts one of the cat candidates on the mat into the extension of the word 'cat', and excludes all the rest. Likewise each intended interpretation picks out one cat candidate, the same one, as the referent of 'Tibbles'. Therefore it is super-true that there is just one cat, Tibbles, on the mat. Because it is super-true, you are entitled to affirm it. And so you may say what you want to say: there is one cat. That is how the method of supervaluations solves the paradox of 1001 cats.

Objection. Just one of the candidates is a cat, no more and no less. But don't try to say which one it is. Nothing you might say would be super-true. For it is exactly this semantic decision that remains unmade; it is exactly in this respect that the intended interpretations differ. Although it is super-true that something is a cat on the mat, there is nothing such that it is super-true of it that *it* is a cat on the mat. (It's like the old puzzle: I owe you a horse, but there's no horse such that I owe you that horse.) This is peculiar.

Reply. So it is. But once you know the reason why, you can learn to accept it.

Objection.[7] Supervaluationism works too well: it stops us from ever stating the problem in the first place. The problem supposedly was that all the many candidates had equal claim to cathood. But under the super-valuationist rule, that may not be said. For under any one way of making the unmade decision, one candidate is picked as a cat. So under any one way of making the decision, the candidates do *not* have equal claim. What's true under all ways of making the decision is super-true. So what's super-true, and what we should have said, is that the candidates do *not* have equal claim. Then what's the problem? And yet the problem was stated. So supervaluationism is mistaken.

Reply. What's mistaken is a fanatical supervaluationism, which automatically applies the supervaluationist rule to any statement whatever, never mind that the statement makes no sense that way. The rule should instead be taken as a defeasible presumption. What defeats it, sometimes, is the cardinal principle of pragmatics: The right way to take what is said, if at all possible, is the way that makes sense of the message. Since the supervaluationist rule would have made hash of our statement of the problem, straightway the rule was suspended. We are good at making these accommodations; we don't even notice when we do it. Under the supervaluationist rule, it's right to say that there's only one cat, and so the candidates have unequal claim. Suspending the rule, it's right to say that the candidates have equal claim, and that all of them alike are not definitely not cats. Suspending the rule, it's even right to say that they are all cats! Is this capitulation to the paradox? – No; it's no harm to admit that in *some* sense there are many cats. What's intolerable is to be without any good and natural sense in which there is only one cat.

Objection.[8] The supervaluationist's notion of indeterminate reference is conceptually derivative from the prior notion of reference *simpliciter.* But if the problem of the many is everywhere, and semantic indecision is inescapable, then reference *simpliciter* never happens. To the extent that we gain concepts by 'fixing the reference' on actual examples, we are in no position to have the concept of reference. Then neither are we in a position to have the derivative concept of indeterminate reference due to semantic indecision.

Reply. We don't need actual examples to have the concept. We have plenty of imaginary examples of reference *simpliciter,* uncomplicated by semantic indecision. These examples are set in sharper worlds than ours: worlds where clouds have no outlying droplets, where cats shed their hairs instantaneously, and so on. When we picked up the concept of reference, in childhood, we probably took for granted that our own world was sharp in just that way. (When not puzzling over the problem of the many, maybe we half-believe it still.) We fixed the reference of 'reference' on these imaginary examples in the sharp world we thought we lived in – and if any theory of reference says that cannot be done, so much the worse for it.

I conclude that the supervaluationist solution to the paradox of 1001 cats, and to the problem of the many generally, is successful. But is it the only successful solution? – I think not. I turn now to the other sort of solution: the kind which concedes that the many are cats, but seeks to deny that the cats are really many.

Relative Identity: The Many Are Not Different Cats

Geach himself favours one such solution. The paradox of 1001 cats serves as a showcase for his doctrine of relative identity.

Everything falls into place if we realize that the number of cats on the mat is the number of *different* cats on the mat; and c_{13}, c_{279}, and c are not three different cats, they are one and the same cat. Though none of these 1001 lumps of feline tissue is the same lump of feline tissue as another, each is the same cat as any other: each of them, then, is a cat, but there is only one cat on the mat, and our original story stands. . . . The price to pay is that we must regard '——— is the same cat as ———' as expressing only a certain equivalence relation, not an absolute identity restricted to cats; but this price, I have elsewhere argued, must be paid anyhow, for there is no such absolute identity as logicians have assumed. (1980, p. 216)

'Same cat' is a relation of partial indiscernibility, restricted to respects of comparison somehow associated with the term 'cat', and discernibility by just a few hairs doesn't count. 'Same lump of feline tissue' is a different relation of partial indiscernibility, and a more discerning one.

I agree that sometimes we say 'same', and mean by it not 'absolute identity' but just some relation of partial indiscernibility. I also agree that sometimes we count by relations of partial indiscernibility. As I once wrote:

If an infirm man wishes to know how many roads he must cross to reach his destination, I will count by identity-along-his-path rather than by identity. By crossing the Chester A. Arthur Parkway and Route 137 at the brief stretch where they have merged, he can cross both by crossing only one road. (1976, p. 27)

I'll happily add that for that brief stretch, the two roads are the same. But though I don't object to this positive part of Geach's view, it doesn't ring true to apply it as he does to the case of the cats.

If you ask me to say whether c_{13}, c_{279}, and c are the same or different, I may indeed be of two minds about how to answer. I might say they're different – after all, I know how they differ! Or I might say they're the same, because the difference is negligible, so I duly ignore it. (Not easy to do while attending to the example as I now am; if I attend to my ignoring of something, *ipso facto* I no longer ignore it.) But if you add the noun phrase, either 'same cat' or 'same lump of feline tissue', it seems to me that I am no less hesitant than before. Just as I was of two minds about 'same', so I am still of two minds about 'same cat' and 'same lump of feline tissue'.

Other cases are different. If you ask me 'same or different?' when you hold Monday's *Melbourne Age* in one hand and Tuesday's *Age* in the other, or when you hold one Monday *Age* in each hand, again I won't know how to answer. But if you ask me 'same or different newspaper?' or 'same or different issue?' or 'same or different copy?' then I'll know just what to say. We can dispute his explanation of what happens, but at least the phenomenon happens exactly as Geach says it does. Not so, I think, for the case of 'same cat' versus 'same lump'.

Something else is lacking in Geach's solution. In other cases where it comes natural to count by a relation other than identity, it seems that identity itself – 'absolute identity' – is not far away. Local identity, as between the Arthur Parkway and Route 137 for the stretch where they have merged, is identity *simpliciter* of spatial parts. Likewise temporary identity, as between a thing and the matter that temporarily constitutes it, is identity *simpliciter* of temporal parts. Qualitative identity is identity *simpliciter* of qualitative character. The newspaper that Monday's *Age* is an issue of and the newspaper that Tuesday's *Age* is an issue of are identical *simpliciter;* likewise my copy and your copy of Monday's *Age* are copies of the identical issue. But Geach never tells us what the 'same cat' relation has to do with identity *simpliciter.*

He wouldn't, of course, because he thinks 'there is no such absolute identity as logicians have assumed'. (Nor would he accept all my examples above; certainly not the one about temporary identity and identity of temporal parts.) But Geach's case against absolute identity is unconvincing. It seems to come down to a challenge: If Geach is determined to construe all that I say in terms of relations of partial indiscernibility, is there any way I can stop him? Can I *force* him to understand? (What's more, can I do it with one hand tied behind my back? Can I do it, for instance, without ever using the second-order quantification that Geach (1967) also challenges?) I suppose not. But I don't see why that should make me doubt that I know the difference between identity and indiscernibility.

We have the concept of identity, *pace* Geach; and if we are to justify denying that the cats are many, we need to show that they are interrelated by a relation closely akin to identity itself. Geach has not shown this, and wouldn't wish to show it. Nevertheless it can be shown, as we shall soon see. But at that point we shall have a solution that bypasses Geach's doctrine of relative identity altogether.

Partial Identity: The Many Are Almost One

What is the opposite of identity? *Non*-identity, we'd offhand say. Anything is identical to itself; otherwise we have two 'different' things, two 'distinct' things; that is, two non-identical things. Of course it's true that things are either identical or non-identical, and never both. But the real opposite of identity is distinctness: not distinctness in the sense of non-identity, but rather distinctness in the sense of non-overlap (what is called 'disjointness' in the jargon of those who reserve 'distinct' to mean 'non-identical'). We have a spectrum of cases. At one end we find the complete identity of a thing with itself: it and itself are entirely identical, not at all distinct. At the opposite end we find the case of two things that are entirely distinct: They have no part in common. In between we find all the cases of partial overlap: things with parts in common and other parts not in common. (Sometimes one of the overlappers is part of the other, sometimes not.) The things are not entirely identical, not entirely distinct, but some of each. They are partially identical, partially distinct. There may be more overlap or less. Some cases are close to the distinctness end of the spectrum: Siamese twins who share only a finger are almost completely distinct, but not quite. Other cases are close to the identity end. For instance, any two of our cat-candidates overlap almost completely. They differ by only a few hairs. They are not quite completely identical, but they are almost completely identical and very far from completely distinct.

It's strange how philosophers have fixed their attention on one end of the spectrum and forgotten how we ordinarily think of identity and distinctness. You'd think the philosophers of common sense and ordinary language would have set us right long ago, but in fact it was Armstrong (1978, Vol. 2, pp. 37–8) who did the job. Overshadowed though it is by Armstrong's still more noteworthy accomplishments, this service still deserves our attention and gratitude.

Assume our cat-candidates are genuine cats. (Set aside, for now, the supervaluationist solution.) Then, strictly speaking, the cats are many. No two of them are completely identical. But any two of them are almost completely identical; their differences are negligible, as I said before. We have many cats, each one almost identical to all the rest.

Remember how we translate statements of number into the language of identity and quantification. 'There is one cat on the mat' becomes 'For some x, x is a cat on the mat, and every cat on the mat is identical to x'. That's false, if we take 'identical' to express the complete and strict identity that lies at the end of the spectrum. But the very extensive overlap of the cats does approximate to complete identity. So what's true is that for some x, x is a cat on the mat, and every cat on the mat is almost identical to x. In this way, the statement that there is one cat on the mat is almost true. The cats are many, but almost one. By a blameless approximation, we may say simply that there is one cat on the mat. Is that true? – Sometimes we'll insist on stricter standards, sometimes we'll be ambivalent, but for most contexts it's true enough. Thus the idea of partial and approximate identity affords another solution to the paradox of 1001 cats.

The added noun phrase has nothing to do with it. Because of their extensive overlap, the many are almost the same cat; they are almost the same lump of feline tissue; and so on for any other noun phrase that applies to them all. Further, the relation of almost-identity, closely akin to the complete identity that we call identity *simpliciter,* is not a relation of partial indiscernibility. Of course we can expect almost-identical things to be very similar in a great many ways: size, shape, location, weight, purring, behaviour, not to mention relational properties like location and ownership. But it is hard to think of any very salient respect in which almost-identical things are guaranteed to be entirely indiscernible. Finally, the relation of almost-identity, in other words extensive overlap, is not in general an equivalence relation. Many steps of almost-identity can take us from one thing to another thing that is entirely distinct from the first. We may hope that almost-identity, when restricted to the many cats as they actually are, will be an equivalence relation; but even that is not entirely guaranteed. It depends on the extent to which the cats differ, and on the threshold for almost-identity (and both of these are matters that we will, very sensibly, leave undecided). What this solution has in common with Geach's is just that we count the cats by a relation other than strict, 'absolute' identity. Beyond that, the theories differ greatly.[9]

One Solution Too Many?

We find ourselves with two solutions, and that is one more than we needed. Shall we now choose between the way of supervaluation and the way of partial identity? I think not. We might better combine them. We shall see how each can assist the other.

Here is how to combine them. In the first place, there are two kinds of intended interpretations of our language. Given many almost-identical cat-candidates, some will put every (good enough) candidate into the extension of 'cat'; others will put exactly one. Context will favour one sort of interpretation or the other, though not every context will settle the matter. Sometimes, especially in our offhand and unphilosophical moments, context will favour the second, one-cat sort of interpretation; and then the supervaluation rule, with nothing to defeat it, will entitle us to say that there is only one cat. But sometimes, for instance when we have been explicitly attending to the many candidates and noting that they are equally catlike, context will favour the first, many-cat sort of interpretation. (If we start with one-cat interpretations, and we say things that the supervaluation rule would make hash of, not only is the rule suspended but also the many-cat interpretations come into play.) But even then, we still want some good sense in which there is just one cat (though we may want a way to say the opposite as well). That is what almost-identity offers.

This is one way that almost-identity helps a combined solution. It is still there even when we discuss the paradox of 1001 cats, and we explicitly choose to say that the many are all cats, and we thereby make the supervaluation solution go away.

Perhaps it helps in another way too. The supervaluation rule is more natural in some applications than in others. For instance it seems artificial to apply it to a case of unrelated homonyms. 'You said you were going to the bank. Is that true? No worries, you bank at the ANZ, it's right down by the river, so what you said was true either way!' – I don't think such a response is utterly forbidden, but it's peculiar in a way that other applications of the supervaluation rule are not. The two interpretations of 'bank' are so different that presumably you did make up your mind which one you meant. So the means for coping with semantic indecision are out of place. The supervaluation rule comes natural only when the alternative interpretations don't differ too much. If they are one-cat interpretations that differ only by picking almost-identical cats, that's one way for them not to differ much.

How, on the other hand, do supervaluations help the combined solution? Why not let almost-identity do the whole job?

For one thing, not every case of the problem of the many is like the paradox of 1001 cats. The almost-identity solution won't always work well.[10] We've touched on one atypical case already: if not a problem of the many, at least a problem of two. Fred's house taken as including the garage, and taken as not including the garage, have equal claim to be his house. The claim had better be good enough, else he has no house. So Fred has two houses. No! We've already seen how to solve this problem by the method of supervaluations. (If that seemed good to you, it shows that the difference between the interpretations was not yet enough to make the supervaluation rule artificial.) But although the two house-candidates overlap very substantially, having all but the garage in common, they do not overlap nearly as extensively as the cats do. Though they are closer to the identity end of the spectrum than the distinctness end, we cannot really say they're almost identical. So likewise we cannot say that the two houses are almost one.

For another thing, take a statement different from the statements of identity and number that have concerned us so far. Introduce a definite description: 'The cat on the mat includes hair h_{17}'. The obvious response to this statement, I suppose, is that it is gappy. It has no definite truth-value, or no definite super-truth-value, as the case may be. But how can we get that answer if we decide that all the cat-candidates are cats, forsake supervaluations, and ask almost-identity to do the whole job? We might subject the definite description to Russellian translation:

(R1) There is something that is identical to all and only cats on the mat, and that includes h_{17}.

Or equivalently:

(R2) Something is identical to all and only cats on the mat, and every cat on the mat includes h_{17}.

Both these translations come out false, because nothing is strictly identical to all and only cats on the mat. That's not the answer we wanted. So we might relax 'identical' to 'almost identical'. When we do, the translations are no longer equivalent: (R1)-relaxed is true, (R2)-relaxed is false. Maybe we're in a state of semantic indecision between (R1)-relaxed and (R2)-relaxed; if so, we could apply the supervaluation rule to get the desired gappiness. Or we might apply the supervaluation rule more directly. Different one-cat interpretations pick out different things as the cat, some that include h_{17} and some that don't. Under any particular one-cat interpretation the Russellian translations are again equivalent, and different one-cat interpretations give them different truth values; so the translations, and likewise the original sentence, suffer super-truth-value gaps. Or more simply, different one-cat interpretations differ in the referent of 'the cat'; some of these referents satisfy 'includes h_{17}' and some don't, so again we get a super-truth-value gap. Whichever way we go, supervaluations give us the gappiness we want. It's hard to see how else to get it.

NOTES

1. See Lewis (1986a, pp. 210–20).
2. This is the solution advanced in Lowe (1982).

3. The dualism of things and their constituters is also meant to solve a modal problem: Even at one moment, the thing might have been made of different matter, so what might have been true of it differs from what might have been true of its matter, so constitution cannot be identity. This problem too has a better solution. We should allow that what is true of a given thing at a given world is a vague and inconstant matter. Conflicting answers, equally correct, may be evoked by different ways of referring to the same thing, e.g., as cat or as cat-constituter. My counterpart theory affords this desirable inconstancy; many rival theories do also. See Lewis (1986a, pp. 248–63).

4. Provided that there exist the many precisifications for us to be undecided between. If you deny this, you will indeed have need of vague objects. See van Inwagen (1990, pp. 213–83).

5. I grant that the hypothesis of vague objects, for all its faults, can at least be made consistent. If there are vague objects, no doubt they sometimes stand in relations of 'vague identity' to one another. We might think that when a and b are vaguely identical vague objects, the identity statement $a = b$ suffers a truth-value gap; but in fact this conception of vague identity belongs to the theory of vagueness as semantic indecision. As Gareth Evans showed, it doesn't mix with the idea that vague identity is due to vagueness in nature. For if a and b are vaguely identical, they differ in respect of vague identity to a; but nothing, however peculiar it may be, differs in any way from itself; so the identity $a = b$ is definitely false. See Evans (1978). (Evans' too-concise paper invites misunderstanding, but his own testimony confirms my interpretation. See Lewis 1988.) To get a consistent theory of vague objects, different from the bastard theory that is Evans's target, we must disconnect 'vague identity' from truth-value gaps in identity statements. Even if $a = b$ is definitely false, a and b can still be 'vaguely identical' in the sense of sharing some but not all of their precisifications.

6. I do not think reference is entirely up to our choice. Some things are by their nature more eligible than others to be referents or objects of thought, and when we do nothing to settle the contest in favour of the less eligible, then the more eligible wins by default; see Lewis (1984). That's no help here: nature is gradual, no handy joint in nature picks out one of the c's from all the rest.

7. Here I'm indebted to remarks of Saul Kripke many years ago. At his request, I note that what I have written here may not correspond exactly to the whole of what he said on that occasion.

8. Here I'm indebted to Andrew Strauss (personal communication, 1989).

9. There is another way we sometimes count by a relation other than strict identity. You draw two diagonals in a square; you ask me how many triangles; I say there are four; you deride me for ignoring the four large triangles and counting only the small ones. But the joke is on you. For I was within my rights as a speaker of ordinary language, and you couldn't see it because you insisted on counting by strict identity. I meant that, for some w, x, y, z, (1) w, x, y, and z are triangles; (2) w and x are distinct, and . . . and so are y and z (six clauses); and (3) for any triangle t, either t and w are not distinct, or . . . or t and z are not distinct (four clauses). And by 'distinct' I meant non-overlap rather than non-identity, so what I said was true.

10. Here I'm indebted to Phillip Bricker (personal communication, 1990).

REFERENCES

Armstrong, D. M. 1978. *Universals and Scientific Realism,* 2 vols. (Cambridge University Press).

Evans, Gareth. 1978. 'Can There be Vague Objects?', *Analysis* 38: 208. Reprinted in *Collected Papers* (Oxford University Press, 1985).

Geach, P. T. 1967. 'Identity', *Review of Metaphysics* 21: 3–12. Reprinted in *Logic Matters* (Oxford: Blackwell, 1972), pp. 238–47.

  1980. *Reference and Generality,* 3rd ed. (Ithaca, NY: Cornell University Press).

Lewis, David. 1976. 'Survival and Identity'. In *The Identities of Persons,* ed. Amélie Rorty (Berkeley: University of California Press), pp. 17–40. Reprinted in Lewis, *Philosophical Papers,* vol. 1 (Oxford University Press, 1983), pp. 55–72.

  1984. 'Putnam's Paradox', *Australasian Journal of Philosophy* 62: 221–36.

  1986a. *On the Plurality of Worlds* (Oxford: Blackwell).

  1988. 'Vague Identity: Evans Misunderstood', *Analysis* 48: 128–30.

Lowe, E. J. 1982. 'The Paradox of the 1,001 Cats', *Analysis* 42: 27–30.

Unger, Peter. 1980. 'The Problem of the Many', *Midwest Studies in Philosophy* 5: 411–67.

van Fraassen, Bas C. 1966. 'Singular Terms, Truth-Value Gaps, and Free Logic', *Journal of Philosophy* 63: 481–95.

van Inwagen, Peter. 1990. *Material Beings* (Ithaca, NY: Cornell University Press).

Reply to Lewis

D. M. ARMSTRONG

Some years ago I happened to ask David Lewis whether he was going to be in Australia during the next northern summer. He replied that he had not at present formed any such intention. But, he added, on inductive grounds I might expect him to be there. He duly turned up, and, indeed, I don't remember his missing one year in the last dozen. It has been a wonderful thing for Australian philosophy. He is a Melbourne man before anything else, but he travels round the cities and the universities of the continent, never failing to attend the Australasian conference. ('Australasia' is the name for the mereological whole composed of Australia, New Zealand and the adjoining islands.) Lewis is pretty assiduous in visiting New Zealand also. The upside-down character of our seasons and so of our academic calendar ensures some philosophical action wherever he goes. Indeed, he often seems to know more about what is happening to philosophy down under than any native.

The presence on a regular basis of this particularly fine yet robust mind, and one very disposed towards intellectual cooperation, has been of incalculable benefit to Australasian philosophy. (I think we have given him something in return.) For myself, although we have many philosopical disagreements along with doctrines that we hold in common, in recent years I have come to owe him more philosophically than any other living philosopher.

1. Partial Identity

Some years ago, as Lewis notes, I rather briefly suggested that the relations of *being a part of* (New South Wales, Australia) and *overlap* (houses with a common or 'party' wall) should be understood as cases of *partial identity*. My idea was that we tend in philosophy to be hypnotized by the extreme cases of *complete identity* (the morning star and the evening star) and *complete nonidentity* (the morning star and the red planet). Because we are so hypnotized, we neglect the intermediate cases, which are best described as cases of partial identity.

I think that an influence here was F. H. Bradley, who frequently spoke of partial identity (see e.g. his 1893 paper). And John Bacon has recently drawn my attention to a passage in Guido Küng (1967, p. 175) which shows that this was not a personal idiosyncrasy of Bradley's. But, indeed, the view strikes me as little more than common sense. Alas, it is far from being generally accepted at present. Most contemporary philosophers seem to think that 'partial identity' can be nothing more than identity (pleonastically: strict, nonpartial identity) of parts. Since such a view implies that (proper) parts are in no way identical with the thing that they are parts of, there will be a tendency among upholders of this view to let parts and wholes drift apart and be considered as things that are merely correlated. Upholders of partial identity, by contrast, will see any such line of thought as involving the mistake of 'metaphysical double vision'.

It may be noted that the whole dispute is a bit difficult to articulate because it is a necessary truth that two things are partially identical if and only if they lack strict identity but do have a common proper part. The dispute is hyperintensional. Is it the left- or the right-hand side of the equivalence that is the metaphysically illuminating one?

In such a dispute, conclusive arguments can hardly be hoped for. But the consideration that moves me is that, in compound things, classical or strict identity appears to be a limit. Take larger and larger parts of some whole in a series that ends in identity with that whole. With the last term in the series an identity, it is both simplifying and natural to think that identity is involved in each term of the series, although an identity that is partial only. We now have as a further argument Lewis's demonstration here that by introducing the notion of 'almost identical' (an entirely natural idiom) we can make headway against the paradox of the 1001 cats.

It may be worthwhile to mention one disagreement between Lewis and myself. Lewis thinks of partial identity as governed solely by the mereological calculus, the so-called 'calculus of individuals'. For him, it seems, the mereological calculus constitutes the extended logic of identity. I, however, admit states of affairs or facts, such things as a's being F and a's having R to b. Such entities, if there are such, are compound but do not have a mereological form of composition. Furthermore, I find the phenomenon of partial identity present among these entities also. It is true that, in order to mark the difference between mereological composition and the composition found in states of affairs, I am accustomed to speak of *constituents* of states of affairs rather than parts. The relation R, for instance, being a universal, may be a constituent of more than one state of affairs. So with respect to states of affairs I should speak of partial identity of constituents rather than a partial identity constituted by a common part. But, I hold, partial identity is still to be found. At one stage I used to think of the mereological calculus as *the* extended logic of identity. But with the recognition that there are other forms of composition besides the mereological, the 'the', at least, becomes inappropriate.

2. *Relative Identity*

I take this opportunity to say something about the notion of relative identity, a notion introduced by Geach and discussed by Lewis in his essay. Lewis says that he agrees with Geach that 'same' does not always mean absolute identity. It may mean nothing more than a relation of partial indiscernibility. I think that this is a most important point about the word 'same'. Not only does identity come in degrees, but when we use the word 'same' we need not be talking about identity at all! Geach calls this other sense of the word same 'relative identity'. Because I cannot think of any better phrase I propose that Geach's terminology be accepted. At the same time, with Lewis and with most other philosophers, I take the fundamental sense of 'same' to be absolute identity. (Geach, of course, holds that all identity is relative identity.) Nor do I wish to commit myself to various other Geachian doctrines concerning relative identity – for instance, the view that the relation of relative identity demands specification by a sortal.

What is right in Geach, then? He is right to maintain that 'relative identity' is constituted by the objects in question belonging to some particular equivalence class (see e.g. Geach 1973, pp. 291–2). The equivalence relation is some salient relation in the situation that may be understood rather than explicitly mentioned. This account of relative identity in terms of equivalence classes constitutes an important explication of this secondary but ubiquitous sense of the word 'same'. The sense is secondary because the explication depends on the notion of the *same* class and the *same* equivalence relation, where the sameness involved is absolute sameness.

Armed with this distinction between absolute and relative sameness, we can make good sense of some things said by past philosophers, in particular Bishop Butler's 'loose and popular' identity (1736, Dissertation: 'Of Personal Identity') and Hume's 'fictitious' or 'feigned' identity (1738/1888, Book 1, Part IV, Section 2). I should here like to mention Peter Anstey, who – as an undergraduate at Sydney University – began the process of giving me insight into the notion of relative identity by remarking that Butler's 'identity' was a matter of equivalence classes. Butler and Hume were talking about common membership of relevant equivalence classes.

Given all this as background, a number of important metaphysical disputes can be illuminatingly stated in the form of the question of whether a certain ordinary-language use of 'same' involves absolute or merely relative identity. I give two examples. First, we say that two numerically different things have the very same property. Those who take 'very same' here to be absolute identity are those who accept universals. But although in the past I have not properly appreciated the point, it is arguable that in this context 'very same' can be explicated in terms of mere equivalence classes. It can be argued, that is, that what we really have is two numerically different properties (different in the absolute sense), properties which belong to an equivalence class whose equivalence relation is exact resemblance. This is a moderate form of Nominalism. Both this and the absolutist position have their attractions. My own choice is still absolute identity.

Again, we say that a thing or person today is the very same thing or person that existed yesterday. This was the problem that Butler and Hume were discussing. Some metaphysicians hold that, in favourable cases at least (unchanging atoms; souls), this is a matter of absolute identity. Others maintain that all that is ever involved is a relative identity. On this second view absolute identity cannot be maintained over time. What we have instead is a class of short-lived objects (time slices) that (more or less) form an equivalence class. The nature of the equivalence relation is a matter of controversy here. Some favour spatiotemporal continuity, others some sort of causal connection between the short-lived objects. But without adjudicating that dispute here, I will just say that I take the relative identity view, thus showing that the cat can jump in different directions in different situations.

The position we reach, then, is this. Absolute identity, real identity, may be strict or it may be partial. As indicated by Lewis, a particularly important case of partial identity is that of *almost* strict identity. Partial identity is symmetrical, but unlike strict identity it is not transitive. Relative identity resembles strict absolute identity in being an equivalence relation, and so is transitive. Considerations of symmetry then suggest that there should be a useful notion of partial relative identity, with an important subcase where the partial relative identity is *almost* strict relative identity. I believe that this is what we find. John Bacon has pointed out to me that Carnap's 'similarity circles' use a symmetrical but not transitive relation (Carnap 1928/1967, Sections 72, 80). And it is clear that in ordinary language we are prepared to call a number of different things 'the same' even where there is no strictly identical or exactly resembling respect of resemblance running through all of the different things (cf. Wittgenstein's 'family resemblances').

These remarks are offered as a contribution to the semantics of the word 'same'.

REFERENCES

Bradley, F. H. 1893. 'On Professor James' Doctrine of Simple Resemblance', *Mind* 2: 83–8.
Butler, Joseph. 1736. *The Analogy of Religion, Natural and Revealed, to the Constitution and Course of Nature* (London: Knapton).
Carnap, Rudolf. 1928. *The Logical Structure of the World,* 2nd ed., tr. Rolf A. George (London: Routledge & Kegan Paul, 1967).
Geach, Peter. 1973. 'Ontological Relativity and Relative Identity'. In *Logic and Ontology,* ed. Milton K. Munitz (New York University Press), pp. 287–302.
Hume, David. 1738. *A Treatise of Human Nature,* ed. L. A. Selby-Bigge (Oxford: Clarendon, 1888).
Küng, Guido. 1967. *Ontology and the Logistic Analysis of Language,* rev. ed., tr. E. C. M. Mays (Dordrecht: Reidel).

II

The Theory of Universals

3

Just Like Quarks? The Status of Repeatables

PETER FORREST

I am in debt to David Armstrong for many things. One of them is for setting a standard as to how metaphysics should be done. He has avoided both the obscurity of a Hegel or a Heidegger, and the symbolese that disfigures so much Anglo-Saxon philosophy. He states his positions with care, and he argues for them with tenacity. He is a model of lucidity and at the same time an original thinker. Armstrong's defence of positions which I disagree with, such as Materialism, is therefore almost as much an inspiration as his defence of positions with which I sympathize, notably in analytic ontology. But it is in this last area that I consider myself indeed a student of Armstrong.[1] And in this essay I shall consider a problem which his work raises for realists about universals. The problem can be stated thus: If we 'follow the argument wherever it leads' then a strong case can be made for an extreme, 'Platonist' realism about universals.[2] But this clashes with the common intuition that universals are not just like quarks, or, more accurately, that realism about them should be qualified in some fashion not required for realism about the theoretical entities of physics.

This essay is in two parts. In the first I argue against a common qualification to realism about universals, namely the Dependence Thesis, which asserts that universals exist because particulars exist. The stronger version of the qualification, rejected by Armstrong, states that universals are in some way composed of particulars, such as possibilia, tropes or nonrepeatable properties. The weaker version of the qualification is the claim, endorsed by him,[3] that universals are abstract entities which exist because states of affairs (a subcategory of particulars) exist, without in any way being *composed* of particulars. As part of my argument against the Dependence Thesis I shall defend uninstantiated universals. In the second half of the essay I qualify my realism about universals by granting that it is only correct relative to what I call the 'ontology convention'.

I

1.1. Repeatables

Because Armstrong restricts the term 'universal' to a repeatable property or relation which is a 'one over many', I find it convenient to avoid the term 'universal'. Instead I use the term 'repeatable', which will be short for 'repeatable property or relation'. Repeatables are properties and relations which are not constrained by their category so that they cannot be multiply instantiated.[4] They are thus distinguished from particulars, which are indeed constrained by their category so that they cannot be multiply instantiated.[5] By realism about repeatables I just mean the thesis that there are repeatables.

In this essay I take realism about repeatables for granted. What concerns me is the extent to which we should *qualify* realism. In the first part of the essay I shall argue against one common qualification, namely the Dependence Thesis, which states that repeatables exist only because particulars (i.e. nonrepeatables) exist. I begin with a survey of some of the commoner ways of defending the Dependence Thesis. Defenders of that thesis can be divided into Aristotelians and moderate nominalists.[6] Aristotelians, such as Armstrong, believe that there are repeatables but emphasize the Inseparability Thesis, namely the 'inseparability of particularity and universality' (1978, vol. 1, p. 111). This thesis is usually taken to imply that there can be no bare (i.e. propertyless) particulars and, more relevant to this essay, that there can be no uninstantiated repeatables. By itself the Inseparability Thesis does not imply the Dependence Thesis. It could be, for instance, that repeatables and particulars are both fundamental categories, and that it is just a brute fact that they are inseparable. In case there are any Aristotelians who accept the Inseparability Thesis but reject the Dependence Thesis, I note that uninstantiated repeatables provide quite as strong an argument against the Inseparability Thesis as against the Dependence Thesis. I assume, however, that Aristotelians treat the Inseparability Thesis as a consequence of the Dependence Thesis. For the purposes of this essay, then, I characterize the Aristotelian position as saying that repeatables, because they are merely abstract entities, depend on particulars. Historically the particulars would have been thought of as material objects, and this would have been combined with the atomistic assumption that relational properties are not constitutive of objects. That leads to the problem with relations: What do they depend on? One solution to this problem is to include the relational properties as (partly) constitutive of objects. Another solution is, like Armstrong, to identify the particulars on which repeatables depend with *states of affairs* (1978, vol. 1, pp. 114f; 1989a, pp. 38ff).

Moderate nominalists concede that there are repeatables but insist that they are composed of particulars. Repeatables might be construed as mereological sums,[7] but the commonest and most plausible claim is that they are classes of particulars. So for definiteness I shall take moderate nominalists to be proposing that repeatables are classes of particulars, and I have in mind three different suggestions. The first is that repeatables are classes of actual or, preferably, actual and merely possible material objects.[8] (The converse, namely that all such classes are repeatables, would not be claimed.[9]) Armstrong calls this position Class Nominalism.

The second position is that repeatables are classes of nonrepeatable properties. To illustrate this, assume that the charge of an electron, E, is (as all current theories suggest) totally without variation. And consider the repeatable *having charge E*. In spite of the total lack of variation, we might claim that every electron has its own nonrepeatable property: the having charge E of this electron. In that case, the repeatable property *having charge E* could be taken to be the class of all the nonrepeatable properties: the having charge E of this electron; the having charge E of that electron; and so on.

Subtly different is the Trope Theory.[10] As I understand it, tropes are not so much properties that familiar objects have as rather mini-substances that would ordinarily be thought of as having a location and one other property. However, on the Trope Theory, these tropes are not analyzed as things with a location and a property, or even as a location having a property, but are treated as that out of which both objects (as mereological sums of co-located tropes) and repeatable properties (as classes of exactly similar tropes) are composed.

Much more could be said about these three positions, including their accounts of relations, but this should be enough to show the sorts of theory I have in mind when I talk of Moderate Nominalism.

In this paper I assume that hypotheses in analytic ontology can be justified by inference to the best explanation, and that the goodness of an explanation depends on a combination of simplicity[11] and the amount which it can explain. I shall not, however, consider comparisons of simplicity. Rather, I concentrate on two things which repeatables explain, namely causal regularities and physical possibilities.[12] I have three reasons for this. First, my space is limited and others, notably Armstrong himself, have provided general discussions of the merits of various hypotheses.[13] Second, there are the threats of Fictionalism and Conventionalism in analytic ontology. Here we may contrast the situation in analytic ontology with the success of many sciences in making accurate and startling predictions. We have, I believe, the very best reasons for limiting the scope of Fictionalism and Conventionalism in the interpretation of science, and so adopting, perhaps with a few qualifications, Scientific Realism. The situation in analytic ontology is somewhat different. Startling predictions are not made. Rather, as in natural theology, we seek to explain already accepted facts. While I insist that hypotheses can be supported by their explanatory power even without startling predictions, I advocate caution when it comes to such explanations. In the case of analytic ontology I am worried lest a great deal of what can be explained in terms of repeatables, such as classes and possibilia, be fictions.[14] My third reason for concentrating on the two explanations I have mentioned is that they suit my purpose, which is to argue against the Dependence Thesis and not only against Moderate Nominalism.

I shall argue that the explanations of causal regularities and of physical possibilities fail if we take repeatables to be classes of particulars. I shall also argue that the explanation of physical possibilities requires uninstantiated repeatables. In this way I provide a case not merely against Moderate Nominalism but also against Armstrong's Aristotelian position.

1.2. Causal Regularities

Armstrong has pointed out that one thing causes another because of its properties, and that this may well be a difficulty for the class nominalist (1978, vol. 1, pp. 42f). However, it is clearly no difficulty for those moderate nominalists who adopt an ontology either of tropes or of nonrepeatable properties. But the story does not end there. We can manipulate things only within and by exploiting the *regularity of causation,* as expressed by constraints that are usually called laws of nature.[15] We believe that these causal regularities are universal in the sense that they cover all times and places;[16] this belief would seem to have been confirmed by modern astronomy. Why, then, are these causal regularities universal? One explanation is that causal regularities are universal because they involve universals.[17] More precisely, the properties by which one thing causes another are *repeatable* properties. Thus, the explanation of why all masses attract, not just some, is that massive objects attract because of the repeatable, *having positive mass.*

This explanation does not depend on the details of the Dretske–Tooley–Armstrong theory of laws of nature (Armstrong 1983a). In particular, it does not require that there be any higher-order repeatables such as a relation of necessitation or probabilification holding between first-order repeatable properties. We could go nominalist at that level and the explanation would still work. Thus consider the schematic case where this F causes there to be this G, and it causes there to be this G because of its having the property F-ness. To avoid various complications let us assume that in this case it is solely because of its having F-ness that it causes there to be a G. Now on Armstrong's account of laws of nature this is treated as an instance of a higher-order repeatable relation of necessitation between F-ness and G-ness. But we do not need that hypothesis in order to explain why not only this F but every other F will cause there to be a G. It is enough that it be something to do with F-ness in this case. So let us say that there is a G because Ω(F-ness), where 'Ω' is a suitable predicate whose analysis need not here concern us.[18] Since F-ness is a repeatable, the F-ness in this case is the very same as the F-ness in other cases. Hence we have Ω(F-ness) in the other case, too. And if in one case there is a G because Ω(F-ness), then no further explanation is required as to why in general there is a G when there is an F. For, by the indiscernibility of identicals, Ω(F-ness) holds in the other case, too. In this way the insight that things have their causal powers because of their properties, combined with the thesis that the properties are repeatable, explains the way in which causal regularities hold at all times and places. Further discussion might indeed convince us that there is a higher-order relation of necessitation, but such discussion is not required for the explanation of the universality of causal regularities.

This explanation cannot be satisfactorily mimicked by moderate nominalists. That is because they treat the repeatable property F-ness as a class of particulars, and it is not by belonging to a class of particulars that one thing causes another.[19] The best that moderate nominalists can do is to state as a meta-law the principle that like causes like. Such a principle is a tenable explanation of low-level generalizations such as that pouring water on fires tends to put them out. But it is not easy to generalize to functional laws – that is, laws which constrain one quantity to be some specified mathematical function of another. For instance, the law that the force of gravitational attraction is proportional to the product of the masses and inversely proportional to the square of the distance can be put in the like-causes-like form only by taking the effect to be not the force but the force multiplied by the square of the distance and divided by the product of the masses. 'Like causes like' is not, I submit, a promising research program.

The universality of functional laws is not easily explained by moderate nominalists, which is a point in favour of Armstrong's theory. However, as he recognizes, functional laws also put some pressure on us to admit uninstantiated universals. For example, suppose that the gas law (that for a given portion of a homogeneous gas, pressure times volume is proportional to temperature) is a genuine universal causal regularity. Then there will be an upper limit to the actual volume of portions of homogeneous gas. Yet, we tend to believe that the law would still govern volumes beyond the limit if they occurred. The law holds of all the portions of gas with volume V_1 because they instantiate the repeatable property, *having volume V_1*. If that explanation is given for the case in which there are many different portions of gas with volume V_1, then for the sake of theoretical uniformity it would be desirable to give the same explanation for some uninstantiated volume V_2.

Armstrong treats the missing values of functional laws counterfactually. (If there were portions of gas with volume V_2, then the repeatable *having volume V_2* would be related in the appropriate way to other repeatables.) This is a drawback, since theoretical uniformity is a desideratum; but I concede that it is a minor drawback. So while causal regularities provide a strong argument against moderate nominalists,[20] they merely put pressure on the Aristotelian position.

1.3. Physical Possibilities

There are two different questions concerning the merely possible. The first is, What is the difference between the merely possible and the impossible? The second is whether there are any nonactual particulars, either possible ones such as the golden mountain or impossible ones such as the golden nongolden mountain.[21] Repeatables can be used to provide us with an answer to the second question. The answer is that there are no nonactual particulars but that the role they play in explanations can, for the most part, be played by suitably complex uninstantiated repeatables. The property of being a golden mountain is not the same as *the* golden mountain. (How can it be, since the property is a repeatable and the mountain a particular?) However, I know of no good reason for insisting that there are nonidentical but indiscernible nonactuals, such as various indistinguishable golden mountains. Hence, where we might seem to need nonactual particulars in our explanations, I submit that uninstantiated repeatables will serve instead.

But do we need nonactuals in explanation? The common-sense position is that we do not. Nor do I think we need them for the purposes of the semantics of modal statements.[22] However, I shall argue that scientific explanations require either nonactual particulars or some substitute for them, such as uninstantiated repeatables. Here I am concerned with the *states* of a physical system,[23] namely the physically possible ways the system

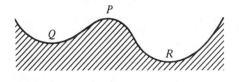

Figure 1

could be. I argue for realism about the system of physically possible states, and so reject any fictionalist or instrumentalist attitude to them.

I begin by noting just how central to any physical theory is the description of the system of states. Expositions of quantum theory, for example, usually begin by telling us how the (pure) states of the system are in one-to-one correspondence with the 1-dimensional subspaces of an infinite-dimensional (Hilbert) space.[24] That the states of a system play a prominent role in physical theories does not by itself show much, although it is suggestive of realism about those states. The states, however, are not merely central to the exposition of physics; they play a nonredundant part in some explanations. I shall concentrate on one such explanation.

Consider the way in which the occurrence of a state may be explained by showing that it is of lower energy than states that would be obtained by small perturbations. For example, consider a ball balanced at point *P* in Figure 1. The forces on it are in equilibrium, but we would be surprised to find it there, and suspect that someone had balanced it. By contrast, we could (partially) explain the occurrence of the ball at point *Q*, simply by noting that the energy is less at *Q* than at nearby points. The same explanation could be provided if it were at *R*. This kind of explanation can be used in all areas of physics, and is appealed to in the Inflationary Big Bang hypothesis.[25] It succeeds even if not all the states that would be obtained by small perturbations actually occur. Even if they do not occur, they are essential for the contrast between the surprising place, *P*, and the unsurprising places, *Q* and *R*. For that contrast requires us to consider the energy of the states that would be obtained by small perturbations.

How could we avoid appealing to nonactual states? Should we rest content with counterfactuals, and say that *P* is a surprising place to find a ball because if it were to be perturbed the ball would go into a lower energy level? This suffers from a common difficulty of attempts to use counterfactuals in order to explain. To be of use in the theoretical explanation of truths that are independent of our attitudes and beliefs, the counterfactuals would themselves have to possess truth independently of our attitudes and beliefs. But in that case we may ask what it is that makes the counter-factuals true. And the answer, whatever it is, could have been given in the first place to account for the contrast between P and Q. The only available answers of this kind are those of Lewis and of Stalnaker, or variants thereof. But surely nothing has been gained if to avoid uninstantiated states we rely on counterfactuals, and then to account for the truth of counterfactuals we invoke possibilia. We should explain in terms of the nonactual the first time round.

Nor will it serve to say that there must be some more detailed explanation involving the precise dynamics of the perturbations. For that would be like Putnam's example of why the 1-inch square peg will not go through the 1-inch round hole (1978, p. 42). No doubt there is a detailed explanation in term of forces, but we rightly prefer the geometric explanation of why the square peg will not go through the round hole. Likewise, it is inappropriate to consider the details of perturbation when we already have a more general explanation in terms of the (local) minimum for the energy.

A much more serious attempt to account for the contrast between the ball at P and the ball at Q is to insist that the contrast can be explained by pointing out that the laws of nature prohibit any small perturbation to lower energy level at Q, but provide no such prohibition at P. But this explanation is incomplete as it stands. For it serves only to explain the unsurprising character of the ball being at Q. We cannot directly explain the surprising character of the ball being at P by saying that the laws of nature are not inconsistent with small perturbations to lower energy levels. They are not inconsistent with the ball being endowed with epiphe-nomenal mental states, either. But if, in some magical fashion, we discovered there were such epiphenomenal mental states, we would surely be surprised. What this shows, I claim, is that there is more to being a possible state of a system than merely being consistent with the laws of nature. A case can be made, then, for realism about the *states* of physical systems, many of which will be nonactual.

I have argued that we need nonactual states. Assuming that we prefer an ontology of repeatables to one of possibilia,[26] this provides a case for uninstantiated repeatables. States of a physical system are (suitably complex) repeatable properties of that system. If the state is nonactual then the property is uninstantiated.

If this argument is successful then it provides a case against Armstrong's position, according to which there are no uninstantiated properties. In addition, it strengthens the case against any version of Moderate Nominalism which does not involve possibilia. For without possibilia,[27] moderate nominalists must take an uninstantiated repeatable to be the empty class.

There is only one empty class but many nonactual states, so this is not a tenable position.

1.4. Uninstantiated Properties and the Dependence Thesis

Armstrong denies that there are any uninstantiated properties. So if I am right about the explanatory power of nonactual states of a physical system, I have an argument against his position. This argument may be supplemented by the desideratum that we give a uniform account of functional laws – a desideratum that cannot be satisfied without uninstantiated repeatables. The question of whether there are any uninstantiated repeatables is interesting in itself. But I am primarily concerned with the Dependence Thesis, namely that repeatables only exist because particulars do. As I shall argue, the mere existence of some uninstantiated repeatables is no objection to the Dependence Thesis. To argue against it we must look more closely at which uninstantiated repeatables we need.

Uninstantiated repeatables are compatible with the Dependence Thesis, for the dependence in question could be indirect. That is, the instantiated repeatables could exist because of the particulars that instantiate them, while uninstantiated repeatables could exist because they are composed of simpler repeatables which are themselves instantiated.[28] For example, there are particles with zero rest mass such as photons, and particles with charge such as electrons, but so far as I know there are no charged particles of zero rest mass. So the conjunctive repeatable property of *being both charged and of zero rest mass* is uninstantiated. On the proposal that I am considering, this conjunctive property exists simply because its conjuncts exist, and they exist because they are instantiated.

I ask, therefore, whether the purposes for which I need uninstantiated repeatables require ones that are not composed of instantiated repeatables. Typically the uninstantiated repeatables will be (conjunctions of) specified degrees of properties (or relations) that admit of varying degrees. Thus, if the universe is finite then there will be many volumes, too large to be instantiated, which nonetheless are required to specify nonactual states of a system. (They will also enter into laws of nature, such as the law relating the pressure, volume and temperature of a gas.) Notice that we cannot obtain such uninstantiated repeatables just by mixing instantiated ones.[29] For we are here assuming that no volume greater than some threshold value is instantiated; we are not concerned with gaps in the range of volumes. Could we say nonetheless that the property of *having volume* V_0 (which is far too large to be instantiated) depends for its existence on other volume properties which are instantiated, say *having volume* $V_0/10$? In the case of volumes and other extensive magnitudes such as length and mass, we could follow Armstrong and treat *having volume V_0* as *being the sum of* 10 *disjoint parts each with volume $V_0/10$.* That would exhibit the dependence of the uninstantiated volume property on instantiated ones.

But what of intensive magnitudes such as the strength of a magnetic field? There may well be an upper bound to the strength of various fields which has never in fact been exceeded. For definiteness consider a magnetic field H.[30] Although this is an intensive magnitude, Armstrong's divide-and-conquer strategy for handling extensive magnitudes might work provided we allow that the field $H_0/10$ could be instantiated 10 times at the same point, resulting in a field of strength H_0. For then excessively large strengths could be handled much as excessively large volumes were. The property of *being a magnetic field of strength H_0* would be treated as the property *having* 10 *co-located parts each with a magnetic field strength $H_0/10$.* This would raise the problem of what the bearers of the field properties were. They might turn out to be points zero distance apart! I judge that the explanatory power of the hypothesis[31] no longer warrants its intellectual cost. And there is a further problem. There might turn out to be an intensive magnitude, such as electric charge, which has only a finite or at most a countable number of instantiated degrees – namely, multiples of quark charges,[32] – and yet we might need to consider states that correspond to a whole continuum of degrees, namely all possible electric charges.[33] And there is no way in which we could compose, say, 1/10 of the charge of a quark out of whole-number multiples of quark charges.

I conclude that the case for uninstantiated repeatables is indeed a case against the Dependence Thesis, on the grounds that not all the uninstantiated repeatables we need are composed of instantiated repeatables.

1.5. On the Case for Dependence

I have made a case for uninstantiated repeatables, and hence a case for rejecting the Dependence Thesis. I now need to consider the case for the Dependence Thesis. Here I know of two arguments to which I should reply. The first I call the argument from the need for location. Its premiss is that everything must have a location (at least in time[34]). Since repeatables are only located indirectly by the locations of their instances, uninstantiated repeatables have no location in either space or time. Clearly this argument is only as strong as the premiss. And why should we believe that? One reason might be that nonlocated entities cannot, it is said, enter into explanations, nor are they directly observable. So, by Ockham's razor, out they go. But consider the reasons I had for proposing uninstantiated repeatables. It was precisely in order to explain what was observable that I invoked them. And I was scrupulous to avoid explanations of anything airy-fairy like modal truths, in favour of explanations based on physics. How then did nonlocated entities enter into explanations of located events? It happened because the explanations are not causal ones. To be sure, if the only nonobservables that we admit are ones directly involved in the causation of what is observable, then – while we might believe in God – we would never accept uninstantiated repeatables. However, I can see no reason to reject explanations, such as the one concerning the possibility of lowering potential energy, just because they are not causal explanations. Against such causation chauvinism it is worth noting that one moral that could be drawn from the Bell inequality is that not all nonaccidental correlations have a causal basis.[35]

Much more threatening than the argument from the need for location is an argument, implicit in Armstrong's work, that I call the threat of transcendence. I shall state it as an argument for the Dependence Thesis, and hence against uninstantiated repeatables. The basic idea is that, if all properties (and relations) were independent of what they are properties of (or relate), then a particular a would instantiate a repeatable F-ness only because a and F-ness are related by the relation of instantiation, $\Re_1$; and so, by definition, F-ness would be a transcendent repeatable.[36] There are various difficulties with transcendent repeatables, but perhaps the most serious is that the relation $\Re_1$ would itself be independent of what it related. Hence it would relate a to F-ness only because it is itself related to a, by $\Re_2^L$ say, and related to F-ness, by $\Re_2^R$ say. But $\Re_2^L$ and $\Re_2^R$ would themselves only relate their instances because they in turn are related, either by $\Re_2^L$ and $\Re_2^R$ again or by some new relations. In either case an infinite regress of 'because' clauses is set up. That is, the promised explanation is never provided but rather continually deferred. This I judge to be a vicious regress.

This argument has no doubt many versions, and some may suspect that I have helped myself to a version which is easy to answer. I plead not guilty. My choice of version has been motivated by the need to make the independence of repeatables from particulars an explicit premiss in the argument. Otherwise, all we have is a regress argument against the existence of *any* repeatables. Such an argument clearly would not support the Dependence Thesis.

In reply to the threat of transcendence, I first make the general point that it is an argument against what I shall call the Independence Thesis, namely that *all* properties (and relations) are independent of what they are properties of (or relate). But the Dependence Thesis says that *none* of

them are independent, so the Independence Thesis and the Dependence
Thesis are contraries, not contradictories. I accept the argument against
the Independence Thesis, but I do not take it to be an argument for the
Dependence Thesis. And if it be asked which properties or relations fail
to be independent, then I reply that the threat of a regress shows that the
relation of instantiation is not independent of what it relates.

My reply to the threat of transcendence raises a new question: What is
the relevant difference between instantiation and (some) other repeatables
which justifies my making an exception of it? I can answer this question
by insisting on the *thickness* of particulars. That is, a particular is not to
be identified with a propertyless substrate. Nor is it to be identified with
the particular abstracted away from some supposedly nonessential properties. Nor is it even to be identified with the particular abstracted away
from its relational properties. A particular is, I submit, a particular-in-a-
situation.[37] Therefore, the fact that a instantiates F-ness is made true by
what a is and what F-ness is. For example, consider the round stone a
and the property of roundness. I take the particular to be the stone in all
its roundness, not some stone-in-itself. Given that the stone is what it is
and that roundness is what it is, it follows automatically that the stone
instantiates roundness. How could it fail to? Hence the relation $\Re_1$ of
instantiation is an internal relation, and more importantly, it occurs precisely because the items it relates – namely, the stone and the property of
roundness – are what they are. To be sure, we could set up a regress of
instantiations as before, but now the explanations are such that each item
is explained by the previous one, not by the next. Hence the regress is not
vicious. Nor is it uneconomic to allow the regress of instantiation relations. For the instantiation relations, being implied by what they relate,
do not offend against Ockham's razor.[38]

With one bound our hero leapt free! My way out of the difficulty seems
too easy. It is therefore worth being quite explicit about the intellectual
costs of my proposal. First, I am taking the basic particulars to be rather different from ordinary material objects, which are not objects-in-a-
situation so much as objects abstracted away from the situation. This
may be compared to Armstrong's position, which is that the basic particulars are states of affairs. If anything, his position is further from common sense than my own. The second intellectual cost is that I must deny
that particulars depend on repeatables.[39] Yet I am also denying the Dependence Thesis, namely that repeatables depend on particulars. So my
ontology is based on a dualism of particulars and repeatables, neither
of which depends on the other. It would be desirable to make all categories depend on one basic category, so in that respect my position is one
desideratum down on Armstrong's. I concede, then, that there is a cost

to admitting uninstantiated repeatables and to denying the Dependence Thesis. The cost is that there are two basic categories, the particular and the repeatable. But I submit that this cost is outweighed by the argument in favour of uninstantiated repeatables.

II

2.1. Paranominalism

In this part of the essay, I argue that there is a conventional element in analytic ontology which provides a qualification to realism about repeatables – a qualification not required for realism about quarks.

I argue for this conventional element by considering a position that I call Paranominalism, which I introduce by means of a discussion of the Ostrich Nominalism attributed to Quine.[40] As Armstrong expresses it, this is the position that '[t]here are no universals but the proposition that *a* is F is perfectly all right as it is' (1978, vol. 1, p. 17). Now Quine distinguishes ontology from ideology. After all paraphrasing has been performed, we can list the kinds to which we apply the predicates;[41] that is the *ontology*. But in addition, there are the 'ideas which can be expressed . . .'; Quine calls this the *ideology* (1953, p. 131). We should be grateful to Quine for getting analytic or postanalytic philosophers to take the ontology seriously. But we should also note that, partly because of his choice of the word 'ideology', the predicates that apply to things have not been taken so seriously. Paranominalists differ from ostrich nominalists in that they take predicates and modalities with the utmost seriousness, but do not offer reductive accounts of predication and of modality. Hence, in addition to a Quinean ontology they would prepare lists of the fundamental categories of predicates, lists of the fundamental modalities, and so on. These would all be treated with just the same seriousness or objectivity as the ontology.

Paranominalism can be made more systematic by introducing ontological reduction as a more inclusive program than analytic ontology. Let us suppose that we have a language Lan. Then, by some process of reduction, we could discover a basic language Bas such that all the true members of Lan hold because of the true members of Bas. This reduction would be expressed by means of schemata of the form: '*S*' is true if *P*. Here '*S*' is a true member of Lan and '*P*' is a true member of Bas. We would then discuss which of these reductions best explains the true members of Lan. Paranominalists take seriously this project of reduction to a basic language, but they insist that there is much more to this language than a list of names; the predicates in Bas are also significant.

2.2. A Verbal Dispute

I now argue that the dispute between paranominalists and realists is a verbal one. To illustrate the nature of this dispute, let us restrict our attention to a language Lan all of whose members are of the subject/predicate form: a is F. For simplicity let us further assume that the predicates are such as a realist would indeed say corresponded to repeatable properties. Then the realist offers a reduction according to which 'a is F' is true because a instantiates F-ness. The language Bas could be chosen to contain a single predicate,[42] namely the dyadic '. . . instantiates ———', but the ontology has two categories: namely, things that can fill the first place and things that can fill the second. The latter is the category of repeatables.[43] By contrast, the paranominalist might offer a reduction in which Bas is a sublanguage of Lan, so that the ontology consists of a single category but the ideology is now described using a long list of predicates.

This dispute is, I suggest, a verbal or conceptual one, not one concerning matters of fact. The long list of predicates required by the paranominalists stands in one-to-one correspondence with the category of repeatables of the realist, and these predicates show us as much about the world as do the repeatables. (To deny this is to lapse back into Ostrich Nominalism.) So what is the difference? The realist has a singleton 'ideology' containing only the predicate 'instantiates'. Does its application indicate some further feature of the world about which the paranominalist is sceptical? No; for, as I argued when defending my position from the threat of transcendence, once we have both – the particular-in-a-situation and the appropriate property – nothing further is required to ensure that the particular instantiates the property.

The argument that the dispute is verbal becomes more complicated when we consider truths which, prima facie, are themselves about properties. The Pap/Jackson Argument[44] exploits this, by pointing to the difficulties of providing nominalist paraphrases of such truths as 'red resembles orange more than it resembles blue' and 'red is a colour'. To these I might add the truth that one thing causes another because of its properties, a truth I invoked in order to explain causal regularities.

On behalf of the paranominalist I now take up the challenge of reducing ('paraphrasing' if you like) such truths. 'Red resembles orange more than it resembles blue' is true if it is possible that some red thing x resembles some orange thing y more than some blue thing z precisely because x is red, y is orange and z is blue. Again, when we consider causal regularities it suffices to assert, for instance, that massive objects attract precisely because they are massive. The example 'red is a colour' is harder to handle. I would begin by reducing it to 'red resembles* itself, blue, yellow and green'. (By 'resembles*' I mean the ancestral of 'resembles'.[45]) Here I acknowledge a certain arbitrariness in the choice of the paradigm colours: red, blue, yellow and green. But arbitrariness does not affect the success of a reduction. I then appeal to my previous reduction of colour resemblances.

Three points concerning these reductions warrant further comment. First, paranominalists must include in the language Bas at least one modal operator; second, the results of the paranominalist reduction tend to be messy; and third, the paranominalist reduction requires 'because' clauses. Concerning the first: Modal operators take the place of uninstantiated repeatables. I claim paranominalists require modal operators to show something about the world which realists describe using uninstantiated repeatables. That there is anything modal or uninstantiated about the world is itself rather surprising, but it has been argued for earlier in this essay.

Concerning the second point, the messy character of paranominalist reductions provides one reason for excluding them by convention in favour of realism about repeatables. It does not, however, provide a reason for rejecting the claim that the dispute is purely verbal, for any position can be messed up without altering the factual content.

Concerning the third point, the use of 'because' clauses shows that the paranominalist description, stated in the basic language Bas, has an undesirable implicit reference to people, here considered as understanders or as explainers. It is as if the realist about repeatables were forever talking about the grounds for the objectivity of discrimination and comparison instead of simply talking about properties. Such an implicit reference to people when discussing the inanimate world is inelegant at best and, at worst, unnecessarily invites some version of Idealism. So we have good reason to adopt a convention to exclude Paranominalism. However, the mere fact that something is described in terms that implicitly (or explicitly) refer to people does not imply that people are really part of what is thus described. Here Quine's example of the use of 'clockwise' comes to mind. Rotations that have nothing to do with clocks and that occurred long before there were any people at all can still be described as clockwise. The anachronism offends, if at all, only against style. Likewise, that a description of the inanimate involves a detour through explanation or understanding does not make it incorrect. In this case, however, the offence is against more than style; there is a lack of perspicuity in such descriptions.

I conclude that the dispute between (my version of) realism about repeatables and (one version of) paranominalism is a verbal one. I have, however, already found some reasons for insisting the Paranominalism should be excluded by convention.

2.3. How Conventional Is Realism about Repeatables?

I have argued that universals (i.e. unreduced repeatables) are not just like quarks because there is a conventional element in the choice of realism over Paranominalism. So, in spite of my rejection of the Dependence Thesis and of my acceptance of uninstantiated repeatables, my position is not a totally unqualified realism. But it should not be assumed that the whole enterprise of ontology is just a matter of choosing the best conventions. For instance, my rejection of the Dependence Thesis is nonconventional. To be sure, the whole discussion of the Dependence Thesis must be understood in the context of a convention that excludes Paranominalism. But in that context the choice between Moderate Nominalism, Armstrong's Aristotelian realism and my more extreme realism is based on the capacity of various ontological theories to explain facts[46] which are not themselves matters of convention. And that is one reason why I have not considered the capacity of various ontological theories to account for numbers, classes, or mere logical possibility. For those topics are themselves as likely to be infected with conventionality as the existence of properties and relations.

2.4. The Ontology Convention

It remains ony to state in greater detail the convention that I propose as the context for discussions of ontology. It is not precise, but serves nonetheless to narrow down the range of ontological theories and so lessen the opportunity for verbal disputes. I shall illustrate it by considering again the simplified case where the truths that concern us are all of the subject/predicate form: a is F. Paranominalists concede that (suitably selected) predicates show us something about the world quite as much as the particulars which they are true of. So, I argued, the dispute between them and me is a verbal one. Roughly speaking, they have put into the ideology what I put into the ontology. I propose as a convention that, again roughly speaking, only the items in the ontology should show us something about the world; I call this the *ontology convention*.

There are complaints about the 'thingified' character of much traditional ontology; although the ontology convention endorses thingification, I am unrepentant. For, I say, the ontology convention serves to promote clear thought. For instance, whether we accept or reject it, the Dretske–Tooley–Armstrong theory of laws of nature is an important theory that makes a factual claim about laws of nature. I challenge readers to discuss that theory in paranominalist terms. You might as well calculate compound interest in your head using roman numerals. Conventions matter.

In addition to promoting clarity, the ontology convention avoids distracting implicit references to people when describing the inanimate world. Finally, it helps us make as clear a distinction as we can between the factual content of truths and their conventional form.

In the attempt to make the ontology convention more precise, I now make explicit my reliance on Wittgenstein's distinction between 'saying' and 'showing'. The project of reduction results in a basic language Bas. A truth in Bas is used to say something. But the language Bas itself shows something, which cannot be said in Bas.[47] What does it show? At one extreme is the Isomorphism Thesis of the early Wittgenstein that, for a suitable basic language Bas_0, thought-independent reality would be structured isomorphically to Bas_0. In that case the correct ontology would be shown in an especially natural way by using Bas_0. The Isomorphism Thesis is, however, rather implausible.[48] At the other extreme is the ostrich nominalist position that the only part of any basic language which shows anything about the world is the list of names for objects. The ontology convention may be compared with both these positions. It tells us to select a basic language Bas in such a way that indeed the only part of it that shows anything is a list of names, but we allow the things named to be as exotic as we please. In particular, the ontology convention would force any defender of the Isomorphism Thesis to use a language Bas that contains names for states of affairs in one-to-one correspondence with the truths of Bas_0.

Conclusions

In the first part of the essay I argued in favour of uninstantiated repeatables and against the Dependence Thesis. This might have suggested a totally unqualified realism. In the second part, however, I endorsed a conventionalist qualification. To be sure, realism about quarks may also be in need of a conventionalist qualification.[49] But the conventionalist element involved in realism about repeatables is not only rather different from any involved in realism about quarks; it is also more striking, owing to a higher proportion of fact to convention. Repeatables are not, then, just like quarks.

NOTES

1. Especially in the selective character of his realism.
2. Plato seems to have believed in *self*-instantiated universals. Hence it is rather inaccurate to call belief in uninstantiated universals Platonism.
3. Armstrong (1989a, Chapter 3, Section II) explicitly states that properties and relations depend on states of affairs.

4. Why not the simpler definition as a property or relation capable of multiple instantiation? There are at least two reasons. The first is that the distinction between repeatable and particular should, I think, be exhaustive by definition as well as exclusive. The second is that I have raised elsewhere (Forrest 199+) the problem of the identity of certain kinds of properties at different positions in curved space. One response to this problem is to allow that the structure of space might prevent the occurrence of multiply instantiated properties. But such prevention would not arise out of the category to which they belong; rather, it would be imposed by the structure of space. I would prefer to include such properties in the same category as those that are indeed capable of multiple instantiation.

5. The category of particulars is not restricted by definition so as to include only substances (i.e. entities incapable of instantiation by anything else). That is because nonrepeatable properties and relations would be particulars but not substances.

6. Moderate Nominalism is moderate in that it does not deny the existence of repeatables. It is Nominalism in that it denies the existence of Armstrongian universals.

7. As Armstrong points out (1978, vol. 1, p. 35), if we took the repeatable *having mass 1 kilogram* as the sum of all objects with mass 1 kilogram, then it would be hard to say what is required for an object to have that property. For it cannot be that an object has the property if it is *part* of the property in question: not every part of the sum 1-kilogram masses itself has mass 1 kilogram. Such difficulties do not arise with the identification of properties as classes or sets. We could identify the property of *having mass 1 kilogram* with the class of all (actual or possible) 1-kilogram objects. In that case, an object has the property just in case it is a member of the class.

8. For the sake of exposition, I consider only physical properties.

9. There are two reasons. First, singletons cannot be identified with repeatable properties; second, we almost certainly need to concentrate on *natural* classes.

10. As expounded in D. C. Williams (1953). The Trope Theory is endorsed by Campbell (1990).

11. Under simplicity I here include elegance, lack of the ad hoc, and so on.

12. If I rejected the Representative Theory of Perception then I would propose a third explanation, for I would then take repeatables to be the direct objects of perception. Uninstantiated repeatables would account for the phenomenology of illusion and hallucination. I do not discuss this because I suspect that neurophysiology is on the side of the Representative Theory. That is, I suspect that we are discovering the physical correlates of the sense-data (see Churchland 1986, pp. 450–8). This, combined with Jackson's (1977) arguments for the Act/Object analysis of sensations, makes me a reluctant believer in the Representative Theory.

13. See for example Armstrong (1989a), Lewis (1983b), and Swoyer (1983, pp. 14–28).

14. Armstrong (1989a) advocates a fictionalist theory of possibilia.

15. I say 'usually called'. My caution here is based on the fact that we may read so much into our concept of laws of nature that it becomes appropriate to question whether there are any. But I shall concentrate simply on the regularity of causation, so that worry is hardly appropriate.

16. Presumptively, that is. Exceptions to causal regularities may occur, but they require some special explanation.
17. An alternative explanation is in terms of God's decrees. Providence requires only such local and superficial regularities as are required to enable humans and any other animals who are persons to order their lives and interact with each other. Providence cannot, therefore, explain the universality of causal regularities. But aesthetic motives might conceivably do so. In this way Theism might conceivably render my explanation redundant. If so, my argument should be interpreted as an ad hominem against atheists.
18. Provided it is referentially transparent.
19. For the reasons that Armstrong gives in his argument against Class Nominalism (1978, vol. 1, pp. 42–3).
20. At least if they are atheists. See note 17.
21. Armstrong (1989a) gives a combinatorial answer to the first, but denies that there are any nonactual things.
22. That a certain ontological theory enables us to give the most plausible semantics for a certain class of statements establishes ontological commitments. But this in no way refutes those who deny the literal truth of the committing statements.
23. The system I am especially concerned with is the whole physical universe.
24. See, for instance, Hughes (1989, Chapter 2).
25. See for example Guth (1983), Linde (1983) and Steinhardt (1983). The diagram representing a ball balanced in an unstable position could just as easily have represented the energy of a Higgs field, with Q the false 'vacuum' and R the true 'vacuum' (cf. the diagram in Guth 1983, p. 183).
26. Discussion of possibilia is beyond the scope of this paper. I rely very much on Armstrong's arguments, which may be divided into two sorts. First there are his direct criticisms of realism about possibilia (Armstrong 1989a). Second, there is his discussion of Class Nominalism (most recently in Armstrong 1989b), which together with the previous section of this essay casts considerable doubt on whether we can use classes of possibilia in place of repeatables. If we cannot, then we should try to use repeatables in place of possibilia.
27. The possibilia in question need not be objects. Realism about possibilia could be combined with, say, a Trope Theory, resulting in nonactual tropes. However, that is not only extravagant but also open to all the objections that Armstrong (1989a) raises to Lewis's theory.
28. Some instantiated repeatables would exist for both reasons.
29. Except in the extended sense in which we allow negative proportions in mixtures.
30. No doubt at high intensities the distinction between electromagnetic and other forces, such as the weak force, break down. In that case, my example is merely a place-holder for the one force of the unified field theory.
31. The hypothesis being considered is the combination of the acceptance of uninstantiated repeatables with the insistence that they depend on instantiated ones.
32. That is, one-third of the charge of an electron.
33. In order to explain why the actual charges are constrained as they are, we might consider states that allow of charges corresponding to all real numbers and then show that the existence of magnetic monopoles so constrains the

charges that they are all multiples of that of a quark (i.e., one-third of the charge of an electron). This is grossly oversimplified, but I am making a point about the sort of reasons we might have for the proposal I describe.

34. Armstrong argues from the stronger thesis that everything is located in space and time. But the argument from the need for location might still appeal to those who believe in God and/or Cartesian minds as located in time but not space.

35. See Forrest (1988, Chapter 3, Section VII).

36. Armstrong uses the term 'transcendent' for repeatables that must be related to particulars in order to have them as instances. I think it would be better to reserve the term for any repeatables that had instances only *because* they were related to them.

37. As a consequence, the essential–accidental distinction becomes problematic. In some cases I would eliminate the distinction, replacing it by the significant-insignificant distinction. In others I would characterize the essential as those properties that must persist if something is to be considered the same thing at a later time.

38. This is a point that Armstrong has often made; indeed, he holds it for all internal relations. For instance, Armstrong (1989a, p. 112) states of various relations that they are 'internal, and so nothing additional to their *relata*'.

39. If I do not, then I am threatened with a version of Bradley's regress. To account for the unity of the properties of an object I would have to posit some kind of relation between them; to account for the unity between this relation and the properties I would need a further relation; and so on.

40. I say 'attributed' because Quine can also be construed as a class nominalist or as a paranominalist.

41. And so quantify over.

42. No satisfactory theory of repeatables could, I fear, get away with a single predicate. But we are looking at a simplified situation.

43. These categories may overlap.

44. See Armstrong (1978, vol. 1, Chapter 6).

45. So x resembles* y just in case either x resembles y or x resembles something which resembles y, or x resembles something which resembles something which resembles y, etc.

46. Such as the universality of causal regularities and the physical relevance of nonactual states.

47. Can it be said at all? I suspect that what we do here, as in many other areas of metaphysics, is to *show* something of the whole by *say*ing it of a part. In particular, if we restrict both Lan (the language to be reduced) and Bas (the basic language that results from the reduction) to languages that do not include anything about thought-independent reality or isomorphism, then we can state quite coherently theses about such an isomorphism.

48. There might or might not be negative states of affairs corresponding to negative truths. Even if there are none, it seems that we shall still require negation in the language Bas_0. This casts doubt on the Isomorphism Thesis. Similar reasoning applies to disjunction and to universal quantification.

49. I have been told that which particles exist is relative to a frame of reference. I am not in a position to judge the accuracy of that claim, but suppose it is correct. In that case, we might well decide to describe the physical world using some especially natural frames, such as the inertial frames specified by the

expansion of the universe. This would be a conventional element in realism about the theoretical entities of physics.

REFERENCES

Armstrong, D. M. 1978. *Universals and Scientific Realism:* vol. 1, *Nominalism and Realism;* vol. 2, *A Theory of Universals* (Cambridge University Press).
1983a. *What is a Law of Nature?* (Cambridge University Press).
1989a. *A Combinatorial Theory of Possibility* (Cambridge University Press).
1989b. *Universals: an Opinionated Introduction* (Boulder, CO: Westview).
Campbell, Keith. 1990. *Abstract Particulars* (Oxford: Blackwell).
Churchland, Patricia S. 1986. *Neurophilosophy: Toward a Unified Science of the Mind / Brain* (Cambridge, MA: MIT Press).
Forrest, Peter. 1988. *Quantum Metaphysics* (Oxford: Blackwell).
199+. 'New Problems with Change and with Repeatable Properties', *Noûs.*
Gibbons, G. W., Hawking, S. W. and Siklos, S. T. C. (eds.) 1983. *The Very Early Universe* (Cambridge University Press).
Guth, Alan H. 1983. 'Phase Transitions in the Very Early Universe'. In Gibbons et al. (1983), pp. 171-204.
Hughes, R. I. G. 1989. *The Structure and Interpretation of Quantum Mechanics* (Cambridge, MA: Harvard University Press).
Jackson, Frank. 1977. *Perception, a Representative Theory* (Cambridge University Press).
Lewis, David. 1983b. 'New Work for a Theory of Universals', *Australasian Journal of Philosophy* 61: 343-77.
Linde, A. D. 1983. 'The New Inflationary Universe Scenario'. In Gibbons et al. (1983), pp. 205-50.
Putnam, Hilary. 1978. *Meaning and the Moral Sciences* (London: Routledge & Kegan Paul).
Quine, W. V. 1953. 'Notes on the Theory of Reference'. In *From a Logical Point of View* (Cambridge: Harvard University Press), pp. 130-8.
Steinhardt, Paul Joseph. 1983. 'Natural Inflation'. In Gibbons et al. (1983), pp. 251-66.
Swoyer, Chris. 1983. 'Realism and Explanation', *Philosophical Inquiry* 5: 14-28.
Williams, D. C. 1953. 'The Elements of Being'. In *Principles of Empirical Realism* (Springfield, IL: Thomas, 1966), pp. 74-109.

Reply to Forrest

D. M. ARMSTRONG

The Department of Traditional and Modern Philosophy at Sydney University never had a great number of graduate students, although some of them were very good. The best of them all was Peter Forrest. He came to us from mathematics. He took that subject as an undergraduate at Oxford, getting a First, and went on to gain a Ph.D. from Harvard. He taught mathematics at the University of Western Australia for a while and then studied philosophy in Tasmania, before coming to us.

He looked much too young to have done all this, not to mention having a wife and children. But within a few weeks, it seemed, he was teaching us as much as we were teaching him. I remember in particular a seminar paper that he read to us on the metaphysics of Duns Scotus, not one of philosophy's easiest authors. Peter could assimilate arguments and positions new to him with astonishing rapidity. He would then go away, and in a very short time produce a whole series of ideas of his own concerning the matters in hand. Some of these ideas were better than others, but the intellectual fertility and ingenuity he displayed was constant. He went on to a research fellowship at the Australian National University, and thence to the Chair of Philosophy at the University of New England in northern New South Wales.

1. Preliminary

The introductory Section 1.1 of Forrest's essay is quite complex, and here I will comment upon one matter only: his use of the phrase 'analytic ontology' to describe what he and I are trying to do. The phrase was introduced by the late Donald Williams of Harvard, an important but somewhat neglected philosopher. Williams contrasted 'analytic ontology' with 'speculative cosmology'. But despite the austere ring of the first phrase and the permissive flavour of the second, Williams was talking about a distinction to be made within fundamental metaphysics. Analytic ontology takes up the deepest and most abstract questions of all, for instance whether everything in the world is purely particular. Speculative cosmology deals with (relatively!) less abstract issues, such as the nature of space and time, the nature of mind, and so forth, matters where observational fact and scientific discovery appear to be more directly relevant.[1]

2. Explaining Causal Regularities

Forrest begins his argument proper by considering the apparent existence of universal causal regularities. He begins by accepting the view that one particular acts causally on another in virtue of certain properties, and certain properties alone, of the particulars involved. Thus, the bodies of the solar system attract each other in virtue of their mass properties; their temperature has little or nothing to do with it. But, of course, if we are to take this truism ontologically seriously, then we shall need to accept that there are, objectively, properties in things.

Suppose that there are such properties. Are they repeatables or are they purely particular entities that exactly resemble each other? Forrest argues that if we assume that properties are repeatables then we can explain the existence of universal causal regularities (something that surely calls for explanation). What is more, he argues that the explanation need not appeal to the higher-order relations between universals postulated by myself and others. Putting it schematically for simplicity, let it be the case that F-ness in a thing universally serves to bring about G-ness in a suitably related thing. Considering a particular instance, there will be *something about* the F-ness that makes it have the effect it has. But, Forrest argues, if the F-ness is the *very same identical thing* in each case, then – by the indiscernibility of identicals – that same *something about* characterizes all the F-ness. But then the *something about* is at least the natural candidate for that which does the job in every instance. What the *something about* actually is can be left for further investigation.

A very beautiful argument, I think. Forrest follows it up by pointing out that the philosopher who holds that each F-ness is a particular is in a much weaker position. The F-ness may exactly resemble each other, but they are not identical. Such a philosopher can do no better by way of explaining the regularity than appeal to the principle that *like causes like*. This principle, though plausible enough intuitively, is exposed to sceptical doubts when it is asked how it in turn comes to be justified.

In any case, however, Forrest has produced a follow-up argument which I think is new. He asks how the like-causes-like principle is to be applied to functional laws. If we consider the first-order nomic connections that we get when specific values are fed into the functional formulae, then the likeness principle applies unpuzzlingly. But it is not at all clear that the functional connection itself instantiates the like-causes-like principle.

As Forrest notes, even those who accept repeatables may be faced with some problems over functional laws if, like me, they deny the existence of uninstantiated repeatables (i.e., uninstantiated universals). For functional laws may involve 'missing values' – that is, values of the 'antecedent universal' that are not instantiated at any time, past, present or future. Some of these missing values may not be nomically possible values: there may be other laws that forbid that particular value. But there may well be (epistemic 'may') nomically possible missing values. Suppose, for instance, that the mass of the universe is finite. It would not seem self-contradictory then to postulate that the universe might have been a few grams more massive. Would it not also be a nomic possibility? If so, among the possible configurations of matter governed by the gravitational equations there would be nomically possible missing values. Forrest would postulate uninstantiated universals to cover these missing values, and he is right to say that it is a (minor) drawback of my view that I must treat the nomic connections that involve these values counterfactually; namely, if (contrary to fact) there were particulars that instantiated certain values then there would be a nomic connection of the form such-and-such.

3. Physical Possibilities

Forrest holds that uninstantiated repeatables (universals) are required if we are to give good scientific explanations of physical systems (in particular of the system formed by the whole physical universe). For, he points out, such explanations characteristically appeal not only to the actual states of the system but also to the whole set of the physically possible states of the system. (See also my reply to Lycan in this volume.) We do not, indeed, require merely possible *tokens* of states. It will suffice, Forrest thinks, if every merely possible state-type is countenanced. But state-types are repeatables, so the merely possible state-types will be uninstantiated repeatables.

This is not the whole of his argument, but it will be convenient to begin by assuming that this is all he has to say in support of uninstantiated repeatables. To an opponent who argued in this way, I would reply by saying that one should start by constructing a theory of *possibility* in the absolute, unrestricted and 'metaphysical' sense of the word. It is at least convenient, I think, to put forward this theory in the form of a theory of possible worlds. I do not, however, think that it is necessary to treat the other worlds besides this one as anything more than convenient fictions. The reason why we need not take the worlds realistically is that they have no causal or nomic links with the actual world. (The same may be said of uninstantiated universals.) The actual world will be no different whether they are there or not. Why, then, give the possible worlds (or the uninstantiated universals) any existence? The principles of the construction of the other worlds are, I think, combinatorial. Combinatorialism would seem to fit in quite well with the way that possible states of physical systems are constructed.

Of course, unless it is held that the laws of nature are unrestrictedly necessary, the notion of 'all the possible worlds' is not the one we need in order to give an account of the physical possibilities of systems. We require instead a restriction to 'all the possible worlds in which all and only the laws of the actual world hold'. But given this restriction, it seems plausible to maintain that reference to merely physically possible states can be dealt with inside a nonrealist (because fictionalist) scheme.

Forrest, however, has a further argument in store. He points out that, among the merely physically possible states, some are less possible than others. His ball balanced at a point is in such a state. A ball could be in such a state, but it is not very probable that it should be so. How, Forrest asks, can we give an account of this difference in probability without giving these merely possible states ontological reality?

I suggest, however, that the fictionalist scheme already adumbrated is equal to the challenge. Consider a set-up on a planet like ours in which a ball is set in motion on a more or less smooth and level plain which, however, contains rounded hollows and rather narrow plateaus. There will be a huge number of empirically (nomically) possible 'boundary conditions' – most of them *merely* possible – that answer to this description. But is it not fairly obvious that in such a set-up the vast majority of this huge number of possible initial conditions will lead to a result where the ball comes to rest at the bottom of a hollow rather than on a plateau? We are dealing with counterfactuals here, but the counterfactuals are 'backed by' (have as truthmakers) the relevant laws of nature applied to each member of the set of empirically possible initial conditions of the sort described. It could even be said that it is a 'law' of systems of this sort that balls set in motion in such a system have a high probability of ending up at rest in a hollow.

I got this idea from a paper by John Earman (1984, Section 6). One thing it can be applied to is the second law of thermodynamics, according to which a closed system tends toward thermodynamical equilibrium. But it is well known that this is, strictly speaking, only a tendency. Initial conditions can be specified in which the closed system would move away from equilibrium. Such conditions, however, form a very small minority of the nomically possible initial conditions, and so can in practice be ignored. But the person who, some years ago, pointed out to me that the second law was an instance of the sort of thing Earman was referring to was . . . Peter Forrest!

4. Intensive Quantities

Although I do not admit uninstantiated universals, I can hardly deny that there might have been other universals besides the ones that actually exist. These possible but nonexistent universals I try to deal with combinatorially in accordance with my combinatorial theory of possibility. Forrest, however, argues (in Section 1.5) as part of his attack on the

Dependence Thesis that *intensive quantities* are not susceptible of combinatorial treatment.

The combinatorialist need not be worried by anything but *irreducibly intensive* quantities. Density, for instance, is an intensive quantity, but it is definable in terms of mass and volume. Volume is extensive. If mass is also extensive, then density is not irreducibly intensive. Forrest takes instead the example of the strength of a magnetic field at a point. Might not such a strength have an upper bound that never in fact has been or will be exceeded? What account will the combinatorialist give of such a possible property?

Extensive properties can be exhibited as structures of non-overlapping parts. But what if we allow, as contemporary philosophy seems inclined to allow, that it is possible for different particulars to occupy exactly the same place at the same time? Intensive quantities could then be treated in just the same way as extensive quantities, except for the fact that the non-overlapping parts would all be in exactly the same place. (In one sense they would overlap but not in a sense that would trouble the combinatorialist.) Forrest judges that 'the explanatory power of [this] hypothesis no longer warrants its intellectual cost' (Section 1.5). I am not so sure. In any case, it does seem plausible that given one degree of an intensive quantity, all other possible degrees should be combinatorially accessible, in this way or some other way.

5. The Threat of Transcendence

Any philosopher who countenances both particulars and universals in his or her ontology is a species of ontological dualist. Such a philosopher may, as a result, be forced to postulate two separate realms of being: a realm of particulars and a realm of universals. Consider, in particular, the situation of one like Forrest, who countenances uninstantiated universals; his uninstantiated universals might have been instantiated. Similarly, it would seem, any instantiated universal of his might have been uninstantiated. Must he not then take the relation of instantiation (or rather the relations of monadic, dyadic, tradic, ..., n-adic instantiation) with the utmost ontological seriousness? For these instantiation relations connect terms that can exist independently of each other, and so they will be 'further things' hooking up particulars to their universals. But then there is trouble. For surely he must treat these instantiation relations as universals themselves. Are they not repeatables? But if they are universals, cannot they too exist uninstantiated? (Consider, in particular, the n-adic instantiation relation where n is a large number.) Then, however, instantiation of these 'realm-linking universals' will demand further instantiation relations to glue them into place between the original particulars and universals. A version of Bradley's regress ensues. But such a regress is either vicious or, at best, viciously uneconomical.

This, I think, is one source of the attraction of a theory that denies the possibility of uninstantiated universals (and that also denies the possibility of bare particulars). Bradleian dilemmas will then at least be harder to generate, and if generated will require less heroic measures to escape. Forrest, however, thinks that he can accept uninstantiated universals and still keep out of trouble by claiming that the instantiation relation or relations are such that *they*, unlike ordinary relations, cannot exist uninstantiated. As he realizes, he needs to follow up this claim by developing a principled distinction between instantiation relations and other relations. He thinks he can do this by 'insisting on the *thickness* of particulars'. A particular, he argues, is not a propertyless substrate but includes all its properties, even all its relational properties; it is a particular-in-a-situation. Given this, the relation between particular and property is an internal one. Forrest then follows me in arguing that internal relations are not something ontologically additional to their terms. Exit, he hopes, any vicious regress.

I myself accept a doctrine of a thick particular. The thin particular is the particular qua particular, the particular in abstraction from all its properties. The thick particular is the particular taken along with all its properties; it is, I hold, a state of affairs: the particular's possessing all these properties. If one accepts conjunctive properties in cases where the properties in question are co-instantiated, then one can roll up all these properties into a single property N (for nature) and take the state of affairs in question to be the particular's having N. But notice that, although it is a necessary truth that the thick particular has whatever properties it has (because these properties help to constitute it), the state of affairs that is (identical with) the thick particular is contingent. For the state of affairs links the thin particular to N, and that is contingent. Notice, furthermore, that the properties involved are all *nonrelational* properties. The particular does not spill out over its spatiotemporal boundaries.

By contrast, Forrest's thick particular is super-thick: it includes all the relations that the particular has to other particulars. It must be that way, according to Forrest, in order to make instantiation an internal relation. It would seem, indeed, that these super-thick particulars may reflect the whole world from their point of view, at any rate if (as seems quite possible) every particular stands in a genuine external relation to every other particular. But from my point of view the greatest difficulty with Forrest's position is that it only papers over the cracks. Behind his necessities, I would say, lie states of affairs where instantiations are contingent. Forrest does indicate that he is taking a different view of particulars from mine. But I regret to say that I have not been able to get a clear view of that different position.

In the second half of his essay, Forrest describes the position he calls Paranominalism and argues that the difference between it and realism about universals is at bottom conventional only. But, as he indicates, this argument depends upon his contention that 'once we have both – the particular-in-a-situation and the appropriate property – nothing further is required to ensure that the particular instantiates the property'. Since I have questioned this, I do not see how to take the dispute any further.

I am glad that Peter has defended realism about universals as the best 'ontology convention'. But I have yet to be convinced that realism about universals involves a convention at all.

NOTE

1. See Williams (1966, p. 74). It so happens that Sydney University was for some years the world centre of Donald Williams studies. David Stove was deeply influenced by Williams's book *The Ground of Induction* (1947). Keith Campbell and I were particularly interested in his empirical metaphysics, and Campbell and Bacon embraced Williams's idea that the world is a construction out of tropes, that is, properties taken as particulars. See Campbell's book *Abstract Particulars* (1990). Forrest got his acquaintance with Williams's work in Sydney.

REFERENCES

Campbell, Keith. 1990. *Abstract Particulars* (Oxford: Blackwell).
Earman, John. 1984. 'Laws of Nature: the Empiricist Challenge'. In *D. M. Armstrong, Profiles,* vol. 4, ed. Radu J. Bogdan (Dordrecht: Reidel), pp. 191–223.
Williams, D. C. 1947. *The Ground of Induction* (Cambridge, MA: Harvard University Press).
    1966. *Principles of Empirical Realism* (Springfield, IL: Thomas).

4

Sets Are Haecceities

JOHN BIGELOW

According to the 1985 Guinness Book of Records, the word 'set' has 58 noun uses, 126 verbal uses and 10 as a participial adjective. The word 'set' is the most ambiguous word in the English language. How on earth did a word so incredibly ambiguous worm its way into the very foundations of rigorous modern mathematics?

In the wake of recent exhumations of long-buried doctrines concerning Platonic or Aristotelian forms, or universals, there have appeared before us a veritable smorgasbord of entities with some claim to be aptly called 'sets'. The leading exhumer of universals, David Armstrong, has argued (1991) that sets are aggregates of things that he calls 'states of affairs': the havings of properties by individuals. I have argued (Bigelow 1988) for a different notion: that a set is a distinctive relation among its members. Later (Bigelow 1990) I adopted yet another viewpoint, arguing that sets are higher-order properties of their members.

It may seem to be a largely verbal question, however, which of the various offered candidates are most aptly called by the dubious honorific 'sets'. Aggregates of states of affairs, and relations, and higher-order properties all exist, I reckon, and it seems hardly worth worrying over which of these are 'really' the sets. And yet, there are some real issues lurking behind this verbal façade. Are any of the rival candidates for the disputed label more deserving of attention than the others? If so, then a good way of attracting the attention they merit would be to call them sets.

Sets, I therefore urge, are higher-order properties of their members. If sets are those properties then, I will argue, it can be understood how it can be that mathematicians have carried on their business for thousands of years without knowing anything about set theory; and yet it can also be understood why sets have, at long last, captured the attention not only of philosophers but also of pure mathematicians. Sets are creatures of abstruse metaphysics, but it takes a rare creature from that zoo to hold the attention of mathematicians for over a hundred years. It is, however, incomprehensible how anyone but medieval monks or Australian realists could take any interest at all in sets if they were really those peculiar creatures of abstruse metaphysics which they are portrayed as being by theories other than the one I will favour. Only if sets are the very special higher-order properties that I will describe can we understand not only why mathematicians took so long to stumble upon them but also why mathematicians have been so obsessed with them ever since.

1. Why Study Sets?

Plato was wrong about many important things: for instance, about what sorts of things the Forms are, and when and where they are to be found. Yet his core conception was entirely right. Mathematics does deal with properties and relations, patterns and structures: things that can be instantiated by many diverse things, things that can be manifested in many different places at one and the same time – and so, things that qualify as universals.

Among the properties and relations studied in mathematics are many that are instantiated by physical properties and relations, such as lengths, areas, volumes, accelerations, forces, masses, and so on. And many of these physical properties and relations are in turn instantiated by physical objects. A Platonist is prone to insist that mathematical patterns have a kind of existence that is not contingent on the presence of any physical manifestation, but this should not blind us to the fact that many mathematical patterns are instantiated by physical things.

Physical objects, like elephants and Italians, humming-birds and Hottentots, have many physical properties and relations: volume and surface area, for example. And the physical properties of these objects stand in important relationships to one another. In particular, such physical properties stand in relations of proportion to one another. There is a relationship between the surface area of the humming-bird and that of the Hottentot; and this may or may not be the same as the relationship that holds between the surface areas of an Italian and an elephant.

Relationships such as proportion will hold not only between surface areas but also between volumes. Conceivably, the relationship between the surface areas of two objects might be the same as the relationship between volumes for two other objects. But it is a fact of considerable biological significance that the relation between surface areas of two objects will not, in general, be the same as the relationship between their volumes. Ignoring differences in shape (say, by supposing an elephant were shaped like an Italian, or vice versa), it turns out that if the elephant has ten times the height then it will have a hundred times the surface area and a thousand times the volume. The volumes of the elephant and the Italian, or the Hottentot and the humming-bird, will be 'more different' than their surface areas. There are several distinct relationships present; furthermore, there are distinctive ways in which these relationships differ from one another. There are also distinctive relationships among these relationships. These facts have consequences of physical significance: for instance, with regard to problems of heat regulation. It is from such fertile soil as this that most of mathematics has grown.

Ratios furnish a clear example of the kind of relations that hold among various physical properties. Consider ratios of areas. Suppose King Lear owns some land and finds a way of dividing this land into two equal regions, one for Regan and one for Goneril. The two portions will not be equal in all respects, but they may be equal in area. This is a relation that holds in virtue of properties of the related regions. Regan's land is equal to Goneril's because it has a determinate area. If Goneril's land had not existed then Regan's land would not have stood in that relationship of equality in area to Goneril's land. But even if Regan's land had not equalled Goneril's, it would still have had the area that it does have. It is because it has the area that it does, and Goneril's has the area that it does, that Regan's land is equal in area to Goneril's.

Equality in area is a relationship between two properties. In this case, we can take the relationship of equality to be simply that of numerical identity between properties. Regan's land has a property – one of Locke's so-called primary properties, in fact – a property that we call *area*. Goneril's land has that very same property.

Suppose Lear's land, before he divided it, was equal in area to that of France (before Joan of Arc, France was very much smaller than it is now). Then the area of Regan's land will not equal that of France. Yet there will be another, equally distinctive relation between the area of Regan's land and the area of France's realm. Regan's land will have an area half that of France. You could divide France into two parts, in the same way foolish Lear did, and each of those parts would have an area equal to that of Regan's land.

More complicated ratios can be defined. Roughly, the area of one land stands in a ratio $n:m$ to that of another when the first can be divided into n parts that are equal in area and the second can be divided into m parts with that same area. Each of these parts has the very same property, I claim. In virtue of this fact, there is a determinate relation between the area of the two aggregates formed by these parts. This relation is a *ratio*.

Ratios hold among an extensive range of properties. Areas stand in ratios to areas, lengths stand in ratios to lengths, masses stand in ratios to masses, velocities stand in ratios to velocities. And numbers stand in ratios to numbers. This is very important. Mathematicians are prone to think of 'the area' of a region as a number. When one area is, say, twice another, they think of this as meaning that the number assigned to one area, when divided by 2, equals the number assigned to the other area.

Yet this is a deep error. The assignment of a number to an area presupposes a prior concept of ratios between areas, and of ratios between numbers. When we assign a number to a region, this is a useful way of describing its area and of identifying its relationships to other areas. But what the assignment of such a number to an area signifies is a fact about relationships among areas, and not a relationship of that area to the number itself. When a number is used to describe an area, what underlies this is the fact that the ratio holding between that number and the number 1 is the very same ratio as that holding between the area in question and some other area arbitrarily chosen as the 'unit area'.

Numbers (natural numbers, that is) are universals that are instantiated by things like pebbles and Pythagoreans, pots and pans, parents and progeny. Pythagoreans thought not only that physical things instantiated numbers; they also thought all the appearances that physical things present to us can be explained entirely by reference to the number properties they instantiate. At any rate, this is one way of reading the scraps handed down from the Pythagorean brotherhood. They may have gone too far in thinking that there are no properties but numbers, but they were not wrong in thinking that things instantiate numbers.

One very amazing thing about numbers is that they are instantiated not only by physical things but also by each other. After you have studied, say, half a dozen numbers, and wondered which of them are odd, which are even, which are triangular numbers, which are squares, and so on, you may then think over what you have been doing, and count how many numbers you have attended to so far. As a consequence, it turns out that there must be infinitely many numbers. It is not logically possible that there should be, say, just two thimbles in existence. If there were two thimbles then they would instantiate the number 2. Neither of them is identical with the number 2. So now count how many things there are: there is the first thimble, and there is the second thimble, and there is the number 2, and none of these is identical to either of the others. So there are three things. The number 3 is instantiated. Now let us take stock again: How many things are there? There are the two thimbles, and the number 2, and the number 3. That makes four things. We are off on an infinite regress. If the world contains two thimbles, then the world contains infinitely many things altogether, since it contains all the numbers; and furthermore all these numbers are instantiated. They are instantiated by one another at least, even if by nothing else.

Thus runs a Pythagorean version of the von Neumann construction of the natural numbers by recursive set-theoretical operations beginning with the empty set. Von Neumann construes each natural number as the set of its predecessors, and the number zero as the empty set, as it has no predecessors. My Pythagorean started with thimbles instead of the empty set, and used those thimbles together with numbers from 2 to *n*, to instantiate *n*. Von Neumann uses set membership instead of instantiation, but the drift is precisely the same.

One very nice thing about natural numbers is that they also instantiate ratios as well as numbers. There is a relationship between, say, 6 and 9. You can divide 6 into two parts which are the same in number, and you can divide 9 into three parts with just that same number in each part. So there is a ratio of 2:3 between the numbers 6 and 9. Exactly the same ratio may hold not only between numbers but also between areas, lengths, velocities and so on. There are many properties that instantiate ratios. But it is nice to find that all possible ratios are guaranteed to be instantiated among numbers. Even if no areas stand in the ratio 117:221, we can nevertheless be sure that that ratio is instantiated at least by pairs of numbers, for instance by the numbers 234 and 442. So even if we were to begin with the supposition that the world contains two thimbles, and we assumed nothing beyond that, we could infer from that minimal assumption the existence of all the natural numbers; and hence we could be assured of instantiations for all the ratios. Any world with at least two thimbles will contain instantiations for all the ratios.

Thus does mathematics feed on itself. If you give a gorilla nothing to eat but two thimbles, it will never grow to be King Kong. But give a Pythagorean two thimbles and they will give you all the ratios. And the Pythagorean gives you all the ratios, not merely as relations that contingently might or might not be instantiated, existing in a Platonic independence from their instances. No, the ratios both exist and are instantiated; they are instantiated by natural numbers. Ratios could not exist without being instantiated – it is a necessary truth that they are instantiated.

There is another reason why ratios could not have existed without being instantiated: they instantiate one another. Not only do the natural numbers 6 and 9 stand in the ratio 2:3, but so do the ratios 2:9 and 1:3 for instance. Ratios stand in ratios.

It is ontologically indecent, the way mathematics feeds on itself. But it is a fact of life – that is just the way things are in mathematics. Yet it is a mistake to think that mathematics is far removed from physical reality. Mathematics deals with properties and relations, such as ratios, which are instantiated by such physical properties and relations as area and velocity. Ratios are relations between physical properties of physical things. These ratios play an integral role in physical theory, so they are themselves physical relations. Physicalists can believe in them without renouncing one jot of their physicalism, say I. Nominalism must be renounced, of course, but physicalists need not be nominalists. For metaphysically realistic physicalists, mathematics is part of physical reality.

Arithmetic instantiates all the ratios. Hence many of the relationships between physical properties are safely instantiated by numbers, whether or not they are instantiated by other physical properties. There are, however, other relationships between physical properties besides ratios. There is, for instance, a distinctive relationship that holds between the circumference and the diameter of any square; there is a distinctive relationship between the circumference and the diameter of any circle; and so on. These relationships may be called proportions.

Some proportions are also ratios. Sometimes the relationship of proportion holding between, say, one length and another, or between one velocity and another, or whatever, is the very same relationship that holds between one natural number and another. Sometimes the proportion between, say, the width and the length of a rectangle is simply the same as the relationship between, say, 1 and 2. That is, the proportion between width and length of a rectangle may simply be the ratio 1:2, which also holds between the natural numbers 1 and 2. So some proportions are instantiated not only by lengths, velocities and so forth, but also by natural numbers. But not all proportions are like that. There are proportions that hold among properties like length and velocity yet do not hold between any two natural numbers. These relations of proportion are not instantiated by natural numbers, and they are not instantiated by ratios either: no two ratios stand to one another in a relation like that in which diagonal stands to circumference for a square, or a pentagon, or a circle.

Relations of proportion, therefore, are not automatically instantiated by numbers alone. Spatial and temporal (or spatiotemporal) properties stand in all these relations of proportion, so we need not think these relations are altogether uninstantiated. However, in order to assure ourselves that they are instantiated, we need to assure ourselves of the existence of things beyond numbers. The full gamut of real numbers rests on things like geometry and dynamics, not just on arithmetic.

When Euclidean geometry came to be challenged as a correct description of physical space, this had a shattering effect on the philosophy of mathematics. Mathematicians want to find instantiations of the various patterns and structures they study, and they had become accustomed to finding instantiations whose existence they could count on without having to take anyone else's word for it. Ratios, for instance, may be instantiated by all sorts of things, from all sorts of subject matters, like geography, history, astronomy, physics, dressmaking, cookery, etc. But when we are doing mathematics, we need not seek assurances about whether or not such things really do instantiate the ratios we want to study. We need not listen to anyone's testimony from any other discipline in order to be sure we have found instantiations for the ratios.

Thus an expectation arises that mathematical patterns will furnish their own instantiations, just as the numbers and ratios do. But some proportions, it seems, are instantiated by space and time but not by numbers or ratios. It is unnerving to find that we cannot be assured of instantiations for all the proportions we need in science without looking beyond mathematics and thereby making ourselves vulnerable to contradiction from experts in other departments. How then can we furnish purely mathematical instantiations for all the proportions that constitute the plenum of real numbers? By set theory. That is what set theory is for.

So it would be nice if we could find purely mathematical entities that instantiate all the real numbers. There is thus a motive for wanting to believe in sets, if their existence can indeed be assured mathematically, and if they can indeed instantiate all the real numbers. But we must beware of wishful thinking. And as philosophers, we should search our consciences for an understanding of what on earth these things are that the mathematicians are studying and calling 'sets'.

The problem is most acute for someone with physicalist leanings. If a physicalist renounces nominalism, then it is possible to embrace mathematical realism without apostasy from physicalism. It is possible to believe in real numbers, provided they are construed as relations between physical properties like mass or velocity. There is a price to be paid by such physicalism, however, if it rests too heavily on the existence of such physical properties as length or velocity: the price is a loss of autonomy for mathematics. The only way this price can be lifted, it seems, is by accepting set theory as furnishing purely mathematical instantiations for all the structures of the system of real numbers.

It would be convenient if we could believe in sets. Then we could be assured that the entire pattern of the field of real numbers is instantiated by purely mathematical entities. We could be assured that this whole pattern would still be instantiated even if there were no such thing as physical space, or even if physical space were finite and not infinitely divisible. It would be nice for the purity and autonomy of pure mathematics if we could believe in sets. Yet how can we? Show me one!

2. Armstrong's Theory

Armstrong has drawn attention to some alleged entities which he thinks are physical enough for a physicalist to believe in with a relatively clear conscience, and yet which he also thinks can be called 'sets' – presumably without radically redefining that word.

Armstrong says sets are aggregates of states of affairs of a special sort. The primary case of a set is a unit set; following Lewis (1991), Armstrong takes any set to be an aggregate of unit sets. And a unit set is the state of affairs of a thing's having some unit-making property. (The property of being a whale, for instance, is a unit-making property, but the property of being snow is not; you can count whales, but you cannot count snow.) A state of affairs, in turn, is something that contains particulars and universals as constituents, combined in a distinctive way.

Suppose we grant that the things Armstrong claims to be sets are things which do in fact exist. Suppose we also grant that they are physical enough for a (nonnominalistic) physicalist to believe in. A question still remains: Is it plausible to suggest that these things are sets?

One question to ask is whether Armstrong's sets can perform the distinctive role of sets within modern mathematics. Could Armstrong sets, if we could be convinced of their existence, provide a rich enough structure to instantiate all the patterns, ratios and proportions that constitute the real numbers?

Yes. Lewis has shown that a structure as rich as set theory can be construed out of the aggregation of certain basic ingredients, provided those initial ingredients possess a certain fairly minimal family of distinctive properties. Armstrong sets, if there are any, would possess the required family of properties. So it is not unreasonable for Armstrong to believe that his putative sets do instantiate the structure of the field of real numbers.

There are two challenges that Armstrong faces up to. The first is that of arguing that his candidates actually can do the mathematical work that is the raison d'être of sets. The other is that of establishing that these candidates are physical enough for a rational person, in this age of science, to believe in.

I do not dispute Armstrong's success on these scores. Yet it would be a mistake to let the defense rest after a successful rejoinder to just those two challenges. Grant that there are physical things that instantiate the patterns of the real number system. Are these things sets? Perhaps, but not necessarily.

Armstrong sets are not the only things which, if they do exist, would instantiate the real number patterns. There are other candidates that would generate those same patterns. And some of those other candidates would have just as strong a claim to count as 'physical'. Faced with rival candidates, each equally 'physical' and believable (if you are not a nominalist), how do you decide which of them are the sets?

Some would urge that this question is misguided, that the only reasonable requirements of a candidate for the title 'set' are that it be something which does exist and which does the mathematical work that sets are expected to do. There is no legitimate additional question about which – among those which meet these requirements – are the 'real' sets. In a sense, all of them are; in a sense none of them are. Or so it may be argued.

That line of thought, however, overlooks one additional way in which we can get a grip on the referent of the word 'sets'. One very important thing we know about sets is that, in the relevant sense of this word, sets are things that mathematicians did not talk about for most of the two thousand years of progress from the ancient Greeks to the last century – or at least, if the things mathematicians were talking about all those years were 'really' sets, then this was something they themselves never suspected. A second very important thing we know about sets is that mathematicians have been talking about them for over a century.

Is it plausible to suppose that mathematicians have been talking about Armstrong sets for over a century? The mere fact that they have not recognized them under that description does not, of course, by itself show that the things mathematicians have been talking about are not Armstrong sets, are not aggregates of the states of affairs of things having unit-making properties. And yet, neither is it obvious that Armstrong sets *are* the things which mathematicians have been talking about. The fact (if it is one) that mathematicians could have done the mathematical work they needed to do if they had chosen to talk about Armstrong sets is not enough to prove that they actually did that work by talking about Armstrong sets. We should consider what other things could have done the same work, and whether it is more plausible that mathematicians might in fact have been talking about those things rather than Armstrong sets.

On the fact of it, it seems implausible that mathematicians should have stumbled on Armstrong sets about a hundred years ago and become obsessed with them ever since. Yet it is hard to back this up with a firm argument to show that mathematicians could not have been referring to Armstrong sets. What I will argue, rather, is that there are other things which mathematicians could have been referring to, and that it is much more plausible that these would be things they stumbled upon late in the history of mathematics and found intrinsically (and mathematically) intriguing ever since.

3. Sets and Essences

If – as I have argued – mathematics deals with universals, with physical properties and relations, then what business do sets have in mathematics?

The answer is that sets, too, are universals. They are universals that came to the attention of mathematicians very naturally, at a specific and very recent stage of the history of mathematics. In an important sense they are highly 'abstract' universals: they are higher-order universals, arising further up the hierarchy of universals than such universals as natural numbers, ratios, and real numbers. It is for this reason not surprising that they came under the spotlight of history only very recently, long after the infancy and adolescence of mathematics. Nevertheless, their higher-order status does not weaken their claim to be universals, as real and existent as mass, velocity or age. Nor does it prevent them from playing a significant role in physical theory. Sets too are physical.

And yet, which universals could sets possibly be? I will first explain what sorts of universals sets would have to be, if they are to be construed as universals. It will then become obvious why it is hard for anyone with any physicalist scruples to be comfortable with the kinds of universals sets would have to be. Any physicalist should find it easy to understand the motivation behind the attempt to cut sets out of science, in the way that for instance Field (1980) tried to do. Yet if sets could be identified with physical properties or relations of some sort or other, then Field's project would be unnecessary. Field's colleague, Penelope Maddy, is on the right track in her defense of Platonism (1989). I will join forces with Maddy and outline another way, somewhat different from hers, in which we may dispel at least some of the supernatural atmosphere that often clouds our perceptions of sets.

An *essence* is something you could not be without. That is, something is an essential property for an individual when the individual could not exist without that property. Shared essences are not an impossibility. If descent from Adam were an essential property for human beings, then it would be a property shared by all and only members of the human species.

An *individual* essence, if there is one, would be something one must have yet cannot share. That is, something is an individual essence for an individual when that individual could not exist without that property, and when furthermore that property could not be possessed by anything other than that individual. It is as the old song said of love and marriage: you can't have one without the other. Possession of the individual essence is necessary for the existence of the individual, and instantiation by that very individual is essential for the presence of that individual essence. Universals often ground similarities, but they also ground differences; individual essences ground only differences and could not possibly ground similarities.

Consider a thing, a say, and its unit set $\{a\}$. Belonging to its own unit set is an individual essence for any thing at all. If anything x is not a member of the unit set $\{a\}$ then that thing x is not a. And conversely, if anything x is not a then that thing x is not a member of the unit set $\{a\}$.

A change of notation will be illuminating. Instead of saying that a thing *a* 'belongs to' the set {*a*}, we should say that thing *a* 'instantiates' the set {*a*}. Set membership is really just instantiation in the special case where the relevant universal being instantiated is a set. Thus, when we say that 'being a member of {*a*}' is an essential property of *a*, this is a roundabout way of saying something crisper: that the unit set {*a*} is itself an essential property of *a*.

Nothing but notation holds us back from saying this; we are inhibited only by the standard use of the term 'is a member of' (rather than 'instantiates') for the link between a set and its members. But no harm will be done by redefining the term 'instantiation' so that it encompasses set membership as a special case. We might put it this way: What content would there be to an insistence that the set-membership relation is not an extension of the instantiation relation? No harm will be done; on the contrary, there will be philosophical benefits to be gained by seeing the set-membership relation as a special case of the instantiation relation. It will then be easier to see set theory in historical perspective, as a recent and natural extension of mathematical ontology.

A unit set is an individual essence of its only member. Many philosophers will have an instinctive loathing for 'individual essences' – empiricists in particular, from the time of Hobbes onward. But that is no reason for them to object to the analysis of a set as an individual essence. On the contrary, it is a reason for thinking that the analysis gets the intuitive notion of a set roughly right. Sets have always been ontologically suspect entities, especially for empiricists, and they have been fishy for exactly the same sorts of reasons that individual essences have been in bad odour since the rise of the sciences at the end of the Middle Ages in Europe.

Unit sets are individual essences; sets more generally are plural essences. Any set, other than the empty set or a unit set, is in one sense unlike an individual essence, in that it does ground a 'sameness' and not just 'uniqueness'; such a set is a 'one over many' universal, in that several distinct things instantiate (are members of) the same set, so the set is something they share in common. Nevertheless, a set with more than one member is strongly analogous to an individual essence. It captures not the uniqueness of any one of its members, but rather the uniqueness of them all collectively.

In the first place, a set is an essential property of each of its members. This is so because, if any thing *x* is not numerically identical with one of the members of a set *A*, then *x* could not possibly instantiate set *A*. Given the members of a set, identity with one of these very things is necessary for instantiation of that set. This makes a set different from other sorts of shared properties. Given the things that instantiate universals like, say, hunger, identity with one of these very things is not necessary for instantiation of that universal: A person could be hungry without having to be numerically identical with one of the things that happen in the actual world to constitute all and only the hungry. A set is a universal that nothing could possibly instantiate without being identical to one of the things that actually instantiate that universal.

So a set is an essential property of its members; but equally, its members are essential to the set. Given the things that actually instantiate a set, it follows that no universal could possibly be identical with that set if it failed to be instantiated by any one of those things, or if it were instantiated by anything that was not numerically identical with one of those things.

Thus, a set could not possibly have failed to be instantiated by the things it is in fact instantiated by – had it had different instances then it would not have been the set it is. Conversely, the members could not all have jointly existed without being members of that set. The instances are essential for the identity of the set, and membership in that set is essential for the joint identities of its members.

Sets, then, are plural essences. A set containing 'these' things is a shared property of those things, but is essentially linked to the numerical identities of those very things. Its identity and theirs are inseparable.

To handle the logic of plural essences most perspicuously, what is required is plural quantification and multigrade predication (see e.g. Sharvy 1968, Morton 1975, Grandy 1976, Massey 1976, and Boolos 1984). However, even in the absence of a full articulation of multigrade predication and plural quantification, it can be seen in outline how sets can be construed as pluralized individual essences.

An important question can now be raised. I am suggesting that sets are plural essences, and in particular that a unit set is an individual essence of its only member. But which individual essence will a unit set be? Nothing has been said to establish that a thing has only one individual essence. An individual essence has been defined to be something an individual must have and cannot share: but no reason has been given why there could not be several such things that it must have and cannot share. If there are several such things, which is the one that constitutes the unit set of that thing?

To illustrate, consider an attempt to articulate what makes a thing unique by giving a sufficiently lengthy and well-chosen conjunction of other properties. For instance, we might begin to articulate what made Descartes the unique person that he was by noting one of his essential properties, say, that he is a thinking thing. This is, however, a property he shares with others, so it is not an individual essence. To find his individual essence, we would need to look for other properties that he has that distinguish him from other thinking things.

We must take care, however, to avoid inclusion of any properties that he has only accidentally, properties he could have lacked without ceasing to be numerically the same person that he is. Otherwise the conjunction formed would fail to be an individual essence, for although such a property might identify Descartes uniquely, nevertheless it would not capture what it is about Descartes that makes him the person that he is. To obtain a conjunction that constitutes an individual essence, we must include only properties that Descartes could not lack; otherwise the conjunction will not be something Descartes could not lack. But we must also include enough conjoined properties to ensure that no one else could possibly share them all.

It is far from obvious that it will be possible to find any such conjunction. Our task would be made much easier if we allow relational properties to play a role here – a person's ancestry, for instance. If we add the origin of an individual to our growing conjunction of essential properties, then it becomes plausible to suppose we are approaching a conjunction that could not possibly be shared, one that logically guarantees uniqueness. This only helps, of course, if we grant that ancestry is essential to identity, and this is something that is not universally granted. I am one of those who endorse Kripke's (1972) thoughts on essence of origins, but others demur. Thus, there is much room for doubt about such things as the essence of origin for individual identity. This doubt about essences casts further doubt on the existence of individual essences. The fewer the properties, like origin, that you are willing to grant as essential, the slimmer your chances of ever obtaining a conjunction which is both essential and necessarily unique.

Whether or not origin is granted to be essential to a thing's identity, another problem faces any attempt to compile an individual essence by conjoining a sequence of essential properties. A general strategy of argument can be mounted to show that no conjunction of sharable properties could ever be an individual essence. Given that each of the conjoined properties is sharable, it can be argued that their conjunction will in principle be sharable too. Such arguments can be found in Adams (1979).

If any conjunction of sharable properties is sharable, then in order to obtain an individual essence we must include some property which is in principle unsharable without being itself analyzable as a conjunction of any sort. Such a property will need to be primitive and unanalyzable. Philosophers call such a property the 'thisness' of a thing, the property that makes the thing what it is. Kaplan (1975) taught us to refer to it by the medieval Latin word for 'thisness': a necessarily unsharable, unanalyzable, primitive essential property of a thing is a 'haecceity'. It may be doubted whether there are any such properties. But if there are any, it is plausible to assume that there is at most one haecceity for each individual. If haecceities are unstructured primitives, it is hard to see what could distinguish one haecceity from another, if they are both necessarily possessed by the very same individual. So it is plausible to grant that there is at most one haecceity for any given thing. This falls short of an argued position, but it is plausible all the same.

This gives us a candidate for the role of the unique individual essence to be identified with the unit set of a thing. A haecceity of an individual will be an individual essence of that individual, and perhaps that is the individual essence which is identical to the unit set of that individual.

Of course, it is open to someone to deny that there are any individual essences. Armstrong defines a 'universal' to be a 'one which runs through many', a 'repeatable'. If *that* is what a universal must be like, then it is hard to see how there could be any such things as individual essences. Hence my strategy of identifying sets with such universals would be ruled out. I think Quine was right to identify sets as special universals, even though they are not 'ones that run through many', but Armstrong takes this to be manifestly wrong-headed.

Etymology, of course, backs Armstrong here – based on the name, 'universals' ought to be ones over manys. Yet the word 'properties' does not have such a powerful etymological pressure towards a repeatability requirement. It does not ring oddly on the ear to say that there may be some 'properties' that make us unique. Some properties might even make us essentially unique. There may be some properties which we could not share. There may be some properties that no one but you could have had. These notions are not absurd from the outset merely on the grounds that 'universals' must be repeatables.

Thus there is a possible theory which holds that there are properties which are essentially 'uniqueness-makers' rather than 'universals'. Armstrong thinks of universals exclusively as the things that ground the samenesses we find around us, but universals also ground differences. Two things are the same in some respect when they share a common property, but they are also different in some respect when one has a property the other lacks. If we focus on difference-makers, there is no impediment to the theory that there are such things as individual essences. Quine's theory that sets are universals cannot be dismissed in the way that Armstrong has done, simply on the grounds that it is obvious that sets are not repeatables.

And yet, why should we believe in sets? Why should we believe in plural essences? And even if you have good reasons for believing in them, a puzzle remains of a more historical sort. Plural essences do not strike the intellect as an obvious choice of subject matter for study by pure mathematicians. One might wonder how it came to pass that such esoteric metaphysical creatures came under the spotlight of mathematical research, and indeed were then plugged into a foundational role beyond the wildest dreams of the medieval monks who discussed them so intensively.

In fact, though I hate to admit it, we have the makings here of a deceptively plausible objection to the conception of sets as plural essences: If sets were plural essences, mathematicians would never have taken an interest in them. But mathematicians did take an interest in sets. Therefore sets are not plural essences. To rebut this objection, and at the same time to find out which plural essences sets could be, we should look to the history of mathematics.

4. Conics and Coextensiveness

One of the most striking and exhilarating things about pure mathematics is the way in which one thing leads to another. It is rather like philosophy in that respect, a seamless web. Mathematics is the study of patterns, that is, of universals, of properties and relations that can be instantiated by things which are in other respects very different from one another, and yet which nevertheless are in an important respect the same. When we find one universal that several things share, it may not be the only universal that those things share. It is sometimes possible to discover other universals – coextensive with the first one – that are shared by those same things. Such a discovery is often of great significance.

The study of conic sections originated, history records, in Plato's Academy, where the academics became fascinated with a problem allegedly presented by an oracle to the people of Delos. There was a cubic altar in Delos, and the oracle advised the people of that city to rebuild it in such a way as to double its volume. A simple problem, it seemed, involving a simple proportion between one physical magnitude and another. Note how the problem has nothing to do with numbers or equations or pure abstractions. It is a thoroughly physical problem.

What was required was to find a sequence of relations between lengths which would connect the edge of the initial cube to the edge of a cube of twice the volume. Now the proportion between these lengths, unlike the required proportion between volumes, is not a ratio. However, this need not make it impossible to find the required sequence of relations. Suppose one line stands in a ratio to another, and the angle between them also stands in a ratio to one complete turn. Then you can use these lines as two sides of a triangle, and compare their lengths with that of the third side. The length of that third side may not be a ratio of either of the other two sides, but by mediation of those sides and the angle between them we have established an indirect relationship between its length and their lengths. By repeated use of this method, it might have been hoped, one could find a sequence of relationships linking the edge of one cube to the edge of its double.

Yet it was discovered, about two thousand years after Plato, that no such sequence of relations could ever yield the relation between the edge of a cube and the edge of its double. Duplication of the cube is, as they say, a construction that cannot be carried out 'with straightedge and compass'. The oracle had set the Greeks off on a millenial wild-goose chase.

Because the Delian problem could not be solved with ratios of lengths and angles (i.e., with triangles or other polygons), this problem led the ancient mathematicians to study other shapes – curved shapes and, in particular, conic sections. By relating the edge of a cube to a conic section, and then by relating some other feature of this conic section to another length, one might thereby establish a sequence of relations connecting the edge of the cube to the edge of its double.

Consider now the points on a conic section. What do all these points share in common? And what distinguishes them all from points that are not on that curve? There are in fact several properties shared by all and only the points on that curve. For example, each point on the curve has the following two relational properties: There is a plane such that each point on the curve is also located on the plane; all the points on the curve share the relationship property of 'being on the plane'. There is also a cone such that each point on the curve is also located on the cone; this is a second relational property shared by all the points on the curve. Hence all points on the curve share a conjunction of two relational properties: each is on the same plane, and on the same cone. Furthermore, this is a common property that distinguishes the points on the curve from all points which are not on the curve. The term 'conic section' encapsulates these two relational properties.

Now note that a cone can have a vertex that is acute-angled, obtuse-angled, or right-angled. Consider first an acute-angled cone. Take one of the curves that lie both on that cone and on some plane, a conic section derived from an acute-angled cone. As we have seen, one of the properties shared by all and only points on this curve is the conjunction of their being on the same plane and their being on this cone. But we may wonder whether there might be another cone which all these points lie upon. Do they all lie not only on the acute-angled cone we began with but also on, say, some obtuse-angled cone? The answer is that given any cone at all, however obtuse or acute, the points on the curve we started with will all share the relational property of being on that cone. Given any conic section and any cone, there is a plane through that cone which yields exactly that conic section. Hence the curves generated by sections of any given cone will be exactly the same as the curves generated by sections of any other given cone. This was discovered, reputedly, by Apollonius of Perga, about two centuries after Plato.

There is philosophical insight to be gained by reflecting on what sort of discovery this was. Apollonius found, for properties of one particular kind, that two different properties of this kind will characterize exactly the same things – that these two properties will be coextensive. Few mathematical discoveries are more exciting than this sort of discovery of exact coextensiveness between two distinct properties.

To further illustrate the point, consider the history of conic sections a little further. About four centuries after Appolonius of Perga, the Delian problem was still unsolved, but another problem was also drawing attention. Pappus of Alexandria was studying not just the problem of doubling the cube but also that of trisecting an angle. This was something else that was found – over a thousand years later – to be impossible using only ratios of lengths and angles (i.e., using only straightedge and compass). This problem led Pappus to consider other shapes, conic sections in particular. Along the way, he discovered another property common to all and only the points on a conic section. (Initially, he discovered this property to be common to all points on a hyperbola, but it holds for ellipses and parabolas as well.)

Given any conic section, there will be a point (a focus) and a line (a directrix) such that each point on the curve stands a distance from the focus and a distance from the directrix, and these two distances always stand in the very same proportion. Points on the same conic section thus share two properties: that of being on the same cone and plane, and that of standing in a fixed proportion of distances from the same point and line. No other points on other curves, or even on other conic sections, are thus related to that same cone and plane, or to that same point and line.

Although conic sections all share something in common, they are also different from one another. What they share is the general property of having some cone and plane, and some point and line, to which they are suitably related – a different pair of cone and plane, and of point and line, in each case, but in each case there are two such pairs. We may then become more specific about the relational properties common to points on the conic. In the first place, we may consider not only relations of these points to a cone and plane but also relations of the cone and plane to each other. The plane may be parallel to one of the straight lines down the side of the cone, or it may deviate from being parallel in one of two different ways. What the points on a parabola have in common is that each is on a cone and also on a plane parallel to one of the straight lines down the side of the cone. What the points on an ellipse (or hyperbola) have in common is that each is on a cone and also on a plane which deviates from being parallel to any of the straight lines down the side of the cone, and which deviates in one way for the ellipse and in the other way for the hyperbola. Note that there are many degrees to which the plane may deviate from being parallel to the edge of a cone; for this reason ellipses and hyperbolas differ in shape, being more or less 'pointy'. But there are no degrees to which a plane may be parallel to the edge of a cone; it is for this reason that all parabolas are of the same shape, differing only in size.

Ellipses, parabolas and hyperbolas are distinguished not only by their relations to a cone and plane, but also by their relational properties with respect to a point and line, a focus and directrix. For any conic section, of any of the three sorts, there is a fixed proportion between the distance of a point on the curve from the focus and its distance from the directrix. The fixed proportion may be less than, equal to, or greater than a proportion of one-to-one. What is distinctive of ellipses is that this fixed proportion is less than one-to-one: each point on the ellipse is closer to the focus than it is to the directrix. For parabolas, each point on the curve is the same distance from a focus as it is from a directrix. For hyperbolas, each point on the curve is further from the focus than from the directrix. Note that there are various degrees to which a proportion may be less than, or more than, that of one-to-one; it is for this reason that ellipses and hyperbolas vary in shape. For parabolas, the proportion is equal to that of one-to-one, and there are no different degrees to which this can be so; thus parabolas are all of the same shape, differing only in size.

There are thus several different sorts of properties that characterize the points on a conic section: relational properties involving a cone and a plane, and relational properties involving a point and a line. One more kind of common property should be mentioned, one which became of overshadowing importance when Descartes sold his Cartesian coordinates to the mathematical community. Pick two lines, at right angles to each other in the same plane as the conic section you wish to study. Then there will be complex relations of proportion which hold between the distance of a point on the curve from one of these two lines and its distance from the other of these two lines. We sum up these relations in equations; for example,

$$y^2 = px - px^2/d \quad \text{(ellipse)},$$
$$y^2 = px \quad \text{(parabola)},$$
$$y^2 = px + px^2/d \quad \text{(hyperbola)}.$$

These equations sum up yet another kind of property which is shared by all and only the points on a conic section. We tend to think today of these equations as expressing relations among numbers, which they do. But we should not forget that these relations are also instantiated by such things as the points on conic sections. Equations offer a striking innovation in notation, but we should not become so mesmerized by symbols that we forget what these symbols are describing. They are describing relationships among numbers, and these very same patterns are also instantiated among such physical quantities as the distances of points on a conic section from a pair of Cartesian axes.

Thus, the equations for conic sections describe yet another class of complex relational properties that are shared by all and only the points on a conic section. Utilizing this new, algebraic notation, it becomes easier to discover countless different relational properties shared by all and only those points. There are many different ways of rewriting the equations for conic sections. The equations just listed appeal to me because they clearly display the intermediate status of the parabola as a limiting case both of an ellipse and of a hyperbola. But there are other equations that are useful for other purposes. A familiar equation for the ellipse, for instance, is:

$$x^2/a^2 + y^2/b^2 = 1.$$

It is far from obvious that the points on an ellipse instantiate not only the relational properties described by this equation but also the relational properties described by the quite different earlier equation

$$y^2 = px - px^2/d.$$

Allowing for shifts of axes and so forth, it turns out that these quite distinct equations describe relational properties that are coextensive. The relations to pairs of axes described by one equation are instantiated by just the same things that also instantiate the different relations to pairs of axes described by the other equation. Furthermore, the things that instantiate these relational properties are 'conic sections', which is to say that they also bear distinctive relations to cone–plane pairs. And they also bear distinctive relations to point–line pairs, of 'focus' and 'directrix'. These discoveries of the coextensiveness of complex patterns of properties and relations excite mathematicians intensely.

5. Sets Are Higher-Order Properties

Coextensiveness is something that crops up very naturally in mathematics. The discovery that two properties are necessarily coextensive is exactly the sort of thing that mathematics constantly strives for.

Sets – that is, plural essences – arise inevitably out of the mathematically crucial relation of coextensiveness. When two properties are coextensive, what is it that they share in common? What they share is their extension, which is a set. What they have in common are their instances, a plurality of things, and it is these things themselves that the coextensive universals have in common. It is, for instance, the points on a conic section that constitute what various quite different complex relational properties share in common. The complex relational properties stand in a relationship to one another, that of coextensiveness, but this relationship among the properties only holds in virtue of their joint relationship to one and the same things – namely, to the very same points that instantiate them. The things in themselves (the points) constitute what coextensive universals have in common, and that is why plural essences are so important in mathematics.

Coextensiveness involves plural essences for the following reason. Imagine two coextensive universals. One might be the property of being a heavenly body which is currently being painted by Giotto; the other might be the property of being a heavenly body which is located both on a certain plane and on a certain cone. When Giotto finishes his painting, the first of these properties changes its extension but the second does not. Halley's comet ceases to have the property of being a heavenly body which is currently being painted by Giotto, but it does not cease to lie both on a certain plane and on a certain cone. These universals are then no longer coextensive. Yet the universal whose extension has not changed will still have the very same thing it had before, in virtue of which it was then coextensive with the other.

We may then suppose that a change occurs in the extension of the second universal. Suppose for instance that Halley's comet finally burns away completely. We may then suppose that the two universals under consideration become coextensive again, both being again instantiated by nothing at all. And yet, although they are again coextensive, as they were before, there is an important sense in which what they share in common is now no longer the same as what they shared before. The only way a universal can share the very same extension that they both once had is by being instantiated by such-and-such things. In our case, this requires that they be instantiated by Halley's comet and by nothing else. Instantiation by any other things, or failure to be instantiated by Halley's comet, guarantees that a universal does not share what our two universals shared before we imagined their extensions varying. Sharing what those universals used to share is necessarily bound to the identity of their instances. That is, what coextensive universals share is a plural essence.

Coextensiveness, then, is the seed from which set theory grows. Note that coextensiveness is something immediately and naturally of great interest to mathematicians, as the history of conics shows. In this respect, coextensiveness is a universal that stands in sharp contrast to a philosophically generated property of primitive thisness, or a haecceity. If individual essences are of interest to mathematicians, it is because they arise from the study of coextensiveness. The fact that they do arise suggests that they are not primitive and unanalyzable plural or individual essences, that they are not in fact haecceities but rather individual essences with enough internal structure for us to get a grip on them by way of the study of coextensiveness of universals.

Coextensiveness, then, is the source of sets; but we need to take a step or two from coextensiveness before we arrive at sets themselves. Coextensiveness is a relation between universals. Set membership is a relation not between those two coextensive universals but rather between another universal – the set – and the things that instantiate all three of these universals. The set of points on a curve is something that is instantiated by the points themselves; coextensiveness is not a property of those points, but is a property of properties of those points. Thus we have yet to find a link between the mathematically magnetic property of coextensiveness and the consequent common property of the things which fall within that common extension.

The link we need is furnished by a very general connection between properties of things and properties of their properties. Things with different but similar properties are themselves, thereby, similar. Having different properties makes them different, but having similar properties is something they share in common. Consider an example: Suppose two things have two different colours; these things are different, because they have different properties. But they also have something in common: their different colour properties do have something in common in both being colours. So the objects with different colours each have a property which is a colour; hence these objects are both coloured, which is something they share in common. If each has a property that has the property of being a colour, then each is coloured. Having a colour entails being coloured.

Similarly, consider the points on one conic section, say on an ellipse, and compare them with the points on another conic section, say on a hyperbola. The points on the ellipse share a property that is not instantiated by the points on the hyperbola. They are, for instance, all closer, and closer to the same degree, to a fixed point than they are to a fixed line. This is a property shared by points on the ellipse which is not shared by points on the hyperbola. Nevertheless, the points on the ellipse do collectively have something in common with the points on the hyperbola: In both cases, they are points on a conic section. The property shared by points on the ellipse is different from that shared by points on the hyperbola, and yet there are properties that these two properties share, properties common to all the distinguishing properties of conic sections. The points on conic sections have common properties, which in turn have common properties. And having different yet similar properties makes them not only different but also similar.

Being a colour is a property of a property; being coloured is a property of an object. Being coloured is a property an object has just when it has one or another of a range of properties, each of which has the further property of being a colour. A property like that of being coloured is sometimes called a 'second-order' property, and is distinguished from 'second-degree' properties. A second-degree property is a property of a property. A second-order property is a property of an object, not a property of a property. Yet a second-order property differs from other properties of the object, from the 'first-order' properties of the object, in virtue of its standing in distinctive entailment relations to properties of its properties.

This can be generalized to cover not only first- and second-order properties but in addition a whole hierarchy of properties. Thus, for instance, the points on an ellipse share something in common, but what they share in common is a property that stands in various entailment relations with properties of properties; in virtue of those entailments, this common property of points on the ellipse is a higher-order property of some level. The points on the ellipse also share properties with points on parabolas and hyperbolas; but these properties will be of a higher order still. The key point to note is that when properties turn out to have something in common, their instances thereby turn out to have something in common, too.

It is by this entailment, between properties of properties and second-order properties, that sets emerged from coextensiveness. Certain universals have something in common when they have their instances in common. Because these universals have a second-degree property in common, their instances thereby have a second-order property in common. That is, because properties have their instances in common, those instances thereby have something else in common. This something else is membership in the same set, the set that constitutes the common extension of those universals.

This is how plural essences came to the light of history: by the study of coextensiveness of universals. From this study, unit sets, or individual essences, emerge as a special case, as does the empty set. Once we have some sets at our disposal, new ones will be discovered, ones that did not appear at the first stage of the study. Random sets are ones unlikely to emerge directly from the study of coextensiveness of universals. After all, the whole idea of a random set is of a set of things whose members have nothing at all in common; or at least, the less the members of a set have in common, the more random the set will be. Thus random sets are not easily construed as 'what coextensive universals have in common', since ideally there will be no coextensive universals with that extension, save for the set itself. Random sets emerge only as an indirect spin-off from a study of coextensiveness. Once we have discovered unit sets, individual essences, we can note that the union of a plurality of these constitutes a new set, whether or not the things in that set have something in common in addition to membership in that set.

In conclusion, then, sets turn out to be much more physical than they appear. The way for a physicalist to make friends with sets without apostasy is by ditching nominalism, the bad company that physicalism and empiricism so often cultivate. We should note that not only do things have common and distinguishing properties and relations, but that those properties and relations in turn have common and distinguishing properties and relations. Some of these higher-level properties and relations, particularly coextensiveness, entail the existence of individual and plural essences. Nothing more than relabelling is then required: We have arrived at set theory.

REFERENCES

Adams, Robert M. 1979. 'Primitive Thisness and Primitive Identity', *Journal of Philosophy* 76: 5–26.

Bigelow, John. 1988. *The Reality of Numbers: A Physicalist's Philosophy of Mathematics* (Oxford: Clarendon).

———— 1990. 'Sets are Universals'. In *Physicalism in Mathematics,* ed. Andrew Irvine (Dordrecht: Kluwer), pp. 291–307.

Boolos, George. 1984. 'To Be is to Be a Value of a Variable (or to Be Some Values of Some Variables)', *Journal of Philosophy* 81: 430–48.

Field, Hartry. 1980. *Science without Numbers* (Princeton University Press).

Grandy, Richard. 1976. 'Anadic Logic and English', *Synthese* 32: 395–402.

Kaplan, David. 1975. 'How to Russell a Frege-Church', *Journal of Philosophy* 72: 716–29. Reprinted in *The Possible and the Actual,* ed. Michael J. Loux (Ithaca, NY: Cornell University Press, 1979), pp. 210–24.

Kripke, Saul. 1972. 'Naming and Necessity', *Semantics of Natural Language,* ed. Donald Davidson and Gilbert Harman (Dordrecht: Reidel), pp. 253–355. Reprinted as a separate volume (Oxford: Blackwell, 1980).

Lewis, David. 1991. *Parts of Classes* (Oxford: Blackwell).

Maddy, Penelope. 1989. 'The Roots of Contemporary Platonism', *Journal of Symbolic Logic* 54: 1121–44.

Massey, Gerald J. 1976. 'Tom, Dick, and Harry, and All the King's Men', *American Philosophical Quarterly* 13: 89–107.

Morton, Adam. 1975. 'Complex Variables and Multigrade Relations', *Noûs* 9: 309–18.

Sharvy, Richard. 1968. 'Why a Class Can't Change its Members', *Noûs* 2: 303–14.

Reply to Bigelow

D. M. ARMSTRONG

In the old days, that is until a few years after the Second World War, Sydney and Melbourne had but one university each. The two cities are, of course, traditional rivals. Strangely enough, this rivalry extended even to the two philosophy departments, where indeed it was particularly sharp. In Sydney were John Anderson and his disciples, the Andersonians. Melbourne was Wittgensteinian, springing from George Paul's wartime years there, followed up by Douglas Gasking and A. C. ('Camo') Jackson, the father of Frank Jackson who writes in this volume. The annual national conference got quite fierce at times as Sydney and Melbourne clashed. In 1956 I made a little bit of history by being the first graduate from Sydney to be appointed to a lectureship in the Melbourne department. (At least I'd been to Oxford in between!)

All this is now changed, much for the better. Sydney and Melbourne philosophers communicate, assist each other by mutual criticism, and are friendly – for all the world as if the two cities they lived in had nothing to do with it. Over the past ten or more years one Melbourne-based philosopher with whom I have had quite a deal to do with is John Bigelow. I greatly admire his intelligence and ingenuity, his apparently effortless mastery of necessary technicalities which he nevertheless presents in an easy and colloquial manner, and the way he has increasingly occupied himself to great effect with central ontological questions.

1. Mathematics

Mathematics, says Bigelow, is concerned with such things as ratios, and ratios hold between (among other things) physical properties of physical things. Ratios are relations, and can hold between physical properties and, via these, the physical things that have the properties. With this I agree whole-heatedly. What I would add, however, is that these ratios are *internal* relations, meaning those that hold in any possible world in which the terms of the relations exist. They supervene on their terms, the physical quantities as it may be. We need to think very carefully, I believe, about the ontological import of this internality, this supervenience. I would say that it shows that the relations in question, although real, are not something over and above the totality of their terms. I don't know whether Bigelow would agree.

Bigelow also calls attention to the way that mathematics feeds upon itself, and can provide from within itself for the existence of all the infinity of ratios, proportions and so on that it requires to work with. Here it may go beyond physically instantiated ratios and proportions. He does just concede in passing that this is 'ontologically indecent', but in the rest of what he says he is rejoicing in this ontological fertility of mathematics. I take it that the ontological indecency is indecency from the standpoint of empiricism. How can we gain all this knowledge of entities a priori?

The problem is a real one, I think. I believe the way to deal with it is to say that mathematical 'existence' is something less than real existence. What is it to say that a certain infinite number exists? It is to say that it is possible (non–self-contradictory) that that number of nonmathematical entities exist. Whatever has mathematical 'existence' will stand in various relations, such as ratios and proportions, to other mathematical existents. But because the relations are internal, we can countenance them also without ontological extravagance. I have argued this at more length elsewhere (Armstrong 1989a, Chapter 9).

2. Sets

Bigelow and I have the following agreements. First, as shown by Lewis, both Bigelow's and my candidates for the true essence of sets will do the mathematical work that sets should do. Second, we agree that both our candidates give reasonably good answers to the question of what that essence is. Third, neither of us thinks much of the strategy of forming an equivalence class out of all the reasonably good answers and then leaving the question at this point. Here I will restrict myself to defending my answer (set out more fully in Armstrong 1991) and criticizing Bigelow's.

My answer is to a great extent a matter of finding a formulation that presents the favoured theory in a way that takes hold of the mind. I suggest the following formulation. A many-membered set is a collection of things, things which are each taken as a unit. It is a further and more technical point that the notion of a collection is here a mereological one. (The relation of set to subset is identical with the mereological relation of whole to proper part, and the relation of intersecting sets is identical with the mereological relation of overlap; see Lewis 1991.) 'Taken as units' may be justly criticized as importing an undesirable element of subjectivity into the notion of a set. So let us say instead that the notion of a set abstracts away from everything about the members except that each is some sort of unit. And what makes a thing a unit? That is a further point, but the suggested answer to it is that the thing has the property of having at least one unit-making property. Following a suggestion from Lewis, I call this property of having a unit-making property *unithood*.

A unit-making property, in turn, is a property that constitutes the thing that has it as one thing of that kind *to the exclusion of another number of things* of that kind. Bigelow's example of *being a whale* will do fine as an instance of a unit-making property. Another is *being a kilogram in mass*. The latter is a more instructive example in some ways, because it does not 'divide its extension' in the way that *being a whale* does (barring Siamese whales). It thus shows how relatively little is required for a unit-making property. Note also that, although each member of a set must have unithood, they do not all have to have unithood by virtue of the same unit-making property.

I submit that, give or take some of the detail, this is a reasonably plausible account of the things mathematicians have in mind when they speak of (many-membered) sets. After all, the central idea is just that these sets are collections of units, of ones. Mathematicians should appreciate the fact that this account preserves the connection between sets and numbers in a direct way. And the account generalizes to unit sets unproblematically.

The account also fits my own metaphysical commitments. I recognize states of affairs, that is, things having properties and things standing in relations to each other. So things having unit-making properties will be states of affairs. These things must further have the higher-order property of having some unit-making property. But since this higher-order property supervenes upon the possession of particular unit-making properties it is, I hold, no further ontological cost. Many-membered sets will be conjunctions of 'atomic' states of affairs (*a* has unithood, *b* has unithood, ...) and so can be said to be (molecular) states of affairs themselves.

This account appears to allow a naturalized epistemology for sets. We perceive states of affairs involving unit-making properties. For instance, we may perceive that there is *a book* on the table. All we must then do is move from this unit-making property of *being a book* to the more abstract property of *having a unit-making property* which is entailed by the original property. We are at least close to being able to perceive a unit set. Most sets are not perceived, of course. But we extrapolate from perceived sets to unperceived sets.

Let us now consider Bigelow's alternative proposal. He suggests that unit sets are individual essences of their members and that many-membered sets are plural essences. Individual essences he then pins down as thisnesses of things, their haecceities.

From my point of view, the objection to this solution is that I do not see the need to postulate haecceities. Consider a small world with two genuinely atomic individuals, each having just one genuinely atomic property. (If there is worry about their connection, relate them by an atomic and symmetrical external relation.) We would have a's being F, b's being G, and a and b related by R. Is there a different world where a change has been made to b's being F and a's being G? As I understand the doctrine of haecceity, this would be a different world. But my own inclination is to say that here we have but one world described twice, containing two particulars, one of which has F and the other G. I do not deny a category of particularity, rather I uphold it. But I do deny what I take the doctrine of haecceity to assert – that there is something about each different particular that makes them internally and secretly different. I would be more sympathetic to an attempt to base the unitary nature of the different members simply on their being different particulars.

What I think Bigelow needs to do is provide some positive arguments for the existence of haecceities. In the nature of the case, the strongest argument for this conclusion would be for it to be shown, or made plausible, that these entities are of value in solving other metaphysical problems.

3. Sets as Universals?

Bigelow and I have a verbal dispute about the use of the word 'universal'. He, like Quine, thinks it is desirable to classify sets as universals, although I do not suppose that he has much sympathy with Quine's reason: that both are 'abstract entities'. His thought seems to be rather that if one can say that two particulars instantiate the very same universal, why cannot one say that two particulars 'instantiate' the very same set – that is, are members of the very same set. I think that this is muddying the wells of discourse. Just consider how different the two relations really are. It is, for instance, quite a feat for two things to instantiate the very same universal, at any rate if we have a 'sparse' theory of universals, which I think both Bigelow and I favour. By contrast, nothing is easier than for two things to be members of the same set. This is connected with the fact that in the universal's case there is a genuine identity holding across the two particulars, while there need be no identity in the set case. I would accept Bigelow's point that the word 'property' does not have any such 'powerful etymological pressure towards a repeatability requirement'. For instance, the quite popular idea that properties exist but are particulars seems to do no violence to the notion of a property. So let us admit a sense of the word 'property' in which it is not, or need not be, a universal. (As a matter of fact, I myself require such a sense in order to capture the notion of a unit-making property, used in giving an account of classes. Few unit-making properties are universals.) But to deny repeatability to universals, as Bigelow's usage would, seems to be courting confusion.

4. Sets and Coextensiveness

I found Bigelow's historical material on the origin of mathematicians' interest in sets instructive. It seems very plausible that it was interest in coextensive properties that directed mathematical attention to sets. (Though I object to his speaking of universals' being coextensive, losing this relation and then regaining it. The extension of a universal, I should have thought, includes past, present and future instances.) But here is a case, it seems to me, where history casts rather little light on essence. Sets were approached through coextensive properties. But sets include what Bigelow calls random sets, sets that have no interesting properties associated with them and in many cases no universals in my sense of the term. (There will in fact be very few sets that are the extensions of these universals.) Indeed, I think that a good way to approach the 'problem of universals' is to ask what marks off your average rough set from those that have, to use G. F. Stout's striking phrase, a distributive unity.

REFERENCES

Armstrong, D. M. 1989a. *A Combinatorial Theory of Possibility* (Cambridge University Press).
    1991. 'Classes are States of Affairs', *Mind* 100: 189–200.
Lewis, David. 1991. *Parts of Classes* (Oxford: Blackwell).

5

Properties and Predicates

D. H. MELLOR

Introduction

I share David Armstrong's (1978, 1989) realism about universals. I agree with him that properties and relations exist, just as the particulars exist which have those properties and relations. I agree with him, moreover, that universals are not to be understood semantically as the meanings, references or extensions of predicates (Armstrong 1978, Introduction). This does not, of course, prevent there being obvious connections between universals and predicates. For example, to every property there obviously corresponds a possible predicate applying to all and only particulars with that property. But it does not follow from this, and is not obviously true, that to every actual predicate there corresponds a single property or relation. Perhaps 'given a predicate, there may be none, one or many universals in virtue of which the predicate applies [and] given a universal, there may be none, one or many predicates which apply in virtue of that universal' (Armstrong 1978, vol. 2, p. 9). So the questions remain: how do universals relate in general to our predicates, and how in particular do they relate to what those predicates mean?

In order to tackle these questions I shall make some assumptions that I defend only briefly if at all. Some are uncontroversial, some merely terminological. Others are more serious, but still I shall not argue for them at length because, although I do believe them, my main interest here is in what they entail.

First of all, although for brevity I shall refer only to properties, I shall take it for granted that what I say also applies mutatis mutandis to relations. On the other hand, I shall not assume that what I say applies to all properties, and specifically not to apparently necessary properties of abstract objects like numbers and sets, such as the oddness of the number 3. I am interested here only in contingent properties of so-called concrete particulars: that is, roughly, particulars that have causes and/or effects and are more or less localized in space and time. 'Concrete', however, is a bad name for them, since the particulars that concern me may well include events (such as explosions) and processes (such as fires and long walks) as well as material objects (such as planets and people). Whether particulars of all these kinds exist and, if so, how they are related to each other are of course contentious questions, but fortunately not ones I need to tackle here. What matters here are contingent properties, not how many or what kinds of particulars have those properties.

Next, I take existence, and the having of properties, to be tenseless but not modal. In other words, I restrict them to the actual world, but not to the present as opposed to the past or future. This assumption too is contentious and does affect some of my conclusions, but only in obvious and uninteresting ways that anyone who disagrees with it can easily work out. In what follows, therefore, I shall take for granted that the class of real people does not, for example, contain the merely possible Danish Prince Hamlet, but does contain all the human ancestors and all the as-yet-unconceived human descendants of everyone alive today.

And as for all these actual human beings, so for the property (if any) of being human which they all share. As a realist about universals, I take the actual properties of actual past, present and future particulars to exist, and to do so whether or not they ever have been or ever will be conceived of by us or by any other thinkers. That is, I reject both nominalism and conceptualism about universals, although again I shall not discuss my reasons for doing so nor for adopting any specific version of realism about universals. What I will discuss is what properties there actually are – an open question for realists, just as what particulars there are is an open question for nominalists – and what, if anything, those properties contribute to the meanings of our predicates.

Properties

I shall start by elaborating on my rejection of the obvious answer to these questions: namely, that properties just are (or are given by) the meanings of our predicates. One reason for denying this is of course that, if they were, they could not *give* our predicates their meanings, any more than particulars could give the meanings of names or other singular terms if that was all they were. But of course they're not. No one thinks the planet Mars just is, or is part of, or defined by, the meaning of the word 'Mars' by which we refer to it. We may indeed give a referential account of that word's meaning, that is, one that takes the planet Mars to be part or all of what the word 'Mars' means. But what makes this a serious thesis about the meaning of that word is precisely that it takes for granted the planet's independent existence and identity: We are using the planet Mars to give the meaning of the word 'Mars', not the other way round.

Similarly with the word 'red'. A referential theory of its meaning might take the property of being red to be part or all of what the word 'red' means. But this again will be a serious thesis about the meaning of that word only if it takes for granted the property's independent existence and identity, that is, if it uses the property to give the meaning of the predicate rather than the other way round.

We may, of course, reject these referential accounts. We may deny that Mars itself is any part of what our word 'Mars' means, perhaps because we think its meaning is given by a definite description (such as 'the red planet') which any planet might satisfy. But this will not make us deny Mars's existence or query its identity. There is more to Mars than its semantic role, and we have more than semantic reasons to believe in its existence. Indeed, this is an understatement. The planet Mars does not depend on its semantic role at all, either for its identity or for its existence: this is why a referential account of the meaning of the word 'Mars', whatever else may be wrong with it, is neither trivial nor viciously circular.

Similarly, I maintain, for the property (if any) of being red. But not everyone will agree. Some philosophers still think that properties, unlike particulars, do depend on their semantic roles: that a property is nothing if not all or part of what some predicate means. Unless the meaning of the predicate 'red' is, includes or entails a corresponding property, then no such property exists. And if it does exist, its identity is given by its role in the meaning of the predicate, not the other way round.

I, like Armstrong, disagree. I think that in this respect properties are just like planets. We have good nonsemantic reasons for believing in them, and there is more to them than their semantic roles – indeed, I consider this another understatement. A contingent universal's existence, like that of Mars, does not depend on its having any semantic role, and its identity does not depend on what that role is. This is why referential accounts of the meanings of predicates, whatever else may be wrong with them, are also neither trivial nor viciously circular.

But what then are the nonsemantic reasons for believing in contingent universals, and what – if not the meanings of predicates – fixes their identity? I take the main reasons for believing in contingent universals to be the roles they play in causation and in laws of nature, and those laws are what I take to give those universals their identity.

One might, of course, think that causation needs universals just because it is one: namely, as Davidson (1967) and others maintain, a relation between particular events, as in 'The explosion *caused* the fire'. I disagree, because I think that what the causation in such cases primarily links are facts, not particulars (Mellor 1987). So I would rather report this example of singular causation by saying 'There was a fire *because* there was an explosion', which represents the causation not by a predicate ('caused') but by a connective ('because'). This of course is yet another contentious claim, but again it's not one I need to defend here; even if causation is not a universal, it will still need universals. For just as Davidson thinks that causation only links particulars with properties that make them instantiate laws of nature, so I think causation only links facts that have just such properties as constituents. And if so, then causation will need universals anyway, and we need not discuss whether it itself is one.

But is this so, and if so, why? Why must causes and effects have or contain properties that figure in laws? I think the reason is that singular causation entails physical probabilities, or chances. Suppose, for example, the causation in this case is deterministic, so that in the circumstances an explosion is both sufficient and necessary for a fire. This means that in the circumstances the chance of a fire occurring is 1 with an explosion and 0 without one. But this, I have argued elsewhere (Mellor 1990), entails that in sufficiently similar circumstances (i) anything sufficiently like the actual explosion would always produce something like the actual fire and (ii) nothing else would ever do so. And this I take to be an existential proposition, entailing that these sufficient similarities exist; in other words, that there are properties C, F and G, of which the actual circumstances (explosion and fire, respectively) are instances, such that it's a law of nature that in C-circumstances, all and only F-events are followed by G-events.

That, briefly, is why I think causation always instantiates laws. Again the argument is contentious, but again I needn't defend it. For all I need is its conclusion, which is much less contentious – and even that contention I shall now try to disarm by disclaiming some common but contentious claims about causation and laws which I don't accept and to which nothing here will commit me.

First, I am not committed to physicalism. Nothing I have to say about causation and laws, or about the particulars and properties involved in them, requires them to be physical. Nor are they required not to be; nothing in what follows will entail either physicalism or its negation.

Next, I am not committed to causal determinism. Causation does not entail deterministic laws, because its connotations don't require causes to be either sufficient or necessary for their effects. I do think they require causes to raise their effects' chances, but they needn't raise them to 1, and they needn't raise them from 0 (Mellor 1988). So although individual circumstances, causes and effects will always need some properties C, F and G to make them instantiate laws, those laws need not be deterministic. They need only entail, for example, that in normal circumstances (e.g. in the presence of oxygen and inflammable material and the absence of other causes of fires) fires have a greater chance of occurring when explosions do than when they don't.

Finally, I am not committed to laws having or entailing any kind of necessity, natural or otherwise – except of course in the common but trivial sense in which calling something naturally or physically necessary just means that it's entailed by a law, or has a chance of 1.

So much for what I am not committed to. What I am committed to is a distinction between laws and statements of laws (see e.g. Armstrong 1983a, p. 8). This distinction is easily (and often) overlooked, as when Humeans say that laws are just true generalizations, like the statement 'All Fs are Gs'. But they could equally well say that all it takes to make this generalization state a law is the fact that all actual Fs are Gs, and call that fact the law. Whether we think of laws as true statements (or sentences or propositions) or as the facts – Humean or otherwise – that make those statements true often doesn't matter, which is no doubt why the difference is often overlooked. But here it does matter, because what law statements contain are predicates (or their meanings), whereas what the facts that make those statements true contain are properties. And clearly what causation needs are the facts, with their constituent properties, not the statements with their predicates. That's why in what follows it is the facts and not the statements which I shall call laws.

I don't, of course, deny the close connection between the properties that laws contain and the predicates we use to state those laws. On the contrary, that connection is, as we shall see, much closer than that between properties and most other predicates. But this is not because the predicates that occur in law statements define the corresponding properties; it's the other way round. For the fact is that we have no semantic (or any other a priori) criterion of identity for the contingent properties that laws contain, any more than we have for contingent particulars. The most we can say a priori is this: for F and F* to be the same property, the predicates 'F' and 'F*' must be coextensive in all possible worlds; otherwise, whether some possible particular is F will depend on which predicate we use to say that it's F, which is absurd.

But this modest a priori truth won't enable us to identify F or any other contingent property. Properties are identified a posteriori by scientific theories, construed as Ramsey sentences, that is, as saying (for example) that *there are* properties C, F and G such that in C-circumstances all F-events have such-and-such a chance of being followed by G-events. If that statement is true, then there are such properties, and there is such a law, of which those properties are constituents. And being a constituent of some such laws is, as I have argued elsewhere (Mellor 1990), all there is to being a property. There is no more to temperatures than the thermodynamic and other laws they occur in; no more to masses and forces than the laws of motion and of its gravitational and other causes; and so on. In other words, if we stated all the laws there are in a single Ramsey sentence S, the properties that S would quantify over are all the properties there are.

And this means that, with one possible exception, S would provide a definite description of all actual contingent properties. The exception (pointed out to me by Jeremy Butterfield) would be a pair of symmetrically related properties P and P* – like being left- and right-handed – identifiable only by ostension. Whether two properties could really differ like this without entering differently into *some* law is not clear to me; but even if they did, S would still quantify over both of them. So even then the contingent properties there are could still be just those that S quantifies over; and from now on that is what I shall assume they are. So our question now becomes: How do these properties relate to the meanings of our predicates?

Predicates

Suppose I see that some thing *a* is red, that is, that the predicate 'red' applies to it. What has happened? Clearly something about *a* has caused me to believe this. But what? In particular, is it just the fact that *a* has the property of being red?

But what does this question mean? What is it for *a* to have the property of being red? What is it, indeed, for there to be such a property? If actual properties are those that our Ramsey sentence S quantifies over, what makes one of them the property of being red? Well, suppose that anything which anyone sees to be rightly called red always has a certain property P, and that its being P is what causes them to see that. Whether there is any such property P is, as we shall see, a very moot point. But suppose for the moment there is. Then clearly, if anything is the property of being red, P is.

But how, if it is this property, does P contribute to the meaning of the word 'red'? Suppose we agree to start by saying that a predicate like 'red' may also be used as a singular term referring to the property (if any) that all and only the particulars it applies to share, as in 'red is a warm colour'. Then if the singular term 'red' refers to anything, it refers to P. So suppose it does refer to P – and does so even though no one knows which property P is, because no one knows enough laws of nature to distinguish P from all other properties.

Some philosophers may deny this possibility because it conflicts with what Evans (1982, Chapter 4) calls Russell's Principle, namely 'that a subject cannot make a judgement about something unless he knows which object his judgement is about' (p. 89). But this principle is false. We can easily make judgements about (and hence refer to) things without anyone knowing which they are. For example, I can easily judge that it's raining now without anyone knowing what time it is, that is, which time my token 'now' refers to. Similarly, when I measure an object's temperature T, I judge in advance that T is what my thermometer will say it is: So I refer to T even before I know which temperature it is, and even if my thermometer fails me and no one ever knows which it is. But if we can use 'now' and 'T' as singular terms to refer to times and temperatures without anyone knowing which times or temperatures they are, we can certainly use 'red' as a singular term to refer to P without anyone knowing which property P is.

So let us suppose we do that. How does our use of 'red' to refer to P relate to our use of 'red' as a predicate? In particular, how does it relate to the predicate's extension, that is, to the particulars it applies to? Obviously they can't *be* the property P, since they are many and P is one. Nor can P be the set of all P-things. For since P is a contingent property, there could be more or fewer P-things, and hence more or fewer red things, than there actually are. But if P were its own extension, and hence that of the predicate 'red', then there couldn't be; so it isn't.

Indeed, P can obviously not be any set of P-things, precisely because being P is what *makes* things members of such sets. What P (like any other universal) is, I maintain, is a constituent of atomic facts, like the fact that *a* is P. I admit of course that what this amounts to – and especially what links *a* and P – are hard and long-standing questions to which I can only respond here by asserting, with Armstrong (1978, vol. 2), that they do have answers, and that those who deny that facts have universal constituents face even harder questions.

But those are not the questions I want to discuss here. The question here is this: If 'red', used as a singular term, refers to P, and if this is what makes 'red', used as a predicate, apply to all and only P-things, then what makes 'red' refer to P? In particular, if 'red' refers to P by having a *sense* that makes it do so, then what gives 'red' that sense?

The obvious answer is that 'red' gets its sense from a kind K of visual sensation that P-things give us when they make us call them red, so that 'red' refers to the property of things which causes us to get sensations of kind K: namely, P. But although this could be how we apply the predicate 'red', it notoriously needn't be. We can learn to see when to apply the predicate 'red' without the P-things it applies to giving all of us sensations of the same kind. Being P must make a difference to how things look to us, but the difference needn't be the same for everyone. I can learn to apply the predicate 'red' by learning to associate it with whatever kind of visual sensations I get from the things that existing users tell me are called red. It is this learned use of the predicate that fixes which kind (or kinds) of sensation this will be for me, not the other way round. And what fixes this learned use, and hence the extension of the predicate 'red', is the property P, because instances of P are in fact what we learn to respond to by applying the predicate 'red'.

But this makes P look less like a referent than a sense, the sense of the predicate 'red': namely, that which fixes its extension. But if it is a sense then again it can't be necessary for us, or any authority we defer to, to know what or which sense this is. For as we've seen, P can fix the extension of our predicate 'red' in this way without anyone knowing which property P is. But this no more prevents P from being a sense than from being a referent, since we no more need to know which senses our words have than we need to know which things they refer to. For suppose the sense of the predicate 'red' was in fact given by sensations of a certain kind K, which it certainly could be, even if it isn't. This wouldn't require us to know which kind of sensation K is; it would only require us to respond reliably to K-sensations by applying the predicate 'red' to the things that caused them. But if that's enough to make K the sense of 'red', then P can also be the sense of 'red'. For all it takes for P to fix the sense of 'red' is for our eyes to make us respond reliably to P-things by calling them red.

Now 'sense' is of course a term of philosophical art, and for some Fregean artists it takes more than this for a word to have a sense (see e.g. Evans 1982, Chapter 1). But if it does, then the predicate 'red' needn't have a sense at all. Yet something about us will still fix the extension of the word as we use it: namely, our having learned to let a thing's being P cause us to call it red. So I prefer to stick to the minimal sense of 'sense' as that which fixes the reference or extension of our words, and allow P to be the sense of our predicate 'red' even though no one knows which property P is.

Suppose then that some property P is, in this minimal sense, the sense of our predicate 'red'. How much of the meaning of the word 'red' does this fix? Not much, and certainly not enough to give us our *concept* of red. For even with words linked as closely to our perceptions as colour predicates are, there is more to understanding them than being able to apply them. To know what 'red' means it isn't enough to know when something is red. We must be able to draw some inferences from that; our predicate 'red' does have some connotations. How does P help to provide them?

The short answer is that it doesn't, at least not directly. That is, *a*'s being P can make us call *a* red without inclining us to infer anything from that fact. For, as we've seen, P can enable us to apply the predicate 'red' without our knowing any of the laws in which P figures. We needn't even know the laws of reflection that make P the property that causes us to call things red, let alone the laws of chemistry that determine what chemical properties will make things P and therefore red. P need not give our predicate 'red' any connotations at all.

But P will constrain its connotations. For we do want our inferences to preserve truth, and when we see that they don't, we give them up. So the inferences we persist in, and eventually make part of the meanings of our predicates, will mostly preserve truth – or at least, they will when their premises and conclusions can be verified by our senses. So at least the verifiable connotations of 'red' will not contradict the laws that P figures in. Indeed, the fact that these connotations generally do preserve truth will generally follow from some of those laws. The connotations of our predicate 'red' will therefore certainly be constrained to some extent by the laws that make P the property it is.

But they will with equal certainty not be constrained enough to make P part of our concept of red. For even if a single property P is in fact what makes us apply the predicate 'red' as we do, this fact is obviously not one of that predicate's connotations. It is no part of our concept of red that all red things share any one property (in my nonsemantic sense), let alone the property P. And rightly so, since there need be no one such property that all red things share. For laws need not, and mostly do not, take the simple form 'In C-circumstancs, all and only Fs are (followed by) Gs', where C, F and G are single properties. In particular, the laws on which our senses rely when we use them to apply predicates like 'red' will almost always have much more complicated antecedents. At the very least, they may easily make things need a negation ($\sim$P), or a disjunction (P $\vee$ Q), or a conjunction (P & Q) of properties to make us call them red – and $\sim$P, P $\vee$ Q and P & Q will not be properties on my account, since the Ramsey sentence S that quantifies over P and Q will not also quantify over them.

But maybe I should allow the existence of complex properties like $\sim$P, P $\vee$ Q and P & Q. For even if *a* and *b* need only be P or Q to be red, it still seems to follow from their both being red that there is something they both are. But that something can't be P or Q, since *a* may be P but not Q and *b* Q but not P. So it looks as if the complex property P $\vee$ Q must exist to be the something that both *a* and *b* are. But this is not so, any more than an actual person (Nobody) must exist in order to be what two empty rooms c and d both contain. The only sense in which it obviously follows that there is something that a and b both are is substitutional: they are both truly called red, just as c and d are both truly said to contain nobody. But on an objectual interpretation of the existential quantifier, it no more obviously follows that there is an actual property that a and b share than that there is an actual occupant whom c and d share.

Yet even if this doesn't follow, it may still be true. It is less obvious that there are no such properties as $\sim P$, $P \vee Q$ and $P \& Q$ than that there is no such person as Nobody. But there really are no such complex properties, as the following argument (taken from Ramsey 1925, pp. 14–15) shows. For suppose there are; that is, suppose there are properties U, V and W such that $\sim P = U$, $P \vee Q = V$ and $P \& Q = W$. Then Ua and $\sim P a$, for example, are the very same state of affairs. But they can't be, because they have different constituents: the first containing U but not P, the second P but not U. And similarly for Va and $P a \vee Q a$, and for Wa and $P a \& Q a$. So there are no such properties as U, V and W – which is not of course to deny the existence of the predicates 'U', 'V' and 'W'.

Armstrong (1978, Chapter 15.1), however, while agreeing that there are no negative or disjunctive properties like $\sim P$ and $P \vee Q$, does think there are conjunctive ones like $P \& Q$. And conjunctive properties are indeed more credible than disjunctive and negative ones, just because they do sustain the existential inference: a and b being P and Q does entail that a and b share a property – indeed two properties, namely P and Q. But this hardly shows that they share a third property $P \& Q$; nor does Armstrong succeed in showing that. His claim that 'it is logically and epistemically possible that all properties are conjunctive properties' (p. 32) just begs the question, while the intuition behind it (that nature may be infinitely complex, so that, for example, there may be no limit to the small-scale structure of matter) needs no complex properties because there need be no limit to the number or complexity of laws of nature, nor hence to the number of properties over which S must quantify. And Armstrong's only other argument (p. 35) is a non sequitur. The fact that $P a \& Q a$ may have effects which don't follow from those of $P a$ and $Q a$ doesn't show that $P \& Q$ is a property; it merely shows that laws of the form 'All $P \& Q$s are . . .' need not follow from laws of the forms 'All Ps are . . .' and 'All Qs are . . .'.

I conclude, then, that there really are no complex properties, and therefore that there need be no one property that all red things share. And once we see that there need be no such property, it is obvious that in fact there isn't. For the property or properties of light that make it red will clearly differ from all the other equally different properties of objects that make them respectively reflect, transmit and emit red light. So our application of the predicate 'red' must in fact rely on at least four laws, with the same consequents – the forming of a belief that something is red – but different antecedents, involving four properties $(P_1, ..., P_4)$ of light and of reflecting, transmitting and emitting objects respectively, which in four corresponding kinds $(C_1, ..., C_4)$ of observational circumstances make them cause such a belief.

There is thus no such property as being red, i.e. no property that all red things share. No one property gives our predicate 'red' its sense in even the minimal sense of fixing its extension, let alone in any more substantial sense of fixing its connotations and hence our concept of red. Even the minimal extension-fixing sense of 'red' must be at least a disjunction, $P_1C_1 \vee \cdots \vee P_4C_4$, of four conjunctions of the properties of the four different kinds of red things that make us call them red together with those of the circumstances in which they do so. But this doesn't make the predicate 'red' ambiguous: as we've seen, since we needn't know what the sense of 'red' is that fixes its extension, we needn't know (or even think) that its sense is disjunctive. Our concept of red no more requires red things to differ in their relevant properties than it requires them to be the same.

Nor will the lack of a property that all red things share make it any harder for us to learn how to apply the predicate 'red'. It obviously won't if what makes us call things red is that they all give us sensations of some kind, even if that kind varies from person to person. For then it is the similarity of those sensations that makes us call all the different things that cause them red, not that of the properties which make those things give us those sensations. So if this is what makes us call things red, it obviously doesn't matter whether all red things share a property or not. But it doesn't matter anyway, even if this isn't what makes us call things red. We can learn to respond reliably to instances of a complex combination of properties like $P_1C_1 \vee \cdots \vee P_4C_4$ just as easily as to instances of a single property P. For, as we've seen, our calling things red isn't an inference from our seeing them to be P, or $P_1C_1 \vee \cdots \vee P_4C_4$; rather, it's a direct effect that we learn to let those things have on us in those circumstances. And however complex the combination of properties involved, we can learn to be affected in this way without having any prior concept either of red or of those properties. For we can learn by example, being corrected by existing users of the predicate, just as the network of parallel distributed processors described by Churchland (1988, Chapter 7.5) can learn by example to use sonar to tell underwater mines from rocks. And just as Churchland's network can learn without containing any representation either of mines or of the properties by which it learns to detect them, so we can learn what to call red without having or acquiring any concept either of red or of the properties to which we learn to respond by calling the things that have them red.

Nothing, therefore, in our learning or use of the predicate 'red' requires it to correspond to any one property of the things we apply it to. And as for 'red', so for almost all our predicates – except some of those we use to state laws of nature. For if, as I have argued, actual properties are those quantified over by the Ramsey sentence S that states all laws, then predicates corresponding to S's predicate variables will in turn correspond to properties. And this gives us reason to think that the simple predicates we use in our law statements – for example, those ascribing masses, temperatures, energies, chemical and biological kinds, mental states and kinds of sensation – correspond to properties. We may of course be wrong, not only because our supposed law statements may be false but also because discovering more laws may convince us that predicates we thought were simple (like 'chlorine') are really complex. But even when a predicate 'P' really is simple, the property P will still not give us its connotations. For even if S identifies P, P doesn't identify S. The laws of nature are contingent: they aren't entailed by even the totality of properties they contain, let alone by any one of them. And although, as we have seen, the laws that contain P will somewhat constrain the connotations of the predicate 'P', they certainly won't provide them. For not only do we not know all those laws (and probably never will), but even if we did, that would still not determine which of them to build into the meanings of the predicates involved.

In short, contingent universals contribute little to the meanings even of the scientific predicates we use to identify them. And to the meanings of most other predicates they contribute even less: not even their extensions. Thus what Wittgenstein said of the predicate 'game' may well be true of every ordinary predicate: No one property is shared by everything it applies to. But that doesn't dispose, as some have thought, of universals and hence of the problems they present; it provides no excuse for nominalism or conceptualism in either metaphysics or semantics. What it does do is show the need to recognize both how much our concepts, and the meanings of our predicates, differ from the actual properties and relations of things, as well as how much, and in what complex ways, they depend on them.

Acknowledgments

Besides the published works mentioned herein, this essay has been considerably influenced by Austin (1939), Wilson (1982) and an unpublished paper by Greg McCulloch. Earlier versions of the essay were discussed at a Conference on Truth and Reference held at the Inter-University Center in Dubrovnik in September 1990 and at the Cambridge University Moral Sciences Club in November 1990. My subsequent revision has been much indebted to comments made in those discussions, especially by Alexander Bird, Jeremy Butterfield, Mike Martin, Greg McCulloch and Roger Teichman, and also to comments made later by Jeremy Butterfield, Tim Crane, Alex Oliver and Peter Weatherall.

REFERENCES

Armstrong, D. M. 1978. *Universals and Scientific Realism,* 2 vols. (Cambridge University Press).

1983a. *What is a Law of Nature?* (Cambridge University Press).

1989b. *Universals: an Opinionated Introduction* (Boulder, CO: Westview Press).

Austin, J. L. 1939. 'Are There *A Priori* Concepts?'. In *Philosophical Papers* (Oxford University Press, 1961), pp. 32–54.

Churchland, Paul M. 1988. *Matter and Consciousness,* rev. ed. (Cambridge, MA: MIT Press).

Davidson, Donald. 1967. 'Causal Relations'. In *Essays on Actions and Events* (Oxford: Clarendon, 1980), pp. 149–62.

Evans, Gareth. 1982. *The Varieties of Reference* (Oxford: Clarendon).

Mellor, D. H. 1987. 'The Singularly Affecting Facts of Causation'. In *Metaphysics and Morality: Essays in Honour of J. J. C. Smart,* ed. Philip Pettit et al. (Oxford: Blackwell), pp. 111–36.

1988. 'On Raising the Chances of Effects'. In *Probability and Causality,* ed. J. H. Fetzer (Dordrecht: Reidel), pp. 229–39.

1990. 'Laws, Chances and Properties', *International Studies in the Philosophy of Science* 4: 159–70.

Ramsey, F. P. 1925. 'Universals'. In *Philosophical Papers* (Cambridge University Press, 1990), pp. 8–30.

Wilson, Mark. 1982. 'Predicate Meets Property', *Philosophical Review* 91: 549–89.

Reply to Mellor

D. M. ARMSTRONG

Hugh Mellor has come out to Australia a number of times, but I think that it was in England that we met. We got to know each other gradually and over the years our philosophical interests converged and friendship grew. In 1985 my wife and I stayed with him in Cambridge for a memorable week. It was memorable, among other things, for a tremendous argument that we had about two Soviet philosophers who paid a quick visit to the university. Noting that they were unaccompanied, I asked Hugh which of them he thought the 'minder' was. Hugh thought this was an inhospitable and generally low suspicion. In the new international situation we may one day be able to throw more light on our dispute!

1. Universals, Causes and Laws

Mellor and I have many, and deep, agreements in ontology. We agree that first-order particulars have properties and relations, where these properties and relations are not at all semantic entities but are rather discovered or hypothesized on the basis of empirical, scientific investigations. These properties and relations, we agree, are not particulars but universals, and their universality is primitive; it is not to be analyzed away in terms of classes, resemblances, possibilia or whatnot. Furthermore, universals are contingent beings. It follows that for us there is no simple semantic relationship between predicates and universals – for instance, no one-to-one correlation. Rather, there are differing semantic relationships in different cases, relationships that can only gradually be brought to light by the combined efforts of logical analysis and scientific investigation.

Mellor goes on to say that he takes the 'main reasons for believing in contingent universals to be the role they play in causation and in laws of nature'. That is a thesis to which I am at least sympathetic. I begin to have a little pause when he goes on to say 'those laws are what I take to give those universals their identity'. Just what does this mean?

Does he mean that it is the whole essence of a universal that it figures in the laws it figures in? This interpretation is supported by his remarks alleging that being a constituent of laws is 'all there is to being a property'. But would not this make laws necessary? Perhaps the laws of our world need not hold 'in every possible world'. But every world that contained just the universals of this world would contain just our laws – the 'weak' necessity of Shoemaker (1984, Chapter 10) and Swoyer (1982). Mellor, however, thinks as I do that laws are contingent.

Perhaps Mellor in these passages has said more than he really wants to say. Perhaps he is really concerned with identification rather than identity. He asks what 'fixes the identity' of contingent universals. Perhaps he thinks that law statements 'fix the reference', as Kripke's phrase has it, of the universals involved. There will, of course, be other ways to fix the reference for universals. 'What we speak of as redness' fixes the reference for a universal or range of universals. But it is plausible to suggest that its 'place in the nomic net' is the deepest and best way we have of identifying universals. (Though the apparent possibility pointed out by Jeremy Butterfield that Mellor mentions – an ingenious adaptation of the 'inverted spectrum' case to the matter at hand – deserves careful consideration.) On this view it is contingent what laws universals enter into, but we have no deeper way of identifying them than by these laws. I am inclined to accept all this, though it should be noted that if there are complex universals (something Mellor denies) then universals may to some extent be used to identify one another.

Passing on, I am puzzled by Mellor's contention that causation is not a universal. The reason he gives for this is that causation should not be represented by predicates, but rather by a connective ('because' in its causal use) that connects facts. Facts, he says elsewhere (Mellor 1991, p. 202) 'make whole sentences, statements, thoughts or propositions true'. At the same time, he denies that this is a correspondence theory of truth ('facts are defined in terms of truth, not vice versa') and says that facts 'are not particulars of any kind'.

I agree that there is such a conception of facts, and that it has its uses. But I think that there is a another conception of facts, one found in the *Tractatus*, in Skyrms (1981) and in my own work, though I use the phrase 'states of affairs'. In this conception facts really do correspond to statements, et cetera, though not in a one-to-one way. They and their constituents (particulars and universals) are my candidate for the truthmakers, the ontological ground, of all truths. Incidentally, such facts are particulars (in most cases) and seem to be the natural relata for singular causal sequences.

Presumably Mellor rejects all this. But suppose instead that we grant that causation is a connection between facts as Mellor conceives them. How does it follow that causation is not a universal? I am not at all clear what the argument is.

We come now to Mellor's contention that singular causation always involves the instantiation of a law. It is clear that if such causation is determined by certain properties of the cause, and if these properties are universals, and if finally these universals have associated with them a certain physical probability (or chance) of bringing about the effect, then the desired result may be deduced. And all these three propositions seem very plausible to me. (I have no difficulty at all with the idea that a deterministic law is just the limiting case – physical probability 1 – of an indeterministic law.) But I doubt if there is any way to extract these three propositions from the notion of singular causation so as to reach the desired conclusion a priori. For even after granting objective chances, why may not the chance be a *single-case* chance? Mellor may reply that causation is linked to the notion of a means to an end (see Mellor 1991, Chapter 13), and that the notion of a means inevitably involves generality. But I think that the link between causality and means–end is inductively established only, and not a priori.

My own position is that *making something happen, producing something, bringing something about,* is a dyadic relation and a universal, one which links facts in the Wittgenstein–Skyrms sense, and which holds in virtue of the universals that these facts contain as constituents. Does the relation admit of further analysis? The view I am attracted to at present is that the relation is a primitive which does not admit of further analysis. We are directly aware of it in certain perceptions (see my reply to Menzies in Chapter 9 of this volume). We find by experience that there are regularities of production. This seems to justify an a posteriori identification of singular causation with instantiation of a (causal) law. (See Heathcote and Armstrong 1991. Following Kripke on identity of constitution, we take the identification to be a necessary one, but that point is less essential.) If all fundamental laws, or all first-order fundamental laws, are causal, then singular causation can be identified with instantiation of a fundamental first-order law.

2. Complex Universals?

I am in a very large measure of agreement with what Mellor has to say about predicates. (I particularly like his last paragraph.) So I will concentrate on one point where we are definitely in disagreement: his conclusion that there really are no complex properties.

I agree with him in rejecting disjunctive and negative properties, but I see no objection to conjunctive and structural properties. It may be (epistemic may) that such complex properties are one and all fully analyzable in terms of simple properties and, in the case of structural properties, simple relations. If that is so, then one can certainly see the force of saying that *the* properties are the simple ones. At the same time this seems to be a somewhat puritanical stand. Conjunctive and structural properties would be repeatables, ones that run through a potential many; they would thus meet one great test for a universal. Consider the position with respect to particulars if it should turn out that they are one and all made up of genuinely atomic atoms. One could see the force in saying that these atoms are the genuine particulars. Yet would one want to say that there really are no such particulars as tables? A natural thing to do would be to distinguish between *basic* particulars and others. Why not do the same for properties?

But this is not the argument on which I would wish to rest the main weight. Mellor records my claim (Armstrong 1978) that 'it is logically and epistemically possible that all properties are conjunctive properties'. At that time I would have made the same claim about structural properties. I would now wish to withdraw the claim about logical possibility (see Armstrong 1989a, Chapter 5, Section 1). My argument for this new conclusion is best presented as a reductio ad absurdum. Consider the supposition that a certain universal is actually simple but might have been complex. A universal is essentially a one that can run through many. How then could we claim that it is the one universal that is actually simple but is complex in 'another possible world'? What we would have, rather, would be two different universals. The structure or lack of structure of a universal is of its essence: internal to its nature. The perception of this point led me to be much more sympathetic than I had previously been to Kripke's contention that there are necessities established, or hypothesized, on empirical grounds.

But I stick to the point that it is epistemically possible that all properties (or relations) should be infinitely complex, whether this be a matter of conjunctions or other structures 'all the way down'. I would hesitate to assign any definite degree of belief to this hypothesis, but I don't see how it can be ruled out by what we now know and rationally believe about the world.

I regret that I cannot see the force of Ramsey's argument against complex universals, at any rate as applied against conjunctive properties. Suppose we have the putative property-identity $P \& Q = W$. Then, as Mellor presents it, Ramsey argues that $Pa \& Qa$ would be the same state of affairs as Wa; but they cannot be, because they contain different constituents. This seems very weak. Might one not argue similarly that the knife cannot be identical with its blade and its handle? The properties P, Q, and W are *partially* identical while P and Q co-instantiated is *strictly* identical to W. (See both Lewis's essay and my reply in Chapter 2 of this volume.)

Mellor appears to concede that, for example, there may be no limit to the small-scale structure of matter. But he claims that this state of affairs could be dealt with without introducing complex properties. Instead, he proposes, we should set no limit to the number of (simple) properties or to the complexity of laws. This, I take it, is the proposal that the 'infinitely complex' be seen as involving an infinite number of simple constituents.

For myself, I would not wish to rule out the epistemic possibility of such an analysis. But, I claim, there is another possibility that must not be ruled out. This is the epistemic possibility that there are no simple constituents at all, not even an infinite number. Consider the case of space. It may be made up on some infinite number of simple points. But spaces may contain spaces as proper parts ad infinitum without being composed of simple things at all. Why might not properties (and relations) be some or all of them like that? Any laws in which such universals figured would have to involve complex universals. Can Mellor rule out this apparent possibility a priori?

As for my argument that laws having antecedent P & Q might not follow from laws about P alone and Q alone ('emergence'), I agree that it does not prove my point. But if there are such laws, it will be very natural to take the antecedent as a unit, as a universal; so conjunctive universals seem at least possible. (Though it is ironic that I am the reductionist physicalist while Mellor rejects physicalism!)

REFERENCES

Armstrong, D. M. 1978. *Universals and Scientific Realism,* 2 vols. (Cambridge University Press).
    1989a. *A Combinatorial Theory of Possibility* (Cambridge University Press).
Heathcote, Adrian and Armstrong, D. M. 1991. 'Causes and Laws', *Noûs* 25: 63–73.
Mellor, D. H. 1991. *Matters of Metaphysics* (Cambridge University Press).
Shoemaker, Sydney. 1984. *Identity, Cause, and Mind* (Cambridge University Press).
Skyrms, Brian. 1981. 'Tractarian Nominalism', *Philosophical Studies* 40: 199–206. Reprinted in Armstrong (1989a), pp. 145–52.
Swoyer, Chris. 1982. 'The Nature of Natural Laws', *Australasian Journal of Philosophy* 60: 203–23.

III

Causality and Laws of Nature

6

Are Causal Laws Contingent?

EVAN FALES

It has been nearly a decade and a half since Fred Dretske, David Armstrong and Michael Tooley, having each rejected the Regularity theory, independently proposed that natural laws are grounded in a second-order relation that somehow binds together universals.[1] (I shall call this the 'DTA theory'). In this way they sought to overcome the major – and notorious – shortcomings of every version of the Regularity theory: how to provide truth conditions for laws that lack instances; how to distinguish laws from accidental generalizations; how to provide truth conditions for the counterfactuals and disposition statements that laws apparently 'support'; how to justify inductive inferences from past events to laws and future events. For each of these puzzles, an apparently key element in the solution seems to be missing from Regularity theories. That missing element is a genuine connection, a relation with more than merely spatial and/or temporal content, linking the antecedent of a law to its consequent. Once such an additional objective element – however understood – is admitted to be essential to the analysis of laws, one is forced to give up the idea that the logical form of laws can be given in terms of quantifiers ranging over events or states of affairs, and truth-functions. What more must be supplied? To this Armstrong, Tooley and Dretske gave the reply: a special, second-order relation between the universals characterizing the antecedent and the consequent of a law. But this is a very general answer, and it leaves much unsettled. In particular, it leaves unsettled the answers to four watershed questions, questions whose answers determine the way in which the DTA theory resolves the challenges faced by Regularity theorists. These questions are:

(1) Are nomic connections between universals necessary or contingent?
(2) Is the nomic connection one of which we are ever directly aware?
(3) Do universals exist only *in rebus,* or may they also exist *ante rem*?
(4) What relationship is there (if any) between causal connection – the connection between events in virtue of which one is the cause of another – and nomic connection?

DTA theorists are divided over the answers to these questions. Armstrong's answer to the first is, as we shall see, not entirely clear. But it seems safe to say, at least, that he denies the *logical* necessity of nomic connections. I say 'seems safe' because the scope of this claim is itself unclear. I shall take up presently the question of how logical necessity is here to be understood.

Armstrong's answer to the second question distinguishes him from almost every other DTA theorist. Armstrong has long maintained that certain causal relations between events are directly perceivable. Whether one should conclude from this that (for Armstrong) nomic connections are also sometimes directly perceivable will depend in part on the answer Armstrong gives to question (4).

To the third question Armstrong gives a clear answer: No universals exist *ante rem*. Platonism is eschewed.

Armstrong has wavered over what answer to give to question (4). For a long time it seemed to him that the DTA theory could be combined with a singularist conception of causation. Single causal connections can be perceived; nomological connections – implying, as they do, regularities – are inferred.[2] And what reason is there to suppose that a causal connection implies a nomological one? But singularism did not seem to Armstrong a plausible position, and he has recently tried to argue that the causal and nomological connections are, at bottom, one and the same.

In this essay I shall focus upon Armstrong's answer to question (1), and I shall argue that causal (and nomological) connections are, in a sense to be investigated, necessary. But the answer to question (1) is not independent of answers to the other three questions. On the contrary: any discussion of one of these questions must embrace a consideration of the others. A necessitarian answer to (1) commits one (I shall argue) either to a form of Platonism or to the view that causal relations are internal; and this is indeed one reason why Armstrong rejects this answer to (1). On the other hand, I believe that only a necessitarian answer can forge a connection between causal and nomological relations, one that offers a satisfactory defence against singularism.

I have said that Armstrong is not a necessaritarian in the logical sense. I must now add a gloss on this claim. A principled way of distinguishing logical from other necessary truths would require a clearer distinction than I can supply between logical form and nonlogical 'content'. But at least I think we may safely take 'a prioricity' as an essential feature of logical truths.

The point is of some importance, because most of those recent philosophers – from Blanshard to Shoemaker[3] – who have held that a causal relation or law is logically necessary have argued that it could be known to obtain a priori, if one were to have a fully adequate conception of the cause and of the effect. But it is clear that to acquire such an adequate conception would require considerable empirical investigation, investigation that would presuppose knowledge of a variety of physical laws. On the other hand, such an adequate conception is surely not presupposed by our ability to pick out, refer to, or meaningfully describe the causally related events in question. Thus, even if causal relations could be inferred from an adequate conception of the related events, such a causal claim would not be an analytic truth. It would not follow merely from the content of the relevant meaning-conventions. As I can imagine no other way in which such truths could be known a priori, I think we are justified in denying that they are truths of logic *even if* they 'follow from' an adequate conception of the related events.

Nevertheless, it is a substantive and interesting thesis that causal truths do so follow; and because this thesis seems on the DTA theory to amount to the claim that causal and nomological connections form part of the real essences of the properties of causally related events, I shall adopt the convention of speaking of this thesis as the thesis that causal and nomological truths are metaphysically necessary. I shall presently examine the merits of this view. But Armstrong is neither a logical nor a metaphysical necessitarian.

That he is nonetheless a necessitarian of *some* sort is suggested by his repeated assertion that nomological and causal relations are relations of necessitation. In a reply to Tweedale,[4] we are told that laws of nature are contingently necessary – that is, necessary in some weaker sense than logical necessity. Moreover, Armstrong links causal necessitation to the fact that a cause produces its effect; and he believes that we sometimes directly perceive relations of causal production:[5]

I would argue . . . that in being aware of a causal sequence we are *ipso facto* aware of necessitation: something making something happen. And I suggest in *What is a Law of Nature?* . . . that this is the *same* necessitation which I hold is found in positive instantiations of laws . . . .

Armstrong's appeal to an awareness of causal necessitation suggests that Lewis and Tweedale[6] are not being entirely fair in charging that Armstrong's necessitarian characterization of these relations is merely an empty label, backed by nothing of substance.

How, though, are we to understand the species of necessity that Armstrong appears to invoke here? There are, I think, just two ways of conceiving this. The first is that truths of the sort 'N(F, G)'[7] have a necessity deriving somehow from the connected universals F and G themselves, although not – given Armstrong's rejection of the views of Shoemaker and Tweedale – a metaphysical necessity. On this picture, nevertheless, the necessity somehow resides in, or stems from the character of, the related universals. A second picture, encouraged by Armstrong's own language, is that necessitation is a characteristic of the causal (= nomological) relation. It is not easy to see how either of these views is to be made intelligible. I shall consider them in turn.

According to the first suggestion, the relation N holds between universals (say between F and G) in virtue of something about those universals, something that makes 'N(F, G)' an a posteriori necessary truth. But this 'something' is not merely the intrinsic nature of F and G; for if that were the case then 'N(F, G)' would be metaphysically necessary. Mustn't it then be some *contingent* characteristics of F and G which determine that they are nomologically related? But if that is so, then 'N(F, G)' is a contingent truth. One might suggest that the characteristics of F and G in virtue of which N holds between them are physically but not logically necessary characteristics, but this represents no progress. One might as well just say that 'N(F, G)' has a sui generis type of necessity – call it physical necessity if you will – and be done with it.[8] This is a viable maneuver, to which I shall return, but it is doubtful that Armstrong would accept it.[9] If he did accept it, he would have a stronger argument than the one he actually employs to show that laws support counterfactuals.

The alternative to this first suggestion is that the nomological relation N is one that its first relatum – say, F – bears only contingently to any other universal – for instance, G – but that, when it obtains, it necessitates G. The idea is that if F exists (has instances) and if the relation N has F as the first of its relata (these being contingent matters), then necessarily the universal G will have instances suitably related in space and time to the instances of F. On this picture, it is not the case that 'N(F, G)' is a necessary truth, nor is it true that $\Box(\forall x)(Fx \supset Gx)$. But when 'N(F, G)' obtains, it necessarily associates Fs with Gs: $(\forall x)[Fx \supset \Box(N(F, G) \supset Gx)]$. The way in which G is associated with F by N could be expressed by the following formula, in which P is a variable ranging over universals:

$$(\forall P)[N(F, P) \supset \Box(P = G)]$$

This formulation points up one of the chief disadvantages of the second alternative. If H is a universal distinct from G, it is evident that F could not be Nly related to H instead of to G. Of course, F may be nomologically related to more than one universal – in particular, it may be nomologically related to H as well as to G. But this will require us to postulate a distinct nomological connector N* in virtue of which that is so. In short, we shall need a distinct nomological relation for each of F's nomological relations – an inelegance which, at the very least, imposes upon us the task of explaining which it is that makes these various relations species of the same genus.

However, the second difficulty with this understanding of necessitation is even more serious. No view on which 'N(F, G)' is strictly contingent (i.e., not necessary in any sense) can account for the fact that laws of nature sustain counterfactuals.[10] The alternative just adumbrated is such a view.

The truth conditions for counterfactuals are hard to specify not only because of their problematic modal features, but also because their evaluation typically involves understanding how the relevant counterfactual circumstance is to be conceived – and this is conditioned by information contained in linguistic conventions, informal contextual cues, and the like. Proponents of nonmodal analyses of counterfactuals tend, understandably, to emphasize the latter factors, hoping indeed to reduce apparently modal features to those factors.

Armstrong's account of how laws support counterfactuals appears to be of this ilk, in spite of his assertions that laws must, if they are to support counterfactuals, be necessary.[11] For he invokes only the idea that laws involve universals to explain why the DTA theory, unlike the Regularity theory, can account for the support given by laws to counterfactuals. Contrasting his own analysis of laws with the Regularity theory, he reasons as follows. On the Regularity theory, the laws that Fs are Gs, expressed by '$(\forall x)(Fx \supset Gx)$', cannot support counterfactuals because the law simply tells us that the extension of F is included in that of G. If, contrary to fact, an individual a were F, then this would constitute a substantive change in the facts upon which the truth value of '$(\forall x)(Fx \supset Gx)$' depends. There is nothing about those facts in virtue of which '$(\forall x)(Fx \supset Gx)$' is actually true that bears upon whether an expansion of the class of Fs would or would not destroy the inclusion of the class of Fs by the class of Gs. So we can't infer from the universal generalization that, if a were F, it would be G. But if the law is founded in a relation N between the universals F and G, then the imagined inclusion of a in the extension of F (a change in the first-order facts) gives us no reason to change the truth value of the law (which would be a change in the second-order facts) – even though the law is contingent. Thus Armstrong states:[12]

It is of the essence that these properties [the ones connected nomologically] be taken to be universals. Only so will the law be a single thing – an atomic fact as Tooley puts it – a thing that remains the same however many or few positive instances fall under the law. It is this that explains why laws sustain counterfactuals. An imagined new instance of the antecedent is not an imagined enlarging of the law, as it is with the Regularity theory. Hence there need to be no question whether the law applies in the imagined new instance.

The necessity of 'N(F, G)' does not appear to play any role in the argument just quoted, unless it be supposed that this necessity flows from the nature of the universals. It is the unity of the nature of a universal – coupled with the fact that 'N(F, G)' is a *singular* statement about universals – that does the work in Armstrong's reasoning. Furthermore, Armstrong goes on to deny that the necessity of laws derives from the natures of the universals they relate.[13] Finally, and of some relevance to the counterfactuals issue, is Armstrong's argument that laws, although contingent, cannot change, since any such change would destroy the unity of the related universals.[14] This argument makes it tempting to think that, for Armstrong, laws, while not logically necessary, are necessary in a sense to be analyzed in terms of the unity of universals.

In view of the difficulty in discerning what Armstrong's position is, I shall proceed as follows. First, I shall argue that laws must indeed be necessary if they are to sustain counterfactuals. Here I shall be agreeing with him. It will follow that Armstrong's actual explanation of how statements like 'N(F, G)' support counterfactuals is not satisfactory, inasmuch as it makes no explicit appeal to necessity. Second, I shall consider the argument for the unchangeability of laws, which I believe to be unsound. Third, I shall present a new argument for Platonism, since the prospects for a necessitarian theory of laws is closely tied to the plausibility of a Platonist theory of universals. Finally, I shall consider what options are available for the necessitarian task of explaining the nature of nomological necessity.

I

First, then, I shall suppose that necessity plays no role in Armstrong's explanation of why laws support counterfactuals. As I am presently construing him, it is simply one fact – namely, that imagined changes in the extension of a universal provide no grounds for supposing the (contingent) nomological relations of that universal to be altered – that provides the rationale for holding those relations fixed as we consider the counterfactual situation. But 'holding fixed' is something *we* do, not the world; alternatively put, the world's doing it constitutes the presence of an objective necessity. Giving an account of law-supported counterfactuals requires, I shall argue, such objective necessities.

We begin with an example that demonstrates the vagaries of counterfactual evaluation. A mother, warning her child, might offer the familiar 'I wouldn't do that if I were you'. And the child, who we may imagine to be as reckless as she is bright, might tempt her mother with this reply: 'Yes you would – if you were me'. This child knows how to manipulate the contextual rules that determine what is to be held fixed in the trip to counterfactual worlds.[15] The mother 'holds fixed' her rationality (i.e., imagines a child possessed of her wisdom); the child 'holds fixed' both her own motives and her recklessness.

Of course the child is trifling with a well-understood convention. But the fact that she can intelligibly do so might appear to offer hope for an anti-necessitarian account of counterfactuals. Surely it is plausible, in particular, to suppose that there might be some analogous convention accompanying the assertion of law-supported counterfactuals, a convention in virtue of which laws support them. The natural suggestion is that there is a contextual rule that lays it down that the law itself is to be held fixed. Moreover – so the story might go – if '$(\forall x)(Fx \supset Gx)$' is an accidental generalization then it is not the case that $N(F, G)$, and so there is no (contingent) nomological relation between F and G to be held fixed as we wander off to inspect nearby possible worlds. That is why accidental generalizations do not support counterfactuals.

This account, while it has some initial attractiveness, cannot be correct – at least not by Armstrong's lights. For one thing, a Regularity theorist can avail himself of precisely the same strategy to account for the difference between laws and accidental generalizations: when we take a regularity to be a law, there is a convention accompanying the corresponding counterfactuals that instructs us to hold the regularity fixed; those that we take to be accidental generalizations are accorded no such treatment.

Second, the convention-based account cannot be correct if the truth conditions for the counterfactuals in question are not merely to reflect human attitudes or conventions, but are further to have an objective basis. What, on the proposed semantics for counterfactuals, could objectively ground the differential 'treatment' of laws and of accidental generalizations?

But wait. Surely Armstrong has a reply to this question not available to the Regularity theorist. For Armstrong (but not for the Regularity theorist), there is an objective fact that distinguishes these two – namely, the obtaining of '$N(F, G)$' when it is a law that Fs are Gs. But this objective difference will not help. The objection against the Regularity theorist was that he sometimes treats '$(\forall x)(Fx \supset Gx)$' as fixed, even though it is taken on those very occasions to be contingent – that is, there is nothing about the world itself that fixes the truth of the generalization across possible worlds. But if '$N(F, G)$' is contingent then, although it gives *one* respect in which laws are distinct from accidental generalizations, there is here, too, nothing that can objectively ground the fixity of the law.

There can be no objective truth conditions for a counterfactual unless there is something fixed across worlds, not as a matter of convention but as a matter of objective fact. Consider once again the parent's warning. What makes that warning true (correctly understood) involves, in part, the requirement that the counterfactual be evaluated with respect to worlds in which the child is supposed to have the mature wisdom of an adult, but otherwise the physical capacities she has in the actual world. Those capacities, and the situation in which the child finds herself, are to be supposed fixed. It is an interpretive convention that determines this, a convention that the child's reply stands on its head. But the convention by itself is powerless to ground the truth of the counterfactual. The counterfactual is true only because, as a matter of fact, mature wisdom naturally dictates a different course of action than that intended by the child. It is no matter of convention that wisdom necessarily dictates a different course of action in these circumstances. This is an objectively necessary fact; and it is essential to the truth of our counterfactual. If what wisdom dictates is itself conventional or contingent – if, for example, it depends upon who possesses wisdom or upon the capricious whims of the agent employing it – then there could be no ground for asserting the counterfactual. Thus, even though conventions play a role in determining the truth conditions for 'I wouldn't do that if I were you', they cannot provide the whole story. Commitments to objective necessity enter as well.

So it is with law-supported counterfactuals. Conventions have a role here, too. They tell us, roughly, to hold fixed all causally relevant aspects of a situation except those to be counterfactually varied. But they could not instruct us to 'hold fixed' the supporting law itself. Were they to do that, the truth of the counterfactual would become a mere artifact of convention (as, for example, it would be if we were to claim that accidental generalizations support counterfactuals in virtue of some newly laid-down convention that fixes the accidental generalizations themselves). To objectively ground a counterfactual, a law must itself be necessary. Only thus will what happens in worlds whose antecedent conditions differ from ours be a matter of objective and determinate fact.

There is, however, one further analogue that Armstrong might hope to exploit. The possession of a dispositional property by a particular will support counterfactuals concerning the behavior of that particular, even when possession of the property is a contingent matter. My automobile has a disposition to start when the key is turned in the ignition. That supports the counterfactual

(1)   If I had turned the key in the ignition five minutes ago, my car would have started.

This disposition of my car is a lamentably contingent one, however. The disposition vanishes, for example, when the temperature drops below 0°F (and also from time to time for other reasons). Nevertheless (1), if I now utter it, seems objectively true. The disposition supports the counterfactual, even though no necessity supports the disposition. Is this not directly analogous to Armstrong's claim that 'N(F, G)' supports counterfactuals, though not itself necessary?

But the support provided by this kind of case is specious. For the support that possession of the disposition provides for the counterfactual depends upon the existence of a law connecting the disposition to its manifestations; and it would be at least begging the question at this point to maintain that that law need not be necessary. If the law is necessary, then we have here an objective necessity that enters into the truth conditions for (1).

But there is a further disanalogy between this case and law-supported counterfactuals, a disanalogy that derives precisely from the contingency with which the disposition is possessed. For it is not difficult to imagine circumstances that make (1) false. It is my established practice to bicycle or walk except in the most inclement weather. This makes it unlikely that I shall attempt to start my car except in weather sufficiently foul to make doubtful the success of the attempt. That information makes it doubtful that (1) is true. What we should say about (1), in fact, depends upon what we should say about the counterfactual

(2)   If I had turned the key in the ignition of my car five minutes ago, the temperature would have been lower than 0°F.

The assignment of a truth value to (2) in the imagined circumstances proves to be difficult. The month being October, a temperature five minutes ago lower than 0°F would be highly unusual, but not impossible. My habits being deeply ingrained, my using the car when it is warmer than that would be extremely unlikely, but also not impossible. The truth value of (2) appears to depend – insofar as this is not a merely conventional matter – upon the balance of these probabilities. But either those probabilities are an objective matter – in which case there must be laws, perhaps probabilistic ones, which determine them – or else the truth value of (2) does not depend upon objective facts at all. If the truth value of (2) does depend upon laws, then these can serve their semantic role vis-à-vis (2) only, once again, if they are necessary and not held fixed by convention.

In either case, then, the analogy to counterfactuals supported by contingently obtaining dispositional properties cannot be of help to Armstrong. This is especially clear where 'N(F, G)' grounds a nondefeasible (or 'iron', in Armstrong's terminology) law. For then, there ought not to be any realizable circumstances under which the truth of the corresponding counterfactuals is cast into doubt.

This argument concerning the truth conditions for counterfactuals is quite general. Abstractly put, its point is simply this. Consider the counterfactual

(3)   If A had been the case, B would have been.

When we evaluate this counterfactual, we imagine the circumstance of A's being the case, and then ask whether in that circumstance B is so as well. But 'A is the case' is a very incomplete specification of a circumstance, and trouble arises because there usually can be circumstances in which both A and B are the case, and also ones in which A is true but B is not. We must therefore refine the question by filling in the circumstances surrounding A. If, upon doing this, we find no case in which A plus the attendant circumstances obtain yet B is false, then (3) is true; otherwise not. But how are the attendant circumstances to be chosen? Perhaps we think of A as obtaining in a circumstance as similar as possible to our world – similar except with respect to whatever, in our world, is incompatible with the occurrence of A. Or perhaps some other strategy is appropriate. But however we do this, there are just two possibilities. Call the attendant circumstances C. Then either $A \& C$ logically entails B or it does not. If C is so stipulated that B is entailed, then of course (3) is true – though in some cases trivially so. Otherwise, B is logically independent of $A \& C$. What, then, ensures that B is the case in every possible world in which $A \& C$ is? Nothing could ensure that, other than some kind of necessary connection between $A \& C$'s obtaining and B's being the case. (Indeed, when $A \& C$ does entail B this is also the case, for then B's obtaining is ensured by the logical necessity of 'If $A \& C$, then B'.)

Analogously, consider Armstrong's counterfactual

(4)   If a had been F, it would have been G.

This counterfactual presupposes the truth of

(5)   If a had been F, it would still have been the case that N(F, G).

But the mere fact that a's being F provides no positive reason for the failure of N(F, G) is not strong enough to establish (5). Armstrong's strategy is to make a case for counting true the counterfactual (which makes explicit the presuppositions of (5))

(6)   Since N(F, G), and since a's being F does not count against N(F, G),
       if a were F, it would be G.

This is an instance of the schema

(7)   Since B, and since A's being the case does not count against B, if A
       were the case then B would be.

Perhaps we do often count counterfactuals like (7) true, even when *B* is contingent and not necessitated by *A* plus attendant circumstances. But there cannot, if I am correct, be any objective grounds for so evaluating instances of (7). Just as *a* might happenstantially have been F, so too 'N(F, G)' might, happenstantially and simultaneously, have been false – if 'N(F, G)' is contingent. And then there is no objective basis for affirming (4).

II

Armstrong can deflect the above criticism, of course, if his account of counterfactual support does after all appeal to nomological necessity. To see whether such a deflection is available, I now turn to what Armstrong says about this type of necessity. Of crucial importance will be whether Armstrong's account of this necessity is irreducably modal, or whether it can be understood in purely nonmodal terms.

Armstrong tells us (1983a, pp. 78ff) that the law that all Fs are Gs is necessary in virtue of the (nomological) relation obtaining between F and G. But how can the existence of such a relation render the law necessary? If we expect to be told at this point that the relation N between F and G holds necessarily, we will be disappointed. It is, rather, the unity of the universals F and G that accounts for the necessity of the law. In particular, this unity is supposed to explain why the law cannot obtain at one time yet fail to obtain at another. To suppose that this is possible – on the ground that N is a contingent relation – is to 'fail to see what a relation between universals is like'. Because F and G are universals, 'it *cannot* be that they have this relation at one time or place, yet lack it at another' [Armstrong's emphasis].[16] If a universal were, *per impossibile,* to have any property or relation when instantiated once that it lacks when instantiated again, it would not be the same – and hence would be a different universal in the two instances, or no genuine universal at all. Thus, the necessity of laws seems to derive from the identity conditions for universals. We should not, however, be misled by Armstrong's express statement that it derives (in our case) from what it is to be an F (and a G).[17] That would suggest that the existence of the relation N between them flows from the particular natures of F-ness and G-ness, and Armstrong's argument does not rely upon these particular natures. It depends rather upon a general identity condition for universals, one that would suggest that *any* property or relation of a universal is necessary to it.[18] It might seem, indeed, that the species of necessity invoked here is metaphysical necessity.

But to interpret Armstrong in this way is to entirely misconceive his point, which rests not on essentialist doctrines about universals but rather on the idea that 'N(F, G)', though contingent, is an eternal singular sentence. 'N(F, G)', if true, is true 'for all time'. Armstrong eschews essentialism, and 'N(F, G)', although true, might not have been.

To make the point plain, Armstrong supplies an analogy. Suppose two spacetime points are contingently related by some relation R. Then, in some possible worlds, they lack that relation. Yet it makes no sense to ask whether they also, in the actual world, lack that relation at some other time or place. For spacetime points are one; they lack spatial or temporal parts. Thus, any sentence mentioning only relations between them is a fortiori an eternal sentence. Similarly, we are to suppose that universals lack such parts, not because universals are points, but rather (I think we must infer) because they are not in space and time at all. This line of reasoning sounds strikingly Platonist, and therefore comports ill with Armstrong's naturalism. In the next section, I shall argue that someone who holds that universals are merely abstractions from states of affairs is committed to holding that universals exist in time and therefore cannot so easily take 'N(F, G)' to be an eternal sentence. For the moment, I wish to remark that the analogy to points is offered as part of an explanation of what it is for a law to be (physically, but not logically) necessary. Physical necessity derives from the fact that laws involve relations between universals; that is, such necessity derives from the nature of universals. Relations between universals are 'necessary' in the sense that, if they are manifested between any pair of instances of those universals in a world, they must be manifested by all instances of those universals *in that world*. To all appearances, this reduces the fact that a law is nomologically necessary to a nonmodal fact – namely, to the unity of universals. We may call this a species of 'necessity' if we wish, but – whatever we call it – it cannot help to explain the fact that laws support objective counterfactuals, statements that must be evaluated with respect to other possible worlds.

III

I now take up the important question of whether universals exist in time. This question, we saw, bears directly on whether 'N(F, G)' can be regarded as an eternal sentence; it bears also upon the prospects for an Aristotelian account of laws of the DTA variety. Here I shall therefore confine myself to asking whether an Aristotelian theory of universals is compatible with the view that universals are not temporal entities, and with some implications of conceding (as I think Aristotelians should) that they are.

Here is an argument for the claim that universals, on the Aristotelian conception of them, are temporal entities:

(1) Universals can (given the Aristotelian conception of them), be created (at a time).

(2) Anything that can be created (at a time) is a temporal being.

(3) Therefore, Aristotelian universals are temporal beings.

I take (2) to be uncontroversial, so my project is to demonstrate (1). Consider two universes, U_1 and U_2, which for the first 10 years of their existence are qualitatively identical. Both universes are governed by the same natural laws, some of which are indeterministic. One of these laws says that when something is F at a time t, it has a 0.0001 probability of being G at the next moment, and a 0.9999 probability of being H instead. Suppose, furthermore, that G is a simple property, and that nothing instantiates G during the first 10 years of either U_1 or U_2. At $t = 10$ years, something in U_1 is F, and similarly in U_2. This F becomes a G in U_1, but it becomes an H in U_2. In U_2, moreover, nothing ever does become G. An Aristotelian must say that G does not exist in U_2 because 'universals are nothing but abstractions from actual states of affairs', and no state of affairs in U_2 exemplifies G.[19] Does G exist in U_1? Certainly. But an Aristotelian must admit, I should think, that even though the sentence 'G exists in U_1' can be so understood as to be timelessly true, it is also true that G does not exist in U_1 until a moment after U_1 is 10 years old. Prior to that time, U_1 and U_2 are qualitatively identical. So G does not exist in the initial 10-year segment of U_1's history, but does exist after that time. G was therefore created in U_1 a moment after U_1's tenth birthday.[20]

If this is correct, then Aristotelian universals are temporal beings. If they have contingent properties, there is no reason why those properties could not change through time. Armstrong's argument does not explicitly appeal to the atemporality of universals, but only to their identity in each of their instances. But for temporal beings, sameness is not destroyed by changes in contingent properties. Armstrong's analogy, the two spacetime points a and b related by some contingent relation R, is indeed an apparent exception, for 'aRb' is contingently but timelessly true. But the reason for this is not hard to find. Spacetime points are nonrepeatable. For Armstrong, indeed, they are paradigm particulars. Furthermore, they have no temporal duration. It is exactly these features of a and b which entail that truths such as 'aRb' are timeless. Thus Armstrong's appeal to 'aRb' trades upon a *dis*analogy between spatiotemporal points and universals. The example cannot be used, therefore, to establish the unchangeability of contingent properties in a repeatable.

Armstrong, no doubt, would reverse the point; for he holds that there are no particulars which are continuants precisely on the ground that such continuants could both have and fail to have a certain property, which is not logically possible. But since (unlike punctiform particulars) universals are repeatable, this reasoning cannot apply to them. The only way of resisting this conclusion, so far as I can see, involves denying that universals exist in space and time.[21]

IV

I have described two imaginary universes, U_1 and U_2, with the aim of showing that the Aristotelian conception of universals is committed to the view that universals exist in time. Quite similar examples can be used to argue that the DTA theory of laws is committed to the existence of uninstantiated universals and hence to Platonism.[22]

I shall briefly present here one such example, similar in many ways to one brought forward by Tooley. Let us suppose our universe to have been one in which, during some initial segment of its history, all of the determinate properties falling under a given determinable were uninstantiated. Such a state of affairs is certainly not logically impossible; for our world, the supposition is not even unrealistic. It seems quite likely that, during some short span of time following the Big Bang, certain fundamental forces, and hence certain ranges of determinate properties, were absent. Let us further suppose these absent properties to have been simple ones.[23] Aristotelian realism implies that neither these determinate properties, nor the determinable under which they fall, had yet begun to exist during that period of time. Since the existence or nonexistence of these properties is contingent, one can say that they were created at the time their first instances appeared.

But in accordance with what principle? Surely their existence (i.e., the coming-to-be of instances of them) was caused by preceding conditions, in accordance with some law. There must have been – or at any rate might have been – something about the prior states of affairs in our universe that brought it about that these instances of novel properties should appear when they did, something which predetermined that, at the very moment in question, these new universals would come into existence.

What is the ground of this fact? Since Armstrong eschews relations between existents and nonexistents, and is no realist concerning mere possibilia, he cannot locate the truth-maker for the laws governing these universal-creating events in a nomological relation between the preexisting universals and the not-yet-existing determinate or determinable ones.

Thus far, the case is in all essentials identical to one of Tooley's, save only that I have tried to make it somewhat realistic.[24] Armstrong's rather uncomfortable response to Tooley's case[25] is to deny that any determinate law governs the creation of such new universals: There is nothing which makes it the case that this new universal (call it G), rather than some other one, shall be created. This response seems unconvincing. Once the new universal has come into existence, surely further instantiations of it will be governed by some definite law. Let us suppose that they are. Shall we say this law itself was not in existence prior to the creation of the first instance of G? Armstrong believes that our tendency to think otherwise results from our (mistaken) inclination to think of universals as necessary beings. But that is not the inclination that produces this intuition. It is not the necessary being of universals but rather the necessity of nomic connections that is surely the source of our intuition. We think it cannot be just a matter of accident that this novel universal, rather than some arbitrary other one, is instantiated under the circumstances.

I want to reinforce that intuition now by offering a variant of Tooley's argument that involves what Armstrong calls a 'contracted' world. Armstrong (1989a) argues that if a simple universal G is never instantiated in a world, then (relative to that world) its existence is logically impossible. Suppose this is correct.[26] A contracted world (with respect to ours) is one that contains no particulars or universals our world lacks, but that lacks some particular(s) and/or universal(s) present in our world. Consider now a contracted world W, similar in all respects to ours save only that it lacks G and contains nothing incompatible with the nonexistence of G; G does not exist in W. Suppose that, in our world, all Fs are Gs in virtue of the deterministic N(F, G); and suppose that only Fs are Gs. F, then, does not exist in W either – although, if F is complex, its constituents might. The differences between our world and W entailed by W's lack of F and G might be momentous, but on the other hand they might be minor indeed. Suppose the latter. Since 'N(F, G)' is true (in our world), it seems obvious that the following counterfactual is true of W:

(8)   If there had been any Fs, there would have been Gs.

Where F is complex and its constituents exist in W, Armstrong is committed to denying the truth of (8) in W. Where F is simple, or some of its constituents are absent from W, Armstrong seems to be committed to holding that (8) is vacuously true of W, since its antecedent is (on his view) logically impossible. But both these judgments certainly seem to be incorrect.[27] This sort of example has one further consequence. Armstrong (1983a, pp. 169–71) saddles necessitarians with the task of providing truth conditions for counterfactuals with impossible antecedents so that they are not vacuous. He thinks it may be possible to do this, but he does not suggest how it is to be done – it is not *his* task, after all. Here I mean to be turning the tables on Armstrong. Given his Aristotelianism and his theory of possibility, he must confront (8).

The necessitarian can, on the other hand, escape having to regard counterfactuals with nomically or logically impossible antecedents as other than vacuously true. The problem for the necessitarian, as Armstrong presents it, was originally raised by Mellor.[28] Mellor considers the functional law that relates the vapour pressure of water to temperature. For each temperature value T_i, the law assigns a vapour pressure V_i, and supports the counterfactual

(9)   If the temperature of this water had been T_i, its vapour pressure would have been V_i.

Mellor substitutes for T_i a temperature whose value exceeds the dissociation temperature for water molecules. Since it is physically impossible for water to exist at this temperature, (9) in this instance has an impossible antecedent. The necessitarian who rules (9) vacuously true on this account must regard equally true the contrary counterfactual whose antecedent matches that of (9), and whose consequent is the negation of the consequent of (9). This is supposed to be an unacceptable conclusion for the necessitarian, who is presumed to agree that the second counterfactual is obviously false.

But why should the necessitarian agree to that? Mellor does not say what the vapour-pressure law for water is, but he apparently indulges in the fantasy of extrapolating the function described by that law at low temperatures in a smooth way to extreme values. In fact, the law does not behave in this way. As the dissociation temperature for water is approached, the vapour pressure curve will become discontinuous. There *is* no vapour-pressure law for water to support either (9) or its contrary at temperatures beyond that point, unless we set $V_i = 0$ on the grounds that water, when absent from the system, exerts no pressure.

Nevertheless, (9) and its contrary are surely well-formed, whatever values are assigned to T_i and V_i. What, then, are their truth values when T_i is, say, 10^6 °C? Let me pose what I think is an analogous question: What are the truth values of

(10)   If Socrates were a number, then some number could philosophize.

and its contrary? We should agree that the semantics of such counterfactuals requires careful analysis. But I see no reason why a necessitarian should not say either that (10) lacks a truth value (on the grounds of reference failure for the designator 'Socrates' in worlds where he is to be supposed identical to a number) or is vacuously, and harmlessly, true. A similar strategy applies to (9).

V

Thus far I have argued for a necessitarian conception of natural law. That conception, of course, has its own problems. Of these, the deepest, I believe, is the challenge of explaining how nomological necessity is to be understood. The DTA theory takes the ground of laws to be relations between universals, and the DTA necessitarian holds these relations to be necessary. Fundamental to seeing how that necessity can be understood is the question of whether this nomic relation N is an internal or an external relation between universals.

Almost all necessitarian theorists hold that nomological relations are internal relations,[29] and it is easy to see why. The internal-relation theory has a ready explanation for the necessity of laws: Laws are necessary because N is an internal relation between universals[30] and is therefore necessary in the same way that all internal relations are necessary. Such relations 'follow from' the natures of the related universals. (If, with Armstrong, we deny that internal relations consist of anything over and above the related universals, the internal-relation view also achieves a significant ontological economy – for then N does not, strictly speaking, designate a universal.)

On the internal-relation theory, knowledge of the existence of a nomological relation between two universals depends upon nothing more than having an adequate conception of the natures of those two universals. Just as a knowledge of *'red'* and *'pink'* suffices to determine that the internal relation *'darker than'* holds between them, so too with causal relations. It is this fact which has led proponents of the internal-relation theory of laws (and of causation) to say that laws are logically necessary. This, as I said earlier, is something of a misnomer, at least if we think of the truths of logic as statements knowable a priori in virtue of their 'form'. Clearly, no narrow conception of logical form can serve to capture what is involved in the existence of internal relations. Furthermore, we can use predicates whose meanings we comprehend to designate universals whose natures we fail to fathom with the completeness required to discern nomological relations. Thus laws of nature are not, on the internal-relation theory, even analytic truths. Nor, therefore, can they be known a priori. On the internal-relation theory, nomic necessity is really a species of metaphysical necessity. Nomic relations hold by virtue of the identities of their relata.

Whatever we call it, this is a species of necessity of which we have some kind of understanding. We can provide analogies to nomic necessity in other internal relations, such as red's being darker than pink. And we can say *what* it is in virtue of which these necessities obtain – namely, the natures or identities of their relata.

For someone of Armstrong's persuasion, the internal-relation theory has another striking advantage. That theory can easily fend off, it seems, the arguments intended to force Armstrong into the arms of Platonism. Those arguments, as shown in Section IV, show that there are laws governing uninstantiated universals. Since Armstrong holds, plausibly, that there cannot be relations between nonexistent universals or between an existent universal and a nonexistent one, he cannot explain how, on the DTA theory, such laws are grounded. He ends, implausibly, by denying that there are or could be any such laws. But he needn't deny this if he were to accept the internal-relation theory. The worry about nonexistent relata, after all, is a worry that concerns only cases in which we have a real relation. But internal relations are not real. Consider, this time, the law that $P(G/F) = 0.001$,[31] a law that might obtain in a world W in which there are Fs but no Gs. What makes this law true of W? The internal-relation theory has a ready answer: it is simply the nature of F. G does not exist in W; nor does the probabilistic nomological relation between F and G. But that relation would not exist even if G did. Moreover, if G existed, it would have a nature; and the law would be a consequence of that nature and F's nature.[32]

These considerations make the internal-relation theory very attractive. Nevertheless, there are powerful reasons to reject it. Those that I shall discuss depend on the assumption that internal relations involve nothing more than the related universals.

The first objection to the internal-relation theory will perhaps have few takers. It rests on Armstrong's minority view (which I share) that we have direct experience of causal relations in the case of pushes and pulls upon our bodies. In these cases of pushes and pulls, causal relations are experienced as forces, and they have distinctive characteristics, such as direction and magnitude. Moreover, they can be experienced even when one of the relata is not distinctly experienced – as in the case of gravitational forces, which can be experienced without our being distinctly aware of their cause. It seems impossible to account for these features of our experience if causal relations are not real, external relations. If causal relations are external, it will be hard to deny that the nomological relations which ground causal laws are external as well. Indeed, for those who would identify the causal relation with the causal nomological relation, this conclusion is inescapable. (In what follows I shall assume this identification and simply use N to denote that relation. This assumption is one that is natural for a necessitarian DTA theorist to make.)

The second difficulty for the internal-relation theory concerns the role of causal (nomological) relations in causal explanation. Specifically, it concerns the fact that causation is a relation that mediates the production of a new existent. Suppose that a's being F causes (a moment later) a's being G, in virtue of a causal relation between F and G.[33] Now a's being F is an instance of F-ness, a's being G is an instance of G-ness, and if a's being F is the cause of a's being G then the first state of affairs and the second involve the presence of the causal relation N in these instances, which mediates the coming into existence of the instance of G. For an Aristotelian, F-ness and G-ness are fully present in each of their instances, but only in their instances. Although we can say that a's being F causes a's being G in virtue of N(F, G), it is clear that it is the presence of F-ness in a that explains the presence of G-ness in a; it is not (we are supposing) some *other* instance of F-ness that is responsible for this. Moreover, the creation of this case of G-ness occurs because there is an instance of causation connecting a's being F to that very instance of G. It could not be merely a relation between the F-ness of a and G-ness in general, for that would not explain why a's being F causes this particular instance of G-ness.[34]

If the causal relation between a's being F and a's being G consists in nothing over and above the existence of these two states of affairs, which is what the internal-relation theory implies, then that conjunctive state of affairs explains the existence of the causal connection N between them. This gets the direction of explanation backwards. For a's being G depends upon the existence of the connection N, not vice versa.[35] By contrast, if N is an external (hence real) relation, it is possible to understand how a's being F can necessitate a's being G in virtue of N(F, G), rather than the existence of the relation in this case being parasitic upon the existence of its relata.

A third difficulty for the internal-relation theory derives from the existence of defeasible ('oaken') laws. Defeasibility reflects the fact that causes can join together in indefinitely many ways, the outcome being a function of their joint operation. It seems that an external-relation theory can accommodate this fact rather naturally, if we think of the causal contribution of a component cause as a kind of force. Causal relations – forces – can be graded in terms of their strength and perhaps other features (e.g. direction). What is then required is an algebra that determines how forces combine, and laws specifying what effect a total force shall have. On such a combinatorial approach, a relatively small number of basic laws may be able to account for an indefinitely large number of possible multicomponent causal interactions.

If, on the other hand, causal relations are internal, this complexity must somehow be built into the structure of each of the universals joined by the causal web. Every lawful combination of causes, and their effects, will have to follow from the natures of the related universals. It is at best difficult to see how an internal-relation theory can provide for this without supposing universals to have tremendously complex natures. Nor, so far as I know, has anyone been able to show specifically how particular causal relations 'follow from' the natures of the universals they connect. This objection is, of course, not decisive.[36] But it does bring out a disadvantage of the theory.

The external-relation theory has disadvantages of its own. For one thing, it seems that this theory cannot avoid Platonism. Second, it is extremely difficult to see what light the external-relation theory can shed on the nature of the necessity (or nonaccidentality) that characterizes causal relations. This was the great strength of the internal-relations theory. If causal relations are not simply a consequence of the natures of universals, what determines that there must be these causal connections and not others? It is tempting to insist that causal relations are somehow necessitated by the natures of the universals they relate, but if they are something additional to these natures then how is this necessitation to be understood?[37]

Perhaps the only response an externalist can give to this question is to say that the necessity of causal relations is primitive and sui generis. Indeed, that is the best that I am able at present to do. This response is not very illuminating, but it may at least be true.

NOTES

1. Armstrong (1978), Tooley (1977), and Dretske (1977).
2. Direct awareness of nomic connections between universals is nevertheless possible 'in principle': see Armstrong (1984, pp. 267–8).
3. And including G. F. Stout, A. C. Ewing, Chris Swoyer, and Martin Tweedale.
4. Armstrong (1984, pp. 261–2). Here, Armstrong agrees with the claim – which I shall defend at some length – that a law "must embody a 'must' if it is to sustain counterfactuals". Yet, surprisingly, Armstrong makes no appeal to necessity when he argues (1983a, p. 103) that N(F, G) sustains counterfactuals. In a recently written reply to van Fraassen (Armstrong 199+b), he deliberately avoids the term 'necessitation' but appeals to our experience of pushes and pulls, in which 'the effect is experienced as *made to happen* by the cause' [Armstrong's emphasis].
5. Armstrong (1984, p. 267). Although Armstrong thinks that one could in principle be directly aware of the fact that such a relation obtains between universals – and hence be directly aware of the obtaining of a law – he thinks that, in fact, laws are always theoretical postulates for us. I shall return to this.
6. David Lewis (1983, p. 366) and Martin Tweedale (1984, pp. 185–6). For related arguments, see Carroll (1987).
7. This affirms the existence of the nomic relation N between universals F and G.
8. Armstrong comes very close to saying this, and being done with it (1983a, p. 92). But he is not quite done with it, for he proceeds to speculate about the connection between N and the experienced singular causal necessity in pushes and pulls.

9. The invocation of de dicto physical necessities (or of anything that entails these) would only serve to highlight what, it could be argued, is a basic problem of circularity in Armstrong's recent (1989a) treatment of logical possibility. The worry there is that Armstrong's analysis of logical possibility in terms of the ways in which particulars and properties could be combined presupposes the very notion of possibility it is intended to articulate. A plausible reply is that at least the idea of combinatorial possibility is philosophically transparent in a way that our pretheoretical concept of logical possibility is not, so a real gain has been posted. If, however, physical necessities – a distinct modal species – are permitted to enter this picture then certain logically possible combinations will not be genuinely possible, and this highlights the fact that neither species of possibility (logical or physical) has been genuinely eliminated in favor of nonmodal notions.

10. Somewhat different arguments to this effect have previously been offered by Swoyer (1982), Tweedale (1984), and Shalkowski (199+).

11. See Armstrong (1983a, p. 50; 1984, p. 261). Armstrong (1983a, p. 77) also suggests that laws must hold in virtue of the *nature* of the universals they connect.

12. Armstrong (199+a). Essentially the same argument is given by Armstrong (1983a, p. 103) with one difference: the counterfactual supposition that a is F is presumed not to give any reason to think that the 'F → G necessity' is destroyed.

13. Armstrong (1983a, Chapter 11).

14. Armstrong (1983a, pp. 78–80).

15. I now adopt, for purposes of exposition, the possible-worlds lingo. But, like Armstrong, I am no possible-worlds realist.

16. Armstrong (1983a, p. 79).

17. Armstrong (1983a, p. 77).

18. On this reading, Armstrong advocates an essentialism with respect to universals of an especially strong kind. But this clearly is not Armstrong's intention.

19. Thus, in U_2, the law that Fs have an 0.0001 probability of being a G is (for Aristotelians) only a 'potential law'.

20. I am inclined to argue on similar grounds that a universal no longer exists (on an Aristotelian account) when it is uninstantiated. But I do not need that further claim here. Armstrong mentions in passing (1983a, p. 164) that he takes both the past and the future to exist, on the grounds that there could not otherwise be relations between present states of affairs and past or future ones. All that is in fact required is the existence of the past. A relation between the present state of affairs and a future one need not be said to obtain until that future state comes to pass. But in any case, the existence of the past and the future would not affect the present point, which concerns the temporality of Aristotelian universals.

21. Also threatened is Armstrong's solution to the problem of induction. Armstrong considers the possibility that 'Fa necessitates Ga', 'Fb necessitates Gb', 'Fc necessitates Gc', etc. are singular states of affairs, and that the law that Fs are Gs is simply the 'sum' of these states. That conception of a law, he recognizes, is merely a variation on the Regularity theory, and it is too weak to solve the problem of induction – for what guarantee can the behaviour of a, b, and c provide that Fd will necessitate Gd? This worry is closely connected to Armstrong's worry that our conception of causation is compatible

with singularism. (See Armstrong 1983a, pp. 93–9 and 199+a). Our concept of cause – which is a concept of one state of affairs necessitating another – derives, according to Armstrong, from our perception of pushes and pulls. How can such single connections between states guarantee the presence of a law? Armstrong's way of surmounting the first of these problems it to understand laws in terms of a necessitation relation that holds *in virtue of the universals* involved, which must (as we saw) be 'the same' in each of their instantiations. The second problem, that of disarming singularism, can then be solved by means of a theoretical postulation of identity between the causal relation and the nomological one. (Because Armstrong holds that we are directly acquainted with instances of the causal relation, this identification is threatened by Kripke's 1972 analogous arguments against the identification of pains with brain states. But Armstrong 1983b, pp. 65–70 finds Kripke's argument unconvincing.) If, however, the existence of a contingent relation between universals at one time is compatible with the nonexistence of that relation at another, then Armstrong's response to both singularism and the problem of induction fails. The upshot of this is that these problems (and that of explaining why laws support counterfactuals) can be solved only by invoking both the unity of universals and the necessity of the relation N. (A general solution to the problem of induction requires much more than this, of course.)

It should be noted, parenthetically, that the existence of singularist causal relations would pose a difficulty, or at least a complication, for Armstrong's reliabilist account of noninferentially justified belief. According to that account, a noninferentially justified belief is justified if the having of that belief is a reliable indicator of the truth of the belief. Reliability requires that there be a nomological connection of a suitable sort between the having of a true belief and the state of affairs in virtue of which that belief is true. Suppose that a present state of affairs causes my belief that that state of affairs obtains. Suppose further that this is a case of singularist causation, i.e. the causal relation in question is an instance of no law. Then the belief that I have is not reliably acquired, on Armstrong's definition of reliability. Moreover, I do not see how the notion of reliability can be broadened so as to enable us to regard such a case of belief acquisition as reliable. It would be a pious hope that law reigns supreme in the operation of human sensory faculties.

22. For familiar arguments of this kind, and Armstrong's responses to them, see Tooley (1977), Tweedale (1984, Section II), Armstrong (1983a, Chapter 8), and Armstrong (1984, pp. 257–8).
23. Or composed of constituent universals that are also uninstantiated.
24. Tooley's case is one in which the new universal never is instantiated, though it might have been. This obviates the possible objection that a universal exists 'always' if it is ever instantiated.
25. Armstrong (1983a, pp. 123–7).
26. I do not accept Armstrong's theory of possibility, but here I am arguing ad hominem.
27. The sort of Platonism demanded by these arguments is not promiscuous. Promiscuous Platonism embraces every universal whose existence is logically possible. Parsimonious Platonism – the kind to which I subscribe – posits only those uninstantiated universals (if any) required to round out the system of natural laws. Other systems of universals may be logically possible, but we have no reason to suppose that they exist.

28. Mellor (1980, pp. 113–14). But see Lewis (1973, pp. 24–6).
29. For a recent example, see Swoyer (1982). Tweedale (1984) is less explicit, but seems also to hold this view.
30. Or, on some versions, between natural kinds.
31. That is, that being F confers a probability of 0.001 of being G.
32. I am not entirely certain that Armstrong would accept this advantage of the internal-relation theory; see Armstrong (1983, pp. 167–8). But his argument there seems to depend on the notion that N is an external relation.
33. Strictly speaking, one should distinguish the causal relation that obtains between events or states of affairs from the relation between universals upon which it depends. For simplicity, I am calling both relations causal.
34. There is an asymmetry in the relation *'being darker than'* that holds between red and pink. This red thing is darker than that pink one, but it is also darker than *every* pink thing.
35. A possible response to this objection would be to build into N a spatiotemporal relation which, given an instance of F, would serve to specify to which instance of G it was causally related. But this move will not help if two instances of G, independently caused, can coexist at the same spatiotemporal location – for then what determines which of these instances of G was produced by which antecedent state of affairs? Moreover, cases of this sort arguably occur, since two bosons can occupy the same spatiotemporal region.
36. The number 1 has little internal complexity, I will grant, yet bears an infinity of internal relations to the other numbers. The internal relations of extensive qualities like those between lengths can be parsimoniously explained by taking advantage of their mappability onto the numbers. If causal relations could be reduced to the operation of a single fundamental force, I suppose a similar strategy could be applied to them.
37. The difficulties we face here are perhaps not surprising. A natural way to explore the problem would be to find analogies and disanalogies to causal necessitation. But it is difficult to find clear cases of (other) necessary relations between universals that are not internal relations. It is equally difficult to find, by way of contrast, contingent (pure) relations between universals. I am not convinced there are any relations of either sort.

REFERENCES

Armstrong, D. M. 1978. *Universals and Scientific Realism:* vol. 2, *A Theory of Universals* (Cambridge University Press).
1983a. *What is a Law of Nature?* (Cambridge University Press).
1983b. 'Recent Work on the Relation of Mind and Brain'. In *Contemporary Philosophy: a New Survey,* vol. 4, *Philosophy of Mind,* ed. G. Fløistad (The Hague: Nijhoff), pp. 45–79.
1984. 'Replies'. In Bogdan (1984), pp. 225–69.
1989a. *A Combinatorial Theory of Possibility* (Cambridge University Press).
199+a. 'Singular Causation and Laws of Nature'.
199+b. 'The Identification Problem and the Inference Problem', *Philosophy and Phenomenological Research.*
Bogdan, Radu J. (ed.) 1984. *D. M. Armstrong, Profiles,* vol. 4 (Dordrecht: Reidel).

Carroll, John W. 1987. 'Ontology and the Laws of Nature', *Australasian Journal of Philosophy* 65: 261–76.

Dretske, Fred I. 1977. 'Laws of Nature', *Philosophy of Science* 44: 248–68.

Kripke, Saul. 1972. 'Naming and Necessity'. In *Semantics of Natural Language*, ed. Donald Davidson and Gilbert Harman (Dordrecht: Reidel), pp. 253–355. Reprinted as a separate volume (Cambridge, MA: Harvard University Press, 1980).

Lewis, David, 1973. *Counterfactuals* (Cambridge, MA: Harvard University Press).

    1983b. 'New Work for a Theory of Universals', *Australasian Journal of Philosophy* 61: 343–77.

Mellor, D. H. 1980. 'Necessities and Universals in Natural Laws', *Science, Belief and Behaviour: Essays in Honour of R. B. Braithwaite*, ed. D. H. Mellor (Cambridge University Press).

Shalkowski, Scott A. 199+. 'Supervenience and Causal Necessity', *Synthese*.

Swoyer, Chris, 1982. 'The Nature of Natural Laws', *Australasian Journal of Philosophy* 60: 203–23.

Tooley, Michael. 1977. 'The Nature of Laws', *Canadian Journal of Philosophy* 7: 667–98.

Tweedale, Martin. 1984. 'Determinable and Substantival Universals'. In Bogdan (1984), pp. 171–89.

Reply to Fales

D. M. ARMSTRONG

Evan Fales teaches at the University of Iowa in Iowa City. Under the leadership of Gustav Bergmann that philosophy department built up a tradition of *unembarrassed* ontological reflection, a tradition that continues to this day. For many years that meant virtual isolation inside the tradition of analytic philosophy, a very honourable isolation as I see it. Now the situation has changed, not quite so fast and dramatically as the change that led to the fall of the Berlin Wall, but dramatically enough. Fales was not trained in Iowa, but it is clear that he feels at home in its traditions. He and I have met, in Iowa and in London, and have corresponded, finding much to agree and to argue about. I salute him as one more manifestation of what shows promise of being 'the ontological turn'.

Fales agrees with me that laws of nature are relations between universals. But he thinks that these relations hold of necessity, while I think that they are contingent. His vigorous but fair criticism, based on his thorough grasp of my position, has made me think hard.

1. Sustaining Counterfactuals

First there is the question of whether, on my view, I can explain why laws 'sustain counterfactuals'. Fales does not think that I can. Despite what I have said earlier, some of which Fales recapitulates, I do not in the course of my explanation wish to appeal to any 'contingent necessity' that laws may or may not have. I think that there is some hard-to-capture necessity about causality, and I think that this or some analagous necessity is involved in laws. But my present idea is that the sustaining of counterfactuals does not demand this necessity as a premiss.

On my view, the law is an atomic or, more strictly, a unitary state of affairs.[1] (I am of course talking about the entity, not the statement that it obtains; the law is a relationship holding between universals.) It is to this unitary characteristic that I appeal in considering the sustaining of counterfactuals. When we contemplate the counterfactual possibility of an instantiation of the antecedent universal, we do not conceive that the law is changed in any way. Hence we see that the consequent universal will be instantiated also.

I think that Fales makes two responses to this. The first of these is that conceiving the law as unchanged, holding it fixed, is mere convention. The law may be a unitary thing, but it is contingent on my account. So why cannot it be thought away or modified, in which case the counterfactual is not sustained? The second response is that what is sauce for the goose is sauce for the gander. If the Armstrong maneuver is any good, why cannot the Regularity theorist take advantage of it and hold his universally quantified proposition fixed? Good questions both.

Let me begin with the second, ad hominem, objection. My answer to this is that the Regularity theorist can keep his version of the law fixed in one way but not in another. It is very significant that it is so natural for him to put his position in terms of a true proposition. He keeps that *semantically* fixed, so perhaps one can say that he keeps the truth condition for the law fixed. But he does not keep the law *ontologically* fixed; he does not keep the truth-maker fixed. As John Bacon has put it in comment, unlike the 'direct' relation between universals, the universal generalization is about the extensions of these universals. These extensions will differ 'from world to world'. The Regularity theorist's truth-maker is therefore a molecular state of affairs, one which he has, in the imagined case, enlarged.

But why does that matter? I think that John Mackie (1966) clearly perceived the problem. A new F, say, has been imagined. But given the Regularity theory, which Mackie held to, what reason is there to think that it, like the actual Fs, will be G? Mackie proposed an ingenious solution. The one who puts forward the counterfactual is in imagination making an inductive inference from the known Fs which are, let us say, all Gs, to the 'unobserved' F which is in all inductive probability a G. Mackie recognized that his solution depended on a solution to the problem of induction *for a Regularity theory*. But I maintain (1983a, Chapter 4, Section 5) that a Regularity theory cannot solve the problem of induction and that in any case Mackie's solution faces certain internal difficulties (Armstrong 1983a, Chapter 4, Section 4). It seems to me that Fales could accept that the Regularity theory had a special difficulty here, though he might not think that it was of much importance in the light of his first objection which, if good, holds against all theories that make laws of nature contingent.

What, then, of this first objection? If laws are not necessary, is not our holding them fixed in reasoning about counterfactual situations quite arbitrary or conventional? Yet does this not conflict with our strong intuition that it is an objective matter that certain counterfactuals, at least, are definitely true or definitely false?

The first thing to wonder about is whether certain nomic counterfactuals do not constitute an ad hominem argument against Fales. There are *counterlegals,* where in the antecedent a law is thought away or in some way altered. Admittedly, these are an obscure and little-investigated species of counterfactual, but scientists and others are to be found proposing that certain statements of this sort are true. Yet for Fales, with his view that laws are metaphysically necessary, these statements have metaphysically impossible antecedents. Fales cannot explain their truth in the way that he explains the truth of more standard counterfactuals. This begins to cast a little doubt on the latter explanation.

To reply more directly to Fales: I simply accept that in standard counterfactuals there is something conventional in our keeping laws 'fixed'. It is a very deep convention, but it is not something absolutely forced upon us. The way the world works, its laws, must have overwhelming importance for creatures in the world. Biologically speaking, the main reason for the existence of conditional thinking is its role in planning. And in planning, the laws of the world, so far as we know them, must be assumed to be unchanged. This, I think, is the reason why, in a possible-world treatment of counterfactuals, resemblance in laws is taken as a major respect of resemblance.

There is no doubt that if this semiconventional holding fixed of laws is routinely involved, then counterfactual discourse is in a measure second-grade discourse. But I think that there is already good reason to take such a view. I discuss the matter a little further in my reply to Smart (Chapter 7 in this volume), where I suggest that there is reason to think that, although truth in general is not to be identified with warranted assertability, truth for counterfactuals is no more than warranted assertability. (In passing, if this is correct then the attempt to found causality on counterfactuality builds on sand.) However, it still seems that – for what it is worth – both my view and Fales's view can explain the assertability of counterfactuals, while a Regularity theory of law has difficulty. This is because for that theory the law in a counterfactual situation must literally be taken as an expanded entity, raising the question by what warrant it is asserted that the imagined case behaves like actual cases.

2. Can Laws Change?

I next consider the question of the unchangeability of laws when they are conceived of as relations between universals. Fales denies that there is any necessity for such unchangeability.

Let us begin by discussing the apparently unrelated matter of the identity of temporal objects over time. Consider a stone today and that stone yesterday. Although, by hypothesis, it is 'the very same stone', this assertion of identity raises certain problems. In particular, the stone yesterday will have certain properties that the stone today lacks and vice versa. For instance, the temperatures of the stone at the two times may be incompatible with each other. But how is this possible if what we are dealing with is the identical subject of predication? (Fales seems insensitive to the problem when he remarks that 'for temporal beings, sameness is not destroyed by changes in contingent properties'.) There are various solutions on offer. One is to argue that the real properties involved are temperatures-at-times. Different temperatures at different times are not incompatible properties. Those like Fales and myself, who take the ontologically basic properties to be universals, will not be much attracted to such a view. Another solution is to take temperatures to be relations that hold between the stone and different times. The clumsiness of such a view is evident enough. Some of us react by introducing the notion of temporal parts and arguing that the temperatures, potentially incompatible, are not actually incompatible because they qualify different parts of the stone.

A fourth reaction, the one we are interested in here, is to partition things that exist through time into two classes. Some things – genuine atoms and souls were the traditional examples – are in their nature completely unchanging; only their environment changes. As a result, a problem such as that of the incompatible temperatures cannot arise for these things. These things are strictly identical over time. Other things, such as stones, have only what Bishop Butler called a 'loose and popular' identity over time. (Actually, I believe that reasonably clear-cut rules can be given for this 'identity'. But it is not the notion of identity for which the logicians have laid down the axioms of identity. See my reply to Lewis in Chapter 2 of this volume.)

Now whatever we say about atoms and souls, it is clear that it is of the essence of universals that they are of their own nature completely unchanging. They are strictly identical over time (and space) if anything is.

Let us now consider a relation that holds between two universals. Let it be a relation that depends upon nothing else except those two universals. This does not mean that the relation must be an internal relation, existing superveniently if the terms exist. But it does mean that the relation does not involve any third or further term, overtly or covertly. Under these circumstances, I suggest, it is not possible that the relation could change over time (or place). Such 'change' would involve the two universals, the two identical things, both having and lacking one and the same relation to each other. But the relation that I (and Fales) postulate to explain the nature of laws of nature is of this strict two-term sort.

It must be admitted that a less 'powerful' relation between universals seems conceivable, one which links the universals in some polyadic relation involving particular times and places (semistrong laws we could call them). This relation could change. Furthermore, the observed uniformity of nature, from which the abductive argument to connections of universals begins, could be hypothesized to be such a mere local uniformity. But once we admit such an hypothesis, we must also consider seriously the hypothesis that the observed uniformity is a mere 'cosmic coincidence' not based on genuine law at all. I take it, however, that we are entitled to dismiss all these pussy-footing hypotheses. The most I will concede is that the question why, nevertheless, we are entitled to assume that the world involves 'strong' laws is a little delicate. But if there are such laws then, it seems to me, the relations of universals involved, even though contingent and so changeable in 'another possible world', are not subject to intraworld change.

3. Uninstantiated Universals

Fales also argues for uninstantiated universals, although, like Tooley, it is (in Fales's phrase) a parsimonious rather than a promiscuous Platonism that he accepts. David Lewis would call it a sparse theory of uninstantiated universals. Only those uninstantiated universals are postulated that are required to round out the system of natural laws. Fales first argues that an Aristotelian realism about universals like mine is committed to the view that universals exist in time. He then says that when a universal comes to be instantiated for the first time – let it be a simple property and let there be a causal law responsible for the instantiation – I ought to agree that before the instantiation the universal did not exist. But then, he continues, the relevant law linking the predetermining universals with the new universal must already exist if the predetermining ones are to act. Yet by hypothesis the new universal does not exist.

I am not very happy about saying that in these circumstances the universal in question does not exist. For me the existential quantifier ranges over past, present and future. Existence is not confined to the present, or to the present together with the past. Still, I can see the force in saying that in the given circumstances the first instantiation of a universal is brought into existence, and so that, in a sense, the universal itself is brought into existence. But cannot it be said that the law and the 'new universal' come into existence at the same instant? It may be added that I hold that laws have no existence outside their instantiations, and that the law is a universal itself, complete in each instantiation. Unless the instantiations of a law stretch back forever, a law must have a first time of instantiation. At that first time both universal and law must 'come into existence' together.

What remains of Fales's case for uninstantiated universals depends upon his endorsement of an important argument of Tooley's. Tooley envisages a possible world in which we would have good reasons, based on parallel cases, to believe that a wholly new universal would emerge in certain circumstances, nomically possible circumstances that never in fact occur at any time at all in the history of that world. Fales gives a more realistic version of Tooley's case. In answer, I allow the truth of the counterfactual that if, say, circumstances P & Q & R were to occur then a wholly new property would be instantiated. At the same time I deny that there *exists* some determinate property that is the property in question. In effect, I concede that the counterfactual has warranted assertibility but deny that there is such an entity as the property in question to which the principle 'to be is to be determinate' can then be applied (see Section 1 of this reply). Fales finds this response 'uncomfortable'. Maybe so. But I think it is less uncomfortable than postulating uninstantiated universals.

It should be noticed, however, that there is a third treatment possible of the Tooley case. This is the view held by C. B. Martin (see Chapter 8 of this volume) that associated with categorical properties we should admit irreducible powers, powers that might never be manifested. The idea would be that properties P, Q and R are such that, if co-instantiated, they have the power to produce a certain property never instantiated at any other time or place. For myself, while hoping to avoid postulating such irreducible powers, I should prefer this account of the Tooley case to that preferred by Tooley himself and Fales. My reason is that the powers would be part of the spacetime framework, while uninstantiated universals would not be.

Fales also uses a variant of Tooley's case. It involves a 'contracted' world, one lacking what is found in the actual world: a simple property

F that is the only producer of property G. He then considers a counter-factual:

(8)   If there had been any Fs, there would have been Gs.

Concerning this case, I agree that if it was a law in the actual world that Fs are Gs then one would see the force in asserting the counterfactual. But Fales thinks that I am committed to saying that (8) is no more than vacuously true. (His point turns on an ad hominem. Given my combina-torial theory of possibility, F becomes an 'alien' universal and such uni-versals, I hold, though thinkable, are not genuinely possible. So for me the antecedent of (8) is impossible.) But if counterfactuals have no better than warranted assertability, it would seem that the law connecting Fs and Gs in the actual world might serve as sufficient ground for asserting (8) in the contracted world.

4. Laws Necessary but External?

Fales holds both that laws of nature are relations between universals and that they hold of necessity. But, although finally undecided, he feels the attraction of the view that these necessary relations are external rather than internal. He offers some interesting arguments against the internal view, at any rate on the orthodox assumption that internal relations in-volve nothing more than the related universals.

His first objection, from the direct perception of pushes and pulls on our bodies (a premiss that both Fales and I hold to, perhaps against the philosophical world), seems to have phenomenological weight. The sec-ond – that the existence of the (token) effect depends on the existence of the token cause together with the connection between the universals, rather than the connection depending on the nature of the token cause and token effect – is ingenious, and deserves attention. I am distinctly dubious about the third objection: that in the case of defeasible laws an unacceptable complexity will have to be built into the universals involved in order to sustain the internal relation. Here I would quote Fales against himself. A little earlier in his argument he states, very rightly I think, that 'we can use predicates whose meaning we comprehend to designate uni-versals whose natures we fail to fathom with the completeness required to discern nomological relations'.

Finally, what should we say about Fales's own suggestion (tentative, he has informed me) that the nomic relation is necessary but external? It would be incompatible with the Humean principle that there can be no necessary connection between distinct existences. That principle, in turn, I would derive from Combinatorialism about possibility. This is for me an argument against Fales. But, unfortunately, it is not an argument for him, or for many others.

NOTE

1. In the past I have said 'atomic'. But John Bacon has pointed out to me that I am happy to allow a conjunctive universal such as F & G as, say, the antecedent term of a law, thus allowing molecular properties as terms of laws. While this is true, a law for me always connects an 'antecedent' universal with a 'consequent' universal to give a single state of affairs. For me, a conjunction of such states of affairs is not a law but a mere conjunction of laws.

REFERENCES

Armstrong, D. M. 1983a. *What is a Law of Nature?* (Cambridge University Press).
Mackie, J. L. 1966. 'Counterfactuals and Causal Laws'. In *Analytical Philosophy, First Series,* ed. R. J. Butler (Oxford: Blackwell), pp. 66–80.

7

Laws of Nature as a Species of Regularities

J. J. C. SMART

In a review in the *Times Literary Supplement* (Armstrong 1989c) of a book by Galen Strawson (1989), David Armstrong refers to the regularity theory of laws of nature as 'a jejune and silly theory', and says that he is pleased to discover from Strawson's book that Hume did not after all hold such a theory. Strawson's book is undoubtedly impressive both as original philosophy and as scholarly commentary on Hume. I am myself not a Hume scholar, nor for that matter a scholar of any other historic figure, but for what it is worth, and speaking as at any rate a lover of Hume's writings, let me say that I still wonder whether when Hume appears to be talking of hidden powers or natural necessities he may merely be talking a bit loosely, and be talking of unobserved regularities at a submicroscopic level. Be that as it may, I do not think that it is jejune or silly to hold a regularity theory, as there are strong intellectual pressures in favour of it. In this essay I cannot deal in detail with all the objections that have been raised against the regularity theory by Armstrong, Michael Tooley, Galen Strawson and others, but I shall try to indicate how I think that we might defend a regularity theory, or some modification of it on lines suggested by F. P. Ramsey (1931) and David Lewis (1973, pp. 73–5).

Sometimes 'law' is used to mean a sentence or proposition, as in 'Newton's laws of motion' or 'Ohm's law'. By philosophers it is often used putatively to refer to something nonlinguistic and nonpropositional, such as a regularity or a relation between universals. I shall mainly follow the latter usage, and for the first usage I shall talk of 'law statements'. I shall also use a hybrid usage, because though I hold that all laws are regularities, I also hold that which regularities are laws depends on which statements are law statements. Roughly, laws are objective regularities but with a whiff of the epistemological.

I am grateful to David Armstrong, John Clendinnen, Brian Ellis, John Forge, Peter Forrest, Ian Hinckfuss, Peter Menzies, Philip Pettit and Michael Tooley, who kindly read and commented on an earlier draft of this paper.

One of my agreements with Armstrong is that I am willing to countenance the existence of something like his (or Tooley's or Dretske's) universals, namely physical properties. These must be sharply distinguished
from what Quine (1960) calls 'attributes'. They are posited entities, unin-
fected by dubious notions of 'meaning'. Let me digress for a moment.

I hold that all science and metaphysics should be expressible in an extensional language, on the lines of Quinean 'canonical notation' (Quine
1960). Thus we should eschew primitive modal operators, and avoid talk
of possible worlds other than the actual world. Quinean canonical notation contains no expressions for attributes and propositions. This is
because of Quine's suspicion of the notions of meaning and synonymy.
Thus an attribute would correspond to a class of synonymous predicates.
Now if a property is an attribute, we should not allow talk of properties in canonical notation. However, physicists do not use the word 'property' in this dubious way. They think of properties as postulated entities.
The postulation of properties seems to be an ongoing feature of physics.
Consider some of the more exotic ones postulated in recent years such
as 'charm' and 'colour', right down to more familiar ones such as spin,
charge and mass, and the hoary old ones, length and period of time.

To describe metrical properties it at first sight seems that we need 'impure numbers', for example 2 centimetres, 4 grams, 5 e.s.u. For canonical notation Quine uses a device due to Carnap for removing these so
that the equations found in the laws of physics use concepts only of pure
mathematics: the physics comes from their conjunction with surrounding physical chitchat (Quine 1960, pp. 244–5). Thus, instead of saying
that something is 5 cm in length we can say it has-a-length-in-centimetres
of 5. (Analogously we can get rid of impure vectors, tensors, functions,
etc.) A problem here is that it seems to leave us with an infinity of structureless predicates. Surely 'has-a-length-in-centimetres of' has a structure,
rather similar to that of 'has-a-mass-in-grams of'. Indeed, such structure
is required on usual linguistic theories which require that language have a
recursive structure. If we postulate properties we can recover the structure. Thus 'This has-a-length-in-centimetres-of 5' comes out as 'This has
(length, standard cm, 5)', where 'has' here is a triadic predicate. Here it
is the determinable quantity 'length' that is mentioned.

Most of the laws of physics are expressed by means of differential equations. So we need infinite sets of numbers, vectors, tensors or whatever.
As Quine (1971) has clearly pointed out, differentiation is an operation
on functions. Thus $(d/dx)\sin x = \cos x$ is more perspicuously written
$D(\lambda x)\sin x = (\lambda x)\cos x$. It is interesting to ask how we should read differential equations occurring in physics. To take a very simple case of

what is only approximately a law, how would we understand '$d^2s/dt^2 = g$', say? We could take it as $D^2(\lambda t)s = (\lambda t)g$, but I think that it is more natural here to take 'd^2s/dt^2' as referring to the *values* of $D^2(\lambda t)s$ for all corresponding ts. Of course, the whole thing becomes much more complicated for interesting cases, such as that of Maxwell's equations. Still, if sets are in our ontology then we are all right. (So also if a more nominalistic philosophy of mathematics could otherwise give us the advantages given to us by set theory.[1]) Differentiation can be extended to differentiation of functions of vectors, tensors, and so on. For example, a vector in n-dimensional space can be treated as an ordered n-tuple of real numbers.

A worrying problem is the arbitrariness of units, as in the case of length in centimetres. Also '$\frac{1}{2}$' for spin looks arbitrary. In many cases we can look forward to a physics in which units are related to physically significant ratios.

If this difficulty can be overcome, there need be no Quinean objection to the postulation of properties. They are not like the bad old 'attributes' whose postulation arises from the notion of meaning. They are postulated for purely physical reasons. We need the new predicate 'has', but this too has nothing to do with misconceptions about meaning. Note that I do not suppose that any property (dyadic, triadic or whatever) corresponds to the 'has'. To suppose such would be to invite infinite regress, which might or might not be harmless. However, postulation of properties should come from science (ultimately, I think, from physics) and not from semantics.

Now physical properties are perhaps the same as Armstrong's universals.[2] If they are then there is a trivial sense in which a law of nature expresses a relation between universals. Thus, suppose that I say that Maxwell's equations (together with associated chat) express a certain relation between various properties, electric current strength, electric field strength, magnetic field strength and positions in space and time. Most of the properties are in fact vector properties; it all gets quite complicated. In fact, the law is stated as saying that these properties are related to one another in such a way that a conjunction of differential equations is true. It is a far cry from Armstrong's typical example of '$(x)(Fx \supset Gx)$', and it suggests that we need a full mathematical ontology. Nevertheless, if we think of Maxwell's law (the law expressed by the conjunction of Maxwell's equations together with accompanying discussion) as a regularity, we can still say that it consists of a relation between properties as well as certain mathematical objects – that is, the relation such that the statement of regularity is true.

Armstrong (1983a, p. 225) is of course aware that it is not in this trivial sense that he asserts that laws are relations between universals. The question is how to distinguish the stronger sort of relation between universals from the relatively trivial sort. Armstrong holds that a law is a contingently necessary relation. He claims to give content to this notion from such things as our experience of pressure on our body and of our experience of the successful operation of our will. This seems to me to be unconvincing.

Moreover, if the relation between universals that constitutes a law is not defined in the trivial way, then as Lewis (1983b) and Bas van Fraassen (1989) have argued, it cannot be a logical deduction from the law statement that the associated regularity statement follows – for example, that '$(x)Fx \supset Gx$' follows from '$N(F, G)$', where 'N' is the necessitation predicate. Note that here 'F' and 'G' are ambiguous: in one context they are dummy predicates, in another dummy names of universals. Replies to some of these criticisms may be found in Armstrong (199+b).

However, it is not my purpose here to argue against Armstrong's theory of laws. I confess that there seems to me to be difficulty for all theories of laws and that the difficulties for Armstrong's may indeed be less than those for any other, and it must remain an important contender in the field. My main purpose here is to give some sort of regularity theory a run for its money.

I must make it clear that I do not restrict regularities to Humean regularities of succession. Nor do I expect regularities to be much on the observational level. The real regularities are likely to be found on the deeper levels of physics and cosmology, where perhaps the difference between general law and particular but cosmic fact becomes unclear. Some regularities may be regularities of coexistence, and some may be of the topology of spacetime. It is extensionality without recourse to possible worlds that I prize in regularity theories. Of course, I have conceded that Armstrong's theory is extensional too, but I also wish to avoid his unanalyzed necessity relations between universals. However, I do not wish to rule out the possibility that a fully worked-out regularity theory of the sort that I propose may end up by being not all that different from a fully worked-out Armstrong type theory.

The regularity theorist must allow that not all regularities are laws. Such a theorist thus has a problem analogous to that of Armstrong's need to distinguish the trivial and nontrivial sense in which laws are relations between universals. I do not wish to define laws merely as regularities; I concede that many regularities are not laws. The ones that are not laws may be called 'accidental' regularities. I also concede that laws support counterfactuals whereas accidental ones do not. An opponent of the regularity theory may not think this much of a concession when I go on to say that I already need a thickened notion of 'law' in order to make the distinction between accidental and nonaccidental regularities, and that my account of counterfactuals is likely to be regarded as a rather emasculated one. Naturally I need to thicken the notion of 'law' in a way that remains within the spirit of a regularity theory. My way of doing this may be seen as a slight modification of the Ramsey–Lewis theory already mentioned, with a bit of pacificatory talk thrown in.

I require a metaphysical postulate of the simplicity of the universe. It is necessary to assign this a positive probability. Such an assignment cannot be validated because all else depends on it, but perhaps it can be vindicated.[3] The more we find simplicities (including regularities and symmetries), the more faith we come to have in the metaphysical postulate. I hold a coherence theory of warranted assertability (though emphatically not of truth). Explanation is a matter of fitting a proposition into our web of belief,[4] and the so-called argument to the best explanation is best thought of as the accepting of propositions that best fit into our web, the fitting sometimes also requiring changes in various strands of that web. We usually modify the web of belief by choosing the simplest system that includes the observational facts, though sometimes we keep the web and explain away some of the observations. This inclusion of observation statements is because their (usual) reliability is itself part of our web. We now believe this because of our knowledge of the physiology of vision and also from evolutionary considerations, so giving weight in assessing coherence to observation statements is part of coherence itself.[5] Thus the search for coherence leads to the continual expansion (as well as modification) of the web (Smart 1989). We of course prize coherence because we believe it to be a guide to truth. This depends on the metaphysical postulate of simplicity. What is needed to make this rather vague and metaphysical description respectable is a Bayesian theory of how the various strands of the web get modified, but the task is beyond my own powers. But though my characterization of a coherence theory of warranted belief may be all too vague, sketchy and metaphorical, I hope that it is neither 'jejune' nor 'silly' and that it can be used in my attempt to defend regularity theory itself against the application of these epithets.

We are already innately programmed, as a result of evolution, to look out for regularities. So our web of belief starts building up before there is any question of whether regularities depend on necessities or any question of justifying induction. As we find more regularities (also, of course, nonregularities) and as we come to philosophizing, our postulate of a simple and regular universe gets some prior probability. Nevertheless, I think that this is not enough to validate induction. The best we can hope for is vindication.

It is impossible in a short essay to comment on all of the arguments put forward by Armstrong, Tooley, Galen Strawson and others against the regularity theory. I shall select a few apparently very strong arguments, and will suggest some replies.

One argument is that if a regularity were not necessary (in some strong sense of this word) then it would be infinitely improbable. Galen Strawson (1989, p. 24) has illustrated this by comparison with the improbability that a random number generator should continue new elements of some simple numerical sequence.[6]

Strawson's example is rhetorically very powerful and is intellectually challenging. Nevertheless, I think that the case of ordinary induction to natural regularities is different. For one thing, argument to the best explanation (or best fitting into our web of belief) is holistic. Even neglecting this, the aforementioned metaphysical postulate that the structure of the universe is simple allows some justification of Bayesian induction to regularities. If we knew that a simple finite sequence 1, 2, 4, 8, 16 had been generated by a random number generator, we would take this to be a coincidence and would not expect the next number to be 32. In an actual case we might take the sequence as evidence that the so-called random number generator was not really a random number generator. Certainly, if it went on to give 2^{i-1} for every ith item up to 2^{100}, I'd be quite sure that the supposed random number generator had something fishy about it and was not a real random number generator at all. Or, alternatively, I'd think that I was dreaming or mad: perhaps I would consult a psychiatrist. It might even be (though heaven forbid!) that I'd desperately try to reconstruct some sort of web of belief by becoming superstitious or something like that. The more sensible reaction would not show that I was not at bottom a regularity theorist. Rather, it would be due to the fact that the good regularities in which I believe are of cosmic import, not generalizations about complex pieces of machinery such as random number generators – or television receivers, say. The roughly regular behaviour of television receivers is explained by reference to very special laws of physics, together with the 'natural history' ('artificial' history?) of the apparatus.

A defender of Strawson's argument might reply that what I have just said begs the question. For if the physical laws that are used to explain the behaviour of a television receiver or a random number generator are mere regularities, then we have no reason to predict their future behaviour. Well, I agree that this is the nub of the problem, but the circuitous return to it, via the story of the random number generator, shows the merely rhetorical force of the story. (Not that I want entirely to disparage the use of rhetoric in philosophy.)

The regularity theorist must assume that the world is simple, in that it contains regularities possibly at some rather deep level. I suggest that such an assumption, if given a finite probability however small, may gain in probability as a result of our success in the past in finding regularities and may be still more augmented by future success. Of course, a philosophical sceptic may always doubt whether even the best-tested regularity will continue in the future. Nevertheless, such a failure to continue would seem an arbitrary occurrence and contrary to the assumption of simplicity. This assumption of simplicity becomes part of our holistic web of belief. I do not mean, of course, that in the beginning, in its little way, a baby explicitly makes a metaphysical assumption. It is enough that a disposition to look out for and to recognize regularities is programmed into it by evolution by natural selection. Rational justification (or perhaps only vindication) can come later after the web of belief has been sufficiently developed.

Evolution, I have said, has caused us to be innately disposed to believe in such regularities. Sometimes this leads us to see regularities when there are none. Should we worry about the possibility that our postulate of simplicity comes from sheer prejudice? There could be an evolutionary explanation for such prejudice. Thus it is better for an animal to have programmed into it the false proposition that all snakes are dangerous than it is to have programmed into it the true proposition that certain species of snakes are dangerous; by the time the animal had decided whether a given snake was dangerous it might have been bitten. There are also experiments by psychologists which purport to lay bare our propensity to impose a spurious order on what is truly chaotic, as when we claim to discern patterns in ink blots. None of this goes against the proposition that our prejudice in favour of regularity starts us off on the road to a more justified belief in regularity.[7] Armstrong, Tooley and Strawson all think that if the regularity theory were correct then induction to regularity would be unjustified, but I have tried to indicate how such induction to regularities might be possible on a coherence and Bayesian theory of warranted assertability. Indeed, since Strawson's necessities and Armstrong's or Tooley's relations between universals are supposed to imply regularities, there is a puzzle for them as to how they could be more fully justified. I do not say, however, that they would have no answer to this, as I have had a similar problem in controversy with van Fraassen over scientific realism (van Fraassen 1980, Chapter 7; Smart 1985; van Fraassen 1989, pp. 147–8).

In connection with our just-mentioned propensity to see regularity where there may be none, one might raise the question of whether the world might at bottom be entirely chaotic. If the universe is infinite it will by chance contain regions that apparently are regular, just as 1, 2, 4, 8, 16, 32 will appear somewhere in an infinite sequence of random numbers. Moreover, chaos theory has led to a realization of the way in which patterns appear that are very like (though not entirely like) patterns we admire in the world – for example of flowers, mountains, eroded deserts and clouds. So in this case there is regularity after all. Even if we allowed indeterministic processes, we cannot envisage complete chaos. Imagine a world of Newtonian atoms moving about and sometimes colliding, more often missing each other, in a way which is completely random. Still, we've just envisaged them as atoms: there must be some laws or similarities at bottom. Complete chaos seems not to be describable. The most we can envisage in any even minimally concrete way is a limited chaos. Still, it is a chilling thought that the regularity we see around us in nature might be a merely chance episode in a universal – even if, in a sense, limited – total chaos.

If this worrying thought were correct, nothing (or next to nothing) would require explanation.[8] Now some of the best explanations are in fact a demonstration that no explanation is required. Consider Galileo's demonstration that acceleration of bodies towards the earth is independent of mass (assuming that air resistance can be neglected), and that Aristotle was wrong in thinking that heavy bodies accelerate more than light bodies (Butterfield 1949, pp. 70–1; Smart 1950). If Aristotle were correct, two tiles glued together or perhaps connected only by a spider's thread should accelerate faster than two just touching one another. This would require explanation. On Galileo's theory there would be nothing to explain – no mysterious efficacies of spider threads, for example.

If the notion of an infinite and entirely chaotic world made sense, the hypothesis that we are in a region of fortuitous pseudo-regularity might be the best and ultimate explanation. I have shed doubts on whether the notion of complete chaos makes sense. One might ask, as a regularity theorist, why are there any regularities at all? After all, although a regularity theorist must hold that regularities may depend on deeper regularities, ultimately the best that could ever happen is to end up with regularities. (Maybe beautiful, simple and symmetrical ones.) For the regularity theorist the question 'Why are there regularities at all?' is self-defeating, and yet sometimes it carries an aura of profundity, just as 'Why is there anything at all?' does. (After all, the simplest universe is the null universe, so it is a mystery why there is anything at all. Theism will not help, because the child's question 'Who made God?' comes up.)

After these chilling speculations, the regularity theory of laws does not in itself seem too threatening. But will it really do? I have discussed Strawson's argument from the analogy of the random number generator. What about the objection that regularity theorists cannot explain why laws support counterfactual conditionals? It seems to me that if we have the right account of counterfactuals then we can envisage circumstances in which any statement, even a statement of particular fact, could support a counterfactual. The view of counterfactuals that I shall advocate was suggested to me by Quine's (1963) account of necessity. It also has affinities to J. L. Mackie's (1962) account of counterfactuals as disguised and incomplete arguments.[9] The view that I advocate is a highly contextual one. Roughly it is that 'If it had been the case that p then it would be the case that q' is true or perhaps just assertable if q follows from p together with certain contextually agreed-upon background assumptions. Though in general I draw a vital distinction between truth conditions and assertability conditions, this distinction is blurred in the case of counterfactuals, which I do not regard as metaphysically important. If we say 'truth conditions' then the view of counterfactuals that I advocate is in effect a metalinguistic one, whereas if we say 'assertability conditions' it is more like Mackie's disguised-argument view.

We can now see that whether a regularity statement supports a counterfactual depends on the contextual assumptions in the particular case. 'If this is a gold sphere it is less than a kilometre in diameter' does not support the counterfactual 'If there were a gold sphere in the Andromeda galaxy it would be less than a kilometre in diameter', because there being a gold sphere a kilometre in diameter is consistent with those regularity statements that we regard as expressing laws of nature – that is, statements that are integrated into theories that we believe, or are such as we believe that they will eventually be so integrated. It is consistent with those statements that cohere into our theoretical structures that there should be higher beings who for reasons best known to themselves construct these huge gold spheres! Again it could be argued that if the universe is infinite then there must be cases in which gold molecules have purely by chance coalesced into a sphere more than a kilometre in diameter. On the other hand, if we are prepared to say that if something were a sphere of one kilometre in diameter it would not be a sphere of uranium 235, this is because of our belief in atomic fission and in the deep physical laws (regularities) that explain this.

It should be noted that the contextual background assumptions vary not only between unrelated counterfactuals but also under syntactical transformations (e.g. contraposition), and so a strict logic of counterfactuals is impossible. Hence – as has been remarked by van Fraassen, who has stressed the contextuality of counterfactuals – it appears to be impossible to find strict truth conditions for counterfactuals, a lesson that Nelson Goodman (1973) has taught us (van Fraasen 1980, pp. 115ff). So when I say that a regularity theorist can agree that laws but not accidential regularities support counterfactual conditionals, this is on certain assumptions about context and moreover is not to concede that counterfactuals need be taken very seriously. So although Goodman was criticizing a view of counterfactuals as a matter of deducibility from sets of assumptions, fundamentally I am on his side.

The sensible regularity theorist will admit that some regularities are not laws, but that there are statements of regularity, which form part of the structure of theory or are explicable in terms of more basic theory, that we call 'laws'. Also, we may allow as laws some regularities that are not yet incorporated into theory but of which we have a hunch that such incorporation is in the offing somewhere. (Consider Ohm's law before the advent of solid-state physics.) I do not think that it is possible to give a tight definition that will separate those regularities that are laws from those that are merely accidental. I am inclined to think of the concept of law as an open-textured[10] one, able to be indicated only by a rough definition. However, it will be noticed that this view of laws is somewhat like that of Ramsey in a paper (1978) only recently published, and as refined by David Lewis. According to Lewis (1973, p. 73), a statement of regularity is a law statement 'if it appears as a theorem (or axiom) in each of the true deductive systems that achieves a best combination of simplicity and strength'.

However, I do not want to stipulate that fundamental physical theory need be presented as a deductive axiomatic system. It may be presented as informally defining a class of models, as has been stressed by many writers from Suppes to van Fraassen. Of course, as a realist I take the physical world to be one of the class. I think also that strength should be elucidated as going beyond mere deductive power and as possible even when detailed deduction or prediction is impossible. Even if the universe were deterministic we could not predict the weather very well; recent chaos theory explains why. (Suppose that the number of steps in a computation goes up exponentially as compared with the interval of time at which a prediction is aimed.) Nevertheless, we can see how the weather patterns are such that they could have arisen as a result of the operation of known physical laws.

I now wish to consider one of Tooley's ingenious objections to regularity theories, and to try to show how a regularity theory of the sort that I am advocating might deal with his case. Tooley (1977, pp. 47–8) imagines a world containing ten types of fundamental particle, and supposes that the behaviour of particles when they collide depends upon the types of particle in question. There are thus 55 possible sorts of interaction. Tooley goes on to suppose that collisions of particles of types X and Y have not been investigated but that laws have been discovered for the other 54 possible types of interaction. He also supposes that each of the 54 laws is basic, not derivable from more ultimate laws. Tooley correctly supposes that on these assumptions it would be reasonable to believe that collisions between particles of types X and Y would also be governed by some basic law. Tooley further supposes that there never have been or will be collisions between X particles and Y particles: by extraordinary chance they all happen to pass one another by. He even envisages a Laplacean calculation from cosmic boundary conditions and laws of motion of the particles that collisions between X and Y particles are impossible. What, asks Tooley, would the regularity theorist say about this?

The problem is that since X and Y particles never collide there would not be a relevant regularity. Nevertheless, it is plausible that there would be a law. It is true that on the regularity view all statements of the form 'If an X particle collides with a Y particle then . . .' would be trivially true, due to falsehood of the antecedent. Nevertheless, I do not see why the regularity theorist should not regard one of these trivially true statements as being a law statement. Remember that while the regularity theorist holds that all laws are regularities, not all regularities are laws. So a statement that was trivially true because of falsity of its antecedent could still count as a regularity statement: a statement of a null-case regularity. And I have suggested that it is the tact of the scientist that enables him or her to decide which such statements should be regarded as law statements – that is, as statements that fit into our web of belief in a suitable way.

Of course, as a metaphysical realist, I make a sharp distinction between truth and warranted assertability. However, I am here prepared to blur this a little because, though the regularities are objective enough, just which regularities correspond to law statements is a matter of the tact and judgment of the scientist, and this imports a whiff of the epistemological. This does not matter much, because I do not think that the word 'law' need occur in the object language of a completed science. Nevertheless, in Tooley's case we can envisage a 'truth-maker' for the law about the X and Y particles: it would be symmetries between the properties of the 55 sorts of particles. Peter Menzies has raised with me the possibility that the law for the X and Y particles might be an awkward loner with no symmetries of consequence between the properties of the X and Y particles and those of the other particles. However it seems to me that if there were no such symmetries then, since the X and Y particles never collide, it would not be the case that this null regularity could be correlated with a law statement. In giving this answer to Menzies I am of course relying on the whiff of epistemology in my separation of law regularities from accidental ones, despite the objectivity of all regularities. If there were two equally good but equally far from simple explanatory laws for the fifty-fifth type of particle, then we would have to lend equal credence to the two explanations and would not know which corresponded to a real regularity.

What about the Laplacean calculation that (*per impossibile*) would show that X and Y particles never collide? This would show only that the law statement was trivially true, a sort of null-case regularity. Well, it could be this and yet also be nontrivial because of 'rounding off' the 54 regularities to make for a symmetrical body of 55 laws. This could save the law statement from being one of the regularity statements that do not express laws.

Tooley envisages that the Laplacean calculation would show that it was impossible for the X and Y particles to collide. I can both accept this and reject it because of my adherence to a contextual account of modality. 'Necessarily p' is true (or perhaps just propoundable) when p *follows from* contextually agreed-upon background assumptions; 'possibly p' is true when p *is consistent with* such assumptions. ('Follows from' and 'is consistent with' are here taken in the sense of logical consequence in first-order predicate logic, or perhaps in a more extended model theory if (for example) an unaxiomatized set theory is also presupposed. They are explicable without properly modal notions. I said 'propoundable' rather than 'assertable' because a disguised argument is not something assertable, and so the more general notion of propoundability seems preferable to that of assertability.) Now in this sense, if we assumed determinism, a regularity theorist could allow that if the contextually agreed-upon background assumptions are taken to include both regularities and initial (boundary) conditions then it is 'necessary' that the X and Y particles never collide. If the contextual assumptions contain only the regularities but not the initial conditions, it is not 'necessary' that the particles never collide.

What about the most fundamental regularities of all, as stated in some final Grand Unified Theory or Theory of Everything to which some cosmologists, such as Hawking, seem to aspire? These would not be necessary in the aforementioned contextual sense. It is hard to face the fact that the ultimate laws must express mere regularities. We do crave necessity. We also crave to know why anything exists at all. But is not possible, so far as I can see, that either craving could be satisfied. Armstrong's theory of laws as relations between universals does not satisfy this craving any more than the regularity theory does, since in his view (and on that of Tooley and Dretske) the relations between universals hold only contingently; they are not logically necessary. If a putative law statement were logically necessary it would be uninformative. Perhaps what the cosmologists seek is something narrower. Perhaps they mean that the laws of the ultimate theory would be necessary only in the sense that they would be consistent with one another, and with the evidence, and would satisfy certain constraints of simplicity, symmetry and the like. It could be that if such a theory were discovered then it would seem highly improbable that there could be an alternative or better theory. A philosophical sceptic might doubt, but then a philosophical sceptic is by definition ready to doubt anything.

Philosophically I try to eschew the notion of causality. I take the view that causality is a useful notion for plumbers, heart surgeons, irrigation engineers and so on, but I do not want it in theoretical physics or cosmology. Regularities and symmetries, yes; causality, no. Nevertheless, in modern cosmology there is a strong sense of the universe developing causally – though not deterministically – in time. On the other hand, quantum mechanics suggests that microprocesses have CPT symmetry. This seems plausible enough. If a positron is an electron pointing the other way in time, and so on, CPT symmetry can be seen as a sort of time symmetry even though it allows violations of T symmetry. If one reverses the direction in time of an electron (reverses charge) then surely one should also reflect rotations in a parity mirror. Nevertheless, cosmologically there is an asymmetry, as when for example symmetry breaking leads to special values of the constraints of nature. Moreover, there is the thermodynamic asymmetry: temporal asymmetry of familiar macroprocesses are explicable compatibly with symmetry of microprocesses. Would the symmetry be restored if the universe were an oscillating one, with big bangs and big squeezes alternating? No, because the thermodynamics of collapse would be different from that of expansion. Perhaps we should think of causality as a macroscopic thermodynamic concept, not applicable to fundamental microprocesses.

A grand unified theory will probably be largely geometrical, not causal. In any case the word 'cause' is not useful in physics: Maxwell's theory, for example, is stated purely mathematically. A totally geometrized grand unified theory would be most intellectually satisfying perhaps, but maybe this is an impossible ideal. It should also be remembered that there are doubts about the universal applicability of the laws of nature.

If theories that the fundamental constants of physics may be different in different regions (small-'u' universes) are to be believed, then the only real universal laws are those proto-laws that hold even at the time of the Big Bang, or perhaps are about the total structure of the spacetime universe. The idea is that the constants of nature are fixed in different small-'u' universes as a result of symmetry breaking, which occurs when symmetrical systems in unstable equilibrium lose their symmetry due to possibly infinitesimal perturbations.

In this essay I have so far avoided discussing the notion of probability, which figures so much in quantum mechanics. Quantum mechanics suggests that the basic laws of the universe are statistical, or rather that, though the ψ wave of a system evolves deterministically, it implies only statistical facts about concrete occurrences. What ψ does is to constrain the statistics of quantum-mechanical goings-on. It is tempting to describe the talk of ψ as referring to some concept of objective chance, and perhaps that is the right way to go. Nevertheless, such a course is not open to a regularity theory of the sort I am trying to defend. If I were happy to postulate objective chances, who would I be to boggle about Armstrong's necessities? (After all, a necessity would just be a limiting case of objective chance.) Van Fraassen and Lewis have raised the problem of how one can infer a universal regularity from an Armstrongian statement of a necessary relation between properties, and analogously there would be the puzzle about how nonstatistical statements about ψ would imply statistical statements about (for example) where a photon will strike a screen. Thus we should take talk about the Schrödinger wave as descriptive of the patterns of statistical regularities in the universe. It is explanatory, in a sense, because it imposes a simple structure on our descriptions of the universe.[11] This may look like a retreat from realism, but in fact it is not: so far as I can see it does nothing to reduce our reasons for thinking of the real existence of those theoretically postulated entities (such as photons, neutrons, etc.) that undergo the regularities, or of such other theoretically postulated entities as spacetime that possess a different type of regularity.

In this I am really just *identifying* objective probability with $\psi^*A\psi$ and the like: it is indeed to deny that we need a separate concept of objective chance. Objective chance is a mysterious thing anyway. We have Lewis's (1986b) 'Principal Principle', which is needed to relate objective chance to subjective probability: a mysterious though necessary link between ontology and epistemology. It seems rather too like getting an 'ought' out of an 'is', but we do seem to need it.

The line taken in the previous two paragraphs looks a bit unsatisfactory, but as Bruce Bairnsfather's Old Bill said (as he and another soldier cowered in a shell hole), 'If you know of a better hole, go to it!' It may, I hope, look less unsatisfactory at some future date when physics and cosmology have become integrated so that the distinction between general law and particular fact may have been transcended.

A main attraction of the regularity theory is its extensionality and actualism. There are no mysterious unanalyzed modal operators and no possible worlds other than the actual world. Armstrong's, Tooley's and Dretske's theories are attractive because they are extensional too: their universals are postulated entities that are part of the universe, quantified over in a first-order way. Their theories are not without difficulty; for example, I have referred to certain objections due to Lewis and van Fraassen. I do not say confidently that such objections cannot be overcome.[12] Indeed, I am being increasingly impressed by the way in which Armstrong's ingenious and subtle accounts of laws, universals and possibility all hang together. No doubt I may not have been convincing in my defense of the regularity theory, but at any rate I hope that I may have done something to refute or at least mitigate the charge that it is a jejune and silly one.

NOTES

1. With help from Peter Forrest, Armstrong has developed a non-Platonistic philosophy of mathematics that depends on his combinatorial theory of possibility. On his view, numbers (rationals and reals) come out as relations between determinate quantities. I have gone the other way and have spoken only of determinable properties and their relations to one another and to ontologically independent mathematical entities. My perhaps unjustified qualms about Armstrong's approach derive largely from wondering whether it will yield all of the set theory required for analysis (the theory of infinite sets of numbers) that seems to be required for physics. It would be good if we could avoid postulating entities neither in space nor in time, though on the other hand I do not see why all entities *should* be in spacetime. (See Armstrong 1989a, Chapter 9; Forrest and Armstrong 1987. Compare also Bigelow and Pargetter 1988 and Bigelow 1988.) John Forge (1986) has even raised a doubt about Armstrong's treatment of functional laws that contain no differential equations.
2. Perhaps they are not the same, since Armstrong holds that both particulars and universals are abstractions from states of affairs. (See note 12.)
3. John Clendinnen (1982) does not agree with me about laws of nature, but his vindication of induction is the sort of thing I have in mind.
4. The phrase 'the web of belief' is of course the title of a book by Quine and Ullian (1970).
5. In this connection perhaps Rescher (1973) should be mentioned. His book is ostensibly about a coherence theory of truth, but I hold that though coherence may be a guide to truth, a coherence theory should be a theory not of truth but of warranted assertability.
6. Strawson has an even more striking example of random generation of pictures on a computing screen, and of sequences of such pictures. However, the simpler example of the random number generator brings out the issues, pro and con, sufficiently well for present purposes.

7. Forge (1990, p. 88) has said that we need not believe in laws but only in regularities, since if we believe in regularities it is possible to 'latch on to these by experiment and observation'. Nor, Forge says, do we need lots of instances. Belief in laws as opposed to regularities, he thinks, adds nothing to our expectation.

8. Peter Forrest has raised the question of whether perhaps total chaos is not the simplest theory but rather an infinitely complex one; even in a deterministic universe, no algorithm could generate it. If we equate complexity with length of algorithm, in deterministic universes more-complex universes would have larger algorithms. This would make all indeterministic universes equally simple. I am inclined to think that we should take a chaotic universe as the most simple and least requiring explanation, and that – while there is good inductive reason for believing that our universe is not completely chaotic – we should consider more or less simple scientific hypotheses as imposing restrictions on this primary chaos. Still, I am not sure of having avoided inconsistency when I use a fundamental postulate of simplicity to yield explanations and yet couple it with a strong propensity to say that a completely chaotic universe would be the most simple and the least requiring explanation.

9. The theory has antecedents in Mill (1843, p. 92), Ramsey (1931, p. 48), and Chisholm (1955). See also van Fraassen (1980, p. 115). Pavel Tichý (1984) has given a very useful critique of various theories involving supplementary premisses, tacit or otherwise, and advocates a tacit-premiss theory in which it is held that the subject need not be consciously aware of or precise about what the tacit premisses are, or even believe them. In this connection he posits a notion of 'propositional office'.

10. For the concept of 'open texture' see Waismann (1945).

11. In this paragraph I am much indebted to Peter Forrest (see Forrest 1988, pp. 109–15). I hope that he will not disapprove of the way I have understood him. Forrest (1985) talks of regularities but does not call them laws because he includes necessity in the concept of a law; he has a 'no law' theory where I have a 'merely regularity' theory (ontologically speaking, anyway), so the difference betwen us in this respect is largely verbal.

12. See, for example, Armstrong (1988a). In this paper Armstrong takes the view that both particulars and universals are 'abstractions' from 'states of affairs'. I am puzzled about the ontological status of 'abstractions', at least if this word is taken in a Lockean sense. I am also not keen to have states of affairs (or 'facts') in my ontology. (See Smart 1986.)

REFERENCES

Armstrong, D. M. 1983a. *What is a Law of Nature?* (Cambridge University Press).
1988a. 'Can a Naturalist Believe in Universals?'. In *Science in Reflection,* vol. 3, ed. Edna Ullmann-Margalit (Dordrecht: Kluwer), pp. 103–15.
1989a. *A Combinatorial Theory of Possibility* (Cambridge University Press).
1989c. Review of Strawson (1989), *Times Literary Supplement,* no. 4525 (22–28 Dec.), 1425.
199+. 'The Identification Problem and the Inference Problem', *Philosophy and Phenomenological Research.* ✻
Bigelow, John. 1988. *The Reality of Numbers: a Physicalist Philosophy of Mathematics* (Oxford: Clarendon).

Bigelow, John and Pargetter, Robert. 1988. 'Quantities', *Philosophical Studies* 54: 287–307.

Butterfield, Herbert. 1949. *The Origins of Modern Science, 1300–1800* (London: Bell).

Chisholm, Roderick M. 1955. 'Law Statements and Counterfactual Inference', *Analysis* 15: 97–105.

Clendinnen, F. J. 1982. 'Rational Expectation and Simplicity'. In *What? Where? When? Why?*, ed. Robert McLaughlin (Dordrecht: Reidel), pp. 1–25.

Dretske, Fred I. 1977. 'Laws of Nature', *Philosophy of Science* 44: 248–68.

Forge, John. 1986. 'David Armstrong on Functional Laws', *Philosophy of Science* 53: 584–7.

1990. 'Can We Dispense with Laws in Science?', *Metascience* 8: 86–93.

Forrest, Peter. 1985. 'What Reasons Do We Have for Believing There Are Laws of Nature?', *Philosophical Inquiry* 7: 1–12.

1988. *Quantum Metaphysics* (Oxford: Blackwell).

Forrest, Peter and Armstrong, D. M. 1987. 'The Nature of Numbers', *Philosophical Papers* 16: 165–86.

Goodman, Nelson. 1973. *Fact, Fiction, and Forecast,* 3rd ed. (Indianapolis: Bobbs-Merrill).

Lewis, David. 1973. *Counterfactuals* (Cambridge, MA: Harvard University Press).

1983b. 'New Work for a Theory of Universals', *Australasian Journal of Philosophy* 61: 343–77.

1986b. 'A Subjectivist's Guide to Objective Chance' with Postscript. In *Philosophical Papers,* vol. 2 (Oxford University Press).

Mackie, J. L. 1962. 'Counterfactuals and Causal Laws'. In *Analytical Philosophy, First Series,* ed. R. J. Butler (Oxford: Blackwell), pp. 66–80.

Mill, John Stuart. 1843. *A System of Logic* (London: Parker).

Quine, W. V. 1960. *Word and Object* (Cambridge, MA: MIT Press).

1963. 'Necessary Truth', in Quine (1976), pp. 48–56.

1971. 'Algebraic Logic and Predicate Functors'. In *Logic and Art: Essays in Honor of Nelson Goodman,* ed. Richard Rudner and Israel Scheffler (Indianapolis: Bobbs-Merrill). Reprinted in Quine (1976), pp. 283–307.

1976. *The Ways of Paradox and Other Essays,* 2nd ed. (Cambridge, MA: Harvard University Press).

Quine, W. V. and Ullian, J. S. 1970. *The Web of Belief* (New York: Random House; rev. ed. 1978).

Ramsey, F. P. 1931. *Foundations of Mathematics* (London: Routledge & Kegan Paul).

1978. 'Universals of Law and Fact'. In *Foundations,* ed. D. H. Mellor (London: Routledge & Kegan Paul).

Rescher, Nicholas. 1973. *The Coherence Theory of Truth* (Oxford: Clarendon).

Smart, J. J. C. 1950. 'Excogitation and Induction', *Australasian Journal of Philosophy* 28: 191–9.

1985. 'Laws of Nature and Cosmic Coincidences', *Philosophical Quarterly* 35: 272–80.

1986. 'How to Turn the *Tractatus* Wittgenstein into (almost) Donald Davidson'. In *Truth and Interpretation: Perspectives on the Philosophy of Donald Davidson,* ed. Ernest LePore (Oxford: Blackwell), pp. 92–100.

1989. 'Explanation – Opening Address'. In *Explanation and its Limits,* ed. Dudley Knowles (Cambridge University Press).

Strawson, Galen. 1989. *The Secret Connexion: Causation, Realism and David Hume* (Oxford: Clarendon).

Tichý, Pavel. 1984. 'Subjunctive Conditionals: Two Parameters vs. Three', *Philosophical Studies* 45: 147–80.

Tooley, Michael. 1977. 'The Nature of Laws', *Canadian Journal of Philosophy* 74: 667–98.

van Fraassen, Bas C. 1980. *The Scientific Image* (Oxford: Clarendon).

1989. *Laws and Symmetry* (Oxford: Clarendon).

Waismann, Friedrich. 1945. 'Verifiability', *Proceedings of the Aristotelian Society,* suppl. vol. 19: 119–50.

Reply to Smart

D. M. ARMSTRONG

One of the pleasures of being a philosopher working in Australia over the past forty years has been to have the company of Jack Smart. My intellectual debt to him is very great. He played no part in my original philosophical formation, which I owe to John Anderson in Sydney from 1947 to 1950, when Smart had not arrived in the country. But after that time his influence was continuous. If we make Wilfrid Sellars's rather profound distinction between the manifest and the scientific image of the world, then it can be said that Anderson was a philosopher of the manifest image. (For instance, he held a Direct Realist and *nonreductive* view of the so-called secondary qualities such as colour.) Smart, of course, is a – one might almost say *the* – philosopher of the scientific image. Despite my Andersonian training I had leanings in the same direction and was encouraged and fortified by the example of Smart, who knew so much more science than I did.

Smart converted me to a central-state materialist view of mental processes. Previously we had both (independently) accepted a Ryle-inspired behaviourism about the mind, seeing no better way to reconcile the existence of mentality with physicalism. I am quite proud of the fact that he later accepted my broadening of the Place–Smart identity theory to cover all mental processes, events and states.

But my deeper debt to Smart is of another sort. It is to the completely open and good-hearted way that he has conducted himself in his writing, in his very extensive philosophical correspondence, and in his personal contacts with other philosophers. Philosophers of any achievement tend towards the egomaniacal. This is probably inevitable in a discipline where there is so much disagreement, and where even collaboration consists for the most part in mutual criticism. Achievement would not be possible under such conditions without a good deal of such self-confidence. Smart himself has a proper sense of the worth of his own thought. But he wears this lightly, and the inevitable and necessary disagreement and criticism is conducted in the most agreeable (and idiosyncratic!) manner. By his example, he has helped us all to create a good environment for philosophy in Australia.

1. The Reality of Properties

Smart begins his essay by objecting to my description, in a review of Galen Strawson's book on Hume, of the regularity theory of laws of nature as 'jejune and silly'. Actually I was referring to the regularity theory of causality, which is not the same thing. Hume speaks little of laws. One who thinks that causes are mere regular sequences will almost certainly take the same view of laws, but it is perfectly possible to reject the regularity view of causation yet hold that laws are mere regularities. I would be prepared to apply the word 'jejune' ('unsatisfying to the mind or soul; dull, insipid, dry; thin, poor; wanting in substance' – S.O.E.D.) to both theories. I would not apply the word 'silly' to the regularity theory of laws. The word was too strong anyway, but what I had in mind was the feature that the regularity theory of causation shares with behaviourism: the way it runs counter to what seem to be the plain facts of experience. Just as we are directly aware of our own mental states, so, it seems to me, we are directly aware of certain cases of token causality. (We could not be directly aware of a cosmic regularity.) Smart's dismissive attitude to causality, which I do not share, may make him insensitive to the distinction between causes and laws.

Leaving this aside, I am delighted to learn that Smart is now prepared to accept properties into his ontology, provided that they are the sorts of thing that appear as properties in physical science. It certainly seems that references to properties (and relations, but Smart may mean his word to cover these) are not eliminable in physics and elsewhere. As Smart says, such properties are to be distinguished sharply from what Quine calls 'attributes', which are semantic creatures correlated with predicates and are rejected by Quine for just that reason. At the same time, unlike Quine and Smart, I find no difficulty in the notion of synonymy and so no difficulty in equivalence classes of synonymous predicates.

Considering Quine's account of metrical properties, which seeks to avoid 'impure numbers' such as 2 centimetres or 4 grams by saying that something has-a-length-in-centimetres of 5, Smart says that this leaves us, most implausibly, with an infinity of structureless predicates. A further difficulty, pointed out by Mortensen (1987, p. 107), is that such an identity statement (as it presumably is) has the consequence that the property of *has-a-mass-in-kilograms of 5* becomes identical with the length property. Smart's suggestion is that we recover the structure by saying 'This has (length, standard cm, 5)' with 'has' a triadic predicate. While agreeing that this is an advance because it introduces properties, I am dubious about two points here. First, I do not like the idea of introducing a pure number as a term in the analysis of the attribution of a physical property to an ordinary particular. I would rather think of the five as a relation (internal and therefore supervenient), a ratio holding between the object's length and the standard centimetre (see Forrrest and Armstrong 1987). Incidentally, I think that this may do something to mitigate the problem raised by Smart a little later on, the problem of the arbitrariness of units. We should certainly hope, as Smart says, for a physics in which units are related to physically significant quantities. But it is not much worry that the object's length should bear different ratios to different units.

Of course, this demands that we introduce determinate lengths as genuine properties. It therefore links up with my second, somewhat unfocussed, worry about the quantity of length in Smart's formula, which, as he emphasizes, is the determinable property. The existence of a set of properties, the determinates of this determinable, seems to me to be clear enough, at any rate the instantiated determinates. But I am far from clear as to whether we should postulate a further property of length (a universal) which is a property of all the determinates, or a universal property possessed by all first-order particulars that have any length.

It seems, nevertheless, that the physical properties which Smart is now inclined to accept are pretty much the same as my universals, although the properties are not embedded in states of affairs as mine are. Whether, given universals, one then wants to postulate irreducibly higher-order relations between them to constitute the laws of nature is, of course, a futher matter. It is perfectly possible to accept universals yet go on to see laws as mere regularities in the way that these universals are instantiated. And, of course, I accept Smart's point that if laws are to be relations between universals then the relationships involved will have to be, in general, much more complicated than the relationship between those old warriors F and G that Tooley, Dretske and I have so often considered. In this respect our account may be said to be somewhat jejune! I will just add in my own defence that I have tried to give an account of functional laws in Armstrong (1983a, Chapter 7). I there took note of the fact that if one substitutes specific values for all the variable magnitudes involved in the law, one then arrives at laws that look like determinates of a determinable, with the original functional law as the determinable. The problem that arises then is, once more, that of giving an account of the determinable. It can hardly be a mere conjunction of all the determinate laws. That would be a 'Humean' theory of the determinable: it would just be a cosmic coincidence that the determinate values fell into this pattern. What one wants, apparently, is a higher-order law, a law governing the determinate laws from which the latter can be deduced. This may involve postulating determinable universals that will constitute the variable quantities, but I find the matter very difficult.

Before ending this section I will just say also that I now rather regret my references to the nomic relation between universals as a 'contingent necessity'. No problem about the contingency, but I think that my continuous references to nomic *necessitation,* though not precisely mistaken, did little explanatory work. I should now prefer to speak of *causation,* of which, I think, we have direct experience in pressure on the body and the operation of the will. The nomic relation between universals, I now think, is to be understood as being the same as (or analogous to) token causation of this experienced sort. It does seem that causation involves modality in some way – the cause *makes* the effect happen – but I do not know how to spell this out.

2. The Regularity Theory of Laws

Smart makes the important suggestion that the Regularity theorist should begin by giving a small but positive probability to the hypothesis that the world is simple. Regularity would be a dimension of simplicity. Bayesian methods can then be used to amplify this probability in the light of continued experience.

Allowing this, it seems that a defender of the relations-between-universals view – and, perhaps, of any 'strong' theory of laws – has the advantage that he or she does not need to begin with an initial assignment that is an act of faith; one can begin from the actual experience of regularities. This is because the strong laws, unlike the 'laws' postulated by a regularity theory, actually explain the regularities. Regularities would seem to be a priori improbable. Hume's doubts about induction seem to be fuelled, in part, by sheer amazement that regularities exist and continue. This fact is explained by, and becomes less amazing in light of, this hypothesis: There is something about the nature of those things that repeat themselves that ensures such repetition. The hypothesis of strong laws can then be given an initial probability on the basis of experience, and Bayesian reasoning on the basis of further confirming experience will increase that probability.

It is true, of course, that the particular account given of strong laws will have to be shown to be intelligible, in the sense of being non–self-contradictory, and superior to any other non–self-contradictory account. I would very readily concede also the point Smart makes that a system of laws – say, as relationships of universals – must itself remain unexplained. But to my instinct this is a far more natural terminus of explanation than a regular world with no explanation for the regularity.

Turning to the subject of counterfactuals, I have a good deal of sympathy with Smart's contextualist-deductive view of counterfactuals. (A sympathy that coexists with a sympathy for a possible-worlds approach in some cases. Since I am a fictionalist about such worlds, I hope that there is no inconsistency here.) I agree with Smart in thinking that counterfactuals are not in themselves metaphysically important, and that the distinction between truth conditions and assertability conditions is blurred for them. One way to bring out the latter point may be to consider the counterfactuals that can be generated when a merely probabilistic law is held constant while it is falsely supposed that an event falling under the antecedent of the law occurred. It can then be said that there was a certain chance that, under these circumstances, the consequent event would have occurred. It can also be added that this event would have occurred or would not have occurred. But suppose it is asked which of these disjuncts is the truth. (To bring out the force of the argument most clearly, let the chance be 0.5.) It would seem that there could be no answer; excluded middle fails. This suggests that counterfactual discourse is second-grade discourse, with a blurring of the distinction between truth and assertability.

My own treatment of the Tooley case mentioned by Smart – where two types of fundamental particle never meet although all other types do, in each case yielding an idiosyncratic pattern of interaction – would be along these same lines. We might have good theoretical reasons to think that if such particles did meet then their interaction would also be idiosyncratic, yet by the nature of the case have no way of saying what that interaction would be. I think we should remain content with the conclusion that the interaction would have been idiosyncratic, and refrain from the conclusion that a definite truth about that idiosyncratic nature exists; warranted assertability only.

Nevertheless, in the ordinary way of business, statements of law do 'support' counterfactuals. Smart himself concedes that laws support counterfactuals whereas 'accidental' regularities do not. I wonder whether this is possible given that laws are nothing but regularities, albeit regularities of a special 'hanging together' sort. The question is whether laws are really held fixed when they are extended to cover a further, though

imaginary, case. They remain fixed semantically; the universally quantified statement of the law does not change. But consider the truth-maker
for the law – that in the world in virtue of which the statement is true –
which is supposed to expand. (There is no such expansion involved if the
law is a relationship between universals.) What assurance do we have,
then, that the new F, as it may be, would be like its fellows in being a G?

This problem was perceived by Mackie, an upholder of the regularity
view. He suggested that in thought we perform an induction, arguing
'from experience' that the new F will resemble the others. I have criticized
this solution elsewhere (Armstrong 1983a, Chapter 4, Section 4).

Smart's discussion of probabilistic laws is brief, but I did like his point
that a regularity theory is in no position to postulate objective chances,
and that those who postulate such chances are in no position to complain
about objective necessities because the latter are no more than chances
set at the value of 1. That seems to me to be entirely correct, even if I do
not draw the same moral from the point that Smart does.

There is much else in Smart's rich essay that I have not discussed, either
from lack of competence or of inspiration. I think that we both agree
that the central difficulty for a regularity theory of law is the distinction
between an accidental and a lawlike regularity. I like to focus on the difference between the sphere of gold that is a mile in diameter and a sphere
of uranium of the same diameter. It is unlikely that the former will ever
exist, but there seems no nomic impossibility involved. The laws of nature, if we know them, tell us that the second sphere is nomically impossible, or (if all fundamental laws are probabilistic only) near enough to
nomically impossible. My sense of the matter is that there is a huge ontological gulf here, where a regularity theory can find only a relatively small
distinction. But the nature of philosophy is that different philosophers
see such matters differently, and there is nothing to do but continue the
argument.

REFERENCES

Armstrong, D. M. 1983a. *What is a Law of Nature?* (Cambridge University Press).
Forrest, Peter and Armstrong, D. M. 1987. 'The Nature of Number', *Philosophical Papers* 16: 165–86.
Mortensen, Chris. 1987. 'Arguing for Universals', *Revue Internationale de Philosophie* 160: 97–111.

8

Power for Realists

C. B. MARTIN

I

David Armstrong and I have been in warm friendship with some testy times, bitter opposition and close alliance. I value our association of more than 35 years as much as any in my philosophical life. His intelligence, force, honesty and candour have been an invaluable resource for me and for the rest of the philosophical world.

The economy, force and directness of Armstrong in discussion was made clear during a seminar in Oxford given by Elizabeth Anscombe. Attempting to show a lack of parallel between the temporal and the spatial, she said, 'The same thing *can't* be in different places'. Armstrong slowly arose to his full and considerable height and, without speaking, stamped his left foot down and then stamped his right foot down and stood straddling. Anscombe stared, then said, 'But, . . .', fell silent, stared again and announced 'I – was – wrong!' Armstrong, who had stood, still straddling, sat down.

In any discussion between Armstrong and myself, If A were criticizing B then B would try to reply to the criticisms, but before very long B would round on A and demand 'What's *your* view?', and A was always expected to have one with twists of its own. With all of this, there was always some territorial spraying of what we thought were our own philosophical trees. Doing philosophy together was not merely an activity but rather a very human and, indeed, personal activity. I still like it that way.

II

Problems concerning the role of causal dispositions have occupied us both. I want to discuss the contrast in our views as they have developed most recently, and say how much my thinking was sharpened and clarified through my good fortune in having a great deal of discussion with Armstrong.

My first interest in causality developed during work on my Ph.D. dissertation in Cambridge and Oxford as part of an attack on the form of phenomenalism put forward by John Wisdom. It took up over one-third of the dissertation and was highly commended – but also (quite reasonably) deemed totally irrelevant – by the examiners, and was omitted in my final submission.

Arriving in Adelaide, I had to teach John Locke and have not wavered since in my convictions that he was largely right in giving powers or dispositionality a central role in ontology and that anything like a Regularist view of causality was entirely wrong, and that this was a matter of the greatest importance.

From the mid-1950s at the University of Adelaide (and as visiting professor at Harvard in 1961 and 1970 and Columbia in 1972, and at the University of Sydney from 1966 to 1971), I gave lectures criticizing the regularity account of causality and arguing for the need of a nonregularist disposition power base as a truth-maker for strong conditionals and counterfactuals, and for the central position of causal dispositions, powers and aptnesses in the account of the ontology of both mental and non-mental concepts.

When J. J. C. Smart and David Armstrong gave 'apt to cause – apt to be caused by' dispositional accounts of basic mental concepts, it seemed evident to me that, under their Humean minimalist, regularist interpretation, the apt-to-cause dispositional concepts could not bear the ontic weight being placed upon them. Untypically, it seemed to me, my two colleagues were not sufficiently ontologically serious. I could not have asked for clearer or more perceptive Humeans than they (and, in particular, Armstrong) during my period in Sydney.

Armstrong attended the seminars on causality I gave for three years in Sydney. For two of those years I gave the seminars jointly with George Molnar, who shared my causal realism and opposition to Regularity Theory. He was a brilliant philosopher and contributed greatly to the clarification and enrichment of my own thinking. The seminars were seminal. In Beauchamp (1974), three members of the seminar – George Molnar, G. C. Nerlich and W. A. Suchting – were contributors.

Armstrong gave up his Humean regularity view some time after I left Sydney in 1971. Smart has remained intransigent, emphasizing that the regularity is, after all, 'cosmic'. In recent years, Armstrong has done important philosophical work on universals and natural law. It is powerful and original and has caused a resurgence of interest in some crucial areas of ontology.

III

U. T. Place, Smart, Armstrong and myself thought of sensations as processes in the brain that had important relationships with other processes and states of the brain. Concerning phenomenological qualities, Place argued, by means of his 'Phenomenological Fallacy' argument, that there were no such qualities, and was an Eliminativist before the term was invented. Smart and Armstrong thought that such qualities at least deserved the courtesy of a reductive (but not an entailment or translational) account. They each saw that such qualities could not be accounted for only in terms of dispositions for relations with the qualities of *other* brain processes or states, but that the 'bottom dollar' had to be in terms of dispositionalities for bodily movements.

I argued, against the form of Identity Theory developed by Place (1956) and the variants developed by Smart and Armstrong, that the qualities of experience were not reducible. (This never inclined me to think that they were not, in a perfectly proper sense, physical and causal *and* located as properties of the brain.) C. D. Broad and Bertrand Russell had given what was later called the 'Absent-Qualia' argument. John Wisdom (1952, pp. 10f) – no doubt, *via* Wittgenstein – used the case of the Inverted Spectrum as a nonsense case providing a reductio ad absurdum of otherwise tempting views. I thought it was a terrific case that made excellent sense, and went on to use it against verificationism and later as an argument against the forms of Identity Theory propounded by Smart and Armstrong; see Smart (1963, pp. 81ff) and Armstrong (1968, pp. 257–60) for their replies. Much later it was dubbed the 'Inverted-Qualia' argument and it sold better.

Certainly I thought that experiential qualities did have causal–dispositional aspects, but I differed from Smart and Armstrong concerning:

(1) the episodic and introspectable experiential qualities being reducible to, or 'constructed' entirely of, their dispositionality; and
(2) the kinds of typifying manifestations for which they are disposed.

With respect to (2), I argued that the typifying manifestations *themselves* must have an experiential component. Even behaviour, as a typifying manifestation, must be under sensory feedback control. Concerning (1), something much more basic and general was involved – namely, the nature of causal dispositionality in the physical as well as the mental domains.

The functionalist attempt to render experiential qualities in terms of dispositionalities is a member of the same family as the operationalist attempt to render the properties of unobservable particles in terms of the dispositionalities of observable objects, and the attempt to render the qualities of the observable objects themselves in terms of dispositionalities concerning their possible operations. The result of such a final step is that every intrinsic categorical quality collapses into dispositionality, and every 'is' is replaced by a 'would be'. Each categorical property that would be manifested by some purported dispositionality is itself a candidate for replacement by some further dispositionality. It is hard to model a real *happening* on such an account. Pure dispositionality is a poor way to interpret any intrinsic property.

Phenomenalism stopped the dispositionalizing with categorical properties of sensations; operationalism concerning unobservables stopped the process with the categorical properties of macroscopic, nonmolecular *plena*. The extreme position of characterizing all qualities operationally was elaborated in its purest form by Bridgman (1927) and Dingle (1950), and intermittently and less consistently and candidly by others since. This epistemically timid and ontologically bold position made every 'is' into a 'would be if' and ceased to be explicitly endorsed. But that left plenty of halfway-house cases in a state of mid-being as 'would be if's. The dispositionalities of both physical and mental entities were expressed in terms of 'Rylean dispositions', the bare counter-to-the-facts fact of the matter that would 'hold' of a person or thing or situation with no need of an ontological base in any state of the individual or situation. I argued for the need of a categorical state truth-maker for these claims of dispositionality. Armstrong agreed, since he shared with me the aversion to ontological evasion and frivolity. We are still in debate concerning the forms such truth-makers should take.

IV

It is not clear how Armstrong's view (1978, p. 161) that a universal may 'probabilify' and 'predispose' by means of a 'connectedness' relation between universals can be made out in terms of what he has to say about universal instantiations.

That is, his universal is *not* an abstract entity but rather exists only in its spatiotemporal scatter of instantiations. Furthermore, only some of its instantiations 'connect' with some instantiations of other universals; the rest of its instantiations may *never* so connect. So, just what is in or about those instantiations that is connectedness if it is not connecting? There seems to be a waffle between 'connecting' and 'connectable'. However, Armstrong cannot be allowed the latter at this level, because it would be introducing unmanifested dispositionality as an unreduced primitive in the universal instantiations.

Since he claims that the dispositionality that accrues between universals is a *contingent* matter, where the actual connectedness does not obtain between some instantiations of universals (perhaps they are not spatio-temporally contiguous), what is there about such instantiations that constitutes their (contingently) having the (unmanifested) disposition or *not* having the (unmanifested) disposition? The universal instantiations manifesting connectedness are logically independent of and spatiotemporally separate from the instantiations of the same universal that are not manifesting connectedness. Claiming that the universal is the One and the Identical in each instantiation does no good. For the being of the One universal *consists* only in the existence of the logically independent and spatiotemporally separate instantiations that Armstrong must allow (and has allowed) to have differing dispositions without ceasing to be instantiations of the same universal.

Armstrong does not make the ludicrous demand that each universal instantiation should manifest all of its dispositions. It would seem, then, that Armstrong has no way of expressing a difference in the world (truthmaker) between instantiations of the same universal (and content) in which the dispositions of those instantiations are (or can be) different. Armstrong's rejection of universals as abstract entities, together with his rejection of uninstantiated universals, seems to end in his view being only a verbal variant of a Tropes view.

The supposed numerically *one* Universal has its only existence in a plurality of logically and spatiotemporally distinct, numerically *many* intermittently existing universal-instantiation particulars. The connection relations or connectednesses between Universals that are the laws of nature, on Armstrong's view, are just the connection-relation instantiations between the logically and spatiotemporally distinct Universals-instantiations particulars, and these connectednesses between Universals through their instantiations are contingent. There is no way, on Armstrong's view, to prohibit the possibility that Universal U-instantiation-X at T_1P_1 should have different connection-relation instantiations from those of Universal U-instantiation-Y at T_2P_2.

Therefore, there is no more grounding (as Armstrong claims there is) for induction *or* abduction concerning connectedness between Universal instantiations in one spacetime segment and between Universal instantiations of the same universals in another spacetime segment than there would be from one trope in one spacetime segment to an exactly similar trope in another segment. They are, in each case, contingent relations between logically and spatiotemporally distinct individuals.

Putting the matter in terms of causal 'laws' only obfuscates the real problems. I have always thought that those who allow (as does Armstrong) that causal laws *could have been* otherwise have nothing - other than mere Regularist Theory hangovers - to block an allowance (the phrase 'bans on mixed worlds' has been recently introduced) that causal laws *could be* otherwise somewhere, sometime in the actual world. Introducing varieties of supervenience adds more vocabulary without more explanation.

It is one short step from this, which I urge Armstrong to take, to a nonreductionist view of the dispositional.

An elementary point needs to be made, though it should be unnecessary. Dispositions are not quasi-existent possibilia. Unmanifested manifestations are flatly nonexistent, and if the nonexistent divides into impossibilia and possibilia then I suppose they number amongst the possibilia, but I see no need for such reification of the nonexistent.

Dispositions are flatly existent. A particular disposition either exists or it doesn't. One can say of an unmanifesting disposition that it straightout exists even if it is not manifesting any manifestation. It is the unmanifested manifestation, not the disposition itself, that is the would-be-if or would-have-been-if. A disposition can come into existence and cease to exist quite apart from whether or not its manifestations exist.

V

Armstrong can allow all of this, but he would not allow the existence of a disposition for any universal instantiation unless somewhere, sometime there is a universal instantiation that is involved in the manifestation of such a disposition. Otherwise, he would have to explicitly allow unreduced dispositionality into his universal instantiations. I have suggested earlier that he has implicitly and unknowingly allowed just such unreduced dispositionality against his own disclaimers.

There is a case that is a counterexample to Armstrong's disallowance. I first devised the case as a counterexample to verificationism. At the same time, I realized that it could be used against many reductive accounts of causal dispositions, and later applied it against Quine's account in *Word and Object* of a disposition (unmanifested) in terms of an object having a structure similar to that of an object manifesting the supposed disposition.

The case is one of a cosmic geographical fact concerning the spatiotemporal spread of kinds of elementary particles (that presumably do not have 'structures'). It is supposed that there are kinds of elementary particles in some spatiotemporal region of the universe, particles different from the kinds in our own region; and that the regions are so vastly distant that the many special dispositions they have for intercourse with one another never have their very special manifestations; and that nothing else in the universe, in the nature of the case, is like them that *does* have the manifestations. Yet they have causal dispositions ready to go.

A very devoted Quinean in discussion replied, 'And if pigs had wings they would fly'. When I complained that he didn't know any better than I did that this wasn't a *true* case, he responded, 'And if pigs had wings they would fly'.

This noninteracting elementary particles case (as well as another argument presented in Martin 1984, pp. 9f) should serve as a counterexample to the view that causal dispositions are to be explained in terms of categorical states in virtue of which counterfactual or probability statements are true. This is so because, in the nature of the case, counterfactuals or probabilities would be left hanging with no relevant actual frequencies. To put it another way: Given that the dispositionality involved is a contingent matter, what would it be about the pure categoricity of the properties of the elementary particles that would make *true* their dispositionality for mutual manifestations *x* rather than *y*, when there are no relevant manifestations either way?

The life of most honest dispositional states is spent mostly in the presence of other dispositional states whose manifestation is the prevention of those former states from having *their* manifestation. Any particular set of manifestation conditions for a kind of manifestation must exclude other sets of manifestation conditions and so prevent the dispositional state from manifesting manifestations suited to the excluded conditions. It is a busy world.

I wish to claim that one should consider disposition and manifestation to be the basic categories by means of which cause and effect are to be explained. A manifestation of a dispositional state should be seen in depth as the tip of a disposition iceberg at the *time,* rather than over a temporal spread perhaps for irrelevant epistemic purposes.

It is not easy to describe even an ordinary case of the manifestation of a causal disposition. The dissolution of salt in water may not be a manifestation of the salt's solubility in water *even if* it is soluble in water and it comes to dissolve in the water, because God (or something) could cause the dissolution before the water had its chance to do the job.

The dispositional state has its character in terms of the pattern and complex variety of alternative manifestations (under a complex range of kinds of manifesting conditions) *to* or *for* which it is directed. The manifestations themselves *are* such only as *from* the depths of the relevant base in the dispositional state, as the dissolving salt case showed.

VI

There are three important ways of categorizing properties with their dispositions.

1. *Interconnectedness* of properties (with their dispositionalities as well as their categoricities) as: (a) simpler properties being constitutive of a more complex property – for example, four-sided and square; (b) distinct properties related contingently and nomologically – for example, freezing

of water and expansion of water; (c) distinct properties related necessarily – for example, equilateral and equiangular.

Exactly how interconnected the properties of particles or of spatiotemporal segments of fields are – and so the properties of the objects they (the particles or field-segments) constitute – is not fully known, nor is it known what form the real necessities of such interconnections must take or what coherent place, if any, there is for the notion of alternative contingencies. The Limit View of properties put forward elsewhere (Martin 1984) and developed in Section VIII does not in itself prohibit an account purely in terms of contingency, necessity, or some judicious mix thereof.

John Locke thought that if we could but discover the workings of the 'finest interstices of nature' we would find the necessary fittings (cf. his graphic example of the key in the lock) between the 'pure' qualities of measure and quantity. For him, the molecular theory of heat as the motion of insensible particles was an approximation to the ultimate necessities of the fittings of nature.

2. *Reciprocity* between properties of different things or parts of things for the manifestation that is their common product – for example, the soluble salt and solvent water for the solution of the salt in the water. The reciprocity of properties with their dispositions for the manifestations that are their common product is deep and complex. This reciprocity has often been expressed (even recently) in terms of unhelpful distinctions such as power to give versus power to receive, agent versus patient, active versus passive, causal conditions versus standing conditions. What? – Standing *by*?!

The important point remains that the manifestation of a given dispositional state will require the cooperation of some other dispositional states amongst its reciprocating partners. The manifestation of the dispositional state of the match needs, amongst others, the cooperation of the reciprocal dispositional state of the enfolding oxygen. This view of the interconnectednesses and reciprocities of properties, largely unknown but existent still, contrasts with the simple-minded view that because nature does not lay out The Cause of each event, causality itself is mind-dependent.

3. *Correlativeness* of dispositions–manifestation, such that for something to be a manifestation it must come from a relevant, deep enough and broad enough disposition base, and for something to be a disposition base it must be so *for* alternative typifying manifestations. Nature comes in package deals. Correlativeness is a largely unexplored but crucially important concept that has major implications in the philosophy of science, philosophy of mind and philosophy of language. It can't be properly stated here.

VII

A weird case of my invention has plagued, puzzled and frustrated me. I don't know for sure if it makes coherent sense, but it is not clearly nonsense. I have felt, over the years, that it was important to think out this case as a kind of test of my views of the workings of causality.

Suppose there is a volume of nothing. I mean just absolute nothing – absolutely empty vacuum. Call it Nothing. It would be, as it were, shaped and sized by its real surrounds, and it seems we could think of it moving. But it now seems to have too many basic primary qualities to retain its nonbeing status. Centuries-old disputes arise again concerning the differentiation of objects and vacua. Aristotle argued they couldn't exist, yet Boyle almost made one.

Perhaps the shape, size and volume of Nothing can be explicated in terms of the real things that surround it. But my puzzle was elsewhere: namely, with its quite undeniable powers and dispositions to affect things that seem to be intrinsically, internally *about* it – indeed, *inside* the real surrounds.

The powers would be many and almost certainly terrible. One wishes to avoid the reification of the Nothing that comes with admission of its frightful powers, capacities and, indeed, forces. And one cannot attribute these powers, as one did the primary qualities, to the real surrounds. It is the *nonbeing* that seems to have such destructive force. That is, if there were nothing whatsover that was in one's physical surrounds and therefore nothing that is or would be supportive of one's existence, one could expect to cease to be.

We should make use of the more basic notion of reciprocating dispositions and mutual manifestations. The production, prevention, or continuance and sustenance of various properties of an entity (or spatiotemporal segment of a field), some of which may be essential for its existence, can be seen as mutual manifestations. They are mutual manifestations of the properties, qua certain dispositions of the entity, with the reciprocal dispositions of its partners. It is a model of reciprocal mutual dependence; if the reciprocal dispositional partners are not present then the mutual manifestation involving the continuance of the properties is not present either.

This may be how it must be in order to avoid the nonsense of a suppositional allowance of powers, forces and causal activity of a reified Nothing.

VIII

It can be shown that, for any property instantiation bearing a disposition, there are more alternative forms of manifestation of that disposition than it ever manifests.

1. For any disposition a property bears, it is ready for indefinitely many kinds (though not just any kind) of manifestation. This is so because of its reciprocity with an indefinite number of possible partners and the variety of alternative manifestation conditions.

2. For any disposition a property bears, its manifestation excludes other possible alternative manifestations. The exclusion is sometimes contingent but sometimes necessary, as in the case of a manifestation in the form of the production, *or* continuance of some determinate property that would necessarily exclude the manifestation of another determinate property under the same determinable obtaining at the same time and place.

3. Pure categoricity of a property or state is as much of a myth and philosophical artifice as is pure dispositionality. Any intrinsic property is Janus-faced, a two-sided coin, and only at the limit of an unrealizable abstraction can one think of these as separate properties in themselves. No intrinsic properties, right down to the ultimate properties of elementary particles or the ultimate properties of spatiotemporal regions of fields, are – in Aquinas's terms – 'in pure act' or purely categorical. They are not, and indeed cannot be, manifesting all of which they are capable.

I have called this the Limit View, though this is misleading because there are no *degrees* within the limit by which a property is categorical or dispositional. 'Dissolves' is no less dispositional than 'is soluble' because different properties obtain for 'in solution' that must in their turn have their dispositionality. Perhaps the term should be the 'Abstractionist View', but that is misleading also. The categoricity and dispositionality of a property or property state are abstractly distinct but actually inseparable, and no nonformal property can manifest all its dispositionality simultaneously.

It isn't that an intrinsic property or quality is purely categorical but dispositionality is 'supervenient' on it, for properties are indissolubly categorical-*cum*-dispositional or dispositional-*cum*-categorical. The dispositionality is as basic and irreducible as is the categoricity, and there is no direction from one as basic in a property to the other as 'supervenient'. To separate one from the other as the really basic property is philosophical artifice and error.

4. Putting the cart in the right position *behind* the horse, one can see how misleading it is to try to explain dispositionality in terms of 'structural states'. The properties of elementary particles or spatiotemporal segments of fields are not structural states. These properties are not in pure act, that is, manifesting at each moment or temporal stage *all* of which they are capable. They have dispositions, not all of which they are always manifesting, and – in the nature of the case, qua elementary particles – their dispositionality is not explained in terms of properties of their constituents.

One should not ask, 'Is there causality at the quantum level?' One should ask the ontologically more basic question, 'Are the properties of quanta in pure act, or are they capable of more than on any particular occasion they do or can manifest?' The answer to the latter is clearly 'Yes'. In this way, one has placed what can and cannot be manifested and how that can change – all of which one should want from causality – in the property instantiations themselves. Only the properties of mathematical entities are in pure act, but of course the entities of physics are not numbers.

This account provides an ontology by which to understand and explain Donald Davidson's insistence that causality concerns events, without denying that characterizations in terms of cause and effect are clumsy ways of indicating the more basic operations of disposition manifestation. If cause and effect are mutual manifestations of reciprocal dispositionalities involved in properties of entities or of segments of fields, then the event status of manifestations is explicit and unarguably obvious. However, when we see causality in terms of the reciprocity of dispositions in their mutual manifestation, we are relieved from attempting the impossible task of separating the cause and the effect, and are able to understand their evident contemporaneity as unproblematic.

Two playing cards standing, leaning together to remain upright, constitute a simple case of causal contemporaneity that is typical throughout nature. Card A's uprightness is operative for card B's uprightness and vice versa. Trying to separate out one prior event as cause and one subsequent event as effect is misguided. The case of the leaning cards is a vivid but standard instance of the ubiquitous mutual manifestation of reciprocal disposition partners. This is just a graphic case; the symmetrical relationship is not necessary for reciprocity of dispositional partners in their mutual manifestations, as can be seen in the case of salt dissolving in water in Section VI.

We do not yet know how tight or how loose is the net of mutual manifestations in the finer interstices of nature; nor what mutual manifestations there may be between spatiotemporally distant reciprocal partners; nor how necessary – or, if contingent, how regular and undiffering – are the kinds of disposition-loadedness of the properties of quanta. (Perhaps there are what could be called 'disposition flutters' to explain and provide truth-makers for what would otherwise be indeterminate or bare mathematizations of probabilities.) At least, we need a model by which to conceptualize the alternatives. I have tried to provide this by means of my Limit View of properties and my Mutual Manifestation View.

Give me, then, my Archimedean point: a realism for the unreduced existence of the dispositionality of properties such that a particular readiness potential can exist, though the manifestation conditions (including the reciprocal disposition partners) do not exist and perhaps never exist. Then an infinity of alternative manifestations is generable, within limits, from that actual point of the infinity of what the readiness potentials are *for*, and also from the even greater infinity of what they are *not* for.

It remains to be seen how much of what is needed can be provided within the resources of this model for modalities without possible worlds and mathematics without numbers. Here, I can only suggest that the model is at least as rich as that of Armstrong's, and does not have the problems that I have found in Armstrong's formulation and use of universals.

REFERENCES

Armstrong, D. M. 1968. *A Materialist Theory of the Mind* (London: Routledge & Kegan Paul).
      1978. *Universals and Scientific Realism:* vol. 2, *A Theory of Universals* (Cambridge University Press).
Beauchamp, Tom L. (ed.). 1974. *Philosophical Problems of Causation* (Belmont, CA: Dickenson).
Bridgman, P. W. 1927. *The Logic of Modern Physics* (New York: Macmillan).
Dingle, Herbert. 1950. 'A Theory of Measurement', *British Journal for the Philosophy of Science* 1: 5–26.
Martin, C. B. 1984. 'Anti-Realism and the World's Undoing', *Pacific Philosophical Quarterly* 65: 3–20.
Place, U. T. 1956. 'Is Consciousness a Brain Process?', *British Journal of Psychology* 47: 44–50.
Smart, J. J. C. 1963. *Philosophy and Scientific Realism* (London: Routledge & Kegan Paul).
Wisdom, John. 1952. *Other Minds* (Oxford: Blackwell).

Reply to Martin

D. M. ARMSTRONG

My philosophical debts to my friend, collaborator and critic Charlie Martin are great indeed. I have tried to discharge them in an article entitled 'C. B. Martin, Counterfactuals, Causality, and Conditions', written for a book dedicated to him (Heil 1989, pp. 7–15). As a result I will be somewhat briefer here. Two themes were central. First there was Martin's demand for a truth-maker, some thing or factor in the world by virtue of which true propositions are true. Martin pressed his demand with special vigour in the case of counterfactuals and attributions of dispositions. He pointed out that phenomenalists about physical objects, Ryleans about dispositions, and operationalists about measurable things were all up to their necks in counterfactuals. Yet they never considered the ontological implications of these statements that they threw around so casually. I didn't like any of these doctrines, and in any case they have since fallen into discredit, but it came as a revelation to me that their upholders were getting away with ontological murder because they were failing to confront the question about the truth-makers for their counterfactuals. In the case of dispositions this led me to categorical states of the disposed thing, and so, in the philosophy of mind, away from the Rylean behaviourism that I had previously espoused.

Second, there was Martin's demonstration (antedating Grice) that perception conceptually involves the causal action of the thing perceived on the perceiver. This he followed up by arguments to show how deeply causality is involved in the analysis of many other mental concepts. For me this was the stimulus to something that Martin thought was going too far: a purely causal account of the mental.

Martin, however, was well ahead of me in rejecting a Humean analysis of the nature of causality itself. I was perhaps not quite so far behind as he suggests in his paper. Already, before my book on the mind was published (1968), I had begun to think that a deflationary account of causation assorted rather ill with a Causal theory of the mind. But I remained agnostic about causality for many years, an agnosticism transcended only when I began to think seriously about universals.

I regret this long hesitation very much. Without it I would have got much more from the seminars on causality that Martin conducted while he was teaching at Sydney. Incidentally, I am glad that he notes the considerable contribution that George Molnar made to those classes. Molnar (1969) published a fine article on the topic of laws, which has deservedly been anthologized. That Molnar left philosophy a few years later was a considerable loss to our profession.

1. The Inverted Spectrum

Martin holds that the qualities of experience are not reducible. For myself, I think that there are no such qualities. There is such a thing as experience, of course, but it does not involve mental qualities. (See, in particular, Farrell 1950.) There are the 'secondary qualities', but I think that they are physical properties, physics-respectable properties, of physical things, and that their secondariness is constituted only by their relative unimportance and idiosyncrasy in the physical scheme of things. (See the reply to Campbell in Chapter 11 of this volume.)

Martin holds that the inverted-spectrum argument is very powerful against the view that experience is qualityless. There are those who have doubted that it is even a meaningful supposition that your colour spectrum could be inverted relative to mine. Let us pass over those doubts that ask whether the colours really have relations that permit systematic and exact inversion, doubts that do not seem too important in this context. Any other doubts seem to me to have been stilled by an elegant argument of Sydney Shoemaker's in a paper 'The Inverted Spectrum' (reprinted 1984). He argues from the possibility of *intra*subjective inversion to the possibility of intersubjective inversion. It is hard to deny the possibility of somebody actually experiencing spectrum inversion in their own case. But if this is possible, must not the question arise of whether somebody else's colour experience corresponds to the first or the second of these spectra – or, indeed, to neither one? So we ought to admit the possibility of an inverted spectrum. But what will the inverted spectrum come to, given a purely causal theory of the mental?

I have attempted to answer this question (Armstrong 1968, Chapter 11, Section IV). I there suggested that it could be a matter of those processes within one mind that are apt for red selection (i.e. red sensations) being type-identical with processes in another mind that are apt for green selection, and of course vice versa. In the two minds, wires would be crossed relative to each other. Red things would furnish red sensations to both minds and green things would furnish green sensations to both. But if A's red sensation had been going on in B's mind it would have been a green sensation, while if B's red sensation had been in A's mind it would have been a red sensation.

I am not aware that Martin has ever commented on this attempt to answer the inverted-spectrum argument. An interesting feature of the answer is that here there would be a reversal – and so a difference – in the pattern of causal functioning, without any difference in the input–output relations. That is one of the reasons why I have always denied that the Causal theory is a purely input–output theory. (The other reason is already implicit in Smart's original account of having a yellowish-orange after-image. He spoke of that experience as merely being '*like* what is going on' in the experience of actually seeing an orange. Evidently, he could not say that the two experiences had the same causal powers.)

Martin says that he rejects 'the functionalist attempt to render experiential qualities in terms of dispositionalities'. But, as I have just been saying, I reject the idea that there *are* experiential qualities. The only qualities we experience, I say, are qualities of physical things, including our bodies. (The point is empirical, but *pace* Martin and, as it happens, John Anderson, I do not think that we experience any qualities that are qualities of the brain.) And I do not think that the qualities of physical things all dissolve into dispositions.

2. Why Martin Ought to Believe in Universals

Those of us who accept properties (which here may be taken to include relations) in our ontology may differ as to whether they are particulars or universals. Those who accept 'strong' (i.e. non-Humean) causes and laws may differ about whether they are contingent or necessary. These differences yield four positions.

(1) Properties are particulars, causes and laws are contingent.
(2) Properties are particulars, causes and laws are necessary.
(3) Properties are universals, causes and laws are 'strong' but contingent. (This is my view.)
(4) Properties are universals, causes and laws are necessary.

Martin holds very strongly that all properties are particulars, so his options are (1) and (2). He holds further (personal communication) that at least some causal connections are necessary, and perhaps all are. (Presumably laws would follow causes.) I myself think that (1) is the worst of the four positions, making an account of laws and a solution to the problem of induction well-nigh impossible. As a result, I think that Martin has a strong motive for moving to a whole-hearted acceptance of (2). But, I now proceed to argue, he might do even better to accept (4).

Martin, like me, rejects the thesis that all properties reduce to dispositions. But associated with all his particularized properties he finds powers, powers standing in intricate relations of mutual reciprocity to further powers linked to other properties, powers which are fully real and present even when they are not being manifested, powers that need never be manifested even where that power type is not manifested at any other place and time. Notice, however, that his powers are as particular as the properties they are associated with.

A main weakness of such a scheme is the difficulty it has in giving an account of the ontology of laws of nature: What could a law then be but one of Hume's dismal regularities? But with universals substituted for particularized properties and powers in Martin's scheme, laws of nature come out very simply as the total range of powers, in all their reciprocity, associated with each universal. (If there are *fundamental* noncausal laws, some further story will have to be told about them.)

If properties and relations are taken as particulars, then one can do no more than take equivalence classes under the equivalence relation of exact similarity (a relation whose properties of symmetry and transitivity cannot be further explained), and then associate different sets of mutually reciprocal powers with each equivalence class. The obvious sceptical doubt that then arises is that different members of the same equivalence class may be associated with different sorts of power. Even if it is granted that the link between property and power is a necessary one, why should it be necessary that distinct (even if exactly resembling) properties should bestow exactly the same powers? Necessity there may be, but we certainly have no a priori insight into the principles of its operation.

Peter Forrest, in Chapter 3 of this volume, points out that the only general principle that those who take properties to be particulars can appeal to here is that of 'like causes like', where this has the sense 'from like causes, like effects'. In contrast with a theory of universals, this principle cannot be understood as 'from same causes, same effects', not at any rate if 'same' here is taken as strict identity. And for the all-important case of functional laws, Forrest argues that it will even be difficult to bring them under the like-causes-like principle.

Contrast the situation where the transition is made to universals. What we have then is different particulars qualified by exactly the same thing. Putting the matter at its very lowest, will it not immediately be natural to think that the same powers are associated with this same thing? Properties, powers and laws will then be linked together in a convincing way.

It would indeed appear that, on a scheme of universals + necessity, all powers and all laws supervene upon the existence of the universals, in the technical sense of supervenience in which 'every possible world' that contains just these universals has just the same laws. At the same time there could be, as Martin thinks it is possible for there to be, laws not deducible from any more general law but which have no positive instantiations. For since the laws flow from the universals alone, there can be nonexistent but possible situations involving certain universals which, if the situations did exist, would necessarily develop along lines not governed by any instantiated law. The full richness of the scheme of interlocking powers that Martin adumbrates in his paper would also seem to be available to him.

Like me, I think that Martin wishes to avoid properties that are not properties of some particular. It would be worrisome for him, therefore, if the substitution of property universals for property particulars were to make uninstantiated universals a possibility. But as far as I can see, any threat of such universals is exactly equal to the threat of unattached property particulars. Martin presumably thinks that his doctrine of dispositionality evades the latter difficulty. If so, then the situation is made no worse by going over to a doctrine of universals.

3. Necessity versus Contingency

I will now offer arguments against Martin's view that causes and laws are necessary. But, in view of the previous section, I will use no arguments that depend upon the assumption that properties are particulars. It will then be time to defend my 'universals + contingency' view against Martin's criticism.

The first problem to be raised is that it may be difficult to uphold a necessitarian view if the fundamental laws of nature are, as it seems that they may be, irreducibly probabilistic. There is first the point that, given the candidate for the cause, the effect does not always follow. Perhaps that difficulty can be met by allowing contingency at that point while insisting that, where the effect does follow, then 'in every possible world' that effect must be of a certain nature. But the deeper difficulty is that it is hard to see how the precise probability is necessary. Suppose the probability is 0.4. Why could it not have been 0.45? In what does the necessity of the alleged necessity consist? Perhaps some very powerful scientific theory would to some degree answer these questions. But that puts the necessitarian theory somewhat at the mercy of science.

Some might raise a more general difficulty for the necessitarian theory here. It might be said that we can easily conceive, we can clearly and distinctly conceive, a cause to exist with a different effect or no effect at all. Similarly, it is easy to conceive the antecedent of a law obtaining with a different consequent or no consequent at all. This argument I reject. It rests upon the old and disastrous Cartesian identification of possibility with clear and distinct conception. At best, clear and distinct conception gives a prima facie reason for thinking that we are faced with a genuine possibility. It can be allowed that such conceiving is a mark of, perhaps constitutes, doxastic possibility. But we are here concerned with ontological possibility.

But I do not think that the argument from conceiving misses the mark entirely. Cause and effect, antecedent and consequent states of affairs in the case of a law, would appear to be 'distinct existences', and it is a plausible view that there are no necessitations holding between distinct existences. I say this not appealing to the authority of David Hume, but because this principle is bound up with a combinatorial theory of possibility, which I think is the most plausible theory of possibility. We may here remain agnostic about the details of such a theory. I take the (fictional) recombination, contraction and expansion of fully distinct elements of actuality to constitute the very essence of possibility (see Armstrong 1989a). But even if this is incorrect, combinatorial rules of this general sort seem to be the only way that one can reach a systematic theory of the structure of possibility and, incidentally, make sense of the idea that conceivability is a first rough test of possibility. Thus I believe that there are quite good reasons to reject a necessitarian theory of cause and of law.

I pass to the matter of defending my contingency + universals view against Martin's criticisms. There are two things to take up. First, Martin argues, against my view of laws of nature as contingent relations between universals, that I can have no assurance that a certain connection of universals that obtains *here* will obtain elsewhere, so that my theory will lack certain advantages that I claim for it. Second, there is the argument from unrealized but empirical possibilities that are not deducible from any instantiated law. This, Martin thinks, should lead me to take powers (dispositions) with full ontological seriousness.

About the first point I shall be brief, since I have already defended myself against this criticism – which is rather regularly made – in my reply to Fales (Chapter 6 in this volume). What I believe my critics overlook is that the relation that I postulate is a higher-order relation holding between certain universals, and that this relation has no further terms. The universals cannot change. And how can the relation between them change? It is contingent (according to me) and so it could be asserted not to obtain, or to be different from the way it actually is, without contradiction. But it cannot, while being a relation between just the universals themselves, be different at different places and times. An analogy that might help is the spatiotemporal relation between two spatiotemporal positions. That would appear to be contingent, but cannot change.

It may still be argued that if the relation is of this nature then it will have no consequences at the level of particulars. But I think that all higher-order properties, relations and states of affairs must have consequences at the levels below them. This is most clearly seen with Russell's 'general facts'. The state of affairs that a certain collection is *all* the lower-order states of affairs acts to exclude any further lower-order states of affairs. Here combinatorialism about possibility has to be limited. Similarly, if a certain sort of state of affairs causes a further sort of state of affairs (a 'relation between universals'), this automatically has consequences at the level of first-order particulars, excluding what would otherwise be certain possibilities.

So, finally, we come to what may be called the Martin–Tooley case. Might not a certain property or properties be big with empirical possibilities that are never realized because the appropriate boundary conditions never obtain? Yet, at the same time, might it not be that from none of the manifested dispositions or instantiated laws do these empirical possibilities flow?

The first thing I would like to draw attention to is what strange things such unmanifested powers would be. In some sense the power contains its unmanifested manifestation. It points to it, for all the world as if it had irreducible intentionality! And yet the manifestation does not exist.

It has a quasi-necessary connection with its manifestations. I do not think that Martin should be too surprised if such an entity disturbs the philosophical conscience of some people, and that as a result they look for alternatives. I can feel the attractions of Martin's view that there are irreducible powers, indeed it is the view I incline to, saving my own. But it is surely worth trying to work out a view where for the powers are substituted 'strong' (but contingent) laws that are always instantiated somewhere or when. It seems clear that such a view will be able to provide truth-makers for the attribution of unmanifested powers, with the possible exception of Martin–Tooley type cases.

It should be noted that these truth-makers are not just a matter of particulars being in suitable categorical states. That is necessary, but there must in addition be 'strong' laws involving those states. These laws will be causal laws, with the categorical states an essential element in the cause. And for the manifestation to really be a manifestation, it must be brought about by that cause (perhaps even 'in the right way') – a reasonably strong replacement for Martin's powers. The world seems little less busy, but with universals it is more united; it does more with less.

Returning to the Martin–Tooley cases, we may divide them into two sorts. First there are cases where we have reason to believe that, say, two particles which never meet would have had a quite idiosyncratic mode of interaction had they had a chance to interact. (Say the world is a world with many emergent laws.) In such a case we can certainly say that there is a true counterfactual: If these particles had met, they would have interacted idiosyncratically. But here truth, I suggest, is no more than warranted assertability. It is not an implausible idea that counterfactual discourse is second-grade discourse; thus, although it is true that there would have been an idiosyncratic outcome, there is no determinate idiosyncratic outcome (forever unknown to us) that would have occurred.

I confess that I am not totally happy with this. If it were just a matter of adjudicating on the case, then my intuitions tend toward Martin's. But if we consider our two overall positions, then I am content to lose on this roundabout, reckoning that I more than make up on the swings. (Every metaphysic that I know of has weaknesses as well as strengths.) It may be noted that the Martin–Tooley cases are, to the extent that I am able to judge, *merely* possible. If the actual structure of fundamental scientific laws turned up cases of this sort, then that might be the time to think again.

The second sort of case, found for instance in Carroll (1987, p. 264), argues from bare possibility. X-particles are, by chance, never found in Y-fields. It is then claimed that there might be a possible law that X-particles in Y-fields have spin up, and another and incompatible possible law that they have spin down. There is no evidence either way. But in a case like this I do not see why we cannot say flatly that these worlds contain neither law.

So I suggest that it is plausible enough to take Martin's powers as shadows cast on the world by strong laws connecting universals. The world certainly presents itself to us as a world of threats and promises. But may this not be a matter of biology? Planning, looking forward, is of the practical essence for intelligent creatures. Such planning involves conditionals. If I do X then Y, but if I refrain from doing X then Z. Treating powers as actual constituents of objects may help to give this planning a much needed imaginative urgency.

REFERENCES

Armstrong, D. M. 1968. *A Materialist Theory of the Mind* (London: Routledge & Kegan Paul).

1989a. *A Combinatorial Theory of Possibility* (Cambridge University Press).

Carroll, John W. 1987. 'Ontology and the Laws of Nature', *Australasian Journal of Philosophy* 65: 261–76.

Farrell, Brian. 1950. 'Experience', *Mind* 50: 170–98.

Heil, John (ed.). 1989. *Cause, Mind, and Reality: Essays Honoring C. B. Martin* (Dordrecht: Kluwer).

Molnar, George. 1969. 'Kneale's Argument Revisited', *Philosophical Review* 78: 79–89. Reprinted in *Philosophical Problems of Causation*, ed. Tom L. Beauchamp (Belmont, CA: Dickenson, 1974).

Shoemaker, Sydney. 1984. *Identity, Cause, and Mind* (Cambridge University Press).

Laws of Nature, Modality and Humean Supervenience

PETER MENZIES

From a philosophical point of view, the most puzzling feature of laws of nature is their modal character. The law that all copper expands when heated involves a physical necessity that is not possessed by a regularity holding as an accidental fact: Every piece of copper *must* expand when heated, whereas every coin in my pocket *just happens* to be a dollar coin. One central philosophical problem has been to account for the apparent physical necessity of laws.

One traditional approach has been to deny that laws are physically necessary in any real sense. This is the approach endorsed by Humean empiricists advocating *regularity theories* of laws. Such empiricists argue that a law of nature *in re* is just a regularity holding among actual occurrences; any appearance of physical necessity is to be explained as a projection of our mental attitudes to the regularities. I think that it has become clear from recent philosophical debate, however, that it is not possible to tame the physical modalities within the actualistic metaphysics of Humean empiricism. The prospects for a regularity approach to laws look very poor. I review the shortcomings of the best regularity theory – David Lewis's – in Section 1.

Another, more recent tradition has been to reject the actualistic metaphysics of Humean empiricism and openly embrace the physical necessity of laws as real. This is the approach adopted by David Armstrong, Fred Dretske and Michael Tooley. These philosophers think that a law of nature consists in an irreducible physical necessity inhering *in re*. In the case of Armstrong's theory, which will be the focus of this paper, it takes the form of a relation of nomic necessitation between universals. Again, I think that recent philosophical discussion has made it clear that necessitation theories like Armstrong's face considerable difficulties concerning the character of their postulated necessary connections and their relation to ordinary empirical regularities. I elaborate on these concerns in Section 2, which reviews Armstrong's theory.

In my opinion, both these well-known approaches to laws are unsatisfactory. In this paper I shall present a new theory of laws that does not force physical modality into the Humean straightjacket nor postulate irreducible necessary connections. The theory will appeal to a primitive concept of modality which we must all possess in virtue of being decision-making agents. This modal concept is that of the possible courses of events within an agent's control or, in other words, the possible outcomes that an agent could bring about by performing an action. I shall argue that a law of nature is a regularity that is experimentally resilient in the sense that it obtains in all such possible courses of events. I present the theory in Section 3, and defend it against some pressing objections in Section 4.

I need to state at the outset a significant limitation I intend to impose on my discussion. I shall confine my discussion to deterministic laws and set aside probabilistic laws altogether. Probabilistic laws introduce complications that cannot be adequately treated in this essay.

1. Lewis's Regularity Theory

Empiricists have traditionally been attracted to the regularity approach to laws of nature, according to which the regularities obtaining among actual occurrences determine which laws of nature hold. They have been attracted to this approach, I think, because of a commitment to a deeper ontological thesis, which David Lewis has called the thesis of *Humean supervenience* after the great denier of necessary conditions. He explains the thesis in the following terms:

Humean supervenience . . . is the doctrine that all there is to the world is a vast mosaic of local matters of particular fact, just one little thing and then another. (But it is no part of the thesis that these local matters are mental.) (1986c, p. ix)

As it applies to the case of laws, the thesis of Humean supervenience implies:

(1)   For any two worlds w_1 and w_2, if w_1 and w_2 agree on local particular facts (and so on regularities), they agree on laws of nature.

The reference to local particular facts in this formulation is deliberately vague, as empiricists differ on exactly which requirements to impose on the subvenient facts. But what seems common to them is the idea that the subvenient facts are to be actual, occurrent facts consisting in the instantiation of an intrinsic property by an individual at a spatiotemporal location. So understood, John Earman has called acceptance of (1) 'the empiricist loyalty test on laws' (1986, p. 85).

Traditional empiricists, then, have regarded it as incumbent on them to find an account of laws which sustains (1). The simplest way of doing so, the way followed by the logical positivists and their immediate successors, is to identify laws with a suitably selected subset of regularities. A theory of laws that is representative of this tradition of thought might go like this: It is a law that A if and only if 'A' is a true lawlike sentence; that is, 'A' has the form of a universal generalization like $\forall x(Fx \supset Gx)$, where 'F' and 'G' are nonpositional, empirical predicates.[1]

Sure enough, this theory of laws makes them conform to the Humean supervenience thesis (1), since two worlds agreeing on local particular facts will also agree on which regularities involving nonpositional, empirical properties hold. But, as a recent barrage of criticism has shown, the theory is not even close to being a decent theory of laws. (See Armstrong 1983a, Chapters 2–4; Dretske 1977; Tooley 1987). For example, the theory fails to meet the most basic condition of adequacy on a theory of laws, namely that it should distinguish between lawful generalizations and accidentally true ones. To appeal to a well-known example of Reichenbach's, there is a clear-cut distinction with respect to lawfulness between the true generalization that all solid spheres of uranium (U235) have a diameter of less than one mile and the let-us-suppose true generalization that all solid spheres of gold have a diameter of less than one mile. The first generalization states a law and the second an accidental fact. But the theory under consideration implies that both generalizations are laws since both are true lawlike sentences. Again, the theory is too indiscriminate in the way it turns all vacuously true generalizations (with appropriate predicates) into laws. Thus, if there are no Fs then it is true that $\forall x(Fx \supset Gx)$; and provided that 'F' and 'G' are nonpositional, empirical predicates, this generalization will count as a law according to the theory. It is true that science does allow vacuous laws such as Newton's first law to the effect that all bodies with no force exerted on them have zero acceleration. But it does so selectively, refusing to admit such frivolities as the true 'lawlike' generalization that all polka-dotted quarks have charm.

Faced with the shortcomings of this simple-minded way of comforming to the supervenience thesis (1), empiricists have resorted to other strategies to vindicate it. By far the most plausible of these is the strategy of arguing that laws are not just the regularities expressed by true lawlike sentences, but rather those regularities that fit together in a coherent system. Mill (1843, Book III, Chapter IV, Section 1) and Ramsey (1978) explored this strategy, But the most sophisticated development of the strategy has been at the hands of David Lewis. He argues that an adequate account of laws must be collective, treating regularities not one at a time but as members of integrated systems of truths: Whether a regularity counts as a law or an accidental fact depends on whether other regularities obtain that fit together with it in a suitable system.

Following Mill and Ramsey, I take a suitable system to be the one that has the virtues we aspire to in our own theory-building, and that has them to the greatest extent possible given the way the world is. It must be entirely true; it must be closed under strict implication; it must be as simple in axiomatization as it can be without sacrificing too much information content; and it must have as much information content as it can without sacrificing too much simplicity. A law is any regularity that earns inclusion in the ideal system. (Or, in case of ties, in every ideal system.)[2] (1983, p. 367)

Lewis intends this to be a theory of nonprobabilistic laws. Recently (1986c, pp. 121–31), he has generalized the theory to cover probabilistic laws, but we shall not discuss the generalized theory except tangentially.

Lewis's theory has many virtues, not least among them being that it ensures that nonprobabilistic laws, at least, conform to the Humean supervenience thesis (1). For two worlds that share the same pattern of local particular fact also share the same systems of regularities; and, since our standards of simplicity and information content apply to all worlds uniformly, they pick out the same ideal system, and so the same laws, for both worlds. The theory also appears to overcome the shortcomings of the simple-minded regularity theory considered earlier. Unlike that theory, it can distinguish between laws and accidental truths by way of the distinction it draws between regularities that find a place in the ideal system and those that do not. It is also much more selective about which vacuously true generalizations express laws: Only those true generalizations belonging to the ideal system can express laws, and a vacuously true generalization can belong to the ideal system only if its contribution to simplicity is sufficiently great to offset its lack of information content.

Is it so clear, however, that Lewis's theory succeeds in these matters as much as it might appear? For example, consider more closely the question of how Lewis's theory makes out the distinction between law and accidental regularity in Reichenbach's familiar example. The theory must say that it is an accidental regularity that all solid spheres of gold have a diameter of less than one mile because it is not incorporated in the ideal system: The loss of simplicity that would result from adding it to the system would not be offset by the gain in information content. But is this really so? As Earman remarks (1986, p. 89), it is not compellingly obvious that the scales tip in this way, whereas it is compellingly obvious that the regularity does not hold as a law. Correspondingly, an ordinary person's certainty that it is a law that all solid spheres of uranium have a diameter of less than one mile is not matched by his degree of certainty that this regularity belongs to the ideal system for the actual world. The latter judgement requires some fine calculations about the balance of simplicity and information content in different systems of fundamental laws for the world – calculations that the ordinary person cannot make with any degree of certainty at all. While these observations do not count as any kind of conclusive objection to Lewis's theory, they do suggest that the theory does not capture the intuitive content of our concept of a law: It makes the issue of whether a regularity holds as a law depend on complicated *extrinsic* considerations regarding its relations to other regularities, whereas this issue seems intuitively to be a simple one depending on the *intrinsic* nature of the regularity.

Still, there are other, more compelling difficulties facing Lewis's theory. One serious difficulty is that the theory does not seem to capture the intuitive physical necessity of laws. It is true that a sense of necessity can be stipulatively defined in Lewis's framework: A proposition can be said to be physically necessary in a world w if and only if it is true in all the worlds in which the laws of w hold. But this sense of necessity does not seem to be strong enough. Van Fraassen makes the point forcefully with an imaginary example (1989, pp. 46–7). He has us imagine a possible world in which there are golden spheres moving in stable orbits around one another, and much smaller iron cubes lying on their surface, and nothing else. This world's regularities are described completely by Newton's mechanics plus the law of gravitation. Intuitive judgements about simplicity and information content dictate that the ideal system for this world should include the statement that all and only spheres are gold. Hence, by the stipulative definition, it is physically necessary in this world that this regularity holds. But this seems wrong. As van Fraassen remarks, we can imagine that there were several little gold cubes among the iron ones, or that several of the gold spheres collided and altered each other's shapes. The example makes the point nicely that simplicity and information content in an ideal system do not add up to genuine physical necessity.

Another serious difficulty for Lewis's theory stems from a much discussed counterexample to it. The example was first described by Tooley (1977, pp. 669–72) and later elaborated by Carroll (1990, pp. 202–4). In this example we are to imagine a world with only one fundamental law, which governs the interaction of particles of type X and fields of type Y. The law states that all X-particles subject to a Y-field have spin up. As it happens, no X-particle ever finds its way into a Y-field in this world, so that the single fundamental law holds vacuously. This nomically barren world is very curious; nonetheless, it seems to be a possible one. Can Lewis's theory explain our intuitive judgement that a world could be governed by a single law of this kind? What is the ideal system for this world on Lewis's theory? One system combining simplicity and information content is the theory axiomatizable in terms of a single axiom that all X-particles subject to Y-fields have spin *up*. But another system with an equal amount of simplicity and information content is the system with the single axiom that all X-particles subject to Y-fields have spin *down*. In cases where two or more systems tie for the best system, Lewis says, the laws are the regularities that are common to all the systems; and if there are no regularities common to all the systems then it is indeterminate what the laws are (1986c, p. 124). But in the case at hand there is no regularity common to two tied systems, so Lewis's theory implies that it is indeterminate what law governs this world. But this is contrary to our initial strong intuition.[3]

This example, I think, is a particularly instructive one. For a small modification of it enables us to see immediately, without having to reflect on any particular theory, that laws of nature violate the Humean supervenience thesis (1). Instead of considering just a single world, let us consider two worlds like that envisaged in the Tooley–Carroll example. Both worlds contain X-particles and Y-fields and nothing else; in both worlds it happens that the particles and the fields never interact; both worlds are governed by a single fundamental law governing the interaction of the particles and the fields. Now it seems completely in accord with the way we intuitively judge that something is a law to suppose that the worlds differ with respect to which law holds: One world is subject to the vacuous law that all X-particles in Y-fields have spin up and the other world is subject to the similarly vacuous law that all X-particles in Y-fields have spin down. This is conceivable even when we suppose that the two worlds agree on all the local particular facts. In view of these judgements, we must conclude that the thesis of Humean supervenience does not hold true of laws. This suggests that the prospects are very poor for any regularity theory, whether naive or sophisticated, since the distinguishing characteristic of such theories is that they are tailor-made to conform to this thesis.

The various difficulties I have discussed point to the central defect of Lewis's theory, and indeed of all regularity theories. The defect is that they fail to capture the *modal character of laws of nature*. Each of the counterexamples above works because it highlights some or other modal ingredient in our pretheoretic concept of a law. For example, our pretheoretic concept is one that distinguishes laws from accidental regularities in terms of the fact that the former involve, as part of their intrinsic nature, a kind of physical necessity that the latter do not possess. Similarly, a regularity can count as law – even though it holds vacuously – because it holds in certain unrealized physically possible situations. It is in virtue of this modal feature of laws that they fail to conform to Humean supervenience: Two worlds agreeing on actual occurrent facts may differ in their modal structure. Lewis's theory fails because all such regularity theories must fail; for they try to fashion modal facts from the thin actualistic resources of Humean empiricism. But to do this is to commit what might be called the actualist fallacy of trying to derive conclusions about the possible and the necessary from premises about the actual. No amount of sophisticated talk of ideal systems that combine simplicity and information content will make this fallacious inference virtuous.

2. Armstrong's Necessitation Theory of Laws

It is a plausible thought that a law is a relation between empirically distinguished or élite properties – natural properties, universals or what have you. It is also a plausible thought that a law involves a kind of physical necessity that distinguishes it from an accidental regularity.

David Armstrong's theory of laws (developed most fully in Armstrong 1983a) combines these thoughts by stating that a law is a relation of nomic necessitation between universals. The theory depends on his realist theory of universals, according to which universals are properties and relations governed by a principle of instantiation which states that each n-adic universal must be instantiated at some point by n particulars. On Armstrong's theory, there need not be a universal corresponding to every meaningful predicate; rather, what universals there are is determined a posteriori on the basis of total science. The law that Fs are Gs is an irreducible second-order relation of necessitation between the first-order universals F-ness and G-ness, symbolized by 'N(F, G)'. This is a nonlogical, contingent sort of necessitation that may fail to hold in a different universe or world. But if it actually holds then, with a proviso to be noted shortly, it is true that the corresponding first-order regularity holds. In other words, this entailment obtains:

(2) $N(F, G) \Rightarrow \forall x(Fx \supset Gx)$.

But the reverse entailment does not, since it takes more for a law to hold than just the holding of a regularity. A notable feature of laws, as explained by Armstrong, is that they do not conform to the Humean supervenience thesis (1) of the previous section. In allowing that there could be two worlds that agree in all local particular facts but differ as to which relations of necessitation hold, Armstrong has foresworn the traditional empiricist commitment to Humean supervenience.

Armstrong's theory overcomes some of the problems confronting Lewis's theory that were mentioned in Section 1. For example, it makes the distinction between law and accidental regularity turn on a difference between their intrinsic natures: A law involves a relation of nomic necessitation between universals, whereas an accidental regularity does not. In this way, our judgement about whether a regularity holds as a law need not depend, as it does in Lewis's theory, on complicated matters concerning its extrinsic relations to other regularities.[4]

Despite its explanatory virtues, Armstrong's theory is afflicted with a number of problems of its own. One important problem concerns the question of how the second-order relations of nomic necessitation are to be understood. If this theory is to clarify our understanding of laws, it needs to provide a philosophically enlightening identification of these relations of nomic necessitation, an identification that makes it clear how these relations confer on laws all the properties we normally associate with them. This is what van Fraassen (1989, pp. 94–9) calls the *identification problem*.

This problem has not gone unaddressed by Armstrong (1988b, In press). He has attempted to provide an identification of the relation of necessitation in terms of our awareness of singular causal relations. He says that Hume was wrong on the question of whether we can perceive singular causal relations: We do, he claims, have direct (noninferential) awareness of singular causal relations through our experience of pressure on our body and our experience of the successful operations of the will. These singular relations involve one state of affairs necessitating another – for example, an impact necessitating the movement of one's body. Of course, we do not perceive laws in the same way; rather, they are inferred on the basis of observed regularities. But he argues that if we suppose that laws involve relations between universals, it is open to us to hypothesize that these relations are identical to the ones we are acquainted with in our experience of singular causation. In his view, there is no circularity in this identification arising from the conceptual tie between singular causation and laws because, contrary to the Humean tradition, he thinks the existence of a singular causal relation does not conceptually presuppose the existence of a covering law.

This answer to the identification problem is most dubious at the point where it asserts that we have direct awareness of the necessitation of singular causation. The Humean point still seems apposite to me: 'All events seem entirely loose and separate. One event follows another, but we never can observe any tie between them. They seem *conjoined,* but never *connected*'. But rather than letting the issue rest on Humean dogma, we will do better to consider some explicit arguments. In the first place, it is implausible to suppose that we can directly perceive singular causal relations – whether or not they involve necessitation – because there is a counterfactual element to these relations that cannot plausibly be claimed to be an object of direct awareness. Compare, for instance, the situation in which my sensation of pressure is caused by the impact on my body with the situation in which the sensation is actually caused by some other causal factor, coincidentally operating at the same time. These situations seem to differ only in terms of what is counterfactually true of them. The first situation is one in which it is true that if the bodily impact had not occurred, I would not have experienced the sensation of pressure, whereas the second situation is one in which this counterfactual is false. In determining the cause of my experience of pressure, I have to be able to determine whether this counterfactual is true or false. But it is clear that I cannot do this on the basis of my perceptual experiences, since the content of my experiences would be the same in both causal situations. It would seem, then, that in arriving at the judgement that my experience of pressure was caused by the bodily impact, I must go beyond what is delivered by my immediate experience – which is to say that I do not, after all, have direct, noninferential awareness of causation in this case.[5]

In the second place, Armstrong's view that we can directly perceive singular causal relations is very difficult to reconcile with a naturalistic causal picture of perception. Whether or not one accepts the full-blown causal theory of perception, the following constraint, which is part of the theory, is plausible in its own right: A subject perceives a state of affairs x only if the state of affairs x causes, by way of some sensory experience, the subject to believe that x obtains. It would be perfectly compatible with this constraint to suppose that a subject perceives the impact of some object on his body, since the impact causes the subject to arrive at the appropriate belief by way of his experience of the sensation of pressure. What is not compatible with this constraint is to suppose that the subject perceived that the impact caused his sensation of pressure. For the purported object of perception – the causal relation – cannot cause the subject to have the relevant belief in the right way for the simple reason that no causal relation of any kind can itself be cause or effect in some other causal relation. It would appear, then, that acceptance of the view that one can perceive causal relations would require a radical departure from a widely endorsed naturalistic constraint on perception.

Another serious and more general problem facing Armstrong's theory is what van Fraassen calls the *inference problem*. It concerns Armstrong's claim that it is logically necessary that if N(F, G) obtains then the first-order regularity $\forall x(Fx \supset Gx)$ obtains; or, equivalently, it is logically necessary that if N(F, G) and Fa obtain then Ga obtains. The logical connections between the second-order state of affairs N(F, G) and the first-order regularity $\forall x(Fx \supset Gx)$, and likewise between the conjunctive state of affairs N(F, G) & Fa and its consequence Ga, are such as to raise disquiet, as David Lewis has remarked:

Whatever N may be, I cannot see how it could be absolutely impossible to have N(F, G) and F*a* without G*a* . . . I am tempted to complain in Humean fashion of alleged necessary connections between distinct existences, especially when first-order states of affairs in the past supposedly join with second-order states of affairs to necessitate first-order states of affairs in the future. That complaint is not clearly right: the sharing of universals detracts from the distinctness of the necessitating and necessitated states of affairs. But I am not appeased. I conclude that necessary connections can be unintelligible even when they are supposed to obtain between existences that are not clearly and wholly distinct. (1983b, p. 366)

Once more Armstrong has faced up to this problem fairly and squarely. In Armstrong (1983a, pp. 86–99) he argues for a number of theses from which it follows that the logical entailments hold.[6] His first thesis is that the law N(F, G) is a second-order state of affairs, but also a first-order relational universal which can itself be instantiated. His second thesis is that there can be necessary connections between states of affairs such as N(F*a*, G*a*), where the relation N is the same as that appearing in laws. His third thesis is that these necessary connections between states of affairs are the relevant instances of the first-order universal N(F, G): just as *Rab* is the instantiation of the first-order universal *R* by the particulars *a* and *b*, so N(F*a*, G*a*) is the instantiation of the first-order universal N(F, G) by the particular states of affairs F*a* and G*a*. Thus, Armstrong assimilates the relation of a law to its instantiations to the relation of a universal to its instances. (Notice that regardless of Lewis' objection, Armstrong needs some account of how a law, construed as a second-order state of affairs, can have instances.)

Granted these three theses, Armstrong argues that the required entailments hold.

It is then clear that if such a relation holds between the universals [in N(F, G)], then it is automatic that each particular F determines that it is a G. That is just the instantiation of the universal N(F, G) in particular cases. The [N(F, G)] represents the law, a state of affairs which is simultaneously a relation. The [$\forall x(Fx \supset Gx)$] represents the uniformity automatically resulting from the instantiation of the universal in its particulars. (1983a, p. 97)

Armstrong's argument in this passage requires some elucidation. Contrary to van Fraassen's claim (1989, p. 107) that the argument is a non sequitur, I think that the argument can be reconstructed so as to validate the logical entailments held in question, provided we grant Armstrong his three theses. If N(F*a*, G*a*) is indeed an instance of N(F, G), then the following principle should hold in the logic of the necessitation relation N:

(3) $N(F, G) \Rightarrow \forall x(Fx \supset N(Fx, Gx))$.

In other words, if it is true that $N(F, G)$ then, for any particular x, if Fx obtains then the instance of the law $N(Fx, Gx)$ should obtain as well. It also seems plausible to accept as a principle of the logic of the relation N that, for any arbitrary particular x,

(4) $N(Fx, Gx) \Rightarrow Fx \& Gx.$

From these logical principles it follows that

(5) $N(F, G) \Rightarrow \forall x(Fx \supset Gx)$

and

(6) $N(F, G) \& Fa \Rightarrow Ga.$

I think it is obvious that Armstrong's argument goes wrong at the very first step, where he claims that the second-order state of affairs is also a first-order universal. Anyone schooled in modern logic is bound to exclaim: How can a state of affairs, which is the ontological correlate of a statement, also be a universal, which is the ontological correlate of a predicate? But Armstrong has heard such exclamations before and has a response (1983a, pp. 89–90). He says that there is no reason why his hierarchy of orders for particulars and universals must follow that of modern logic. Within his hierarchy, it would indeed be inconsistent to say that $N(F, G)$ is a state of affairs and also a universal of the same order. But what he is saying is that $N(F, G)$ is a second-order state of affairs and a first-order universal. In support of this claim, he draws the following analogy: in the state of affairs Rab, the first-order particulars a and b, together with the first-order universal R, yield a state of affairs which is a first-order particular. In the state of affairs $N(F, G)$, the second-order particulars F and G, together with the second-order dyadic universal N, yield a state of affairs that considerations of symmetry suggest is a second-order particular, which is just to say a first-order universal.

Armstrong may well thumb his nose at modern logic, but the question remains whether he is justified in doing so. By allowing states of affairs to play doubled-up roles, Armstrong pays the price of an extremely complicated hierarchy of orders. For example, consider the second-order state of affairs *one kilogram's being a mass,* which results from the application of the second-order universal *being a mass* to the first-order universal *being one kilogram.* On Armstrong's account, this second-order state of affairs should be a first-order universal. But is it monadic or dyadic? What first-order particulars does it apply to? If first-order particulars can instantiate first-order universals such as being one kilogram and also universals such as one kilogram's being a mass, can they possess both kinds of universal at the same time? These questions are ones to which I cannot see any answers that are not purely ad hoc.

In any case, I doubt whether Armstrong's conception of universals allows him to appeal to this nonstandard hierarchy of orders in the first place. For Armstrong, both particulars and universals (of whatever order) have a kind of derivative existence, being abstractions from states of affairs (of the appropriate order).

The particularity of a particular, and equally its properties and relations, are abstractions from states of affairs, but not vicious ones. The particularity of a is a nonvicious abstraction from all the states of affairs in which a figures. The property F (or F-ness) is a nonvicious abstraction from all the states of affairs where some particular has F. The factors of particularity and universality are really there in states of affairs. (1983a, p. 84)

This conception of particulars and universals as abstractions from states of affairs is quite central to Armstrong's views, being required to stave off Bradley's regress argument. But this conception points to an essential difference in categorial nature between universals and states of affairs. This difference can be expressed by saying that states of affairs, in forming the abstraction base for universals and particulars, are in some sense complete or saturated (to use Frege's terminology); but universals, in being abstracted from states of affairs, are by their nature incomplete or unsaturated, requiring particulars of the appropriate kind to complete them. If this is correct, then it is a fundamental confusion of categories to think that something can be both complete like a state of affairs and incomplete like a universal. In conclusion, I believe that Armstrong's argument for the controversial logical entailments fails at the very first step, leaving us without any explanation of these entailments and moreover without an account of how laws can have instances.

3. Laws and Experimental Modalities

We have reached an impasse in our discussion. We cannot embrace either of the two traditional approaches to laws. Regularity theories are ruled out because such theories - even a sophisticated one like Lewis's - fail to capture the modal character of laws. Necessitation theories like Armstrong's are ruled out because they appear to be unable to provide satisfactory solutions to the identification and inference problems, among others.

We need a new departure. In this and the following section I plan to outline what I hope is a more promising approach to laws, an approach that does not suffer the drawbacks of either the regularity or the necessitation approaches. Perhaps the best entrée to this new theory is provided by a common-sense observation about the difference between laws and accidental regularities. The intuitive reflection is that a law of nature, but not an accidental regularity, is robust or *resilient under actual and hypothetical experimentation*. That is to say, a law – unlike an accidental regularity – is a uniformity that would continue to hold under actual and possible experimental testing. This seems to fit neatly the classic examples such as Reichenbach's. Thus, it is an experimentally resilient regularity that all solid spheres of uranium have a diameter of less than one mile, because any experimental attempt to construct a larger body of uranium would be spectacularly frustrated when the critical mass of uranium was exceeded. But this is not so with the regularity that all solid spheres of gold have a diameter of less than one mile, since there would be no obstacle, in principle, to our experimentally constructing a gold sphere of larger proportions.

How is this observation to be cashed out into a full-scale theory of laws? How is the notion of resiliency under actual and hypothetical experimentation to be explained? I think that we can begin to answer these questions by considering a certain modal concept that we all possess in virtue of being decision makers. In deliberation, we naturally make use of the concept of the possible outcomes of our actions. Thus, in deciding whether to open the window or leave it closed, I may consider such sequences of possible outcomes as follows: the window is open at t_1 & fresh air comes in at t_2 & my papers blow away at t_3; and the window is closed at t_1 & fresh air does not come in at t_2 & my papers do not blow away at t_3. I shall call such sequences of events courses of events.[7] More precisely, I shall say that a *course of events* (at a certain level of abstraction) is a conjunction of temporally ordered first-order possible situations – events or states of affairs – such that every possible situation (at the relevant level of abstraction) or its negative counterpart is a conjunct. Now in making a decision, I consider those possible courses of events that are now within my control and ignore those that are now outside my control. Intuitively speaking, a course of events is *within my present control* just in case I can now bring about the course of events by performing some action. We can represent the kind of possibility that attaches to courses of events that are within my present control by the symbol $\Diamond$. Michael McDermott (1991), who has studied this kind of modality in connection with conditionals, argues that it obeys the characteristic axiom of the modal logic S5. Where $\Box A$ is defined as $\sim \Diamond \sim A$, it seems to be true that $\Diamond A \supset \Box \Diamond A$: If A is now within my power, it is not now within my power that A be not now within my power.

The concept of a possible course of events within one's control is a plausible candidate for being a conceptual primitive. It is certainly a concept one must possess as a precondition of being a decision maker, and so a concept one is likely to acquire at an early stage of conceptual development. How exactly does one acquire the concept? We can already discount one answer to this question. If it is doubtful that the concept of necessitation is acquired through perception, it is just as doubtful that the concept of a possible course of events within one's control is acquired through perception. The simple answer to the question is that we acquire the concept through the complex and not-entirely-perceptual experience of deliberation and action – the experience of weighing up different options by considering their outcomes and then realizing the chosen option. On the basis of this experience, one recognizes that there are many courses of events within one's control besides the one that one will actually realize. Even if I choose to open the window and so bring about the first course of events just mentioned, the second course of events was within my control at the time of decision. It is this sense of there being many alternative possible courses of events within one's control at the time of deliberation that lies, I shall argue, behind the modal character of laws of nature.

But to elaborate this point it is necessary to generalize the present-tense, first-person concept of the possible courses of events within my control *now*. Evidently we also possess more general concepts that apply to other times and other agents. Not only do we possess the concept of the possible courses of events within our control now, but also the concepts of those that were within our control in the past and those that will be within our control in the future. Also, by analogizing from one's own situation to that of other agents, one can fashion the concept of the possible courses of events that are, were, or will be within the control of some other agent. We also recognize that an agent's control over events can be enhanced by appropriate manipulative aids; that is to say, an agent who is suitably equipped with the relevant instruments, tools or experimental devices can bring about possible courses of events that an unequipped agent cannot. By allowing the use of manipulative aids in this way, we can abstract away from the brute limitations of a normal human agent's manipulative abilities. Of course, only those manipulative aids that are practically feasible – that could actually be constructed by agents – are relevant to our discussion of the possibilities open to suitably equipped agents.

Given the generalization of the basic decision-making concept along these dimensions, we can introduce the concept that will occupy centre stage in our subsequent discussions. Let us say that *x* is an *experimentally possible course of events* if and only if some suitably equipped agent could at some time bring about *x* by performing some act. An experimentally possible course of events is like a logically possible world in that it represents an extended sequence of possible, sometimes nonactual, events. But it is unlike a possible world in that it does not represent a complete alternative universe that is concrete in every detail; rather, it represents a localized sequence of first-order events and states of affairs, described at a certain level of abstraction. Again, it is unlike a possible world in that it does not represent a merely logically possible sequence of events that could be totally unlike any sequence of events that takes place in the actual world; rather, it represents the way the actual world would develop were some suitably equipped free agent to choose to act in a certain way and, as such, it is constrained by the underlying character of the actual world.[8]

Mimicking the style of possible-worlds semantics, we can recursively define the conditions under which a proposition is true in an experimentally possible course of events. Starting with atomic propositions, we can say that an atomic proposition is true in a possible course of events just in case the situation described by the proposition is a conjunct of the course of events. The truth conditions of logically complex propositions involving negation, conjunction and universal quantification can be defined in the usual way. The truth conditions of certain modal operators can also be stated within this framework of possible courses of events. Let us say that it is *experimentally possible that A*, symbolized as $\Diamond A$, just in case the proposition A is true in some experimentally possible course of events. The necessity operator, symbolized as $\Box$, will be understood as its dual, so that $\Box A$ will be understood to be true just in case the proposition A is true in every experimentally possible course of events. We can express this by saying that it is *experimentally necessary that A*.

The experimental modalities seem perfectly suited to capturing the idea that a law of nature is a regularity that is resilient under actual and hypothetical experimentation. For if a regularity is so resilient then no agent – not even an agent whose manipulative abilities are enhanced by experimental aids – can bring about a course of events in which the regularity breaks down: In other words, the regularity holds in all experimentally possible courses of events. Conversely, if a regularity is not so resilient, that will be because the regularity fails to hold in some course of events that a suitably equipped agent could contrive to realize – more succinctly, because it fails in some experimentally possible course of events.

These reflections suggest the following truth condition for statements of law:

(7)   *It is a law that* $\forall x(Fx \supset Gx)$ if and only if (i) it is experimentally necessary that $\forall x(Fx \supset Gx)$ and (ii) it is not logically necessary that $\forall x(Fx \supset Gx)$.

The additional clause is to ensure that logical truths holding of necessity in all experimentally possible courses of events do not come out as laws of nature. This truth condition also captures a concept that is correlative with that of a law of nature. If a proposition is experimentally but not logically necessary, let us say that it is *physically necessary.* The welcome upshot of this is that all laws count as physically necessary.

This theory of laws explains many features of our concept of a law. It is worthwhile enumerating some of its explanatory successes. In the first place, it yields a simple, clear-cut account of our intuitions about the difference between laws and accidental regularities. For example, we judge it to be an accidental fact that all the coins in Goodman's pocket are always silver, because we know that some agent could simply insert a bronze coin in his pocket and so break the regularity. All the same, observe how our judgement would change if (by some extraordinary turn of events) the regularity should turn out to be experimentally robust, so that it held in all experimentally possible courses of events. Suppose it turned out that, no matter what sort of coin was put in Goodman's pocket, whenever anyone extracted a coin from his pocket it proved to be a silver one. We would be very surprised to make this discovery about his pocket, especially if other pockets with similar properties did not behave in the same way. But if the regularity proved to be experimentally resilient, we would judge it to be a law. Whether a regularity counts as a law, on this theory, does not depend on complicated extrinsic considerations regarding its relations with other regularities; it depends solely on its intrinsic character, in particular on whether it is physically necessary in the sense explained.

In the second place, the theory explains the idea that some physical possibilities may never be realized. A case in point is described by Popper's example about moas, the flightless New Zealand birds that have been extinct for centuries. Popper has us imagine that a certain virus present in the New Zealand environment caused all moas to die before they were fifty, even though there was nothing in their physical constitution that prevented them from living longer. Naive regularity theories have difficulty in explaining why it was physically possible for moas to live beyond age fifty, since they take it to be a law, and so physically necessary, that all moas do not survive beyond fifty. But the present theory does not have any difficulty here. For agents could conceivably have intervened experimentally to rid some moas of their virus, and in the resulting experimentally possible courses of events the moas could be expected to survive beyond fifty. The unrealized physical possibilities are simply those experimentally possible courses of events that no agent ever realizes.

In the third place, the theory allows for the possibility of so-called local laws, a type of law strictly prohibited in Armstrong's theory because it involves positional properties that are not universals. An example of a local law would be the imaginary law about Goodman's pocket that was mentioned earlier. Another example has been described by Tooley:

All the fruit in Smith's garden at any time are apples. When one attempts to take an orange into the garden, it turns into an elephant. Bananas so treated become apples as they cross the boundary, while pears are resisted by a force that cannot be overcome. Cherry trees planted in the garden bear apples, or they bear nothing at all. If all these things were true, there would be a very strong case for its being a law that all the fruit in Smith's garden are apples. And this case would be in no way undermined if it were found that no other gardens, however similar to Smith's in all other respects, exhibited behavior of the sort just described. (1977, p. 686)

Tooley's description makes it evident that the regularity regarding the fruit in Smith's garden is resilient under actual experimentation. From the fact that it holds in all possible courses of events that agents have actually realized, we inductively surmise that it holds also in the ones that have not been realized and so count it as a law.

In the fourth place, the theory provides a straightforward explanation of the way in which statements of law support counterfactuals. The law that all copper expands when heated is physically necessary according to the present theory because the statement that $\forall x(x$ is a piece of heated copper $\supset x$ expands) is true in all experimentally possible courses of events. Now consider an individual piece of copper, a, which has not and never will be heated. However, an agent could have heated it, in which case we know it would have expanded, since the universal generalization holds in all experimentally possible courses of events. Accordingly, we are entitled to assert that if a were heated then it would expand. It is essential to this explanation that the antecedent of the counterfactual be physically possible. If a were not a piece of copper but rather an electron, or a quadratic equation or a human being, it would not be experimentally possible that a be a piece of heated copper; and in this case the counterfactual 'If a were a piece of heated copper, a would expand' is not genuinely entertainable; it seems to lack a truth value. But if it is physically necessary that $\forall x(Fx \supset Gx)$ and also physically possible that Fa, then the counterfactual $Fa \,\square\!\!\rightarrow Ga$ holds.[9] Observe that this explanation depends on the fact that the law statement describes a regularity that holds in *all* experimentally possible courses of events: If the statement reported an accidental regularity, we would not be entitled to infer that the consequent would be realized in *any* physically possible course of events that realized the antecedent.

In the fifth place, the account provides satisfying solutions to the identification problem and the inference problem. Recall that the first is the problem of identifying in a philosophically enlightening way the condition by virtue of which a regularity counts as a law. The present theory states that a law is a regularity that holds in all experimentally possible courses of events. The concept of an experimentally possible course of events should be a comparatively transparent one. After all, each of us must, as agents, possess the concept of the events within our control, or (in other words) the concept of the events we can bring about by performing some act. An experimentally possible course of events is just a temporally ordered sequence of events within the control of some suitably equipped agent at some time.

The inference problem is the problem of showing how laws connect up with the occurrent happenings that are the means by which we come to have knowledge of them in the first instance. The present theory makes this matter no more problematic than the inference from $\Box \forall x(Fx \supset Gx)$ to $\forall x(Fx \supset Gx)$. A law is a regularity holding in all experimentally possible courses of events, and so a fortiori in the actual course of events. Observe that the actual course of events may be one which an agent has brought about in the minimal sense of refraining from intervening in the workings of nature so that the natural course of events takes place. But a significant feature of the theory is that it allows for the actual events that serve as the confirmation base for law statements to be the result of active intervention by experimenters. This will almost invariably be the case with real scientific theories that formulate relationships between a number of variables under the idealizing assumption that no other causally relevant variables have a significant influence.[10] In these cases, the experimentally possible courses of events will be ones that require the active intervention of the experimenters to shield the experimental set-ups from the influence of the other causal variables.

The theory of laws presented so far deals only with the laws holding in the actual world, neglecting the laws holding in other possible worlds. Yet, as van Fraassen's example and the Tooley–Carroll example illustrate, the thought that other worlds are law-governed is readily intelligible. Indeed, these examples illustrate the further point that laws of nature may hold in possible worlds that contain no agents whatsoever. How is the present theory to be amended to deal with such cases?

The required emendation is achieved by defining a more general concept of an experimentally possible course of events, one that ranges in its application beyond the actual world to other possible worlds. A plausible suggestion for this more general definition is the following: x is *an experimentally possible course of events in world* w if and only if w is such that an actual human agent, equipped as necessary with actual experimental aids, could bring about x by performing some act in w'. This definition has the right character. It makes the notion of an experimentally possible course of events in world w depend on the underlying character of w itself, while linking the notion to the abilities of actual agents. This familiar rigidification strategy[11] – the strategy of explaining the concept in terms of the capacities of actual agents – overcomes the apparent difficulty generated by possible worlds that are devoid of agents: Even though these worlds contain no agents, the experimentally possible courses of events holding in them are fixed by what actual agents could do in such worlds. Given this extended definition of an experimentally possible course of events, we can generalize the theory of laws as follows:

(8)   *It is a law that* $\forall x(Fx \supset Gx)$ *in* w if and only if (i) $\forall x(Fx \supset Gx)$ holds in all experimentally possible courses of events in w and (ii) it is not logically necessary that $\forall x(Fx \supset Gx)$.

This amended theory has no difficulty explaining our judgements about the laws governing imaginary worlds that are very different from our own in being completely devoid of agents. It can explain, for instance, why we think that in the simplified world of van Fraassen's example it is only accidentally true that all and only the spheres are gold. For it would seem that this regularity would not be experimentally resilient in that world: The world, as described by van Fraassen, is such that experimenters could be imagined to intervene in the workings of the world so as to ensure that the regularity breaks down – for example, by bringing about shape-altering collisions between the gold spheres. Similarly, the theory explains our inclination to suppose that the sparse world of the Tooley–Carroll example could be governed by the vacuous law that all X-particles subject to Y-fields have spin up. This would be so if the world were such that the regularity was experimentally resilient in it; and indeed, it does seem quite conceivable that were we present in the world and were we to bring about interactions between X-particles and Y-fields in it, the X-particles would always have spin up.

An important consequence of the amended theory is that it implies that the Humean supervenience thesis fails for laws of nature. The theory allows that there could be two worlds agreeing on all their occurrent happenings but differing in their laws. As we saw earlier, the Tooley–Carroll example can be modified to provide an example of this. To repeat the details of this modified example: Suppose two worlds contain only X-particles and Y-fields which, as it turns out, never interact; and that both worlds are governed by a single fundamental law about the interaction of the particles and the fields. It could be that these worlds are governed by different laws: The vacuous law that all X-particles in Y-fields have spin up holds in one world and the different vacuous law that all X-particles in Y-fields have spin down holds in the other. On the present theory, this is perfectly intelligible. One world makes the regularity that all X-particles in Y-fields have spin up experimentally resilient, whereas the other world makes the regularity that X-particles in Y-fields have spin down experimentally resilient. In other words, while the worlds agree with respect to what happens in the experimentally possible course of events that is actualized in each, they differ with respect to what happens in their unrealized experimentally possible courses of events. In this way, the present theory supports the earlier diagnosis of the reasons for the failure of Humean supervenience: the diagnosis that laws possess a modal character that is underdetermined by even global patterns of occurrent happenings.

4. Some Objections Disarmed

This section will be devoted to addressing some pressing objections to the proposed theory of laws. The three objections to be considered touch on features of the theory that may cast doubt on it in the minds of philosophers. My hope is that the rebuttal of the objections will dispel these doubts about the theory and help to clarify its character.

The first objection is that, by failing to bear out the Humean supervenience thesis, the theory makes laws unknowable. According to the theory, laws transcend all local occurrent fact, but if this is so then they are no less mysterious than the relations of nomic necessitation that Armstrong postulates as truth-makers for laws. How can humans ever acquire knowledge of these strange entities?

The point made here about laws is made more generally about other kinds of entities that appear to fail Humean supervenience. Traditional empiricists argue that, insofar as an entity does not conform to Humean supervenience, it runs the risk of lapsing into unknowability. Earman (1986, p. 86) has formulated, without explicitly endorsing, an argument that goes some way towards articulating the 'threat of unknowability' worry. The two-premissed argument runs as follows: We can in principle know directly (noninferentially) only occurrent facts; what is underdetermined by everything that we can in principle know directly is unknowable in principle; therefore, what is underdetermined by the occurrent facts is unknowable in principle.

One response to this argument – a response favoured by Tooley (1987, pp. 129–37) – is to claim that the argument does not apply in all instances because its second premiss is not in general true. It is useful, Tooley argues, to draw an analogy with the debate over realism about common-sense physical objects (desks, trees, rocks) or about scientific theoretical objects (quarks, electrons, genes). The strict empiricist will object that such entities are in principle unknowable since their existence is underdetermined by all possible sensory experience. Realists respond that such underdetermination is not fatal because there are general reasons for believing in the existence of such entities, reasons which are not vitiated by the fact of underdetermination. The suggestion, then, is that a realist about laws can take a leaf from the realist's book, arguing that the general reasons for believing in the existence of observation-transcendent physical objects also carry over to believing in the existence of observation-transcendent laws. In this way, realism about laws is in no worse position than realism generally.

I do not find this line of reply to the 'threat of unknowability' argument at all helpful. For the most persuasive reasons in favour of realism about common-sense physical objects and scientific theoretical objects do not apply in the case of laws of nature. To my mind the most persuasive arguments in favour of general realism are those which point to the fact that common-sense physical objects and scientific theoretical objects possess causal powers: We know from everyday experience and experimental investigations that we can manipulate tables and chairs, genes and quarks to produce certain effects. Knowing that they are causes, we can infer that they exist.[12] But this inference is unavailable in the case of laws, since they do not occupy a place in the causal order: While some laws – the causal laws – may formulate the causal powers of other things, they do not themselves have any causal powers of their own. Thus, it seems implausible to respond to the 'threat of unknowability' argument by drawing an analogy with the realist's defense of common-sense physical objects and scientific theoretical objects. There is a disanalogy between laws and these other kinds of entity precisely with respect to the sort of property that enables the latter to circumvent the charge of unknowability.

The flaw in the empiricist's argument, in my view, is not in the second premiss but rather in the first premiss, which states that we can in principle have direct knowledge only of occurrent facts. If the empiricist's argument is to tell against the conception of laws embodied in the present theory, the conclusion of the argument must be read as stating that what is underdetermined by the occurrent facts *of the actual course of events* is unknowable in principle. (For the laws of nature on the present theory are not underdetermined by what happens in all the experimentally possible courses of events.) Consequently, if the first premiss of the argument is to link up with its conclusion, it must be read as stating that we can in principle have direct knowledge only of the occurrent facts of the actual course of events. But in the light of the framework of the present theory we can see that this premiss is false. To the extent that it is within our power to realize experimentally possible courses of events besides the actual one, it is within our power to observe what happens in these courses of events. We can in principle observe what happens in other experimentally possible courses of events simply by choosing to bring them about. It is simply false, then, to say that we can in principle observe only the occurrent facts of the actual course of events.

The second objection to the proposed theory of laws is that it looks as though it covertly smuggles in counterfactual constructions at several vital points. For example, it would appear that the notion of an experimentally possible course of events is an implicitly counterfactual one: for such a course of events is simply the sequence of events that *would* occur if some suitably equipped agent were to perform some act. This implicit appeal to counterfactuals is a problem precisely because counterfactuals, by consensus, are themselves to be understood in terms of laws of nature. Consequently, in making essential an appeal to counterfactuals, the theory is guilty of a vicious circularity.

It is indeed true that a common assumption has been that counterfactuals are to be analyzed partly in terms of laws of nature. For example, the popular possible-worlds approach attempts to analyze counterfactuals in terms of similarity relations between possible worlds, with similarity with respect to laws of nature playing an important role in most analyses. This kind of similarity is especially important in the case of forward-tracking counterfactuals[13] like those purportedly implicated in the present theory of laws. Suppose that the counterfactual $A \Box \rightarrow B$, where A refers to a stretch of time t, is to be read in the forward-tracking manner. One widely accepted suggestion concerning the possible worlds relevant to the evaluation of this counterfactual is the following:

> The worlds that are *overall most similar* to the actual world are those worlds w such that (i) A is true in w; (ii) w is exactly like the actual world at all times before a short transition period shortly before t; (iii) w conforms to the actual laws of nature at all times after t; and (iv) during t and the preceding transition period, w differs no more from the actual world than it must to permit A to hold.[14]

The counterfactual $A \Box \rightarrow B$, then, is true in the actual world if and only if the consequent B is true in every such world w. The significant point from our present perspective is that these truth conditions make reference to laws of nature in clause (iii).

In response to this second objection, however, I wish to dispute both the claim that the notion of an experimentally possible course of events must be understood in terms of a forward-tracking counterfactual construction, and also the claim that such a counterfactual construction can only be understood given a prior grasp of the concept of a law of nature.

My view is that both forward-tracking counterfactuals and laws of nature must be explained in terms of the logically prior concept of an experimentally possible course of events. The previous section was devoted to explaining the connection between laws of nature and experimentally possible courses of events. It remains to be shown how forward-tracking counterfactuals can be explained in terms of experimentally possible courses of events. This explanation should serve to undercut the widely held view that the analysis of such counterfactuals must proceed in terms of laws of nature.

Let us confine our attention in the first instance to a special class of forward-tracking counterfactuals – those whose antecedents describe a possible action of some agent. The explanation in terms of experimentally possible courses of events is very straightforward for these special counterfactuals, and in any case it is these counterfactuals that are of immediate relevance to our discussion of laws. Let us suppose that $A \mathbin{\square\!\!\rightarrow} B$ is one such counterfactual, where A describes a possible action that agent S could perform at time t. Then I suggest that a suitable truth condition for this counterfactual is the following: It is true that $A \mathbin{\square\!\!\rightarrow} B$ if and only if B holds in all the experimentally possible courses of events that the agent S could bring about by performing A at t. This truth condition has the virtue of simplicity. Moreover, it is one that can lay claim to explaining the counterfactual construction in terms of a genuinely more primitive concept. As argued earlier, the concept of an experimentally possible course of events is one that we must possess in order to be decision makers and so one that we are likely to acquire at an early stage in our conceptual development.

An impressive virtue of the simple theory is that it explains the plausibility of the standard possible-worlds account. The standard account is very specific about which respects of similarity between possible worlds are relevant to the evaluation of forward-tracking counterfactuals. One might wonder why these respects of similarity, and not others, are relevant. The simple account proposed here supplies the required explanation. We can broach this explanation by considering how the experimentally possible courses of events of this theory would be described within a possible-worlds framework. If one were to think – mistakenly, in my view – of these courses of events as possible worlds, how would one describe the nonactual experimentally possible courses of events that an agent *could* bring about by performing action A at time t? First, as these courses of events are brought about by the agent's performing A, the corresponding possible worlds would be ones in which A is true. Second, since the agent's performing A cannot affect or change the past, the corresponding possible worlds could be described as holding fixed the past of the actual world until a time, shortly before t, when the agent decides to perform A. Third, given that the character of the possible courses of events depends on the way in which the actual world would evolve after t, the corresponding possible worlds could be characterized as conforming to the laws of nature of the actual world after t. Fourth, since these non-actual courses of events differ minimally from the actual course of events during the period from the agent's decision to perform A to his realization of A, the corresponding possible worlds could reasonably be described as differing from the actual world during this period by no more than is required to permit A to hold.

Of course, these possible worlds are exactly those that enter into the standard possible-worlds account of forward-tracking counterfactuals. We can make sense of this fact if we think of the standard account as really a projection within the possible-worlds framework of the proposed theory. What establishes the conceptual priority of the proposed theory over the possible-worlds account is the fact that it represents a much more plausible hypothesis about the way in which subjects acquire mastery of forward-tracking counterfactuals. It is more reasonable to suppose that subjects learn to use such counterfactuals by thinking in terms of experimentally possible courses of events than in terms of complex similarity relations between possible worlds. If this is so, we have good reason for thinking that the present theory of laws in terms of experimentally possible courses of events is not vitiated by any circular reference to laws of nature. This reason is not defeated by the fact that the natural projection of the concept of an experimentally possible course of events in the possible-worlds framework employs the concept of a law of nature.

It will doubtless be observed that this theory of counterfactuals applies only to the special subclass of forward-tracking counterfactuals whose antecedents specify a possible action of some agent. It will also be observed that there are many forward-tracking counterfactuals that fall outside this special class. Even though these other counterfactuals are not of immediate relevance to our discussion, it is important to establishing the credentials of the theory that some brief account be given of how the theory can be extended to handle them.

The key to extending the theory is to generalize the notion of an experimentally possible course of events. In the special case where the antecedent of the counterfactual $A \square \rightarrow B$ specifies a possible action of an agent S, the theory refers to the experimentally possible courses of events that can be brought about by S's performance of A. What is significant about these possible courses of events is that they are initiated by an antecedent-realizing action that can be conceived as a departure from the ordinary course of events: We intuitively see the action as deriving from a source that is independent of, and external to, the natural course of events. In order to generalize the notion of an experimentally possible course of events, we need to find some general analogue of an antecedent-realizing action. What could this be? I suggest that the concept of an *antecedent-realizing miracle* has many of the right features. Like an action, a miracle is thought of as an external intervention in the natural course of events, so an antecedent-realizing miracle will initiate courses of events that depart from actuality in the same way that an antecedent-realizing action does. The generalized notion of a course of events that can be brought about by an antecedent-realizing miracle can then be used to analyze forward-tracking counterfactuals as follows: $A \,\square\!\!\rightarrow B$ is true if and only if B is true in all possible courses of events that can be brought about by an A-realizing miracle. There is much in this account that requires elaboration, but this brief sketch must suffice for our present purposes.

The third objection to the proposed theory of laws I would like to consider is the objection that the theory depends on mistaken verificationist assumptions. It may be conceded that experimental interventions that bring about departures from the actual course of events play an important role in the verification of law statements. If a law statement describes a regularity that holds in all the specially controlled situations that experimenters have created to test it, this provides a very good indication that the law statement is true. But it is the cardinal mistake of verificationism, it will be objected, to think that the meaning of law statements is to be given in terms of their test conditions. As a further twist to the objection, it may be claimed that the theory mistakenly impugns the objectivity of laws by linking them with test conditions that implicate the existence of subjects. Does this not make the existence of laws depend in some idealist fashion on the existence of human subjects?

In response to this objection, I should say that the guiding idea for the present theory does not lie in any semantic theory linking meaning with conditions of verification or warranted assertibility. On the contrary, the theory is straightforwardly truth-conditional: It seeks to explain the concept of a law of nature by stating the conditions under which a law statement is intuitively held to be true. If the present theory invites comparison with any other kind of theory, it is with traditional theories of secondary quality concepts. Consider, for example, a standard dispositional theory of colour that states that something is red just in case it is such as to look red to a normal observer under standard conditions. This theory states perfectly straightforward truth conditions for the concept of redness, but it does so by linking the concept with a certain test for detecting instances of the concept – in this case, the test of seeing how the thing looks. (Of course, it is recognized that the test is not incorrigible: The way a thing looks to a subject does not indicate anything about its colour if the subject is not normal or the conditions of observation are not standard.) The present theory of laws should be seen, I suggest, as similar to such a theory in this respect: It states truth conditions for the concept of a law of nature in terms of a certain test – in this case, the test of seeing whether the regularity continues to hold in experimentally contrived departures from the actual course of events. But it would be just as much of a mistake to think that the present theory of laws is covertly committed to verificationism as it would be to think that the standard dispositional theory of colour is wedded to verificationist assumptions.

Other philosophers have seen that the analogy with colour is very useful for explaining philosophically interesting concepts. For example, they have sought to extrapolate the standard dispositional treatment of colour to the concept of value, arguing that an a priori biconditional holds for value like the biconditionals holding for colour. Thus, some such biconditional as the following is offered: Something is valuable if and only if it would evoke approval from an ideal subject under conditions of ideal information and critical reflection.[15] Concepts that support an a priori biconditional of this kind have been called *response-dependent concepts*.[16] The essential feature of such concepts is that they involve a test response which is essentially mental in character, whether it be sensory, cognitive or affective.

However, I think that there is another, more general way of developing the analogy with the standard dispositional theory of colour. On this way of developing the analogy, the significant feature of the standard treatment is that it explains the concept by way of a distinctive kind of test for detecting the presence of colour – a test that implicates human subjects because it involves the exercise of some subject's natural capacities. Concepts that are like the concept of colour in this respect might be called *subject-implicating, test-constrained* concepts. On this way of looking at things, it would be an inessential feature of such concepts that the test sometimes involves the exercise of a mental capacity. This general class of concepts would include response-dependent concepts as a special class, but it would also include the non–response-dependent concept of law, as it is understood on the present theory. For even though this concept of a law does not advert to any mental test response, it does give a privileged role to a subject-implicating test.[17]

Against this background we can see whether the charge is justified that the present theory of laws impugns the objectivity of laws, insofar as it makes the existence of a law depend on the results of some subject-implicating test. At first sight, it might seem that the theory implies that laws would not exist if there were no agents, or would be different if agents had different manipulative capacities. Of course, similar accusations have been lodged against dispositional theories of colour and value. But these theories typically answer such accusations by appealing to a rigidification strategy that links the concepts of colour and value to the capacities of actual existing subjects. Thus, a dispositional theory of colour that is immune to this accusation might read: Something is red just in case it is such that it would look red to an *actual* normal subject under *actual* standard conditions. Since the present theory of laws applies the same rigidification strategy, it too sidesteps the charge of being excessively subjective.

All the same, theories that explain concepts in a subject-implicating way often have a surprising character. For they show that concepts that do not on their face have anything to do with human subjects turn out nonetheless to implicate them. The element of surprise is not so great in the case of the concepts of colour and value, as it has always looked as if these might be prime candidates for some anthropocentric treatment. But it is more surprising, I think, that the concept of law should prove to be subject-implicating. The concept does not on its face make any reference to human subjects or their capacities. Yet we cannot, I have argued, make sense of the necessity thought to attach to laws without appealing to the concept of the possible courses of events that human agents can bring about by their actions.

It is true that there is a tradition of empiricism that takes up the 'felt-determination' aspect of Hume's doctrine about causation and emphasizes the role of human cognitive attitudes and practices. Representatives of this tradition are Goodman, who wrote (1954, p. 21): 'I want only to emphasize the Humean idea that rather than a sentence being used for prediction because it is a law, it is called a law because it is used for prediction'; and Ayer, who claimed (1956, p. 162) that the difference between a law and an accidental regularity 'lies not so much on the side of the facts which make them true or false, as in the attitude of those who put them forward'. The line that is usually run by these empiricists is that laws *in re* are simply regularities and their putative physical necessity is simply a projection of our theoretical cognitive attitudes. These theories do make laws subject-implicating in some sense, but they are hampered by the restricted Humean conception of human subjects as essentially passive observers of, and theorizers about, the world. What is missing in the traditional Humean vision is the idea we have experience of the world, not just as passive observers and theorizers, but as potent agents capable of actively intervening and shaping the world after our own will.

To conclude our answer to this objection: The present theory of laws should not be seen as committed to a verificationist theory of meaning. Rather, it should be seen as offering an explanation of the concept of law that is analogous in a certain respect to the standard dispositional explanation of colour: The explanation highlights the way in which the concept is constrained by a certain kind of subject-implicating test. The theory has no truck with idealist claims to the effect that laws would not exist if there were no human agents, or that the laws would be different if human agents had different manipulative capacities. The rigidification strategy ensures that the theory avoids these obvious pitfalls. But there is a certain sense in which the present theory does fall short of a full-blooded realism about laws. This is so because it holds that there are a priori restrictions on the extent to which our tests can lead us astray about laws. The concept dictates that laws cannot transcend the most refined tests involving the realization of all experimentally possible courses of events. It is an interesting question whether this falling short of a full-blooded realism still leaves the concept of a law of nature with an appropriate degree of objectivity.[18] But that is a question for another occasion.[19]

NOTES

1. This is the Naive Regularity Theory discussed by Molnar (1969) and Armstrong (1983a). A nonpositional predicate is one that does not include the name of any individual; an empirical predicate is one whose instantiation can be confirmed directly or indirectly by either observation or measurement.
2. Lewis first formulated his theory in Lewis (1973), where he summarized it thus: 'A contingent generalization is a law of nature if and only if it appears as a theorem (or axiom) in each of the true deductive systems that achieves a best combination of simplicity and strength' (p. 73). The theory described in the main text is the same as the 1973 theory, but the later formulation is more useful for my purposes.
3. For a useful examination and rebuttal of various responses to this argument, see Carroll (1990, pp. 203–6).
4. Armstrong's own comparison between his theory and theories falling within the regularity approach is to be found in Armstrong (1983a, pp. 99–107).
5. The point of this argument is not that our judgements about causation are corrigible and so cannot be the deliverances of immediate experience. Rather, the point is that judgements about causation involve decisions about the truth value of counterfactuals, decisions which cannot be determined on the basis of perceptual experience alone.
6. Armstrong has presented his solution to the inference problem in recent publications in a more summary fashion. In the most recent (In press), he says this: 'If this [the postulation that the necessitation relation involved in laws is the same as what we are aware of in singular causation] is satisfactory then it seems that the inference problem is solved. For if a certain type of state of affairs has certain causal effects, how can it not be that the tokens of this type

cause tokens of that type of effect? The inference is analytic or conceptual'. I have chosen to discuss Armstrong's less recent discussion of the inference problem on the grounds that it contains a more detailed solution, one that this short discussion must be seen as summarizing.

7. The assumption of determinism that is being made in this essay dictates that each act can initiate only one possible course of events. In a context where this assumption were suspended, it would be appropriate to suppose that each act could give rise to many possible sequences of outcomes.

8. The use of counterfactuals in characterizing the notion of an experimentally possible course of events is almost unavoidable; this may suggest that the notion is an implicitly counterfactual one. Given that standard accounts of counterfactuals analyze them in terms of laws of nature, one may object that any account of laws that appeals to the notion of an experimentally possible world will involve a vicious circularity. This objection is answered in Section 4.

9. I take this thesis about the connection between counterfactuals and laws to be uncontroversial. For arguments in support of this thesis see Pollock (1984, pp. 116-40). Another way of establishing the connection between laws and counterfactuals is discussed in Section 4.

10. For discussion of this feature of real-life scientific theories see Joseph (1980), Cartwright (1983), and Suppe (1989).

11. The rigidification strategy was originally discussed by Davies and Humberstone (1980).

12. For a defence of realism about scientific theoretical entities along these lines, see Cartwright (1983) and Hacking (1983).

13. Another widely used term for these counterfactuals is 'non-backtracking counterfactuals'; see Lewis's (1979) discussion.

14. This specification of the relevant aspects of similarity for forward-tracking counterfactuals follows a suggestion of Lewis (1979, p. 39). (He does not, however, completely endorse the suggestion because he thinks that it rules out the possibility of a backwards counterfactual dependence of the past on the present. He offers a more general account of the relevant respects of similarity which agrees with this suggested account in ordinary cases that do not involve backwards counterfactual dependences.) Many philosophers have suggested possible-worlds analyses of forward-tracking counterfactuals along similar lines; see for instance Bennett (1974), Jackson (1977) and McCall (1984).

15. For a discussion of dispositional theories of value, see Lewis (1989) and Johnston (1989).

16. The term 'response-dependence' was introduced by Johnston (1989). For a more extensive discussion of the utility and justification of treating concepts as response-dependent, see Johnston (In press). Wright's 'extension-determining concepts' coincide more or less with Johnston's 'response-dependent concepts'; see Wright (In press) and Johnston (In press) for a discussion of the relationship between their approaches.

17. In Menzies and Price (In press) it is argued that the concept of singular causation is a subject-implicating, test-constrained concept. We draw on the analogy with the dispositional theory of colour to defend an agency account of causation against charges of covert verificationism and subjectivity.

18. For an enlightening discussion of the issue of whether a response-dependent treatment of some area of discourse is consistent with a full-blooded realism about it, see Pettit (1991).

19. Earlier, very different versions of this essay have been read at seminars at the ANU, the University of Sydney and the 1990 meeting of the Australasian Association of Philosophy. Thanks are due to Frank Jackson, Michael Mc-Dermott, Huw Price, Michael Tooley, Jack Smart and especially David Armstrong and Philip Pettit.

REFERENCES

Armstrong, D. M. 1983a. *What Is a Law of Nature?* (Cambridge University Press).
    1988b. Reply to van Fraassen's 'Armstrong on Laws and Probabilities', *Australasian Journal of Philosophy* 66: 224-9.
    In press. 'The Identification Problem and the Inference Problem', *Philosophy and Phenomenological Research*.
Ayer, A. J. 1956. 'What Is a Law of Nature?', *Revue Internationale de Philosophie* 10: 144-65. Reprinted in Ayer, *The Concept of a Person* (London: Macmillan, 1963).
Bennett, Jonathan. 1974. Review of Lewis 1973. In *Canadian Journal of Philosophy* 4: 381-402.
Carroll, John W. 1990. 'The Humean Tradition', *Philosophical Review* 99: 185-219.
Cartwright, Nancy. 1983. *How the Laws of Physics Lie* (Oxford: Clarendon).
Davies, Martin and Humberstone, Lloyd. 1980. 'Two Notions of Necessity', *Philosophical Studies* 38: 1-30.
Dretske, Fred I. 1977. 'Laws of Nature', *Philosophy of Science* 44: 248-68.
Earman, John. 1986. *A Primer on Determinism* (Dordrecht: Reidel).
Goodman, Nelson. 1954. *Fact, Fiction, and Forecast* (Atlantic Highlands, NJ: Athlone).
Hacking, Ian. 1983. *Representing and Intervening* (Cambridge University Press).
Jackson, Frank. 1977. 'A Causal Theory of Counterfactuals', *Australasian Journal of Philosophy* 55: 3-21.
Johnston, Mark. 1989. 'Dispositional Theories of Value', *Proceedings of the Aristotelian Society,* suppl. vol. 63: 139-74.
    In press. 'Objectivity Refigured: Pragmatism without Verificationism', *Reality: Representation and Projection,* ed. John Haldane and Crispin Wright (Oxford University Press).
Joseph, G. 1980. 'The Many Sciences and the One World', *Journal of Philosophy* 77: 773-90.
Lewis, David. 1973. *Counterfactuals* (Cambridge, MA: Harvard University Press).
    1979. 'Counterfactual Dependence and Time's Arrow', *Noûs* 13: 455-76. Reprinted in Lewis 1986, pp. 32-52 [repr. pages cited].
    1983b. 'New Work for a Theory of Universals', *Australasian Journal of Philosophy* 61: 343-77.
    1986c. *Philosophical Papers,* vol. 2 (Oxford University Press).
    1989. 'Dispositional Theories of Value', *Proceedings of the Aristotelian Society,* suppl. vol. 63: 113-37.

McCall, Storrs. 1984. 'Counterfactuals Based on Real Possible Worlds', *Noûs* 18: 463–77.

McDermott, Michael. 1991. 'Conditionals', unpublished manuscript, Philosophy Department, University of Sydney.

Menzies, Peter and Price, Huw. In press. 'Causation as a Secondary Quality', *British Journal for the Philosophy of Science.*

Mill, John Stuart, 1843. *A System of Logic* (London: Parker).

Molnar, George. 1969. 'Kneale's Argument Revisisted', *Philosophical Review* 78: 79–89. Reprinted in *Philosophical Problems of Causation,* ed. Tom L. Beauchamp (Belmont, CA: Dickenson, 1974).

Pettit, Philip. 1991. 'Realism and Response-Dependence', *Mind* 100: 587–626.

Pollock, John. 1984. *The Foundations of Philosophical Semantics* (Princeton University Press).

Ramsey, F. P. 1978. 'Universals of Laws and of Fact', *Foundations,* ed. D. H. Mellor (London: Routledge & Kegan Paul).

Suppe, Frederic. 1989. *The Semantic Conception of Theories and Scientific Realism* (Urbana: University of Illinois Press).

Tooley, Michael. 1977. 'The Nature of Laws', *Canadian Journal of Philosophy* 67: 667–98.

1987. *Causation: a Realist Approach* (Oxford: Clarendon).

van Fraassen, Bas C. 1989. *Laws and Symmetry* (Oxford: Clarendon).

Wright, Crispin. In press. 'Order of Determination, Response-Dependence, and the Euthyphro Contrast', *Reality: Representation and Projection,* ed. John Haldane and Crispin Wright (Oxford University Press).

Reply to Menzies

D. M. ARMSTRONG

Peter Menzies was for some time a member of the department at Sydney. It was a great pleasure, both intellectually and personally, to have him there. At one point he gave an excellent series of seminars on causation, and that topic has continued to be his main research interest. I have found his present paper on laws a very stimulating one.

1. Criticism of the Regularity Theory of Laws

Menzies begins by criticizing the Regularity theory (of laws, not causes), concentrating upon what I agree is its strongest version, the Ramsey-Lewis variant. For the most part I agree with Menzies's criticisms, but I would like to enter one caveat. Menzies follows Tooley and Carroll in giving the case of a world with only one fundamental law: particles of type X have spin up in fields of type Y. Xs and Ys, however, never meet, so the law is not instantiated. Another world is like the first world, except that the uninstantiated law gives X-particles spin down. Two different possible worlds, apparently, but the claim is that the Regularity theory, even in Lewis's version, can give no account of the difference.

I think that we should treat this argument a little cautiously. It may be granted that the two worlds and their difference are *conceivable,* but it is not quite so obvious that here we have two different *possible* worlds. For to allow these as possibilities seems to involve postulating entities that some might think twice before postulating. Tooley would deal with the situation by postulating a relationship between the universals X and Y, a different relation for each world, relations that would ensure different outcomes if, contrary to fact, Xs and Ys ever met. Menzies is sceptical about such relations. Others would postulate irreducible but unmanifested powers associated with the universals X and Y. Is Menzies prepared to do this? If not, what proposal does he have? He will need to ensure that any proposal he endorses is consistent with his own account of laws and of causality.

2. Criticism of Armstrong's Theory of Laws

Menzies organizes his criticism of my theory of laws by using van Fraassen's suggestion that any theory which tries to see laws of nature as a relation or relations between universals faces two problems: the *identification* and the *inference* problem. First, the identification problem: As Menzies says, I try to solve this problem by pointing to what I take to be our direct awareness of singular causation in certain favourable cases. In his very interesting book translated as *The Perception of Causality* (1963), the Louvain psychologist A. Michotte argued that there is experimental evidence for just such direct awareness. The majority of analytical philosophers, however, follow Hume in denying the existence of such awareness. Menzies is with the majority.

Michotte concentrates on visual cases, but from my point of view these cases, though fascinating, are controversial because one can see how it can be argued that the perceptions in question involve inference of an unconscious sort made on the basis of purely visual cues. As Michotte himself points out, it is much harder to deny that there is noninferential perception of causality in the case of tactual perception. I think that the case of awareness of pressure on our own body is the most difficult case for a Humean. The content of a sensation of pressure seems, phenomenologically, to involve nothing more than pressure on our body. And pressure is a causal notion.

Menzies has two interesting arguments, of a relatively a priori sort, for denying that we are directly (noninferentially) aware of singular causation in the perception of pressure, or, for that matter, anywhere else. First he says that 'it is implausible to suppose that we can directly perceive singular causal relations . . . because there is a counterfactual element to these relations that cannot plausibly be claimed to be an object of direct awareness'.

I readily concede that a counterfactual is involved. It is important to see, however, that the counterfactual is singular only, and has nothing to do with general laws. The point is important because, if the counterfactual did involve an unrestricted universal quantification, it would be most implausible that our awareness of singular causation is direct. Menzies renders the counterfactual as 'If the bodily impact had not occurred, I would not have experienced the sensation of pressure'. This may be a little too strong, because a ceteris paribus clause seems to be in order, ruling out (for example) a back-up cause that would have brought about the sensation of pressure if the bodily impact had not occurred. But, passing this over, I see no reason to rule out direct awareness of an event having such restricted counterfactual implications.

What needs discussion at this point is the theory of perception. According to me, perception is a flow of (subverbal) information or misinformation about the current state of the organism's body and environment. Once one takes such a view, I think it becomes relatively easy to see how one could have, among one's noninferential perceptions, perception of a happening with the required counterfactual implications.

Almost nothing can concern the organism more directly than to receive up-to-date information about pressures upon its body. Why, then, should not nature work out a system whereby pressures on some part of the body should register in the brain that pressure, understood as pressure and so involving counterfactual implications, was occurring at that spot? Such registration would have to be broadly reliable to be useful. But sometimes registration might occur and yet be caused by something that is not pressure.

I wonder if Menzies is influenced, consciously or unconsciously, by the idea that the direct or noninferential object of perception is always a *thing* of some sort, or perhaps a thing having some occurrent quality, and nothing else? Direct perception would then have to be counterfactual-free. I see no reason to accept this picture of perception. It may be a last, lingering influence of the sense-datum theory. It is not the least advantage of the information-flow theory of perception that it delivers us from this picture, thus allowing a noninferential perception of causal action on the body.

But Menzies has a second argument. How, he asks, can a causal relation, allegedly the thing noninferentially perceived, act causally on the mind to produce awareness of itself? In answer to this query, consider first the perception of other relations. Suppose that we perceive that *a* is to the left of *b*. What happens, I take it, is that the state of affairs of *a*'s being to the left of *b* causes the state of affairs which is the perception of this very state of affairs. Diagramatically:

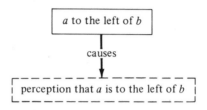

I don't know how this happens – perhaps psychologists do know – but it seems very clear that it does happen. Otherwise, we would not perceive relations. Now is it really so impossible that '*a* causes *b*' should be substituted in the top box? Some object presses on our flesh. That whole situation causes perception of the situation. How does this happen? Leave that matter to psychology and neurophysiology.

But perhaps the situation is a bit different. Perhaps what we are given in noninferential perception of pressure is not so much a situation of the sort '*a* causes *b*' but rather, as it were, only one end, the effect end, of the causal relation. Perhaps all that we are aware of is our body being pressed upon. Being pressed upon entails that something presses, so if our perception is veridical then there is something doing the pressing. But perhaps, once collateral information (from other senses, etc.) is abstracted from, the pressure sensation involves nothing more than a quite indeterminate awareness of something or other doing the pressing. This may be a more realistic picture of the perception of pressure.

Once more, it helps greatly to wheel in an information-flow conception of perception. We are noninferentially aware that our body has the relational property of *being pressed upon*. ('We are under attack'.) Why need there be any awareness of that which is doing the pressing, beyond its bare existence?

I have done no more here than try to answer the particular arguments that Menzies uses against the direct perception of causality. But if we assume that there is such perception, then an answer to the identification problem appears. We must not indeed take it that awareness of singular causation is awareness of the instantiation of a law. I have been convinced by Elizabeth Anscombe (1971), among others, that there is no a priori or conceptual connection holding between singular causation and instantiation of a law. Nevertheless, as Adrian Heathcote has pointed out (Heathcote and Armstrong 1991), this is no bar to making a plausible a posteriori identification of singular causation and law instantiation. With this identification in place, it can then further be suggested, again as a plausible hypothesis, that the *mustness* involved in alleged nomic connection of properties is identical with, or bears a close analogy to, the mustness present in singular causation. The mustness – that is, the modal nature – of singular causation is signalled, though not I think constituted by, the singular counterfactuals that statements of singular causation sustain. The hypothesized connections between universals sustain counterfactuals of the same sort, except that they involve types of states of affairs rather than tokens.

So much, I hope, for the identification problem. As I see it, the inference problem is not then too difficult to solve. Instead of state of affairs *a* causing state of affairs *b* at the level of particulars, we have a hypothesis that a certain type of state of affairs causes a further type of state of affairs. It is a hypothesis that there can be a causal connection between types (i.e., between universals), a hypothesis meant to explain the regular successions, and so on, at the level of particular states of affairs. But if the hypothesis be entertained, it would seem analytic that if it holds then it must be reflected in successions and so forth at the level of first-order states of affairs.

Such links between universals do raise the question of 'necessary connections between distinct existences'. Not between the universals themselves, if it can be maintained (as I think it can) that physical necessity is not absolute necessity. But if there is a deterministic link between universals F and G such that, say, an F physically must be a G, or at least must be a G in default of further (positive) defeating conditions, then Fs that are non-Gs are ruled out, at least in the absence of defeating conditions. This sticks in the Humean gizzard.

I believe, however, that with regard to the relations between higher-order and lower-order entities, such as relations between universals and relations between states of affairs, the Humean principle must be given up. For particulars, universals and states of affairs at the same level, the principle holds. But with higher-level entities, something is always ruled out at a lower level. I first became aware that 'always' seems correct here in connection with what Russell called 'general facts' and which I call facts (states of affairs) of totality. For instance, for a certain class or aggregate of electrons it is the case that it is *all* the electrons. With Russell, I do not think that this fact supervenes on the electrons themselves; the fact is an irreducibly higher-order one. But as I failed to see until

David Lewis pointed it out to me, if we admit such a fact or state of affairs into our ontology then we have something that excludes; it excludes the existence of any further electrons. Bad news for facts of totality, Lewis thought. But I thought that Russell's argument was too strong to be rejected, and that in any case such exclusion did not seem particularly paradoxical. The exclusion of certain states of affairs at the first-order level by nomic connections of universals at a higher level seems also reasonably intuitive when we remember what a universal is. And as far as I can see at present, the higher level always excludes at a lower level.

The topic of higher-order entities – nonsupervenient properties and relations of properties and relations, nonsupervenient states of affairs concerning states of affairs – is a difficult and ill-explored one. Menzies very reasonably raises various puzzles and difficulties. He asks, as others have asked before him, how a state of affairs of one property nomically determining another can at the same time be a universal, as I claim is the case. For the first is the ontological correlate of a statement, the second the ontological correlate of a predicate.

I don't think that there is too much difficulty here. Consider:

(1) The building collapsed.
(2) The building's collapse caused the financial collapse.

Here the ontological correlate of a statement and a subject term would appear to be the same. Again:

(3) This colour is agreeable.
(4) The dress is this agreeable colour.

Here the ontological correlate of a statement and a predicate might well be the same.

Properties of properties are particularly puzzling, and I sometimes wonder if first-order universals fall under any nonsupervenient properties as opposed to relations. But suppose that the property of being one kilogram in mass really falls under the nonsupervenient property of being a mass. Menzies rightly says that on my view this second-order state of affairs is a first-order universal. It must obviously be a monadic universal, and it will qualify those first-order particulars (and only those) whose mass is one kilogram. I don't see that these answers are ad hoc, or particularly implausible. (I am not claiming that they are particularly plausible either. Spoils to the victor.)

Finally, Menzies uses my idea that universals are abstractions from states of affairs in order to launch an ad hominem criticism of the idea that some universals are themselves states of affairs. Universals are abstractions and states of affairs are not, so no universals are states of affairs. I think that Menzies shows that I have been careless here. But why should I not back up a little and say that only *first-order* states of affairs are non-abstract? Someone like Michael Tooley, who allows uninstantiated nomic relations between universals, will have nonabstract second-order states of affairs. But I (perhaps wrongly) deny the existence of uninstantiated laws – although, of course, I allow that truth conditions can be specified for statements that have the surface form of saying that such laws exist. My corrected view will be that in that state of affairs which constitutes a law, the universals that it contains are abstractions from the law. The law in turn is an abstraction from its instantiations in first-order states of affairs.

3. Menzies's Account of Laws of Nature

Menzies's account of laws in terms of what is experimentally possible is an interesting addition to the currently available accounts of laws. I note that it joins the class of theories that make laws nonsupervenient upon local matters of fact. But I find the demotion of law to the status of secondary quality a trifle distressing – my own instinct is to make laws completely objective – but I don't know that I have an argument to back up my instinct.

I do wonder about the status of causation in Menzies's theory. The notion of an experiment is one that involves causality essentially. Into a certain set-up the experimenter introduces a further factor in order to see what effect it will have. If causation in its turn essentially involves laws (whether this is a truth certified a priori or a posteriori does not seem to matter), then the theory appears to be involved in vicious circularity. Does Menzies hold that singular causation is essentially singular? That, I think, is a tenable position – I held the view myself for some years – although I do not think it is a very comfortable one.

A deeper worry is the question of the status of nomic possibilities in Menzies's theory. Consider a certain token experimental set-up. A human agent or a miracle-working God may introduce a new factor into the situation. For each of the innumerable factors that could be introduced into the situation there will be a host of possibilities. But given Determinism, only one of these possibilities will be an empirical possibility. Now what marks off this empirical possibility from the other nonempirical possibilities for that set-up plus that added factor? Does it exist, while the other possibilities do not? That would be a heavy extra ontological burden. But if the empirical possibility does not exist, is it just an unanalyzable truth that that possibility, unlike the others, is empirical? That would come perilously close to having a truth with nothing in the world to make it a truth.

A further problem arises when the attempt is made to pass from tokens to types. Suppose that the situation is repeated, at least in all nomically relevant respects, with the added factor also identical in relevant respects. What guarantee is there that the empirically possible outcome is the same as in the first token of the situation? Menzies might complain that this is just the problem of induction, which creates difficulties for everybody. I will just point out, however, that the introduction of relationships between *universals* seems to give promise of solving the problem that Menzies would have.

REFERENCES

Anscombe, G. E. M. 1971. *Causality and Determination,* Inaugural Lecture (Cambridge University Press). Reprinted in *Causation and Conditionals,* ed. Ernest Sosa (Oxford University Press, 1975), pp. 63–81.

Heathcote, Adrian and Armstrong, D. M. 1991. 'Causes and Laws', *Noûs* 25: 63–73.

Michotte, A. 1963. *The Perception of Causality,* tr. T. R. Miles (London: Methuen).

IV

Consciousness and Secondary Qualities

10

Block's Challenge

FRANK JACKSON

An English test umpire is reported to have said that Jack Hobbes was the greatest batsman he had ever seen, though Bradman was the greatest run-making machine. The umpire was making a conceptual mistake. The point of batting is to make runs. Similarly, the point of intelligence is to generate intelligent responses. In this lies the plausibility of functionalist and behaviourist approaches to intelligence. Being intelligent comes down, when all is said and done, to facts about behaving intelligently.

My concern in this essay is to defend this conception of what it is to be intelligent from an interesting and influential example due to Ned Block.[1] This example is widely supposed to dispose of behavioural approaches to intelligence.[2] I will argue, however, that the example is quite compatible with an essentially behavioural or functionalist approach to intelligence. The mistake, I will argue, has been to understand behavioural or functionalist approaches to intelligence in an unduly narrow way. I will address at the end of the essay the question of whether what I say actually contradicts the letter of Block's paper. It certainly contradicts the moral typically drawn from what Block says, and this is the main focus of what follows.

1

We can all agree that the information processing that goes on inside someone is vital for their being intelligent. Sympathy for behaviourism about intelligence should be sympathy for the idea that being intelligent is a matter of being internally such as to make true certain facts about behavioural dispositions and capacities. True, some hold that 'bare' dispositions are logically possible, and some go further and hold that, for example, force fields are actual examples of bare dispositions; but no one thinks that the kinds of dispositions and capacities distinctive of intelligence could possibly be bare dispositions. In D. M. Armstrong's terminology, we must be realists and not phenomenalists about the dispositions distinctive of intelligence.[3] The live issue, therefore, is not whether what goes on inside an intelligent person matters for that person's being intelligent; it is whether it matters in a way that outruns how what goes on inside relates to and sustains the facts about behavioural capacities and dispositions typically associated with intelligence. What is at issue is whether or not what goes on inside only matters inasmuch as it sustains the appropriate facts about behavioural dispositions.

The issue can be approached by distinguishing stimulus–response (SR) functionalism from internally autonomous (IA) functionalism. Both versions of functionalism think of mental states in general, and a piece of intelligent thought in particular, as internal states of persons defined by the usual three kinds of clauses: input clauses, output clauses and internal-role clauses. The difference is over whether (or for which mental states) the internal-role clauses are *autonomous,* in the sense that their holding or not holding is independent of the total input–output story, that is, independent of how they relate to the sustaining of behavioural capacities and dispositions.

Consider, to illustrate the distinction, a functionalist who holds that what a person believes at a time supervenes on the total story about the subject's internally sustained actual and potential dispositions to behave at the time, *except* that a necessary condition of being a subject to which belief can be ascribed is that the subject obey certain rationality constraints, including (let's say, by way of over-simple illustration) a tendency to believe that most crows are black shortly after acquiring the belief that many crows have been sighted and they have all been black. Such a functionalist gives internal causal roles a central place in her account – as she must to be properly called a functionalist – for she insists that evolving according to certain rationality constraints is a necessary condition for being a belief. But the roles, or at least the role illustrated, are not autonomous. The internal role could be described in terms of the causal evolution of internally sustained behavioural dispositions. Although diachronic as well as synchronic facts about the internal sustaining of input–output facts enter the picture, the picture is still one in terms of the sustaining of input–output facts. Such a functionalist is, therefore, a SR-functionalist and not an IA-functionalist about belief.[4]

In terms of the distinction between SR-functionalism and IA-functionalism, the moral typically drawn from Block's example can be put as that we should be IA-functionalists about intelligence. His example shows, it is claimed, that what goes on inside matters for being intelligent in a way that outruns how it connects with facts about the sustaining of actual and potential behavioural dispositions.[5] And what we will be defending is SR-functionalism about intelligence from his example.

2

Saying that intelligence comes down to facts about behaving intelligently is vague. The best way to remove the vagueness is informative but risky – it is to attempt a convincing analysis of exactly what makes a piece or pattern of behaviour intelligent, and of rationality in general.[6] The exercise is informative, or at least potentially informative, because it sets out to tell us what intelligence is. It is risky because the question of exactly what constitutes intelligence is hard, and any suggestion is bound to be controversial and open to objection.

There is a less risky – and correspondingly less informative – way of arguing that intelligence is, when all is said and done, a matter of behaving intelligently. It is to find a plausible supervenience thesis that appropriately connects intelligence and behaviour. Suppose, for instance, that we define a behaviour-in-circumstances duplicate of S to be a creature which is internally such that, for every actual and possible input that a subject S is or might be subjected to, it responds behaviourally in exactly the same way as S would. We might then suggest the following supervenience thesis:

> If S is a normally embodied, intelligent creature free to move about his environment, then any behaviour-in-circumstances duplicate of S must be intelligent.

Let's call this the first supervenience thesis. It is limited in a number of ways. It does not say what counts as intelligent behaviour; it only offers a sufficient condition for being intelligent, and a circular one at that. It is silent about how people bound in chains, or who are partially or totally paralyzed (or who are 'brains in vats') – people, that is, who are *not* normally embodied creatures free to move about their environments – could count as intelligent. But it does entail the SR-functionalist position on intelligence. If it is true, then the obtaining of a certain internally sustained totality of behavioural dispositions – the totality shared with the intelligent S – must be sufficient for intelligence. For if the sustaining of that totality of behavioural dispositions were not sufficient for intelligence, it would be possible to be a behaviour-in-circumstances duplicate of S and yet fail to be intelligent.

What Block shows, in effect, is that the first supervenience thesis is false. He describes a recipe for making a behaviour in circumstances duplicate of our intelligent, normally embodied S but which is not intelligent. I will describe his recipe, and then go on to suggest the reason why a thing made according to it is unintelligent. This reason points us towards

a second supervenience thesis and why we should appeal to this second
thesis in order to capture the core of the SR-functionalist position about
intelligence.

3

Block introduces the key idea behind his recipe for making an unintelligent input–output duplicate of an intelligent normally embodied person
by describing a way of playing good chess, in the sense of winning chess,
without actually having any understanding at all of chess.

Suppose that you are playing black to an opponent's white. There are
only finitely many possible (legal) first moves by white that could confront you. For each of these first moves there are only finitely many replies that you might make, and for each of these replies by you, there are
only a finite number of second moves that your opponent might make.
And so on and so forth. This means that *in principle* an expert chess
player could write down a look-up tree by which you could play. The first
row contains every possible opening move by white, and has written next
to each a good reply by you as black. The second row is divided into subrows, one for each of the opening moves by white, and each subrow contains every possible second move by white given your reply, and has written next to that second move a good reply by you for your second move
as black. And so on and so forth. The crucial point is that you have a
huge array which you can search systematically and which, for any and
every possible sequence of moves by white, has written next to it a good
response to make as black to every move by white in the sequence. A
point which will be important later is that any two distinct sequences of
moves by white take you to different places in the look-up tree. If the sequences are the same length, you will be taken to different places in a
given row (indeed, to different places in the ith row if the sequence is i
members long); if the sequences are of different lengths, you will be taken
to different rows.

Playing chess when you are black by look-up tree is simply doing what
the tree we have just described tells you to do at every stage. Obviously,
we could in the same general way describe a look-up tree to follow when
you are white. Playing by look-up tree will ensure that you play good
chess – how good will depend on the ability at chess of the person who
wrote up the array – but, Block urges, your good performance will show
absolutely nothing about your ability at chess. Playing chess by look-up
tree is compatible with a complete lack of understanding of or ability at
chess. Of course, that you use the look-up tree correctly and know that
following the look-up tree is a good idea if you want to win both point to

your general intelligence, but not to your having any understanding of chess.

As it stands, the fact that you could play 'good' chess by look-up tree and yet understand nothing about chess (over and above an ability to read correctly the notation used in the look-up tree) shows nothing against a SR-functionalist approach to intelligence. A person who plays chess by look-up tree will display quite enough input–output failures to sustain the charge that he does not understand chess. To give a single example to make the point: Part of what is involved in understanding chess is understanding how the nature of the rules of chess connect, with which moves are good and which moves are bad. But suppose that a small change is proposed in the rules – say, that for the next game castling be disallowed. A genuinely good chess player in the sense of someone who understands chess will still perform well, while anyone playing by look-up tree will be all at sea. The point, however, of the chess example is to introduce what I will call (as has become traditional) the Blockhead example. And in this example there are no input–output failures over and above those displayed by people we all agree to be intelligent.

4

Blockhead, as we might put it, plays the game of life by look-up tree. The recipe for making Blockhead runs as follows. Take an intelligent normally embodied person, our S. The surface of S's body is inevitably limited in its discriminatory capacities. Although there may be infinitely many different inputs to which his body may be subjected at its periphery at any one time, we need only list finitely many inputs (or input intervals, really) to cover every possibility by way of behavioural output. Cutting any finer would be behaviourally irrelevant. This means that we can write out an array which gives what S would do subject to any and every possible sequence of peripheral inputs, in the same general way we imagined for the chess example. The first row consists of every possible peripheral input that S might be subjected to at the first moment of his life. Against each input in this row is written what S would do were he subjected to the input. The second row is divided into subrows, one for each input in the first row, and it contains every possible input that S might be subjected to, given that he was subjected to the corresponding first input; and against each entry in the second row is written what S would do were he subjected to the input following the corresponding first input; and so on and so forth. We end up with a searchable array that has at every position in it what S would do were he subjected to the sequence of inputs which takes us to that point in the array.

Now imagine this array implanted inside a creature called 'Blockhead' which has a body exernally like S's, and that Blockhead works by look-up tree in the following sense. When the first peripheral input strikes Blockhead, Blockhead searches the first row and carries out the response written down there; that is, Blockhead does what S would have done if subjected to that input as first input. Its search mechanism then goes to the subrow in the second row corresponding to that first input. When the second input strikes Blockhead, it searches that subrow for the second input, and does what is written there. And so on and so forth. Clearly, for any and every possible sequence of peripheral inputs, Blockhead will do exactly what S would do. And since causation is local, this means that for any and every possible possible sequence of inputs, peripheral or distal, Blockhead and S are precisely equivalent in what they would do in every actual and possible circumstance. And yet, as Block and many others following him say, surely Blockhead has no intelligence whatever; or, as Block in fact put it, it has the intelligence of a toaster.[7]

5

I have just agreed with Block that Blockhead lacks intelligence. But in fact the intuition to that effect could well be denied. What I have in mind here is not the point that the example is impossible in any except the most rarefied sense. You could not write down a look-up tree for draughts, let alone for chess, and let alone for the whole of a life; and even if you could, it could not be searched in real time. There are far, far too many possibilities that need to be covered. But I do not think that this really matters, provided you accept the method of possible cases at all. For Block's example is not hard to understand. It is not one of those enormously complex, hard-to-grasp cases where one feels inclined to trust theory more than intuition. Rather, the point I have in mind arises from the fact that there is an obvious reason why we regard getting answers by look-up tree as in general not displaying intelligence and understanding in the relevant domain. There is a characteristic inflexibility about successful performances based on look-up trees. We have already noted that playing chess by look-up tree is in serious trouble when even minor changes to the rules are proposed. Or consider someone who does not understand what the square root of a number is while being able to produce the square root of a range of numbers by using a table of square roots. He will be unable to make even a start on giving the square root of a number not in the table – that is, he will not be able to 'go on' in the right way – and should the table contain a mistake he will be quite unable to locate or correct it.

Now because those who get answers by look-up tree will have distinctive deficits in their capacities, deficits which would or could be exposed by various tests, it might well be argued that it is these deficits which make it the case that the successful performances of the user of a look-up tree fail to reveal understanding and intelligence concerning the subject matter in question. It is the deficits, and not the role of the look-up tree as such, that are essentialy responsible for the lack of intelligence.

The point is that if we are to go along with Block (as I think we should) in holding that Blockhead is unintelligent, we must give the reason why Blockhead is unintelligent. It is not enough simply to cite the fact that Blockhead works by look-up tree. True, anything that works by look-up tree is unintelligent in the sense that anything that has any chance at all of actually existing that works by look-up tree is unintelligent. But arguably this is because of the behavioural deficits inevitably associated with working by look-up tree, not because of the fact of working by look-up tree itself.

I think that we can say why Blockhead is unintelligent. We can, that is, identify a property ineluctably associated with working by look-up tree which is transparently inconsistent with being intelligent. But first we need before us a point familiar from discussions of personal identity.

6

Consider two molecule-for-molecule identical twins: Tweedledum and Tweedledee. And suppose that they are raised in separate environments that are molecule-for-molecule identical for the whole of their lives. Their lives, both mental and physical, march in parallel from start to finish. When one is thinking that snow is white, so is the other; when one is intentionally reaching for a glass of water, so is the other; and so on and so forth.[8] Accordingly, if you want to know what Tweedledum is doing or thinking at 12 noon, examing Tweedledee is just as good as examining Tweedledum himself. Tweedledum's biography might just as well have been Tweedledee's biography, and so on and so forth. Does all this mean that there are not two persons here? The answer of course is 'No.' True, the similarity Tweedledum on Tuesday has to Tweedledum on Monday is no greater, and no less, than the similarity that Tweedledum on Tuesday has to Tweedledee on Monday; but there is an enormously important difference all the same. The way Tweedledum is on Tuesday is causally dependent upon the way Tweedledum is on Monday, and not upon the way Tweedledee is on Monday. Although the way Tweedledee is on Monday is good for predicting the way Tweedledum is on Tuesday, there is no *causal path* from the way Tweedledee is on Monday to the way Tweedledum is on Tuesday.

We are simply noting here the accepted point that part of what makes a person a continuing subject of experience is the way earlier thoughts give rise to later thoughts. This means that a string of thoughts cannot in itself make a thinker no matter how similar the thoughts are, individual thought by individual thought, to the thoughts of a genuine thinker. Consider the case of an epiphenomenal person. Epi is an exact copy of me which is re-made moment by moment in some suitable medium. The way I am, molecule for molecule, at any given time T causes the way Epi is at T (or T plus whatever the transmission time is).[9] In consequence, the way Epi is at a time is not caused by the way it was previously. It is the way that I am at the relevant time that does all the causing for each and every moment of Epi's life.

I take it that it is obvious that Epi does not do any thinking. Certain causal connections between thoughts are necessary for thinking, just as they are for personal identity, and although Epi's thoughts march in parallel with mine, I am thinking and Epi is not. (I am talking here as if Epi has thoughts but does not do any thinking because its thoughts at one time do not cause its thoughts at another. Alternatively, and perhaps better, we could say that it does not have 'thoughts' properly speaking, but rather has thoughts* – states that would be thoughts if they stood in the appropriate causal relations to other thoughts*.)

This means that we could have used Epi instead of Blockhead to refute the first supervenience thesis. Epi would behave exactly as I would in all possible situations; but whereas I am a normally embodied thinker with intelligence, Epi neither thinks nor is intelligent. Epi highlights what has been left out of the story about intelligence by those who favour the first supervenience thesis – namely, that diachronic facts about the sustaining of behavioural capacities matter as well as synchronic facts.

7

I suggest that the reason Blockhead is not intelligent is that it does not think, and the reason it does not think is the same as the reason Epi does not think. Its thoughts (or thoughts*) are not appropriately causally connected. We noted earlier that a crucial feature of the way Blockhead works is that any two distinct strings of inputs go to distinct places in the look-up tree. Moreover, the response specified at any given place in the tree does not causally depend on, nor does it cause, the response specified at any other place in the tree. If we altered the response specified at any given point, the responses specified everywhere else in the tree would be unchanged. But this means that the internal nature of Blockhead which causally sustains its capacity at some particular time to give intelligent responses is not causally dependent on the internal nature of Blockhead which causally sustains its capacity to give intelligent responses at any earlier time; more generally, the basis of Blockhead's dispositional nature at one time is not causally responsible for the basis of Blockhead's dispositional nature at any other time.

There is of course a single thing inside Blockhead responsible for its capacities at the various times to give intelligent responses – namely, the huge look-up tree. But the parts that come into play at the various times are causally independent of each other in the same way that the internal states of Epi at various times are causally independent of each other. What Blockhead is thinking (or thinking*) at any one time is not caused by what it is thinking (or thinking*) at any earlier time. Part of what makes you and me intelligent is the fact that had our thoughts yesterday been different in certain ways, our thoughts today would have been appropriately different – an intelligent person is in part someone who, in addition to thinking what she ought to today given what she thought yesterday, would think today what she ought to had she thought quite differently yesterday. True, what Blockhead is thinking is caused by what inputs it has received in the past along with the nature of the huge array inside it, because its input history determines which part of the array is in play. But that is quite different from what it is thinking now being appropriately causally dependent on what it thought in the past. Blockhead is like someone in a huge hotel, each room of which contains an 'input–output book'. When she receives an input she performs the output specified by the book in the room she is in and then moves to a new room. It might be that the room she moves to depends on the input she receives and on the output she performs, but the 'content' of the book in the second room is causally independent of the content of the book in the first room. There is no causal dependence between the input–output stories in the various books.

8

We introduced the first supervenience thesis as a first, Turing-style stab at capturing the essence of an SR-functionalist approach to intelligence. We can now say why the first supervenience thesis is inadequate. A creature can be exactly like a normally embodied, intelligent S in what it would do in circumstances, and yet be totally unlike S in how what is true of it at one time concerning what it would do in circumstances causally interconnects with what is true of it at other times concerning what it would do in circumstances; and, what is more, be totally unlike in ways which warrant denying that it thinks. But this shows that neither Blockhead nor Epi refutes SR-functionalism about intelligence. They rather reveal what is wrong with seeking to capture the essential claim of SR-functionalism about intelligence through the first supervenience thesis. The SR-functionalist holds that being intelligent comes down to facts about behaviour in circumstances. Now, although the facts about what inputs would lead to what outputs at every moment of a creature's life are clearly highly relevant for being intelligent, they do not exhaust the facts about behaviour in circumstances that are relevant. The lesson of Epi and Blockhead is that causal connections between what sustains behavior in circumstances at different times are essential to being a thinker, and so are highly relevant to being intelligent. Because diachronic as well as synchronic facts about the sustaining of behavioural dispositions matter for intelligence, we need to include facts about causal connections among what sustains the input–output facts in the supervenience base, as in the following, second supervenience thesis:

> If S is a normally embodied, intelligent creature free to move about his or her environment then any duplicate of S, with regard (a) to the totality of actual and possible behaviour in circumstances at times sustained by its internal nature and (b) to the way the totality of behavioural dispositions at one time causally depends on what sustains the totality of behavioural dispositions at earlier times, is also intelligent.[10]

I suggest that this second supervenience thesis is what is needed to capture the essence of an SR-functionalist approach to intelligence. It tells us that a certain totality of facts (a 'bigger' totality than in the first supervenience thesis) about internally sustained behavioural dispositions – namely, the totality of facts in common between S and any duplicate in the sense specified in clauses (a) and (b) – is logically sufficient for intelligence. But although the totality of facts is bigger, it remains true that what goes on inside only matters inasmuch as it grounds the relevant facts about behavioural dispositions. It is just that diachronic as well as synchronic facts about such groundings have been included.

9

In what way are we disagreeing with what Block claims in his article? We are certainly disagreeing with the moral commonly drawn from his article, namely, that what we called SR-functionalism about intelligence must be replaced by IA-functionalism about intelligence. But the relationship between what we are saying and what he actually says in the article is open to interpretation. Here is the crucial passage:

> I mean psychologism to involve the doctrine that two systems could have actual and potential behavior typical of familiar intelligent beings, that the two systems could be exactly alike in their actual and potential behavior, and in their behavioral dispositions and capacities and counterfactual behavioral properties . . . yet

there could be a difference in the information processing that mediates their stimuli and responses that determines that one is not at all intelligent while the other is fully intelligent.

This paper makes two claims: first, psychologism is true, and thus a natural behaviorist analysis of intelligence is false . . . . (Block 1981, p. 5)

The passage could be read as giving Block's *definition* of psychologism, the definition being in effect that psychologism is the denial of what is pretty much what we called the first supervenience thesis. Read this way, we are not disagreeing with Block over psychologism. We agree that it is true. Our disagreement is rather with the inference that a substantive point has been made against natural behaviourist analyses of intelligence. As we saw, sympathizers with behaviourist analyses of intelligence can and should reject the first supervenience thesis. It is the second supervenience thesis that an upholder of a generally behaviouristic approach to intelligence should espouse.

Alternatively, the passage could be read as advancing, as the crucial *test* for deciding whether intelligence can be understood in essentially behavioural terms, the acceptability of the first supervenience thesis. On this reading, 'psychologism' is the name for any theory which denies that intelligence can be understood in essentially behavioural terms. On this reading we disagree over which test is crucial and over psychologism. Block holds that the Blockhead example shows that psychologism is true, whereas we hold that the Blockhead example does not show that psychologism is true, and further that the Blockhead example, along with the example of Epi, shows that the acceptability of the first supervenience thesis is not the crucial question for those who espouse an essentially behaviourist analysis of intelligence.[11]

NOTES

1. Most fully developed in Block (1981).
2. See, e.g., Clark (1989, Chapter 3) and the references therein.
3. Armstrong (1968, pp. 85f). Armstrong holds that we ought to be realists about all dispositions, on the ground that bare dispositions are logically impossible.
4. I am indebted here to discussions with Aubrey Townsend.
5. Actual and potential behavioural dispositions, because we want to allow paralyzed people to count as intelligent, and they are only potentially disposed to make intelligent responses. The argument to follow will, however, skirt the complications raised by these cases.
6. See, e.g., Bennett (1964).
7. See, e.g., Block (1981, p. 21) as well as Clark (1989, Chapter 3) and the references therein.
8. Perhaps they differ in certain demonstrative and certain self-reflexive thoughts, but that will not affect the points to follow.

9. The example is different from Christopher Peacocke's example of a being with a Martian controller, described in the last chapter of Peacocke (1983). The way I am causes not Epi's responses but rather the way Epi is internally. Indeed, my role in the example is essentially rhetorical. In order to make the points that follow, Epi could simply be described as a series of 'adjacent' states, none of which causes any of its successors and each of which sustains a rich input–output story.

10. Incidentally, Armstrong gives causal connections between mental states a prominent role in his analyses of various mental states; see particularly Section XI, 'Mental Actions', in Armstrong (1968, Chapter 7).

11. I am indebted to numerous discussions, and must mention David Braddon-Mitchell, Karen Neander, Martin Davies and Philip Pettit.

REFERENCES

Armstrong, D. M. 1968. *A Materialist Theory of the Mind* (London: Routledge & Kegan Paul).

Bennett, Jonathan. 1964. *Rationality* (London: Routledge & Kegan Paul).

Block, Ned. 1981. 'Psychologism and Behaviorism', *Philosophical Review* 90: 5–43.

Clark, Andy. 1989. *Microcognition* (Cambridge, MA: MIT Press).

Peacocke, Christopher. 1983. *Sense and Content* (Oxford University Press).

Reply to Jackson

D. M. ARMSTRONG

Frank Jackson's first year as a philosophy undergraduate at Melbourne University coincided with my last year as a lecturer there. Unfortunately, I did not have the pleasure of teaching him. I was, however, one of the examiners of his doctoral dissertation, which became his book *Perception: a Representative Theory* (1977). It was certainly the best Ph.D. that I have ever examined.

I don't have a great deal to say about his present paper. When Frank criticizes an argument it tends to stay criticized, and he has answered Block completely to my satisfaction. It is interesting to see how powerful in very many fields is the technique of formulating and examining supervenience theses. I think that a good deal of its power, as Jackson points out for the particular case in hand, is its very unambitiousness, which makes it suitable for the work of analysis. The fact that no claim is made about the analysis of what supervenes and what it supervenes on, and the fact that a supervenience thesis is just a thesis whose truth or falsity must be determined (if it can be determined) by further arguments, has a calming effect on the discussion. Smaller winnings but surer gains.

It seems perfectly clear, once the argument has been laid out, that Block's counterexample shows that an account of intelligence in terms of behaviour and dispositions to behave will allow an unintelligent Blockhead. At the same time, it seems perfectly clear that what is conspicuously wrong with Blockhead is that his inner states are not causally linked to each other in some intimate and sophisticated way, diachronically and synchronically. So it remains a thesis that Block has not overthrown that a purely causal theory will suffice as a theory of intelligence.

I must admit, though, after championing a Causal theory of mental concepts for many years, that I have become convinced (mainly by Bill Lycan) that the phenomenon of intentionality, obviously involved in intelligent behaviour, escapes a purely causal analysis of the sort I used to peddle. What is needed is a causal–teleological theory, and a naturalistic theory of teleology. (Though it may still be argued that the teleological theory involved should be causal.)

I will just add something on the topic of dispositions. Unless we stretch the notion of disposition a bit, they seem to be a somewhat blunt instrument for a causal theory to work with. I think that dispositions have 'categorical bases'. I am not so sure as I once was that other accounts are logically impossible (see Jackson's note 3). But, as Jackson says, it does seem important for an account of mental concepts that the dispositions involved are not 'bare'. Nevertheless, granting this, the ordinary concept of a disposition does not demand that the categorical base be *structured*. Structure may be involved in the causal power of the base, but the concept of a base does not demand it. All that is necessary is that, in standard circumstances, the base, plus the initiating cause if it occurs, should bring about the manifestation of the disposition. That would not be enough, for example, for belief. We need beliefs to be structures of some sort, structures whose internal complexity mirrors the way that the concepts hang together in the belief. Consider the inferring of belief from belief. It could not be a matter of unstructured state bringing about an unstructured state. There must be a structure and that structure must play an essential causal role, a very sophisticated role, in the causal sequence that is the inferring in the head.

I don't think that there is anything here that Jackson would wish to deny. But the human mind is the most complex and sophisticated object of which we have knowledge. We may hope to evolve very sophisticated concepts in an attempt to explain its workings. Indeed, the mental concepts that we already have are the most complex and sophisticated of all our nontechnical concepts, the most complex and sophisticated of all of the concepts of the 'manifest image'. So there is a danger that, when we try to analyze the mental, our using a (relatively) coarse concept like that of a disposition may point our analyses in the wrong direction.

REFERENCE

Jackson, Frank. 1977. *Perception: a Representative Theory* (Cambridge University Press).

11

David Armstrong and Realism about Colour

KEITH CAMPBELL

The philosophy of colour is, for David Armstrong, one of the many aspects of the general program of arriving at a scientifically plausible world view that he has pursued with such pertinacity over the years. He has always seen the main problem about colour in what are fundamentally Galileo's terms: Colour is a salient feature of the manifest material world, with a phenomenology both rich and apparently deeply intersubjective. But it turns out to have no comfortable home in the scientifically informed description of that inanimate world which physics presents and which is the most credible of all extant world schemes.

The problem of colour, in other words, has always been for him a systematic problem. Today, a dominant concern with the systematic integration of science, metaphysics and epistemology may seem not particularly noteworthy. It was not always thus: I still remember with gratitude attending an Oxford seminar in 1962, conducted by Armstrong with Brian Medlin, which taught me (along with much else) that the natural bias of my own mind towards system in philosophy was not necessarily an unfortunate anachronism.

Armstrong's thought about colour has been conditioned not only by the search for system; it has been made more difficult by a further condition that he has always imposed: The system may admit no nonmaterial realm of concrete substances. So the classic Lockean strategy, that of providing a refuge for colour in the immaterial perceiving minds of creatures with colour vision, has never been a serious option for him. As a man to whom half-measures have never appealed, he has sought a full-fledged physicalist naturalism, thus ruling out any dual-aspect or epiphenomenal way of accommodating those ontic troublemakers, the transient colours seen by those with colour vision.

It is not that Armstrong does not believe in minds. On the contrary, he holds that minds are substances we know to exist. The problem is that, with minds being functional systems whose categorical basis consists in nervous tissue, there is no more comfortable a place for the colours in the brain than there is on the surfaces of the material objects that seem to bear them. This is perhaps why he has not pursued the position of Galileo himself, for whom the doctrine that colours are secondary does not itself involve any commitment to the immaterial. As Lloyd Reinhardt taught me, Galileo maintained in 'The Assayer' that colours '. . . hold their residence solely in the sensitive body; so that if the animal were removed, every such quality would be abolished and annihilated' (1623, p. 275).

The core of the complaint against colours, as is well known, is their apparent failure to take a working role in the world's causal net. They seem not to belong, as G. F. Stout so memorably put it, to the 'executive order of nature' (1904, p. 153). Accepting that, and accepting the Platonic notion that power is the mark of being, we seem to be left with the conclusion that the colours have no being, at least in the causal nexus of Nature. That is the metaphysical problem about colour.

Before assessing Armstrong's treatment of that problem, let us trace its history a little. For that history provides a cameo of another theme characteristic of Armstrong's work: the continuity of scientific and philosophic problems, and the relevance of contingent truths to the credibility of any responsible metaphysic.

Successive discoveries about colour reveal successive difficulties for the unreflective realism about colours which comes naturally to us. By *realism* about colour I mean the view that colours are properties of the natural world of space, time, matter and energy. More than that: Realism is the thesis that colours are, in some substantial sense which is easy enough to grasp but rather tricky to spell out, physical properties – that is, properties belonging to the same family as shape, temperature and texture characterizing the public, inanimate world around us.

Colour realism admits of several variants, depending on whether it is bodies, or surfaces, or light waves that are identified as the real bearers of colour. And there are differences over whether colour properties are categorical or dispositional, and over whether or not colour is taken to be a reducible physical property.

As every philosopher knows, what colour an object looks to have depends on many factors, some of which involve human, or near-human, observers with their distinctive perceptual make-up. In specifying an object's colour, we do well to keep this in mind. It is often convenient to distinguish an object's *standing* colour from its *transient* colour appearances. The standing colour is relatively invariant; it changes only when the object itself is suitably modified (with a fresh coat of paint, for example), and it is identified – as puce, or golden yellow, or whatever – by reference to standard observers and standard conditions of observation. The object's transient colours, by contrast, are a mixed bunch, varying from illuminant to illuminant, surrounding to surrounding, and according to the state, attitude and distance of the observer.

Rather than the bald

Object X is turquoise,

we should say

Object X is turquoise, under illumination I, in surrounding visual field F, for observer O, in state S.

The mere fact that particularities of an observer – being a normal trichromat and not colour-blind, for example, who has not just spent ten minutes in a room suffused with pink light – make a difference to the colour appearances of an object does not *of itself* tell against the physical status of colour. It provides no real embarrassment for colour realism.

To see this, consider the parallel,

Object X is too heavy to lift, in gravitational field I, in surroundings F, for lifter O, in state S.

Whether O has normal arms, whether O is suffering a hangover, are particularities of the lifter which make a difference to whether the property *too heavy to lift* belongs to object X. But they do no more than indicate that *too heavy too lift* is an uninteresting (because anthroporelative) physical property. Anthroporelativism carries no metaphysical punch. It does not, of itself, point to any unusual status. Objects too heavy to lift furnish no hints of a subjective and nonphysical realm.

Moreover, the existence of both standing and transient colours, which by no means always coincide, provides no serious embarrassments for realism either. Too heavy to lift, after all, displays the same structure: Under standardized normal conditions, any object either is or is not too heavy to lift, and this standing condition varies only with relevant changes of mass in the object itself. The object's transient liftability changes with every change in the gravitational field, the grip of the lifter and that lifter's degree of exhaustion. The problems in realist theories of colour lie not in the mere facts of variability nor of anthroporelativism, but in the particular ways in which the role of the observer undercuts the common-sense attitude to colours as objective characteristics of physical objects.

The development of a viable theory of colour has consisted in the successive elimination of various realist views, which are ruled out as we gain a deeper understanding of the processes of colour vision. It is in this way an instructive test case illustrating the way sound philosophical doctrine evolves in the light of contingent discoveries.

Hardin's recent book, *Color for Philosophers: Unweaving the Rainbow,*[1] is an admirable object lesson to that effect. But Hardin does more than that; he provides one further step in the process of eliminating realism that has been going on for centuries. As I hope to show, Hardin's discussion does indeed furnish real embarrassments for the realism Armstrong upholds.

Nonreductive Realism

The most straightforward view of colours is that they are what they seem, to the rather unreflective mind, on most normal occasions. On this view colours are properties in their own right, most often properties of surfaces of solid objects. Colours exist – alongside sizes, shapes and hardnesses – as independent, sui generis, physical, observer-independent characteristics.

Such a view suffers, inter alia, from terminal epistemic incredibility. Colours, so interpreted, play no role in our perception of colour, which is mediated exclusively by the frequency and intensity of light waves. So there is no way in which the perceiving mind could be given its grasp of these independent physical colour features.

This did not have to be so; it is a contingent matter how perception works. This brand of nonreductive realism just backs the wrong hypothesis. Vision might have worked on Epicurean principles. On Epicurus's theory, sight worked as smell actually does. To remind you: A small piece of what you smell actually detaches itself from the thing you smell, and enters your nose. According to Epicurus, a very thin surface film of the object you see detaches itself and makes its way into your eyes.[2] If that did indeed happen, awareness of colours nonreductively conceived would at least be possible, since the sample of the object that entered your eye would bring with it a sample of the colour seen. But vision, in particular colour vision, does not work that way. No sample of the surface gets into your eye. This is just as well, or watching the flames as they dance would be a good deal less pleasurable than it is.

A more sophisticated variant of nonreductive realism could be developed from a less idealist version of the philosophy of James Ward. In *Naturalism and Agnosticism* he sets forth an account of the core of physical science, Newtonian mechanics, as inherently selective.[3] Physics does indeed deal with the physical world, and is concerned to describe the way in which that world evolves over time. But physics develops by concentrating exclusively on the quantitative, measurable physical properties. In this, it is selective; it will not do simply to identify the many qualitative physical realities with convenient quantitative ones. Qualities have only quantitative equivalents. So whatever its pretensions, this way of proceeding in science actually develops an abstract picture of physical reality, not necessarily inaccurate, but schematic. Although Ward never makes any express comment on the status of colour, he does hold that the sensations are not merely subjective. We can gloss this: Colour is real, and just as physical as anything else is, but it does not figure in the mechanistic economy of physical science because it is not quantitative in the requisite way.

Since all explanations offered in physical science appeal to the quantitative features on which it is focussed, we can understand why colour, being nonquantitative, will not figure in any explanatory contexts. In particular, it will not figure in physical explanations of the processes of colour vision.

To account for the apparently comprehensive success of quantitative characteristics in specifying the executive order of nature, one could allow that colour, while real, is not fully independent. It only occurs in conjunction with certain other physical factors which do belong in selective physical science. Colours and their scientific counterparts always go about in pairs, like constables in tough neighbourhoods. We come to a knowledge of colour, in some way we do not understand, through the action of its counterpart on the visual system.

The general notion of physical science as proceeding by selective abstraction has a certain appeal, but it is not going to yield a satisfactory account of colour. The basic reason for this is again a contingent matter of how colour vision works. The colours we see do not keep sufficiently close company with their alleged genuinely scientific physical concomitants. There is too much variation in the colours seen in the absence of any appropriate variation in the proposed scientific concomitants.

Some experiments of Edwin Land provide elegant testimony of this.[4] Land set up what he called color Mondrians, complex arrays of rectangles of different shapes, sizes and colours. Two of these, carefully made to be as like one another as possible, were set up side by side. Three narrow band projectors – of short, middle and long wavelength, making up an additive primary triple – were focussed on one patch from each Mondrian, one white patch and one green.[5]

The flux entering the eye from the white patch was accurately determined. The intensities of the projectors focussed on the green patch on the second Mondrian were then adjusted until the flux from the green patch exactly matched that from the white. Yet, the green patch continued to look green, indeed just as green as ever. Land claims that not only white but also a gray, a yellow or whatever patch can have the flux it sends to the eye adjusted in this way to match the green patch's, without the apparent colour of the second patch changing towards green (1977, p. 111).

Notice that we are dealing here with *standing* colours, which are remaining stable. So there is great disparity in colour seen (green, or white, or gray, or yellow), but there is no disparity at all in the relevant scientific physical concomitant – the pattern of frequency and intensity in the light waves entering the eye.

Reductive Realisms

Categorical Realisms

i. Wavelength Realism. Those same experiments of Land's also tell against a still too-common mistake: that colour is a categorical property not of surfaces, as it appears, but rather of the light by which we see the surfaces. We might call this misapprehension 'Newton's legacy', since his work with the spectrum produced by shining sunlight through a prism gave the view its currency.

It is true that, in a wide range of conditions and for normal observers, each different narrow band of wavelengths of visible light has its own distinctive spectral hue. But light with many different wavelength compositions can also appear to all normal observers to have exactly the same hue. (Lights of different compositions which in this way look alike are known as *metamers.* By extension, surfaces reflecting metameric light compositions are called metamers also.)

Any flux entering the eye which is a metamer of a given narrow-band light can be usefully described as having the centre of that narrow band as its dominant wavelength. But metamers exist with any proportion whatever of the so-called dominant wavelength, right down to zero. As Hardin remarks, 100% 577-nm light looks pure yellow to many, and 577 nm is its dominant wavelength (1986, p. 28). Yet, as he proceeds to point out, light which is 50% 540 nm (on its own, this would be green) and 50% 670 nm (on its own, red) is indistinguishable from our original yellow light and has the same dominant wavelength. But this composite light has a composition of 0% 577 nm.

Metamers are numerous, and surprisingly various in their composition. It is the on-going failure to find any common physical, nonperceptual thread uniting the flux compositions of all the metamers of any given hue which to my mind provides the definitive refutation of wavelength realism. Moreover, an important group of nonspectral colours, notably the purples, have no dominant wavelength in this sense, so wavelength realism would have to dismiss them as some type of pseudo-colour.

If that were not bad enough, the theory that colour is a physical property of light stumbles further when we consider the phenomena of colour mixtures. Turquoise, or bluish green, for example, is a colour that looks like a mixture of blue and green. It appears to have those colours as components. Orange, or reddish yellow, likewise. But if colour were literally a matter of the wavelength composition of light, daylight should look as if it had every colour as a component, which obviously it does not. Colour mixtures will prove important again, at a later point in the discussion.

ii. Reflectance Realism. Land's work on metamers led him to reason as follows: If the colour seen can remain constant while the flux entering the eye is varied, then colour judgements must be made on some information which the flux carries, but which is not itself changing when the flux changes (1977, pp. 115f). He proposed that what is significant is not the actual flux sent from the surface to the eye, but the relation between what falls on the surface and what comes from it. Each opaque surface reflects a certain proportion of the light falling on it. Except for white, gray, and black surfaces, this proportion varies from wavelength to wavelength across the visible range, and is known as the surface's *reflectance* at that wavelength. Surfaces with chromatic hue are selective reflectors, each with its distinctive reflectance curve. White, gray and black are nonselective reflectors.

Because human beings have three linked receptor systems in their retinas, each maximally sensitive to a different (though overlapping) section of the visible range, a reflectance triple that specifies the reflectance at the central wavelengths of each of the three systems thus specifies a colour. That the metamers under a given set of conditions form families, all of whose members have reflectance triples that share some straightforward common formula, is – so far as I know – still a viable hypothesis.

Humans, and other creatures with comparable colour vision, must judge reflectance from the flux that enters the eye. To do this, they will need to make hypotheses about the illumination falling on the surfaces that they can see. How this can be done is a challenging, but not impossible, part of the theory Land tried to develop (1977, p. 119). Reflectance realism is not terminally epistemically incredible. Nevertheless, it won't do.

There are two main reasons for this. First, reflectance realism is grievously incomplete. It deals only with the case of opaque bodies whose surfaces are seen by reflected light. But colours occur under a wide variety of other physical circumstances. Incandescence, gas excitation, scattering, refraction, ion exchange, accelerated electric charge and moiré effects all produce colour (Hardin 1986, p. 2). Moreover, these processes typically produce colours that exactly match those available by selective reflection, yet in none of these cases is a reflectance triple at all relevant to the effect. Many items that have colour in these slightly unusual ways have no reflectance curve at all, being transparent, translucent or too small. There seems to me a negligible prospect that any physical basis will be found common and peculiar to each distinguishable hue when we include, as we must, all these different ways of having colour.

I leave aside, in this argument, the even more recherché colour production methods, which involve spinning black-and-white discs at certain special speeds, or producing coloured shadows by stimulating complementary after-images. These exotic phenomena may well be described as illusions of colour. Setting those aside, what we are dealing with are ordinary coloured items: gemstones, the sea and the sky, the wings of beetles, lasers and street lighting. No theory that must discount all these kinds of colours as in some way ersatz can be satisfactory.

It seems that we shall not be able to escape the conclusion that the unity of specific colours, that common and peculiar aspect that is shared by all and only examples of the same shade, must lie in the observer's response to the physical facts, rather than in those facts themselves. This conclusion becomes even more irresistible when we confront the second major weakness in reflectance realism: its incompetence in dealing with simultaneous contrast. This is an ubiquitous phenomenon, even though in everyday life we are scarcely conscious of it.

What simultaneous contrast means is this: The colour that a patch in the visual field will appear to have is a function of not only its own characteristics and the flux it sends eyewards, but also of the flux characteristics of the surrounding areas. The immediately neighbouring areas have the most marked influence, but the entire field plays a part in determining the perceived colour of any patch in it. Simultaneous contrast works for both intensity and hue. Hardin quotes Delacroix on this matter, which is of necessity very familiar to painters: 'Give me mud, let me surround it as I think fit, and it shall be the radiant flesh of Venus' (Hardin 1986, p. 49).

The most remarkable effects of simultaneous contrast concern blacks, browns, and olive greens. These are all colours in perfectly good standing in their own right, but they are severely anomalous for any reflectance realism, for none of them has a distinctive reflectance triple.

No difference between orange and brown can be found in the coloured surface itself. The difference between the two lies in their setting: Where a patch is bright in comparison with its surroundings, it will look orange. On the other hand, where the surroundings are comparatively bright, the patch will look brown. The absolute values of the relevant physical properties of the patches that look brown do not differ from the absolute values of the patches that look orange. A greenish yellow, the hue of not fully ripe lemons, and olive green stand in the same relation to one another.

The case of black is particularly striking. Black is not just the colour one sees in the absence of light. The absence of light gives you an experience of a rather dark gray, known in the trade as 'brain gray' since it arises from the base rate of firing of visual-system neurons. This base rate can be depressed by inhibitory processes, but that is not what is required for the experience of black. Black coal in sunlight is much blacker than white paper in shadow, yet the coal sends more flux to the eye than the paper.

Think about how we get black on the television. Many scenes show a blacker, glossier, darker black than the switched-off screen. Yet every colour, including black, occurs only if the entire screen, including the black patches, is made brighter than in the switched-off state. Black is black because it is darker than its surrounds. Black is a product of simultaneous contrast. For the whole white–gray–black sequence, reflectance-triple theory has nothing helpful to say.

Once again, the unity of a colour – in this case, what all the blacks share but which grays and whites don't have – does not lie just in the physical state of the surface in question. Although painful for the reflectance realist, that the context is doing an unsuspected amount of the work in our seeing olive, brown, black and white does not in itself point in a subjectivist direction.

What the variety of physical bases of colour and the facts of simultaneous contrast point to, rather, is the claim which Hardin insists on, and both Smart and Armstrong concede together with Armstrong's defenders Jackson and Pargetter: The unity of the colours lies in the unity of the response they engender in creatures with a colour vision system like ours. It does not reside in any extra-animate physical reality.[6]

Dispositional Realism with Variations: The Return of John Locke

For all that, the colour realist is not yet defeated. Locke, you remember, identified secondary qualities in bodies, including colours, as powers of those bodies to produce the appropriate experiences in us. Secondary qualities simpliciter are qualities of the ideas that perception produces in the mind.[7] J. J. C. Smart (1961) once adopted a relative of this position: Locke's mentalistic ideas are replaced by behaviouristic capacities to discriminate, but – more significantly from a realist point of view – Smart located the colour simpliciter at the external end of the causal process.

In this scheme, the items which are truly coloured are not, as with Locke, states of ourselves, but of the surfaces (or whatever) that we see. These items are marshalled into their natural classes not by any intrinsic commonalities, but by the commonality of the effects they are apt to produce. Colours are dispositional properties of physical objects. The disposition is towards an effect in perceivers rather than on other inanimate objects; here lies the distinction between secondary and primary qualities. We are familiar enough, these days, with the notion that a disposition can have a whole variety of physical embodiments. So the physical variety of the objects that to us look alike in colour is no embarrassment.

Later, Smart moved to a more unequivocal realism: For an object to be (for example) red is for it to have those physical properties in virtue of which, as a matter of fact, it is apt to look red. For different red objects, the relevant physical properties may be different.

Disjunctive Realism

David Armstrong (1987) and Jackson with Pargetter (1987) have taken up this basic theme. They concentrate on the categorical basis of the disposition to make something look red. The colour red is identified with the categorical basis. (Different philosophies of dispositions differ over whether there is any real distinction between a disposition and its basis. However that may be, it is the basis which is here identified with the colour.) Redness is what causes (in the right way) objects to look red.

The merit of opting for the categorical basis over the disposition of which it is the basis, for those who do make a distinction, is that dispositions are inferred whereas colours are perceived (Jackson and Pargetter 1987, p. 131). If colours are perceived, they must be categorical. If their unity lies in their effects on us then the categorical property must be one that is picked out by such effects. So the physical property of objects in virtue of which, for us in this world, they look red is their redness.

On the Armstrong–Jackson–Pargetter theory, as for Smart, colour is in one sense indeed a secondary quality. For 'the fundamental ground for ascribing a certain colour to something is the colour it looks to have' (Jackson and Pargetter 1987, p. 132). Such essential reference to how things seem to observers is never required for the ascription of any genuinely primary quality.

But in another sense, colour is as primary as shape or solidity (Armstrong 1987, p. 11). For it is a feature of an object which that object has whether or not there are any perceivers at all, still less any with colour vision, still less any with colour vision that works as ours does. The property of being red is a property (disjunctive, gerrymandered overall, but perfectly definite in any given case) which the object that has it would have in a perfectly inanimate world. In this world, it makes the object look red. In another, it may not have that effect, but it would be the same property. So there is nothing inherently subjective about those properties which have the effect of making their bearers look coloured.

This is an anthropocentric realism, but a realism nonetheless. Its proponents are confident that, because they make no attempt to find a basis for unity in the inanimate physical sphere, they will be immune from the kinds of criticisms canvassed herein, which we might call, in general, *disjunctivist* criticisms. These hold that any reductive realism locating the colour in the physical surface will be hopelessly disjunctive, with no principle bounding the number or variety of disjuncts. This will require us to be hopelessly untrue to the experience of colour vision, holding that there are indefinitely many different colours where we can ever only detect one. Or it will require of us to be hopelessly ambivalent about the character of some physical properties, affirming that colours are physical properties while denying there is anything significant that is common and peculiar to the physical reality of any given colour.

Armstrong wrestles with what he calls the *idiosyncracy* difficulty, as well as the already familiar disjunctive difficulty (Armstrong 1987, pp. 8f). Idiosyncracy is what we have dubbed anthroporelativism. For reasons given previously, I entirely agree that this is no real embarrassment to realism about colours.

For the disjunctive difficulty – setting aside the more general metaphysical concern that there are problems about admitting disjunctive properties as genuine properties at all – Smart, Armstrong, Jackson, and Pargetter all adopt what is essentially a neo-Lockean strategy: The property is an objectively physical one, but its identity and unity are settled by its subjective effects.

This neo-Lockean strategy will work only so far as the identification of colour with what causes things to look coloured will work. That identification will succeed only if every feature of some particular case of a colour, say turquoise, can be matched with a feature of the physical property which, on the occasion in question, causes it to look turquoise. But the proposed identification does not succeed. Colours have properties not to be found in their physical causes.

This brings us to the opponent-processing theory of colour vision. Opponent processing is responsible for the existence of colours as complementary pairs, for the existence of apparently pure and apparently composite colours, for many of the experienced resemblances between colours, for the existence of nonspectral colours and for the nonexistence of certain mixed colours. So it is of the greatest importance to the nature of colour, and to a satisfactory account of colour as a phenomenon.

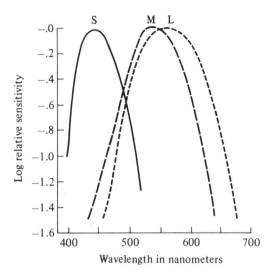

Figure 1. Normalized spectral sensitivity functions for the three human and macaque monkey cone types: shortwave (S), middlewave (M), and longwave (L). The sensitivity at each wavelength is proportional to the probability that the cone type will absorb a quantum of light at that wavelength. From C. L. Hardin, *Color for Philosophers,* Hackett Publishing Company, 1988, Indianapolis, IN and Cambridge, MA.

We all have two visual systems that operate more or less independently; one is based on the rods, the other on the cones. The rods give achromatic (black-and-white) vision only, and are adapted for low-acuity operation at low levels of illumination. The cone system provides both achromatic and chromatic vision, with higher acuity, but requires higher energy levels for it to operate. It alone subserves colour vision (Hardin 1986, pp. 26ff). The base structure of the cone system consists in three subsystems, each one responsive across a different section of the visible spectrum (see Figure 1).

In normal situations, the light from every part of the visible environment includes rays at most visible wavelengths. So it is normal for all three subsystems to be stimulated at once by any given visible object. But they will be differentially stimulated; it is on the ratios of their outputs that the system goes to work. Any incident light within a subsystem's range of sensitivity produces exactly the same response, if any at all, from the cones. So there is an immediate and severe loss of wavelength information in the processing.

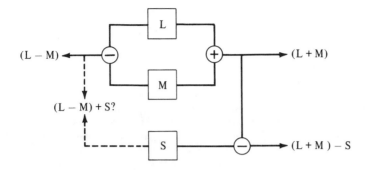

Figure 2. A schematic representation of a quantitative opponent theory. From C. L. Hardin, *Color for Philosophers,* Hackett Publishing Company, 1988, Indianapolis, IN and Cambridge, MA.

This is in part offset by the critical fact that the outputs from the three subsystems are combined both additively, by summation, and by difference also. The output of one subsystem can either stimulate or inhibit the output of others. To make room for a strong inhibitory signal, stronger than what it works to inhibit, the whole system needs a base rate of neural firing, which occurs in the absence of any input and which can be increased by a stimulating input and depressed by inhibition.

Following Hardin, and labelling the three subsystems L, M and S for brevity, a possible scheme for their integration is provided in Figure 2 (Hardin 1986, p. 34). Then we can propose the following neural code.

$(L+M)$ is the achromatic signal:

$(L+M) > 0$ codes whiteness;

$(L+M) < 0$ codes blackness;

$(L+M) = 0$ codes 'brain gray', as do all zero values.

$(L-M)$ is the red–green signal:

$(L-M) > 0$ codes redness;

$(L-M) < 0$ codes greenness.

$(L+M) - S$ is the yellow–blue signal:

$(L+M) - S > 0$ codes yellowness;

$(L+M) - S < 0$ codes blueness.

The relative sensitivity of the L, M and S subsystems at different points across the visible wavelengths results in the three response curves (achromatic, red–green and blue–yellow) depicted in Figure 3. At almost every wavelength, all three systems are making a contribution to our total colour visual response.

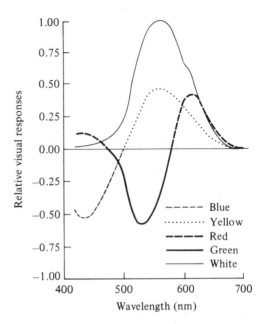

Figure 3. Chromatic and achromatic responses for an equal-energy spectrum and a single observer. From C. L. Hardin, *Colour for Philosophers,* Hackett Publishing Company, 1988, Indianapolis, IN and Cambridge, MA.

    The structure is an opponent-processing one in this sense: An output that codes for red cannot also code for green; these are mutually exclusive. Similarly, yellow and blue codings exclude one another. An output can include neither, but it cannot include both. Here, in the contingent details of the operation of our nervous system, lies the explanation for an otherwise baffling fact in the phenomenology: Some colour mixtures are possible, while others are excluded. There are no greenish reds, and there are no bluish yellows. On the other hand, where the colours are coded on different channels, they mix readily. There are plenty of bluish reds and yellowish reds, and there are plenty of greenish blues and greenish yellows.

    Why are there just these mixed colours and not others? There is no clue to be found outside the colour vision mechanisms of humans and those who see as we do. No matter how enlightened, we could never have predicted the patterns of perceived colour mixture from any consideration of the physics of surfaces and light rays. Moreover, given a little practice, people can reach impressive noncollusive agreement on what the hue components of a given stimulus are. To characterize all the different colours we can see, the four salient ones – red, blue, yellow and green – are severally necessary and jointly sufficient. Furthermore, these four salient colours are the only ones that occur phenomenologically pure, that is, with no apparent admixture of any other. These are the unique colours.

An explanation of this lies close to hand in opponent-processing theory. The unique colours are seen when the stimulus's dominant wavelength is one where either the red–green or the blue–yellow chromatic output curve (see Figure 3) crosses the zero line (Hardin 1986, p. 37). At 475 nm, for example, the red–green curve crosses the zero line, so the perceived colour will have no red component and no green component either. The blue-yellow curve is at -0.25, emphatically and unequivocally blue. There is, of course, no yellow component. So what is seen at dominant wavelength 475 nm is an unmixed blue. At 500 nm, a pure green is seen; at 590 nm, a pure yellow. Note that we can't get a fully pure red using a monochromatic light source, or an equivalent of a monochromatic source. For there is always some residual yellow at the long end of the visual spectrum; a pure red needs a 'dollop' of blue to cancel the yellow. Here is a detail that tellingly supports the basic processing story.

There are exactly four unique colours. Why? Not for any reason that makes the dominant wavelengths of the unique colours physically distinctive. From the point of view of the physics of the inanimate world, there is nothing special about those points on the spectrum. And there is nothing physically distinctive about those combinations of wavelengths that yield a colour mixture, when compared with those that yield a unique hue.

This matter of the phenomenology of colour mixture is not to be dismissed lightly. For the resemblances among the colours, as we experience them, rest entirely on our sense of the red, blue, green, or yellow components in how they seem to us to be made up. But it is with colours as with anything else: Patterns of resemblance are patterns of internal relations. These are not contingent matters, but touch on the very constitution of the resembling hues.

From Figure 3 it is also possible to see why colours have complements at all. Here we are concerned with complementary pairs of monochromatic (or dominant-wavelength) light; complementaries among pigments are a different matter. For light, a complementary colour is one which, when added to a given colour, yields white. A typical colour C has two nonzero components, one on the red–green and one on the blue–yellow channel. C's complement $C^\wedge$ will neutralize both these components, reducing both to zero and leaving only the achromatic response. It is facts about us, not facts about what we are looking at, which determine that there are complementary colours and also what the complementary colour is in any given case.

These aspects of colour vision – that there are just the four unique hues, that there are just the mixtures and resemblances that there are, and that every colour has exactly one complementary – are so intimately a part of the nature of colours as we experience them that one is tempted to say they belong to the essence of the colours. Whether or not that is a fortunate way to express the matter, any reductive realism that involves identifying colours with physical features of surfaces or light waves must omit these aspects or relegate them to some accidental, marginal status. They must appear as the most contingent of side issues, since they have no basis in the external physics of the situation. Such a dismissive stance is unacceptable. Armstrong (1987, p. 12) very rightly expresses uneasiness about the fit between the phenomenology of colour vision and a reductive, disjunctive physical realism.

We have now found two classes of reasons for such uneasiness. First, the facts about simultaneous contrast require any objectivist reductive realism to hold that black and gray are really the same colour and that so are brown and orange, and yellow-green and olive green. Second, the facts about opponent processing require any reductive objectivist realism to relegate to a marginal status the central truths about colour purity and colour mixture, about colour resemblance, and about colour complementarity.

So, characteristics that are central to the nature of colours belong not to the physical but instead to the psychoneural side of the processes of colour vision. What is the moral to be drawn from this? Armstrong's disjunctive realism is the most recent in that long line of realist theses about colour which prove inadequate to the scientific facts as our grasp of them improves.

The Problem of the Alternatives

Yet the story does not end quite yet. What has been said so far suggests that if colours are to be given a physical identification then it will have to involve, essentially, those neural states and processes that do carry the distinctions between brown and orange, or between pure and mixed colours, that have proved so elusive in the physics of the outside world. That is just the moral that Hardin, for example, draws.

Subjectivism

At least one important necessary condition of any subjectivist account of colour seems to me to be this: A subjectivist thesis must have as a consequence that, in the absence of perceivers with colour vision, there are no colours. Subjectivism requires that sunsets have not been red since time immemorial, but only since the appropriate living forms evolved.

That may be counterintuitive, but any embarrassment is balanced by counterintuitive results on the other side: What, for example, is the 'real' colour of an object, given the surprises about colour which the microscope can give us? Or what is the true colour of an object, given the transformations in perceived colour that occur under selective fatigue of one of our three-cone receptor systems?

Subjectivism comes in at least three forms, all of which must be, in one way or another, projectivist. It is of the essence of every subjectivism to hold that whatever does literally bear the colour properties, it is not the bodies (or the surfaces, or the light sources) that seem to. So appearances must deceive; anyone who thinks that grass is green – in the full, genuine, literal and metaphysical interpretation of that proposition – must be making a mistake.

Every projection theory is an error theory. They all hold that because grass acts on us so that it looks green, we wrongly suppose that it is green. We project greenness onto the cause of looking-green, and so fall into error. All subjectivisms are projectivist, so they are all error theories.

That by itself is not fatal. But error theories are fall-back positions. They do not recommend themselves as inherently plausible; they are positions to which one is forced, reluctantly, by the untenability of the alternatives. This is true of error theories in general – in ethics, for example. And it is true for colour. Indeed, error theory about colour is not just a fall-back option; it is a desperation option. Just how desperate an option it is can be glimpsed from a review of each of its variants.

i. Dualism. This is the nonreductive alternative, almost orthodox in the period of Galileo and Locke, now idiosyncratic. It is defended by Moreland Perkins (1983) and by Brian O'Shaughnessy (1985), who both claim, as this alternative requires, that the true, direct bearers of the colour qualities are perceptual states of mind. Colour is not an illusion; it is a state of mind. The only error consists in misascribing the colour to its external stimulus. Dualism has enough crosses to bear without my dwelling on them here.

ii. Reductionism. Hardin's idea is that we can capture all that is essential, and indeed all that is true, about colours by holding that for an object to have a colour is for it to set up in us the appropriate neural states and processes. The colours themselves (redness, deep carmine, burnt sienna, . . .) are the structured neural states and processes that have the distinctive characteristics we recognize as purity, mixture, complementarity, likeness and difference, warmth and chill, rest and agitation, and so on.[8] This is a physicalist naturalism, and meets the objections to realist naturalism. So much in its favour. But it won't do, either.

A New Spectrum-Shift Argument

The problem is all too familiar: The neural side of the proposed identification consists in a system of patterned resemblances – relations between neural states. Thus $L > M$ codes redness, while $L < M$ codes greenness and $(L + M) > S$ codes yellowness. Hence, in seeing red, green or yellow we are receiving inputs that involve common elements in different ratios.

Now I do not propose to make anything of the fact that the phenomenology of red, green and yellow does not include any intuitive grasp of ratios among common elements (although it is intriguing to speculate that some such grasp lies behind our recognition of the fact that all colours belong under the same determinable). Armstrong's (1987, pp. 10ff) insistence on the 'headless-woman' analogy should suffice to dissuade anyone inclined to reason from the absence of the apprehension of a given aspect to the apprehension of its absence.

What is evident, I submit, is that there is nothing inherently red rather than yellow about the input $L > M$, which codes redness. 'Codes' is a good word here. That what we experience should be the redness of red is a contingent, gratuitous and gratifying extra.

The possibility of spectrum shifts is often appealed to in this context. But the opponent-processing theory of colour vision gives us an alternative, and deeper, way of making the same point. Imagine a perceiver with responses transposed. That is, suppose a perceiver codes yellow and blue (instead of red and green) on the $L - M$ channel, and red and green (instead of yellow and blue) on the $(L + M) - S$ channel.

The diagram of Figure 3 will still represent the perceiver's responses: There will still be just four unique colours, and the patterns of resemblance among the mixed colours will also still be there. Judgements as to what pairs of colours are complementary will agree. The colour vocabulary such a perceiver uses in colour descriptions will match that of normally sighted persons. Even the 'tone' of the colours will be replicated: the anomalous perceiver will agree that green (= blue) is cool and restful, while red (= yellow) is vibrant and stimulating.

All this serves to point up the truth that it is well to say that the channel relationships only code for the colours, rather than encapsulating them. Reductionism will succeed only if it can banish the qualia. And the qualia refuse to go away. This puts us between a rock and a hard place. Dualism and reductionism seem equally unacceptable. This leads one to the following.

iii. Full-Scale Error Theory. According to this view, the experience of the world as coloured involves a double mistake. In the first place, no colour is a physical property of the environment; contrary to how things seem, objects in the outer world would not be coloured were there no perceivers with colour vision. (Objectivism is false.) In the second place, no sense data – or visual field patches understood as psychological states of perceivers – are coloured either. (Subjectivism in the Lockean tradition is false.) Human perceivers have complex neural states that are projected as colours.

Projection is the first error. Experiencing what is projected as yellow, or turquoise, or whatever, is the second. There are no colours. Here we have a desperation option indeed. Armstrong's philosophy of colour, like many a position in philosophy, draws a good deal of its appeal from the manifest difficulties in each of its rivals.

NOTES

1. Hardin (1986). A great deal of the information about colour vision referred to in this essay I have learned from a study of Hardin's book, to which I am generally indebted.
2. 'For the flow of atoms from the surface of bodies is continuous, yet it cannot be detected by any lessening in the size of the object. . . . The flow of images preserves for a long time the position and order of the atoms in the solid body, though it is occasionally confused. . . . Now we must suppose too that it is when something enters us from external objects that we not only see but think of their shapes. For external objects could not make on us an impression of the nature of their own colour and shape by means of the air which lies between us and them, nor again by the rays or effluences of any sort which pass from us to them – nearly so well as if models, similar in colour and shape, leave the objects and enter according to their respective size either into our sight or into our mind . . .'. Epicurus (circa 300 B.C.).
3. Ward (1906). Much of Volume I is devoted to this theme. For example, 'There are no processes in the real world that are entirely mechanical . . . (pp. 83–4). '[T]he hypothesis of molecular [i.e. microreductive] physics is that all the qualitative variety of the external world can be resolved into quantitative relations of time, space, and mass, that is, of mass and motion. . . . the descriptions of molar [= macro] physics are abstract: *one* property of bodies, that of massiveness, of which we can have sensible evidence, is taken; the *remaining* properties are simply left out of account. But the descriptions of molecular physics taken together are not in this sense abstract. They leave no properties out of account; on the contrary, they transform everything qualitative into quantitative equivalents' (pp. 97–8).
4. An accessible account of these is to be found in Land (1977).
5. An additive primary triple is a set of three monochromatic lights which, when mixed in different proportions (with sometimes an addition of white), can produce a match for every colour a normal human being can distinguish. There are many such triples, not just the familiar pure red, green and blue.
6. Hardin (1986, pp. 1–6); Smart (1975); Armstrong (1987); Jackson and Pargetter (1987).

7. Locke (1690, Book II, Chapter viii, Sections 10–23).
8. Hardin (1986, pp. 111–12). It is not quite clear whether Hardin adopts a reductivist or a full-scale error theory (see the final subsection iii). 'We are to be eliminativists with respect to color as a property of objects, but reductivists with respect to color experiences'. Yet, on the preceding page: 'in the ultimate sense, there are no colors'. And, a few lines above that, 'We are normally in chromatic perceptual states'.

REFERENCES

Armstrong, D. M. 1987. 'Smart and the Secondary Qualities'. In *Metaphysics and Morality: Essays in Honour of J. J. C. Smart,* ed. Philip Pettit, Richard Sylvan and Jean Norman (Oxford: Blackwell), pp. 1–15.

Epicurus, c. 300 B.C., *Letter to Herodotus,* tr. Cyril Bailey. In *The Stoic and Epicurean Philosophers,* ed. Whitney J. Oates (New York: Random House, 1940), pp. 3–33.

Galileo Galilei. 1623. 'The Assayer' [excerpts]. In *Discoveries and Opinions of Galileo,* tr. Stillman Drake (Garden City, NY: Doubleday Anchor, 1957), pp. 229–80.

Hardin, C. L. 1986. *Color for Philosophers: Unweaving the Rainbow* (Indianapolis: Hackett).

Jackson, Frank and Pargetter, Robert. 1987. 'An Objectivist's Guide to Subjectivism about Colour', *Revue Internationale de Philosophie* 41: 127–41.

Land, Edwin H. 1977. 'The Retinex Theory of Color Vision', *Scientific American* 237, no. 6: 108–28.

Locke, John. 1690. *An Essay Concerning Human Understanding* (London: Bassett).

O'Shaughnessy, Brian. 1985. 'Seeing the Light', *Proceedings of the Aristotelian Society* 85: 193–218.

Perkins, Moreland. 1983. *Sensing the World* (Indianapolis: Hackett).

Smart, J. J. C. 1961. 'Colours', *Philosophy* 36: 128–42.

1975. 'On Some Criticisms of a Physicalist Theory of Colors'. In *Philosophical Aspects of the Mind–Body Problem,* ed. Chung-Ying Cheng (Honolulu: University Press of Hawaii), pp. 54–63.

Stout, G. F. 1904. 'Primary and Secondary Qualities', *Proceedings of the Aristotelian Society* 4: 141–60.

Ward, James. 1906. *Naturalism and Agnosticism,* 2 vols. (London: Black).

Reply to Campbell

D. M. ARMSTRONG

During Michaelmas term in 1962 I was in Oxford as part of a sabbatical year from Melbourne. Brian Medlin was a research fellow at New College and, as Campbell mentions, Brian and I gave a seminar on Central-State Materialism. It created some interest among the graduate students, especially those from overseas, but not, I think, among the dons. Tony Quinton, however, did attend and read us a paper. Among the students was a graduate from Wellington, New Zealand – Keith Campbell. He was not far from graduating, had won the John Locke Prize and was clearly a very good philosopher.

The Melbourne department was making a new appointment. The most promising applicants were, as it happened, all in England and a committee had been set up under the chairmanship of Stuart Hampshire to interview them in London. As I was the only member of the department who was in England at the time, Professor Gibson asked me to join the committee and sent me copies of the applications. They didn't seem very exciting. The phenomenal expansion of the Western universities was getting under way, and there was a desperate shortage of good and trained philosophers.

A very few days before the meeting in London I was talking to Keith at a party and getting more impressed by the minute. I mentioned the job in Melbourne and, somewhat to my surprise, he exhibited great interest. (I remember him complaining about the fact that the sky in England seemed only a few feet above one.) The result was that in a day or so I cabled Gibson that I had found a candidate who was much stronger than the ones already in the field. Keith was added to the list of those to be interviewed, and the committee did not have the slightest doubt about who should be appointed.

In 1964 I went to the Chair at Sydney and shortly afterwards, by great good luck, Keith was interested in coming to Sydney as a Senior Lecturer, although he had already obtained that promotion in Melbourne. Apart from the quality, clarity and ease of his teaching and writing, one of Keith's great contributions to philosophy at Sydney was what he did in the horrible political struggle that broke out in the department in the early seventies. Keith had tried to stand aside from the brawl to some degree, but after the so-called strike had been met eventually by a capitulation of the University authorities, it seemed that all the good philosophers would look for jobs elsewhere or else take early retirement. Keith came forward with a scheme to create two departments. The rest of us were pretty well exhausted by the long struggle, by all the meetings, pamphlets, telephone calls, telegrams and anger. For the next few weeks Keith steadied us and took us through all that had to be done to persuade the Vice-chancellor and University administrators generally. The result was the creation of the Department of Traditional and Modern Philosophy in which Keith, myself and others have enjoyed many good years.

Colours

At the beginning of his essay Campbell provides an excellent account of my general approach to the philosophy of colour, both accurate and imaginative at the same time. He combines this with a history of those discoveries about colour which create difficulties for those of us who would like to be direct (but reductive) Realists about colour. Here I find it harder to assess the worth of what he has to say, because I have been accustomed to get much of my information on such matters from Campbell himself. I do note that he now finds difficulties in the seductive reflectance-triple theory of Edwin Land.

At a certain point, however, I do begin to protest with some authority. This is the point at which Campbell tries to associate me with a physicalized version of Locke's theory of colour and, in particular, the neo-Lockeanism advocated in a joint article by Jackson and Pargetter. Locke, when he is speaking most carefully, is a half-hearted Realist about colour. Colour is a property of physical things, but they have this property in virtue of their power to excite appropriate sensations in our minds. Locke makes this half-retreat to the mind in the case of all the secondary qualities. He is not influenced, I think, by specific difficulties about colour. And as Campbell notes, he is not a physicalist about sensations. Jackson and Pargetter, however, if I understand them, are influenced by specific difficulties about colour; further, they think of the colour sensation as a physical process in the brain. (It is my impression that most contemporary Physicalists hold to some form of this 'Lockean' theory.)

I reject such theories. I do not think that being red is to be analyzed in terms of 'the categorical basis of the disposition to make something look red' (Campbell). In my most recent attempt to say something about colour I said that the concept of colour 'does not yield any necessary connection between red objects and any sort of perceptual experience, such as looking red to normal perceivers in normal viewing conditions' (Armstrong 1987, p. 11). Here I part with the Lockeans.

It seems to me that I am pretty well compelled (though not unwillingly) to take up this position because of my theory of what sensations are. I hold that to have a red sensation is to acquire the information (the term is meant to cover misinformation) that there is something red at some more or less specific place in the perceiver's environment. (The information, although registered, may be overruled by 'higher' cognitive centres with access to wider information, thus permitting the phenomenon of 'perception without belief'.) This account of sensation is propositional. It seems to me to be supported (without being established) by such phenomena as the indeterminacy of sensations and the failure of transitivity of exact resemblance that can occur when, for example, surface A and B look to be exactly the same shade of colour and so do B and C, yet A and C are discriminable. Given this propositional (although of course non-verbal) account of sensation, I cannot without circularity analyze the notion of redness in terms of red sensations. Some may hold that having certain sensations under certain conditions is at least a reference fixer for the corresponding colour term. It seems to me that I am barred from saying even that.

What I did and do accept about colour, though, is what Campbell calls 'disjunctive realism'. Physical redness is not merely an idiosyncratic property of no particular physical (as opposed to biological) significance. It is, or may well be, an irreducibly disjunctive property (because of the metamers, as Campbell explains). I was held up from embracing this view for some time by taking properties to be universals, as I maintain that there are good reasons for denying that there are any disjunctive universals. I have since come to realize, though, that there is no objection to admitting disjunctive properties provided that they are not identified with universals. Most, perhaps all, perceptual properties are disjunctive, as are most of the properties mentioned in ordinary discourse. This involves no ontological cost, I hold, because disjunctive properties supervene on the universal properties.

To this may be added the reflection that quite different causes may have the same effect. A number of different sorts of physical cause might all create the same sort of sensation in an organism, so that the organism would classify these physical causes together. There is then room for redness to be a property of external things that is, as Smart memorably put it, 'hellishly disjunctive'.

The question for me, then, is whether the evidence marshalled by Campbell for the opponent-processing theory (courtesy of Hardin) should make me abandon my position. Campbell is kind enough to do some of my work for me by pointing to the difficulties that attend the alternatives. Dualism – the view that the colour qualities are extra properties, emergent properties, properties that do not supervene on the purely physical (physics-respectable) properties – is subject to horrendous scientific difficulties, whether the properties are taken to be nonrelational properties of the perceived objects or of the neural processes that constitute the perceiving of the objects. The latter involves a 'projection' or error theory.

The identification of colour qualia with purely physical properties of neural processes must also appeal to projection. But in addition, Campbell points out (and it is a pleasant irony), that theory faces its own inverted-spectrum problem. You could switch the coding between the yellow–blue channel and the red–green channel yet preserve all normal colour discriminations.

I am not sure, however, that this should daunt a determined physicalist. Could he not accept the possibility of such switching? The wires are crossed relative to each other. The pair of sensations that you call 'yellow' and 'blue' another calls 'red' and 'green', and vice versa. But whatever the pair is called, it is just the one thing, even if it is playing a different causal role. It is a certain type of neurological structure. In general, I do not believe that inverted spectra pose a threat to physicalist schemes, although they may threaten a strict input–output theory. (See Armstrong 1968, Chapter 11, Section IV.)

I believe, however, that projection poses more difficulty than its supporters realize. Talk about projection in the case of the foulness of a toadstool or a crime seems appropriate enough. But how imprecise the projection is! Asked to indicate the spatial boundaries of the foulness, it is likely that one could do little more than indicate the spatial boundaries of the toadstool. Contrast the colour of surfaces. The alleged projection is exceedingly precise. In general, there will be noncollusive agreement between perceivers that the boundary of a colour change occurs just *here*. At this point it is worth remembering that 'projection' is but a metaphor. What is happening according to a projection theorist is that we *mistakenly* take the physical surface to be coloured. But if each of our brains picks out just the same precise surface area to make a mistake about, then must not something about the area itself be cuing us off? And then why can't this something be the colour of the surface?

So encouraged (rather mildly), let us go back to the difficulties that Campbell finds for a physicalist direct Realist theory of colour in a disjunctive property form. He offers, I think, two classes of reasons. I will take his second class first. He says that opponent processing forces a reductive objectivist to give only marginal status to the phenomenologically central features of colour: their purity, mixture, resemblance and complementarity. This does not worry me too much. Colour could well be a very unimportant and extremely idiosyncratic physical property. The perceived relationships between the colours could be very unimportant, and idiosyncratic, relations between these properties. (These relationships might nevertheless be necessary because flowing internally from the nature of the unimportant and idiosyncratic properties.) Not a delightful position, but a tenable one, I hope. We could appeal to that wonderful maid of all work, the Headless Woman, to explain why these unimportant properties seem so prominent in colour perception. What is not perceived seems not to be there, and what *is* perceived fills the phenomenological stage and so the mental stage.

In addition, I would hope – indeed, expect – that the colour properties would turn out to have some biological value. For instance, in the state of nature the condition of potential food may be signalled by its colour. Again, the differentiations provided by differences of colour may perhaps play an important part in recognizing persons and objects.

More worrying, perhaps, are the facts about simultaneous contrast that Campbell points to. If perceived colour depends upon contrast with the colour of the surrounding surface in a way that destroys the difference between black and gray, between brown and orange, and between yellow-green and olive green, then things do not look so good for colour realism. I take it, though, that there is still an objective distinction between black and gray paint, brown and orange paint, and so on. I take it further that where the colour of the surrounding surface affects the perceived colour of what is surrounded, this phenomenon is a fairly small-scale affair. If a large expanse, such as half a wall, is painted with certified brown paint, and the other half with orange paint, then I take it that in ordinary lighting conditions the difference will be clear enough in most colour environments. Perhaps if Delacroix surrounds mud with paint as he thinks fit, and produces 'the radiant flesh of Venus', this is an *illusion*.

So I'm not giving up on an objectivist theory of colour just yet.

REFERENCES

Armstrong, D. M. 1968. *A Materialist Theory of the Mind* (London: Routledge & Kegan Paul).

1987. 'Smart and the Secondary Qualities'. In *Metaphysics and Morality: Essays in Honour of J. J. C. Smart,* ed. Philip Pettit, Richard Sylvan and Jean Norman (Oxford: Blackwell), pp. 1–15.

Bibliography of the Works of
D. M. Armstrong

A. BOOKS

(1) 1960. *Berkeley's Theory of Vision: a Critical Examination of Bishop Berkeley's Essay towards a New Theory of Vision.* Melbourne: Melbourne University Press.

(1a) 1988. Reprinted in series *The Philosophy of George Berkeley,* vol. 6, ed. George Pitcher. New York and London: Garland.

(2) 1961. *Perception and the Physical World.* London: Routledge & Kegan Paul.

(2a) 1966. In Spanish as *La Percepción y el Mundo Físico,* tr. Pedro Garcia Ferrero. Madrid: Editorial Tecnos.

(3) 1962. *Bodily Sensations.* London: Routledge & Kegan Paul.

(4) 1968. *A Materialist Theory of the Mind.* London: Routledge & Kegan Paul.

(4a) Forthcoming. Paperback edition, with a new Preface by D.M.A. London: Routledge.

(4b) 1982. In Polish as *Materialistyczna Teoria Umysłu,* tr. Halina Krahelska. Warszawa: Państowe Wydawnictwo Naukowe.

(4c) 1988. 'Perception and Belief', extracted from (4). In *Perceptual Knowledge,* ed. Jonathan Dancy. Oxford: Oxford University Press, pp. 127–44.

(5) 1973. *Belief, Truth and Knowledge.* Cambridge: Cambridge University Press.

(5a) 1978. 'Beliefs as States', extracted from (5). In *Dispositions,* ed. Raimo Tuomela. Dordrecht: Reidel, pp. 411–25.

(5b) 1990. 'The Infinite Regress of Reasons', extracted from (5). In *The Experience of Philosophy,* ed. Daniel Kolak and Raymond Martin. Belmont, CA: Wadsworth, pp. 168–74.

(6) 1978. *Universals and Scientific Realism,* 2 vols: *Nominalism and Realism* and *A Theory of Universals.* Cambridge: Cambridge University Press.

(6a) 1988. In Spanish as *Los Universales y el Realismo Científico,* tr. J.-A. Robles. México: Universidad Nacional Autónoma de México.

(7) 1980. *The Nature of Mind, and other Essays.* St. Lucia, Queensland: Queensland University Press; Ithaca, NY: Cornell University Press (1981); Brighton, Sussex: Harvester Press (1981).

(8) 1983. *What Is a Law of Nature?* Cambridge: Cambridge University Press.

(9) 1984. (with Normal Malcolm) *Consciousness and Causality: a Debate on the Nature of Mind.* Oxford: Basil Blackwell.

(9a) 1986. In Japanese, tr. Hiroshi Kurosaki. Tokyo: Sangyo Tosho.

(10) 1989. *Universals: an Opinionated Introduction.* Boulder, CO: Westview Press.

(11) 1989. *A Combinatorial Theory of Possibility.* Cambridge: Cambridge University Press.

B. BOOKS EDITED

(1) 1965. *Berkeley's Philosophical Writings.* New York: Macmillan; London: Collier-Macmillan.

(2) 1968. (with C. B. Martin) *Locke and Berkeley: A Collection of Critical Essays.* London: Macmillan; New York: Doubleday; Notre Dame, IN: University of Notre Dame Press.

C. ARTICLES

(1) 1954. 'Berkeley's Puzzle about the Water that Seems both Hot and Cold', *Analysis* 15: 44–6.

(2) 1955. 'Illusions of Sense', *Australasian Journal of Philosophy* 33: 88–106.

(3) 1963. 'Absolute and Relative Motion', *Mind* 72: 209–23.

(4) 1963. 'Is Introspective Knowledge Incorrigible?', *Philosophical Review* 72: 417–32.

(4a) 1991. Reprinted in *The Nature of Mind,* ed. David M. Rosenthal. New York: Oxford University Press, pp. 126–32.

(5) 1965. 'The Freedom of the Will', *The Pluralist* (Sydney) 2: 21–5.

(6) 1965. 'A Theory of Perception'. In *Scientific Psychology,* ed. B. Wolman and E. Nagel. New York: Basic Books, pp. 489–505.

(7) 1965. (with R. N. Spann) 'The Knopfelmacher Case', *Minerva* 3: 334–44.

(8) 1966. 'The Nature of Mind', *Arts* (Proceedings of The Sydney University Arts Association) 3: 37–48.

(8a) 1968. Reprinted (abridged) in *Question* 1: 70–82.

(8b) 1970. Reprinted in *Mind/Brain Identity,* ed. C. V. Borst. London: Macmillan, pp. 67–79.

(8c) 1980. Reprinted in *Readings in Philosophy of Psychology,* vol. 1. Cambridge, MA: Harvard University Press, pp. 191–9.

(8d) 1980. Reprinted in *The Nature of Mind,* q.v. A(7), pp. 1–15.

(8e) 1983. Reprinted in *Persons and their World,* by Jeffrey Olen. New York: Random House, pp. 259–64.

(8f) 1991. Reprinted in *Metaphysics: Classic and Contemporary Readings,* ed. Ronald C. Hoy and L. Nathan Oaklander. Belmont, CA: Wadsworth, pp. 234–41.

(9) 1966. 'The Politics of Liberty', *Honi Soit* (Sydney University), April 21 and 28.

(9a) 1969. Reprinted in *Solidarity* (Manila) 4(2), Feb., pp. 21–8.

(10) 1967. 'The Humphreys Affair', *The Bulletin* (Sydney), May 13, p. 30.

(11) 1968. 'The Headless Woman Illusion and the Defence of Materialism', *Analysis* 29: 48-9.

(12) 1968. 'The Secondary Qualities', *Australasian Journal of Philosophy* 46: 225-41.

(13) 1969. 'Colour Realism and the Argument from Microscopes'. In *Contemporary Philosophy in Australia,* ed. R. Brown and C. D. Rollins. London: Allen & Unwin, pp. 119-31.

(13a) 1980. Reprinted in *The Nature of Mind,* q.v. A(7), pp. 104-18.

(14) 1969. 'Does Knowledge Entail Belief?', *Proceedings of the Aristotelian Society* 70: 21-36.

(15) 1970. 'The Limits of Protest', *Sydney Morning Herald,* April 17, p. 2.

(16) 1971. 'Meaning and Communication', *Philosophical Review* 80: 427-47.

(16a) 1979. In German, in *Handlung, Kommunikation, Bedeutung,* ed. G. Meggle. Frankfurt: Suhrkamp, pp. 112-36.

(17) 1971. 'The Nature of our Democracy', *The Union Recorder* (Sydney University) 51(23), Sept. 23, pp. 3-5.

(17a) 1971. Reprinted in *The Australian Liberal,* Nov., pp. 5-6.

(17b) 1972. Reprinted in *Dialectic* (Journal of the Newcastle University Philosophy Club) 7: 1-9.

(18) 1972. 'Materialism, Properties and Predicates', *The Monist* 56: 163-76.

(19) 1973. 'Acting and Trying', *Philosophical Papers* 2: 1-15.

(19a) 1980. Reprinted in *The Nature of Mind,* q.v. A(7), pp. 68-88.

(20) 1973. 'Continuity and Change in Philosophy', *Quadrant* 17 (Sept.-Dec.): 19-23.

(21) 1973. 'Epistemological Foundations for a Materialist Theory of the Mind', *Philosophy of Science* 40: 178-93.

(21a) 1973. Reprinted in *Dialectic* (Journal of the Newcastle University Philosophy Club) 9: 1-19.

(21b) 1980. Reprinted in *The Nature of Mind,* q.v. A(7), pp. 32-54.

(22) 1973. 'Language and Mind'. In *Linguistics and Mind,* ed. D. Douglas. Sydney: Sydney University Extension Board, pp. 1-10.

(23) 1974. 'Infinite Regress Arguments and the Problem of Universals', *Australasian Journal of Philosophy* 52: 191-201.

(23a) 1980. In Spanish, in *El Problema de los Universales,* ed. and tr. J.-A. Robles. México: Universidad Nacional Autónoma de México, pp. 203-16.

(24) 1975. 'Towards a Theory of Properties: Work in Progress on the Problem of Universals', *Philosophy* 50: 145-55.

(25) 1976. 'Immediate Perception'. In *Essays in Memory of Imre Lakatos* (Boston Studies in the Philosophy of Science, vol. 39), ed. R. S. Cohen, P. K. Feyerabend and M. Wartofsky. Dordrecht: Reidel, pp. 23-35.

(25a) 1980. Reprinted in *The Nature of Mind,* q.v. A(7), pp. 119-31.

(26) 1976. 'Modern Materialism and the Mind', *Proceedings of the Russellian Society* (Sydney University) 1: 44-55.

(27) 1976. 'The Nature of Tradition'. In *Liberty and Politics,* ed. O. Harries. Sydney: Worker's Educational Association of N.S.W.; Pergamon Press (Australia), pp. 7-19.

(27a) 1980. Reprinted in *The Nature of Mind,* q.v. A(7), pp. 89–103.

(28) 1977. 'The Causal Theory of the Mind', *Neue Hefte für Philosophie* 11: 82–95 (Göttingen: Vandenhoeck and Ruprecht).

(28a) 1980. Reprinted in *The Nature of Mind,* q.v. A(7), pp. 16–31.

(28b) 1990. Reprinted in *Mind and Cognition, a Reader,* ed. W. G. Lycan. Oxford: Basil Blackwell, pp. 37–47.

(28c) 1991. Reprinted in *The Nature of Mind,* ed. David M. Rosenthal. New York: Oxford University Press, pp. 181–8.

(29) 1977. 'On Metaphysics'. In 'Fifty Years of John Anderson', *Quadrant* 21 (May): 65–9.

(30) 1977. 'The Problem of Universals', *Proceedings of the Russellian Society* (Sydney University) 2: 11–22.

(31) 1977. 'Naturalism, Materialism and First Philosophy'. In *Ist systematische Philosophie möglich?* (Proceedings of the Stuttgarter Hegel-Kongress, 1975), ed. Dieter Henrich. Bonn: Bouvier Verlag Herbert Grundmann, pp. 411–25.

(31a) 1977. 'Remarks Read at the Conference'. In *Ist systematische Philosophie möglich?* q.v. C(31), p. 427.

(31b) 1978. Reprinted in *Philosophia* 8: 261–76.

(31c) 1978. Reprinted in *Dialectic* (Journal of the Newcastle University Philosophy Club) 12: 1–14.

(31d) 1980. Reprinted in *The Nature of Mind,* q.v. A(7), 149–65.

(32) 1978. 'What is Consciousness?', *Proceedings of the Russellian Society* (Sydney University) 3: 65–76.

(32a) 1980. Reprinted in *The Nature of Mind,* q.v. A(7), pp. 55–67.

(33) 1979. 'Perception, Sense Data and Causality'. In *Perception and Identity: Essays Presented to A. J. Ayer with His Replies to Them,* ed. G. F. Macdonald. London: Macmillan, pp. 84–98.

(33a) 1980. Reprinted in *The Nature of Mind,* q.v. A(7), pp. 132–48.

(34) 1979. 'Three Types of Consciousness'. In *Brain and Mind* (Ciba Foundation Series 69, N.S.). Amsterdam: Excerpta Medica, pp. 235–41.

(35) 1979. 'Laws of Nature', *Proceedings of the Russellian Society* (Sydney University) 4: 46–61.

(36) 1980. 'Identity through Time'. In *Time and Cause: Essays Presented to Richard Taylor,* ed. Peter van Inwagen. Dordrecht: Reidel, pp. 67–78.

(36a) 1991. Reprinted in *Metaphysics: Classic and Contemporary Readings,* ed. Ronald C. Hoy and L. Nathan Oaklander. Belmont, CA: Wadsworth, pp. 147–54.

(37) 1980. 'Against Ostrich Nominalism: A Reply to Michael Devitt', *Pacific Philosophical Quarterly* 61: 440–9.

(38) 1980. 'Letter from Prague', *Quadrant* 24 (Dec.): 25–7.

(39) 1982. 'Laws of Nature as Relations between Universals, and as Universals', *Philosophical Topics* 13: 7–24.

(39a) 1982. Reprinted in *Dialectic* (Journal of the Newcastle University Philosophy Club) 19: 17–36.

(40) 1982. 'Metaphysics and Supervenience', *Crítica* 14: 3–18.

(40a) 1984. In German as 'Naturalistische Metaphysik'. In *Moderne Naturphilosophie,* ed. Bernulf Kanitscheider. Würzburg: Könighausen & Neumann, pp. 83–94.

(41) 1983. 'Recent Work on the Relation of Mind and Brain'. In *Contemporary Philosophy: A New Survey,* vol. IV, Philosophy of the Mind, ed. G. Fløistad. The Hague: Martinus Nijhoff, pp. 45–79.

(42) 1983. 'Do Things Have Temporal Parts?', *Proceedings of the Russellian Society* (Sydney University) 8: 25–35.

(42a) 1983. Reprinted in *Cogito* (Journal of the University of New South Wales Socratic Society) 1(5): 57–68.

(43) 1984. (with Peter Forrest) 'An Argument against David Lewis' Theory of Possible Worlds', *Australasian Journal of Philosophy* 62: 164–8.

(44) 1984. 'Self-Profile'. In *D. M. Armstrong* (Profiles, vol. 4), ed. Radu J. Bogdan. Dordrecht: Reidel, pp. 3–51.

(44a) 1983. 'An Intellectual Autobiography', abbreviated version of (44), *Quadrant* 27 (Jan.–Feb.): 89–102; (Mar.): 68–78.

(45) 1984. 'Replies' (to contributors). In *D. M. Armstrong,* q.v. C(44), pp. 225–69.

(46) 1984. 'Bibliography of D. M. Armstrong' (with abstracts of books and major articles). In *D. M. Armstrong,* q.v. C(44), pp. 273–300.

(47) 1985. 'A Polish Diary', *Quadrant* 29 (Aug.): 52–7.

(47a) 1986. Reprinted in *The Salisbury Review* 4 (Jan.): 20–5.

(48) 1986. 'Baza Epistemica', Roumanian translation by Sorin Vieru of 'The Epistemic Base' (not published in English), *Stiintele Sociale si Politice Peste Hotare* 1: 41–65 (Bucuresti).

(49) 1987. 'The Nature of Possibility', *Canadian Journal of Philosophy* 16: 575–94.

(50) 1987. 'Smart and the Secondary Qualities'. In *Metaphysics and Morality: Essays in Honour of J. J. C. Smart,* ed. Philip Pettit, Richard Sylvan and Jean Norman. Oxford: Basil Blackwell, pp. 1–15.

(51) 1987. (with Peter Forrest) 'The Nature of Number', *Philosophical Papers* 16: 165–86.

(52) 1988. 'Are Quantities Relations?: A Reply to Bigelow and Pargetter', *Philosophical Studies* 54: 305–16.

(53) 1988. 'Can a Naturalist Believe in Universals?'. In *Science in Reflection,* vol. 3, ed. Edna Ullmann-Margalit. Dordrecht: Kluwer, pp. 103–15.

(53a) 1986. In Roumanian as 'Naturalismul si convingerea in existenta universalor', tr. Sorin Vieru, *Stiintele Sociale si Politice Peste Hotare* 2: 59–76 (Bucuresti).

(54) 1988. Contribution to Symposium: 'The Role of the Basics and the Classical Disciplines in Education'. In *P.A.C.T. Occasional Education Series,* no. 2, ed. Don Moore, pp. 17–20.

(55) 1989. 'C. B. Martin, Counterfactuals, Causality, and Conditionals'. In *Cause, Mind, and Reality, Essays Honoring C. B. Martin,* ed. John Heil. Dordrecht: Kluwer, pp. 7–15.

(56) 1989. 'My Second Polish Diary', *Quadrant* 33 (Nov.): 6–13.

(57) 1989. (with Storrs McCall) 'God's Lottery', *Analysis* 49: 223–4.

(58) 1991. 'Intentionality, Perception, and Causality: Reflections on John Searle's *Intentionality*'. In *John Searle and his Critics,* ed. Ernest Lepore and Robert van Gulick. Oxford: Basil Blackwell, pp. 149–58.

(59) 1991. 'Classes Are States of Affairs', *Mind* 100: 189–200.

(60) 1991. (with Adrian Heathcote) 'Causes and Laws'. *Noûs* 25: 63–73.

(61) 1991. 'What Makes Induction Rational?', *Dialogue* 30: 503–11.

(62) 1992. 'Properties'. In *Language, Truth and Ontology,* ed. Kevin Mulligan. Dordrecht: Kluwer, pp. 14–27.

D. DISCUSSIONS AND NOTES

(1) 1956. 'Discussion: Berkeley's *New Theory of Vision*', *Journal of the History of Ideas* 17: 127–9.

(2) 1959. 'Discussion: Mr. Arthedeva and Naive Realism', *Australasian Journal of Philosophy* 37: 67–70.

(3) 1963. 'Discussion: Max Deutscher and Perception', *Australasian Journal of Philosophy* 41: 246–9.

(4) 1963. 'Discussion: Vesey on Sensations of Heat', *Australasian Journal of Philosophy* 41: 359–62.

(5) 1964. 'Discussion: Vesey on Bodily Sensations', *Australasian Journal of Philosophy* 42: 247–8.

(6) 1968. 'Student Activism in a Free Society', *Vestes* (Sydney) 11 (July): 138–40.

(7) 1969. 'Dispositions are Causes' (Reply to Roger Squires), *Analysis* 30: 23–6.

(8) 1975. 'Beliefs and Desires as Causes of Action: A Reply to Donald Davidson', *Philosophical Papers* 4: 1–7.

(9) 1975. 'Fission at Sydney University', *The International Council on the Future of the University: Newsletter* 2 (Jan.): 1, 10, 14.

(10) 1975. 'Those Sydney Blues', *The University of Sydney Archives: Record* 3 (Sept.): 125–7.

(11) 1976. 'Incorrigibility, Materialism and Causation' (Reply to George Pappas), *Philosophical Studies* 30: 125–7.

(12) 1976. 'On the University Crisis', *The International Council on the Future of the University: Newsletter* 3 (May): 1.

(13) 1978. 'On Passing the Buck' (Commentary on Roland Pucetti and Robert W. Dykes, 'Sensory Cortex and the Mind–Brain Problem'), *The Behavioral and Brain Sciences* 3: 346.

(14) 1983. 'Indeterminism, Proximal Stimuli, and Perception' (Commentary on Fred I. Dretske, *Knowledge and the Flow of Information*), *The Behavioral and Brain Sciences* 6: 64–5.

(15) 1984. 'Barry Humphries: At *Quadrant,* at Fifty', *Quadrant* 28 (May): 12.

(16) 1985. 'The Heart of Berkeley's Metaphysics?: A Reply to Ernest Sosa', *Hermathena* 139: 162–4.

(16a) 1986. Reprinted in *George Berkeley, Essays and Replies,* ed. David Berman. Dublin: Irish Academic Press and Hermathena.

(17) 1985. Foreword to David A. J. Seargent, *Plurality and Continuity.* The Hague: Martinus Nijhoff, pp. xii–xiii.

(18) 1986. 'In Defence of Structural Universals' (Reply to David Lewis), *Australasian Journal of Philosophy* 64: 85–8.

(19) 1986. Contribution to 'Tributes to Richard Krygier', *Quadrant* 30 (Nov.): 22.

(20) 1987. 'Comments on Swoyer and Forge'. In *Measurement, Realism and Objectivity,* ed. John Forge. Dordrecht: Reidel, pp. 311–17.

(21) 1987. 'Knowledge: Naturalistic Analyses'; 'Mental Concepts: the Causal Analysis'; 'Mind–Body Problem: Philosophical Theories'. Entries in *The Oxford Companion to the Mind,* ed. Richard L. Gregory. Oxford: Oxford University Press.

(22) 1987. 'Reply to Stephens' Review' (of *Consciousness and Causality* in same issue), *Behaviourism* 15: 157–9.

(23) 1988. 'Are Dispositions Ultimate?: Reply to Franklin', *Philosophical Quarterly* 38: 84–6.

(24) 1988. 'Reply to van Fraassen's 'Armstrong on Laws and Probabilities'', *Australasian Journal of Philosophy* 66: 224–9.

(25) 1989. 'Commodore J. M. Armstrong, C.B.E, D.S.O., R.A.N., 1900–1988', *Naval Historical Review* (Journal of the Naval Historical Society of Australia) N.S. 9(8): 15–17.

(26) 1989. Reply to Geoffrey Blainey's 'Australian Universities: Some Fashions and Faults', *Seminar on the Sociology of Culture 1989,* La Trobe University, Victoria, Australia, pp. 8–10.

(27) 1991. 'Arda Denkel's Resemblance Nominalism', *Philosophical Quarterly* 41: 478–82.

(28) 1991. 'Searle's Neo-Cartesian Theory of Consciousness'. In *Consciousness* (Philosophical Issues, no. 1), ed. Enrique Villanueva. Attascadero, CA: Ridgeview, pp. 65–71.

(29) Forthcoming. 'The Identification Problem and the Inference Problem' (Reply to van Fraassen), *Philosophy and Phenomenological Research.*

E. CRITICAL NOTICES AND REVIEWS

(1) 1950. 'Bleak Prospect for 1984'. Review of *1984,* by George Orwell, *Honi Soit* (Sydney University), June 15, p. 5.

(2) 1958. 'Critical Notice: A. J. Ayer's *The Problem of Knowledge*', *Australasian Journal of Philosophy* 36: 128–45.

(3) 1958. 'Anderson and Andersonianism'. Review of special issue of *The Australian Highway, The Observer* (Sydney), Oct. 4, p. 535.

(4) 1959. 'Russell the Sage'. Review of *My Philosophical Development* and *Wisdom of the West,* by Bertrand Russell, *The Observer* (Sydney), Nov. 28, p. 31.

(5) 1966. Critical Notice: 'Richard Taylor's *Action and Purpose*', *Australasian Journal of Philosophy* 44: 231–40.

(6)   1966. Review of *Vietnam Seen from East and West,* ed. Sibnarayan Ray, *Oz* (Sydney), July.

(7)   1967. Review of *Brain and Mind,* ed. J. R. Smythies, *Philosophical Review* 76: 246-9.

(8)   1969. Review of *Human Action, Conceptual and Empirical Issues,* ed. Theodore Mischel, *British Journal for the Philosophy of Science* 21: 117-19.

(9)   1970. Review of *Berkeley's Renovation of Philosophy,* by Gavin Ardley, *Philosophical Quarterly* 20: 181.

(10)   1972. 'B. F. Skinner's Plastic Man'. Review of *Beyond Freedom and Dignity,* by B. F. Skinner, *Quadrant* 16 (July-Aug.): 46-50.

(11)   1973. Review of *A Modern Introduction to Philosophy,* ed. Paul Edwards and Arthur Pap, *Australasian Journal of Philosophy* 51: 270.

(12)   1976. 'Russell the Robust'. Review of *The Life of Bertrand Russell,* by Ronald W. Clark, *Quadrant* 20 (Mar.): 57-8.

(13)   1976. Review of *The Achilles of Rationalist Arguments,* by B. J. Mijuskovic, *Journal of Religious History* 9: 103-4.

(14)   1976. 'Reflections on Chomsky'. Review of *Reflections on Language,* by Noam Chomsky, *Quadrant* 20 (Aug.): 72-5.

(15)   1977. 'Freddy'. Review of *Part of My Life,* by A. J. Ayer, *Quadrant* 21 (Nov.): 73-4.

(16)   1978. Review of *The Self and its Brain,* by Karl Popper and John Eccles, *Times Literary Supplement,* Feb. 17. pp. 183-4.

(16a) 1978. Reprinted (with minor alterations) in *Quadrant* 22 (July): 18-22.

(17)   1979. Review of *Cerebral Logic,* by Charles W. Needham, *Australian & New Zealand Journal of Psychiatry* 13: 276.

(18)   1979. 'Program and Performance'. Review of *Programs of the Brain,* by J. Z. Young, *Quadrant* 23 (Apr.): 63-5.

(19)   1980. Review of *Persons and Minds,* by Joseph Margolis, *Philosophy of the Social Sciences* 10: 129-50.

(20)   1980. 'The Nature of Creativity'. Review of *Liberty and Language,* by Geoffrey Sampson, *Quadrant* 24 (May): 51-4.

(21)   1982. Review of *Scientific Materialism,* by Mario Bunge, *Australasian Journal of Philosophy* 60: 373-4.

(22)   1982. 'A Search for Values'. Review of *Philosophical Explanations,* by Robert Nozick, *Quadrant* 26 (June): 65-70.

(23)   1982. Review of *A Case for Idealism,* by John Foster, *Times Literary Supplement,* Oct. 22, p. 1170.

(24)   1982. Review of *Tradition,* by Edward Shils, *Quadrant* 26 (Oct.): 71-3.

(25)   1983. Review of *Berkeley: Critical and Interpretive Essays,* ed. Colin M. Turbayne, *Australasian Journal of Philosophy* 61: 439-42.

(26)   1984. Review of *Space, Time and Causality,* ed. Richard Swinburne, *Philosophy* 59: 539-41.

(27)   1984. 'Reinhardt Grossmann's Ontology'. Critical Notice of *The Categorial Structure of the World,* by Reinhardt Grossmann, *Critical Philosophy* 2: 63-76.

(28) 1984. Review of *The Vindication of Absolute Idealism,* by Timothy Sprigge, *Australasian Journal of Philosophy* 62: 376-7.

(29) 1986. Review of *The Concept of Physical Law,* by Norman Swartz, *Times Literary Supplement,* Mar. 7, p. 253.

(30) 1986. Review of *Identity, Cause and Mind,* by Sydney Shoemaker, *Australasian Journal of Philosophy* 64: 236-7.

(31) 1986. Review of *Ayer* (The Arguments of the Philosophers Series), by John Foster, *Mind* 95: 387-9.

(32) 1987. 'Metaphysical Scotland'. Review of *The Democratic Intellect in Crisis,* by George Davie, *Quadrant* 31 (May): 77-8.

(33) 1987. Review of *The Closing of the American Mind,* by Allan Bloom, *Quadrant* 31 (Nov.): 12-16.

(34) 1989. Review of *The Secret Connexion – Causation, Realism, and David Hume,* by Galen Strawson, *Times Literary Supplement,* Dec. 22-28, p. 1425.

(35) 1991. Review of *Necessity, Essence and Individuation: a Defence of Conventionalism,* by Alan Sidelle, *Philosophical Books* 32: 106-8.

(36) 1991. 'The Role of Philosophy'. Review of *Our Place in the Universe,* by J. J. C. Smart, *Metascience,* Pilot Issue, pp. 71-2.

(37) 1992. 'Missing the Major Villains'. Review of *The Decline of the University,* by Philip de Lacey and Gabriël Moens, *Policy* 8: 50-1.

(38) Forthcoming. Review of *Causation and Universals,* by Evan Fales, *Australasian Journal of Philosophy.*

(39) Forthcoming. Review of *Science and Necessity,* by John Bigelow and Robert Pargetter, *Australasian Journal of Philosophy.*

(40) Forthcoming. Review of *The Immaterial Self: A Defence of the Cartesian Dualist Conception of the Mind,* by John Foster, *The Philosophical Review.*

(41) Forthcoming. Review of *Locke,* by Michael Ayers, *Mind.*

Index